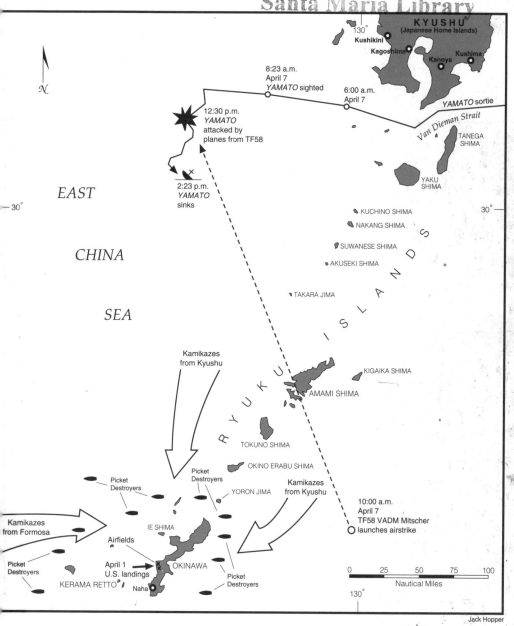

𝒩

KYUSHU
(Japanese Home Islands)
130°
Kushikini
Kagoshima
Kanoya   Kushima

8:23 a.m.
April 7
YAMATO sighted

6:00 a.m.
April 7

YAMATO sortie

Van Dieman Strait

12:30 p.m.
YAMATO
attacked by
planes from TF58

TANEGA
SHIMA

YAKU
SHIMA

EAST

2:23 p.m.
YAMATO
sinks

30°   30°

KUCHINO SHIMA

NAKANG SHIMA

CHINA

SUWANESE SHIMA

AKUSEKI SHIMA

SEA

TAKARA JIMA

R Y U K U   I S L A N D S

Kamikazes
from Kyushu

KIGAIKA SHIMA

AMAMI SHIMA

TOKUNO SHIMA

OKINO ERABU SHIMA

Picket
Destroyers

Picket
Destroyers

YORON JIMA

Kamikazes
from Kyushu

10:00 a.m.
April 7
TF58 VADM Mitscher
launches airstrike

Picket
Destroyers

Kamikazes
from Formosa

IE SHIMA

Airfields

April 1
U.S. landings

OKINAWA

Picket
Destroyers

KERAMA RETTO   Naha

Picket
Destroyers

0   25   50   75   100
Nautical Miles

130°

Jack Hopper

HELLCATS

HELLCATS

A Novel of War in the Pacific

BARRETT TILLMAN

BRASSEY'S

Washington • London

Library of Congress Cataloging-in-Publication Data
Tillman, Barrett.
Hellcats: a novel of war in the Pacific/Barrett Tillman.
p. cm.
Includes bibliographical references.
ISBN 1-57488-093-4
1. World War, 1939–1945—Aerial operations, American—Fiction.
2. Hellcat (Fighter planes)—Fiction.
I. Title.
PS3570.I39H4 1996
813´.54—dc20   95-49922

10 9 8 7 6 5 4 3 2 1

Printed in the United States of America

DEDICATED TO THESE TEN, TO THE SQUADRON MATES THEY REPRESENT,
AND TO THOSE WHO STILL REMEMBER THEM AS FOREVER YOUNG

Lieutenant Karl B. Satterfield (age 28)
VF-5, USS *Yorktown* (CV-10)
Killed in combat over Kwajalein Atoll, 4 December 1943

Lieutenant George Formanek, Jr. (24)
VF-30, USS *Monterey* (CVL-26)
Struck trees while strafing over New Guinea, 23 April 1944

Lieutenant Commander Ernest W. Wood, Jr. (28)
CVLG-27, USS *Princeton* (CVL-23)
Lost to structural failure in combat near the Marianas, 19 June 1944

Ensign Frank T. Vitkusky (27)
VF-14, USS *Wasp* (CV-18)
Lost in water landing, Western Pacific, 12 July 1944

Ensign Joseph Kelley (24)
VF-19, USS *Lexington* (CV-16)
Murdered by Japanese cannibals in the Bonin Islands, 5 August 1944

Ensign Kenneth "C" Chase (20)
VF-11, USS *Hornet* (CV-12)
Killed by Japanese anti-aircraft fire near Okinawa, 10 October 1944

Ensign Jack S. Berkheimer (20)
VF(N)-41, USS *Independence* (CVL-22)
Killed in night intercept over the Philippines, 16 December 1944

Ensign Paul K. Spradling (22)
VF-82, USS *Bennington* (CV-20)
Killed by U.S. anti-aircraft gunners off Japan, 16 February 1945

Lieutenant (j.g.) Irl "V" Sonner (25)
VF-29, USS *Cabot* (CVL-28)
Killed in flight-deck crash, Western Pacific, 22 March 1945

Lieutenant (j.g.) John J. Sargent, Jr. (26)
Formerly of VF-18, USS *Bunker Hill* (CV-17)
Killed in kamikaze attack off Okinawa, 11 May 1945

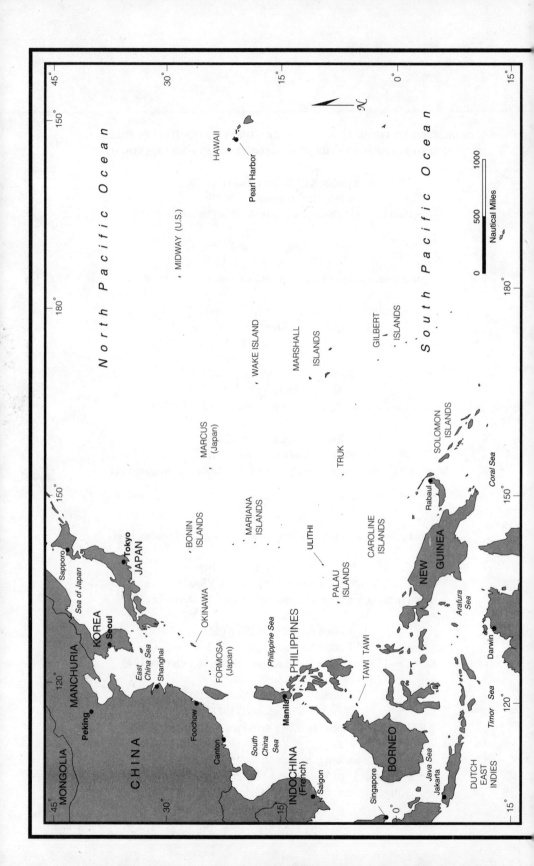

Glossary

ACIO	Air combat intelligence officer
AirPac	Naval Air Forces Pacific
bogey	Unidentified aircraft
BOQ	Bachelor officers' quarters
BuAer	Navy Bureau of Aeronautics
BuOrd	Navy Bureau of Ordnance
CAG	Commander of air group
CAP	Combat air patrol
CAS	Close air support
chutai	Tactical group of eight Japanese fighters
CIC	Combat information center
Clara	Fighter direction officer call: Radar screen is clear of bogeys
CNO	Chief of Naval Operations
ComFair	Commander Fleet Aircraft
ComFairWest	Commander, Fleet Aircraft, West Coast
CV	Fleet aircraft carrier, usually Essex class
CVE	Escort aircraft carrier
CVG	Aircraft carrier air group
CVL	Light aircraft carrier, Independence class
FDO	Fighter direction officer
ForceCAP	Task force combat air patrol
hikokitai	Japanese carrier-based air group
hikotai	Subordinate unit to *hikokitai* and *kokutai,* squadron
HVAR	High-velocity aerial rocket
IFF	Radar beacon: Identification, friend or foe
IJNS	Imperial Japanese Naval Ship
kokutai	Japanese land-based air group

LSO	Landing signal officer
NAF	Naval Aircraft Factory, Philadelphia
NAP	Naval aviation pilot, noncommissioned aviator
NAS	Naval air station
NCO	Noncommissioned officer
RadCAP	Radar picket patrol
RAG	Replacement air group
RO	Radar operator
RP	Radar picket (station) or rocket projectile
shotai	Tactical group of Japanese fighters
Snap	Visual shipboard fighter direction
VB	Navy bombing squadron
VBF	Navy fighting-bombing squadron
VC	Navy composite squadron
VF	Navy fighting squadron
VMF	Marine fighting squadron
VT	Navy torpedo squadron
XO	Executive officer (also "exec")

U.S. AIRCRAFT

F6F-3/5 Hellcat   Single-seat, single-engine carrier fighter built by Grumman. The most successful naval fighter of World War II, it accounted for more Japanese aircraft and produced more aces than any other American airplane. It was also produced in the -3E/N and -5E/N night-fighter models. Top speed of F6F-5 in level flight: 390 mph/332 knots.

F4U-1D Corsair   Single-seat, single-engine fighter-bomber by Vought. Primarily flown by the Marine Corps from land bases, it also proved itself as a carrier aircraft and was produced by Goodyear as the FG-1D. Top speed: 417 mph/354 knots.

SB2C-1/4 Helldiver   Two-seat, single-engine carrier scout-bomber by Curtiss. Top speed of the SB2C-4: 295 mph/250 knots.

SBD-3/5 Dauntless   Two-seat, single-engine carrier scout-bomber by Douglas. Top speed of the SBD-5: 250 mph/215 knots.

TBM-3 Avenger   Eastern Aircraft model of Grumman's TBF-1. A four-seat (normally three crew), single-engine carrier torpedo bomber. Top speed: 267 mph/225 knots.

JAPANESE AIRCRAFT

A6M2-N Type 2 Fighter Seaplane   Single-seat, single-engine floatplane version of the A6M Zero carrier fighter built by Nakajima. Code-named Rufe by Allied intelligence. Top speed: 270 mph/235 knots.

A6M5 Type Zero, Model 52   Single-seat, single-engine carrier fighter by Mitsubishi. The late-war upgraded version of the famed Zero Fighter. Code-named Zeke. Top speed: 350 mph/305 knots.

B6N1 Carrier Attack Aircraft Two-seat, single-engine torpedo bomber by Nakajima. Code-named Jill. Top speed: 290 mph/250 knots.

D3A2 Type 99 Carrier Bomber Two-seat, single-engine dive-bomber slightly upgraded from the Aichi D3A1 of 1940. Code-named Val. Top speed: 267 mph/232 knots.

D4Y1 Carrier Bomber Two-seat, single engine dive-bomber and reconnaissance plane by Aichi. Code-named Judy. Top speed: 343 mph/292 knots.

N1K2-J Naval Fighter Single-seat, single-engine land-based interceptor developed from Kawanishi's N1K1 floatplane. Code-named George. Top speed: 370 mph/320 knots.

Ki-43-II Type 1 Fighter Single-seat army fighter by Nakajima. Code-named Oscar. Top speed: 329 mph/280 knots.

Ki-61-I Type 3 Fighter Single-seat army fighter by Kawasaki. Code-named Tony. Top speed: 368 mph/313 knots.

Preface

Hellcats is the product of documented history and my own imagination. Notable among those who contributed to this novel—and therefore know the difference—are fighter aces Ed Copeland and Elvin Lindsay (VF-19), Bill Leonard (Task Force 38), Blake Moranville (VF-11), and Alex Vraciu (VF-6 and 16), who lived some of the events depicted here. Over the years dozens of additional aviators contributed recollections from twenty-one other Hellcat squadrons, including four night-fighter units. Former fighter directors John Monsarrat, Henry Rowe, and the late John Connally responded to detailed queries on their esoteric wartime trade with patience and humor.

Japanese material, beyond that readily available, came via Henry Sakaida and directly from Saburo Sakai, with thanks to interpreter Jim Crossley.

Access to surviving aircraft—primarily an F6F-3 Hellcat and a *Shiden Kai* Model 21—came through my former boss and longtime friend Doug Champlin in Mesa, Arizona. Freedom to roam an Essex-class carrier was kindly provided by Dr. Steve Ewing aboard USS *Yorktown* (CV-10) in Charleston, South Carolina.

A grateful dip of the wing goes to Mike and Chris Dillon of Dillon Precision in Scottsdale, Arizona. Their kindness and generosity, always extraordinary, literally went to new heights when they enabled the author to make two dive-bombing sorties with inert ordnance. The T-34Bs in the Dillon stable are immaculately maintained and a complete joy to fly.

Special acknowledgment is due Dr. Dean C. Allard, former Director of Naval History, who was so supportive for two decades, and Roy Gross-nick's Naval Aviation History Office.

Computer support was provided—again—by John Gresham, with extra effort by Dwin Craig. Both gentlemen fought the continuing war against the Dell NL25.

Most of the ships and squadrons depicted in this novel never existed. There was no Air Group 59 in World War II, nor a USS *Reprisal,* though that name was assigned to an Essex-class carrier (CV-35) that was never completed. To my knowledge, no U.S. Navy squadron called itself the Sunsetters, and the reader should infer no connection between that fictional unit and the World War II VF-11 Sundowners. The author enjoys the exalted status of Honorary Sundowner, and wears the squadron's distinctive patch on his flight jacket, with gratitude and with pride.

Barrett Tillman
August 1995

PART I

"I am more and more convinced, as I grow older, that what a squadron does before it gets into combat has far more influence on its ultimate performance than most people realize. Once the shooting starts, there isn't much time for training."

Captain T. Hugh Winters, USN (Ret.)
Commander, Carrier Air Group 19, 1944–45

ONE

February 1944

THURSDAY, 17 FEBRUARY
TRUK ATOLL, CAROLINE ISLANDS

The Hellcats streamed out of the dawn, pushing 300 knots through a rose-tinted sky. Below them Truk Atoll lay dark and drowsy on the surface of the sea, barely visible as waves broke over the coral reef. In the cockpits of seventy white-starred Grummans, sharp young eyes lanced the gloom in search of aircraft bearing red suns.

At the van of the fighter sweep were two dozen F6F-3s led by a thirty-two-year-old lieutenant commander known to his Annapolis classmates as Killer. But today he was "Reaper Leader," staking his claim as the first American carrier aviator over the Japanese naval air base at Truk Atoll, considered the Gibraltar of the Pacific. His eleven pilots from the aircraft carrier code-named Bobcat Base were similarly eager, as were those from Jungle and Felix bases.

Safe under an umbrella of twenty-two Hellcats from Dexter Base, Killer's fighters orbited Moen Island at thirteen thousand feet, sizing up the situation. Truk Radio had gone off the air at 0714—fifty minutes ago—and any doubt of what that meant was quickly erased. Moen spat out a first few tracers that sparkled through the dawn, too low to threaten the Hellcats but accurate enough to direct interceptors. Knowing that surprise had been lost, Killer nosed down toward the bomber strip, intent on destroying the torpedo-armed Type One land-attack planes where they sat.

Then he saw the Japanese fighters nosing upward to stop him, and the fight was on.

Flight Chief Petty Officer Hiroyoshi Sakaida seldom thought of Carmen Miranda anymore. As he shoved the power to his Type Two sea fighter, the Nakajima floatplane variant of the Mitsubishi Zero, he wondered why the "Brazilian Bombshell" should come to mind at this moment. True, he had always been a movie fan, and there was a time when Sakaida's Latin American rhumba routines had left his shipmates doubled over with laughter. Especially when he had wrapped a bandana around his head with bananas or other tropical fruit on top of it.

Sakaida realized that he had not performed that act more than twice in the twelve months since Japan evacuated Guadalcanal.

As his fighter accelerated on the step, Sakaida felt the centerline float lift from the water. He kept his left arm stiff against the throttle and propeller controls and nudged the stick backward with his right hand. Ordinarily he would have shot a glance at his engine instruments, but during a combat takeoff into a barely visible sky he wanted all his human sensors directed outside the cockpit.

His initial scan detected nothing above him, but Hiroyoshi Sakaida was too experienced a fighter pilot to take such things for granted. Less than an hour before, he had been shaken from his cot with word of many unidentified aircraft inbound, and that could mean only one of two things—a very nervous radar operator or the first enemy attack on Truk.

The order to scramble had brought a jumble of sensations: darkness, noise, confusion—and palpable fear. Truk was beyond the range of even the Seventh Air Force B-24s that had been pounding the Marshall Islands from newly conquered Tarawa Atoll in the Gilberts. So the intruders had to be carrier aircraft—certainly flown by competent, dangerous opponents. Sakaida had tangled with American naval fighters several times since 1942, and he gave them ungrudging respect. Sometimes he dreamed of the Grumman Wildcat that had caught his cruiser-based Type Zero reconnaissance floatplane near Midway early that June. It had been a close-run thing, and he would not have survived to report the position of the carrier *Yorktown* if not for the blessed clouds near the U.S. task force.

Glancing left and right, he saw the irregular wakes on the water where his squadron mates had lifted off, and sought a companion. As he climbed higher the sky lightened and visibility improved marginally. He saw the familiar silhouette of another sea fighter ahead of him and turned to join it. Belatedly he remembered to charge his guns: two 7.7s firing through the propeller and two 20-millimeters in the wings.

Sakaida slightly reduced power to his Sakae 12 radial engine and reached up to shut the canopy hatch. He missed the handle, looked up to grasp it, and saw the Grummans. His mind registered, *No time!* No time to call a warning on the damnably inefficient radio, no time to maneuver, no time to do anything but slew his ungainly floatplane and trade gunfire nose to nose.

The leading enemy fighter's wings sparkled abruptly, lancing spearpoints of .50-caliber tracer ammunition through the sky. The intended victim, Sakaida's still-unidentified partner, violently nosed over to avoid the volley. Sakaida instantly knew that the closure rate was too great to draw a bead on the assailant, but he triggered a burst from his machine guns anyway. He smelled the familiar tang of burned gunpowder in the cockpit, then the first two Americans were gone, flashing out of sight below him.

Something's different, he realized. These fighters were not the familiar Grummans he had encountered at Midway and fought in the Solomons—what the Yankees called Type F4F. These seemed bigger, yet somehow sleeker. *And they're so fast! It must be the new fighter model F6F.* Sakaida knew better than to try to dive after the first pair of Hellcats. He would never catch them, and besides, there were certainly others plunging down on him from the upper darkness.

Assuming the following Grummans would be in close trail behind the leaders, Sakaida turned 90 degrees left and kept climbing. Altitude was his best friend just now. Height meant room to dive away if necessary, time to evaluate a situation without getting trapped as he had been over that Guadalcanal-bound convoy when Grummans had nearly killed him and sent his friend Ensign Yasuke Kono torching into the waters of New Georgia Sound in the Solomons.

The sun was up now, and Sakaida was appalled at what he saw. The sky was alive with fighters painted hostile tricolor blue and friendly olive green. Several fires burned on the water of the thirty-mile-wide lagoon and there were parachutes in the air. Sakaida moved in the cockpit like a perpetual-motion machine, swiveling his head and squirming in his seat in an effort to see everything within five hundred meters.

Two more Grummans slashed at him from above. Another sea fighter crossed his nose and the Hellcats diverted toward the nearer target. The American leader knew his gunnery. He fired two or three short bursts and the Nakajima rolled over and fell toward the lagoon. Sakaida glimpsed the number 19 on the Grumman's fuselage, but its speed carried it away before Sakaida could get in a shot. He choked down the frustration he felt and diverted his rage by concentrating on survival.

Cloud-hopping around the periphery of Truk Lagoon, Sakaida locked his eyes on a low-level dogfight. He saw several Grummans engaged with Zeros and sea fighters, and with an insurance glance over his shoulder he descended toward them.

Still beyond effective range, Sakaida discerned one fighter shooting into another. At first he could identify neither, but as he cut the corner of their turn he identified the shooter as an F6F. The victor zoom-climbed away from his victim, unknowingly denying Sakaida a shot. Sakaida made a mental note of where the Japanese would fall, and gawked as he realized it was another Grumman. *The Yankees are not infallible after all!*

Below to his right, Sakaida saw the dogfight still in progress. A low, snaking line of Grummans, Zeros, and sea fighters wound inward upon itself with demonic frenzy, frequently punctuated by gunsmoke and muzzle flashes. After another concerned glance above, Sakaida dived into the fight just as a Zero hit the water and skidded to destruction in foamy white spray. The sea fighter behind the lead Hellcat clearly scored hits, then was shot to pieces by the American's wingman. Debris rained down into the azure waters of the lagoon.

Apparently the second American stopped to admire his handiwork, as he rolled into a medium-banked turn to watch the death of the enemy plane code-named Rufe. That vanity gave Sakaida time to fill his range-finder with the F6F's wingspan, quickly level his own wings, and open fire with all four guns. At two hundred meters he saw aluminum pieces fly off the big Grumman, which slowed visibly. He decided to press his advantage and closed in, triggering long bursts that pounded his ears as the Type 97 machine guns chattered away. He realized that his Type 99 cannon were now empty.

A dirty-brown smoke plume trailed back from beneath the F6F's cowling, then the carrier fighter fell off to starboard. Sakaida pulled up, saw the splash, and surprised himself with a high-pitched, atavistic shriek.

Incredibly, the air seemed empty. Sakaida had experienced the sensation once or twice before, but never like this. How a densely packed, low-altitude combat could disperse so rapidly he never understood, but he seemed alone. For the first time in—how long?—he reduced power to his abused engine.

Then it quit. Belatedly, he realized that some of the smoke in his cockpit was tinted with the odor of heated engine oil. He ran his eyes over his gauges, saw that the cylinder-head temp was well into the yellow and oil pressure falling toward zero. *There's no time,* he told himself again. At barely four hundred meters altitude he pulled the mixture to idle-cutoff, cut the magnetos, shut off his fuel selector, and turned into the wind.

Sakaida felt horribly vulnerable, gliding straight ahead, without power.

He was as dead as his ancestors if another Grumman came by, completely unable to defend himself. But he managed a good landing, bouncing slightly in the chop and coasting to a halt a few miles off Moen Island.

He unstrapped, slid from the cockpit and lay on the port wing root. Peering forward, he saw oil streaks leading from the cowling back along the centerline float mount. Two or three holes were visible on that side—neat, round punctures of the aircraft's skin with paint chipped away where .50-caliber rounds had entered. Sakaida slowly shook his head, cursing fervently and expertly to himself. *Fool! You didn't even know when you were hit!* In more than half a dozen combats, that had never happened before. He told himself that he would remember this date with that frantic June 4, 1942, near Midway.

Hiroyoshi Sakaida slumped on the wing, his back against the fuselage. He checked his watch and noted that his morning's excitement had lasted barely twenty minutes. But he heard more aircraft engines in the sky and realized that the battle was going to continue.

Less than three hours later, when a motor launch took him to shore, the only airplanes overhead sported white stars on their square-tipped wings. Sakaida's mind drifted again as he wondered what it would be like to rhumba with Carmen Miranda.

FRIDAY, 18 FEBRUARY
NAVAL AIR STATION PEARL HARBOR

"Benny, you gotta help me. I'll do anything to get out of antisubmarine work. Can't you ease me into a new bombing or fighter squadron?" Lieutenant Phil Rogers's voice carried a plaintive note that the AirPac detailer found both alarming and amusing. Lieutenant Commander Ben Nichols, onetime fighter pilot, had known Rogers aboard USS *Saratoga,* before the war. That seemed eons ago—nearly three years.

Nichols tapped the phone cradle two or three times as if testing the line. "Uh, excuse me. Is this Lieutenant Rogers of Composite Squadron 54 on the escort carrier *Alazon Bay*? The same Buck Rogers who last year pleaded on bended knee for assignment to an antisub squadron?"

At the other end of the line, Rogers flinched visibly. *Ouch,* he thought. *Touché.* His mind raced, seeking an explanation for his change of heart. Nothing occurred to him so he took the aviator's last resort. He told the truth.

"C'mon, Benny. I'm dying of boredom." Another thought occurred to him. Maybe asking for sympathy would help. "Remember, I got torpedoed three times in eight frigging months—twice on the Sara, and the *Yorktown* at Midway. You can't blame me for wanting a crack at Jap subs."

Nichols remembered. Poor old *Saratoga;* she and *Enterprise* were the only two prewar carriers remaining in the Pacific. Nichols mentally checked off the flattops lost so far in this war: *Lexington* at Coral Sea, *Yorktown* at Midway, *Wasp* torpedoed off Guadalcanal, *Hornet* at Santa Cruz. And luckless Sara: holed by Japanese submarines off Hawaii in January '42, then again near the Solomons that August. Phil Rogers and his original squadron, Bombing Squadron 3, had been aboard both times. In between, VB-3 had spelled one of *Yorktown*'s exhausted squadrons for Midway in June. There she had survived crippling air attacks only to succumb to another goddamn sub. No wonder Rogers had wanted revenge.

"All right, you've convinced me," Nichols heard himself say. "But you're not fooling me, Rogers. You're just feeling sorry for yourself, driving one of those pregnant sharks instead of your old Speedy Three."

Phil Rogers laughed into the phone. "You got me there." The big-bellied Grumman TBF-1 had everything an antisubmarine plane needed: range, payload, and a three-man crew to divide the workload. But it lacked the grace, the sheer fun of the Douglas SBD-3, the Dauntless, which Bombing 3 had flown to glory at Midway and Eastern Solomons. The Curtiss SB2C-1 Helldiver was slowly replacing the SBD-5 as the current carrier dive-bomber, and even though the Helldiver was troublesome, Rogers would gladly accept a '2C assignment as a way out of the sluggish TBF and its deadly dull antisubmarine mission.

"Thanks, Benny," he concluded. "I owe you one."

"Damn right," Nichols replied. "Don't you forget it."

DUBLON ISLAND, TRUK ATOLL

Sakaida stood at the head of the bombed seaplane ramp and stared blankly into the lagoon. The Americans finally had gone; that was the good news. But the bad news was visible every direction Sakaida turned his head. When the last Yankee warship steamed over the horizon that afternoon, Truk was a smoldering mess. Some thirty ships, including two cruisers and a large tanker, had been sunk by air or surface attack, and much of the atoll's facilities had been bombed, strafed, or shelled into rubble.

For the aviators it was not difficult to assess the toll. By dusk on the second day, perhaps a half dozen aircraft remained from the four fighter units based there. Eventually the word got around. Sakaida had heard that Air Group 204 counted eighteen pilots dead or missing. Air Group 501's fighter squadron wrote off eleven Zeros and Air Group 201's small contingent had lost all eight. The sea fighters of Air Group 902, short four pilots, now were without operable aircraft.

Sakaida felt a presence behind him and turned to see his longtime wingmate, Flight Petty Officer Masao Mizuno. They were, not close friends—Mizuno was more reserved than Sakaida—but they had flown sea fighters together since the old *Kamikawa Maru* seaplane tender had arrived in the Solomons back in the fall of '42. Looking at Mizuno's face, clouded with the shadow of a lingering oil fire, Sakaida reflected that his friends now were chosen for him. Those who survived were eligible.

"The search boats have returned," Mizuno said in a soft voice. He looked down, bit his lip, then raised his gaze over Sakaida's shoulder. "They found no one."

It was not surprising news. Since yesterday's morning combat there had been little hope that the missing float-fighter pilots would turn up. The unit commander, Lieutenant Michiji Kawano, was among the known dead. Three noncommissioned pilots also were gone, including the well-regarded Aleutians veteran Yoshio Suzuki. *He fought the twin-engine Lockheeds,* Sakaida thought, *but the new Grummans killed him.*

"I've been thinking about the new enemy fighters," Sakaida said. "We will have to develop new tactics."

Mizuno had not flown yesterday, and, with only six fighters left, no-body had taken off today. The Americans' capabilities were astonishing. They had even launched night bombing missions from their carriers and sunk ships almost with impunity. Undoubtedly the TBF-1 Avengers had radar—how else could they bomb accurately in the dark?

"We need new planes for ourselves," Mizuno replied bitterly. The Type Two float fighter was only a stopgap measure, dating from late 1941. Intended to provide temporary air cover at advanced bases lacking runways, it never was meant to defeat conventional fighters.

Sakaida seemed not to hear. "These Americans fly well. They use their superior speed wisely, and they always fight in pairs." Sakaida had got that one Hellcat only because its pilot was fixated on his own victim.

Mizuno was not impressed. "I heard that we captured some Yankees," he said. Objectivity was not his forte; the spite in his voice was audible. "They deserve to die for . . . this." He jerked his head at the rubble behind him.

For an instant Sakaida perked up. Though he had seen Hollywood films before the war, he had never met an American, much less an aviator. It might be interesting to speak to one, even through an interpreter. *No, it would never be permitted,* he realized. Besides, the poor fellows already were undergoing interrogation, then they would surely be killed. It was pro-cedure—everybody knew that. He decided to change the subject. "I am al-most going to miss this place."

"So you're really leaving us?" Mizuno asked.

"It was bound to happen, Masao. After this . . ." Sakaida swept a hand at the wrecked atoll. The air group now was only an administrative entity, fated to be dissolved.

"Yes, I know. You are the lucky one, I would say. We'll all be reassigned when the *kokutai* is disbanded next month." He managed a smile. "At least you are getting your wish for carrier duty."

Sakaida could hardly believe it himself. He recalled the time when he sailed as a cruiser-based floatplane pilot in the Carrier Striking Force, in Operation Hawaii and then at Midway, Operation MI. In those days he had only dreamed of flying a Zero fighter. But now, his considerable experience and modest success demanded assignment to the Mobile Fleet, where fledglings already filled the cockpits of fighters, bombers, and attack planes.

Sakaida felt an uneasiness—an urge to be done with this parting. "Farewell, Masao. We'll meet again I'm sure."

Mizuno shook hands. "Yes, I'll be seeing you at the Yasukuni Shrine."

Hiroyoshi Sakaida took a last look at the familiar face, then turned away. Yasukuni Shrine in Tokyo was where the ashes of Nippon's warriors were returned from the front.

March 1944

THURSDAY, 2 MARCH
OITA NAVAL BASE, KYUSHU ISLAND

Sakaida found only disappointment after returning to Japan.

First he learned that home leave would not be possible. It was a considerable distance from Kyushu to his mountain village on Honshu—a thousand kilometers—and there was just no time. "Besides," a petty officer had told him, "you will not be missing anything. Even the best restaurants are closing because geishas and waitresses are needed for factory work."

Nor was Sakaida much impressed with Second Carrier Division or its aviation component, Air Group 652. Upon reporting for transition training at Oita Base, he found an understrength, ill-equipped organization badly in need of increasingly rare assets—trained aviators. During the indoctrination lecture Sakaida was shocked to realize that he—who had never landed aboard a carrier—was easily one of the most experienced pilots.

By making friends in the base personnel department—he donated some "borrowed" sake to the office staff—Sakaida learned the lay of the land. One of the petty officers took him aside. "Your *Hikokitai* 652 is a brand-new unit," the man explained. "The commander is Commander Suzuki, who had the Second Carrier Division fighters at Rabaul. They were cut up in just three weeks of land-based combat, then retreated to Truk. They arrived here last month and reformed." He averted his gaze at that point. "They're at the bottom of the list for rebuilding."

* * *

"You men have a lot to learn," began the briefing officer, Lieutenant Commander Hiroyoshi Yoshimura, the squadron commander. He was an old hand, previously division officer of *Ryuho* Fighter Squadron, a veteran of the Rabaul attrition, and now leader of *Hikotai* 321, the fighter division assigned to IJNS *Junyo,* flagship of Carrier Division Two.

"Most of you are low-time pilots recently assigned to us from carrier attack and bomber aircraft. Your average is fewer than three hundred hours in the air, but most of you will have to qualify in Zero fighters." At that news an animated buzzing hummed through the room, but Yoshimura ended it with an icy edge to his voice. "Our authorized strength is eighty-one fighters, thirty-six dive-bombers, and twenty-seven torpedo attack bombers for *Junyo, Hiyo,* and *Ryuho.* We will not have nearly that many planes until next month or later, so everybody will have to double up."

Yoshimura stood on the stage with his arms akimbo, surveying the rapt audience. Sakaida swiveled his head during the lull, seeing what his leader saw. Young faces: eager, attentive, determined. Sakaida felt a shiver beneath his uniform, thinking of Midway, Guadalcanal, Rabaul, and Truk. *The Americans have chopped up fliers with three times the experience of these boys. How can they hope to survive?*

It began to dawn on Hiroyoshi Sakaida that fulfillment of his dream of becoming a carrier pilot might not be so attractive after all.

SUNDAY, 5 MARCH
WEST PALM BEACH, FLORIDA

Kathleen Foster Rogers was baking a pie when the doorbell rang. Flustered, she looked around for a towel to wipe the flour from her hands and, finding none, scurried from the kitchen. "Coming," she called in a contralto voice. Instinctively she raised a hand to touch her gray-streaked hair, then caught herself. She hastily rubbed both hands on her apron, opened the door and felt her heart rise in her throat, pushing an audible gasp from her lips.

"Hi, Mom." Phil Rogers stood amid his baggage, grinning the little-boy smile he had shown when he got the paper route on his own; when he hit that homer against Lake Worth. He was about to shout "Surprise!" when his mother leapt at him. Her arms cinched so tight around his neck that he was startled by her strength. She was still only forty-eight, though thirty pounds heavier than when she had given birth to her first son twenty-five years before.

The pressure on his neck increased and Rogers tried to unwind himself. But he smelled the familiar scent, heard her sigh, "Oh, Philip," and blinked back the moisture forming in his eyes. Only she had ever called him that. By the time they untangled and stepped inside, mother and son were both misty-eyed and chattering to each other.

"Is Dad here?"

"You told your father that you wouldn't arrive until tonight!"

"Right after I called I bummed a ride from Dallas on a TBF headed for NAS Miami. It left two hours before the R4D."

Mrs. Rogers ignored the incomprehensible alphabet soup. Torpedo plane or transport—it made no difference. "Your father is downtown, probably telling all his cronies you're coming home." She touched the two rows of ribbons beneath his golden wings. "You know, he'll want to show you off."

Rogers groaned, giving an exaggerated toss of his head. "Ah, Jes— ... whiz." He flushed slightly in embarrassment. Ready-room language would land him in hot water, son or no son, Navy Cross or no Navy Cross.

Ignoring the inelegant recovery, Mrs. Rogers placed her floured fingertips on his braided sleeve. "Phil, you can't blame us for being proud of you. Besides, we haven't seen you in almost *three* years. . . ." The emphasis was unmistakable.

"Yeah, I know, Mom." *Please don't start that again.* He lowered his gaze to his shoes. It had taken his parents months to forgive him for not trying to get home in the two weeks after he left Bombing 3 in late '42. They had not understood the difficulties of wartime transportation from Hawaii to the West Coast, let alone to Florida. Rumor was that two hundred pounds of Spam would bump a junior officer with a Double-A travel priority.

Nor had they appreciated the depth of his feelings for Sallyann Downey, though his letters were full of her. His father, who had served in the Great War, undoubtedly grasped the essentials—a willing young woman in Hawaii, versus five or six days at home. But Stephen John Rogers had been just as disappointed as his wife. Both inferred that the idyllic Hawaiian relationship had ended when Miss Downey, a Honolulu librarian, accepted a job offer in her native Portland, Oregon.

Rogers sought to change the subject. "What about Ray? Can he get back for a while?"

"Oh, no, dear. He's at McDill Field, and doesn't think he can get leave while you're here. But he called and said if you can get over there he'll be glad to show you around."

Rogers cheered up. His younger brother, an Army Air Forces second lieutenant, was completing B-26 crew training near Tampa. Bitterly disappointed at not making the cut for flight school, he had accepted bombardier training. Phil Rogers suspected that his own success as a dive-bomber pilot had nudged his brother into the same line of work.

"Well, that's okay," he told his mother. "I won't mind hobnobbing with the Army." *It'll give me a reason to get away from here after a few days.*

THURSDAY, 9 MARCH
OVER THE INLAND SEA

Sakaida felt at home in the Zero Model 52's tight cockpit. With more than three hundred hours in the floatplane version, his preliminary checkout in the shipboard fighter had been routine, and he was far ahead of his squadron mates. In fact, Lieutenant Commander Yoshimura had detailed Sakaida to oversee a group of rookies as they logged their first flights in the *Riesen.*

But much of Sakaida's closely held confidence evaporated when he saw IJNS *Junyo* from 1,300 meters up. From there, her 24,000 tons seemed insignificant—and her 210-by-28-meter flight deck looked positively microscopic.

Field-landing practice theoretically had prepared the fledgling carrier aviators for this moment. Sakaida was familiar with the carrier traffic pattern and had confidence in the simple landing-aid system, but still . . . *It's so small!*

He reduced power to the Sakae 21 engine, ran through his landing checklist, and descended into the pattern over the ship. As fourth in line he checked his spacing, extending his downwind leg to allow the preceding Zero plenty of room. During flight operations at sea, a premium was placed upon tight intervals. But here, doing it for the first time, Sakaida did not want to crowd anyone, and he certainly did not want some junior pilot crowding him.

Rolling out on final approach over the ship's 20-knot wake, Sakaida checked again to ensure his landing gear was down and locked. He had to trust that his tailhook was extended, but the briefings had stressed that if it wasn't, a sailor waving a red flag would convey that essential information.

Two hundred meters from the diagonal-striped deck edge, Sakaida had the two lights. By keeping the blue lights properly aligned, he slipped easily down the 5.5-degree glideslope designed for carrier fighters. The heavier carrier bombers and attack planes employed a slightly shallower 5-degree approach, but both glideslopes intercepted the flight deck at the third of six arresting wires.

Leaning slightly into the slipstream from his open cockpit, Sakaida was surprised at how stable the Zero acted astern of the ship. He had heard that some carriers generated turbulence at this point in the approach, but of course *Junyo,* like many Imperial Navy carriers, had no island structure. And her starboard-mounted smokestacks vented exhaust slightly downward, further reducing complications. All in all, quite a sensible arrangement.

Crossing the ramp, Sakaida resisted the urge to flare as he would ashore. Bringing the nose up only slightly, he saw the signal lights show red at the instant before touchdown. Then he felt the hook snag the second wire, which ran out to its limit as he was tossed forward against his shoulder harness. For an instant he was confused at the abrupt halt, then it dawned on him. *I did it! My first carrier landing!*

A flight-deck director was signaling at Sakaida, and none too politely, either. Belatedly, the pilot remembered to throttle back and ease the tension on the wire. Looking aft, he saw a sailor dash toward his tail to disengage the hook so the fighter could be taxied forward.

Hiroyoshi Sakaida, carrier pilot, raised his flaps and added power to clear the landing area. He was still smiling oafishly when he parked his Zero forward in preparation for his first launch.

SATURDAY, 11 MARCH
WEST PALM BEACH

Phil Rogers quickly discovered the downside to being a returning hero. The demands on his time were astonishing: speaking invitations from the American Legion post, his old Boy Scout troop, and his high school; two requests for newspaper interviews and one from a radio station. And then there were the relatives.

Finally, after two days, he had to lay down the law: no more than one commitment every other day, family included. "In fact," he told his parents at dinner the third evening, "I'm going to streamline things. I want to do as many of these events as possible at one time. You, know have in the relatives, classmates, reporters, the works."

Stephen Rogers looked across the table at his wife, and they exchanged knowing glances. Phil saw the look and knew its meaning, but he'd stood his ground. "Mom, Dad, please. I'm supposed to be on leave—getting some rest. I haven't even been able to sleep in without the damn—darn doorbell or the phone ringing." His father quickly sipped some coffee to hide a smile.

Kathleen opened her mouth to object—family meetings were special—when Stephen interjected. Placing a hand on Phil's arm, he said, "All right, son. We'll do it your way."

Having made that pact, now Phil was obliged to honor it. He had not expected his mother to organize a day-long event on such short notice, but he ruefully acknowledged her formidable powers of coordination. Not only were the aunts, uncles, and cousins out in force, so were Stephen's Legion pals, two reporters, and several former classmates. That did not even count Reverend Mason, who never missed a chance to utter his favorite redundancy while lauding Philip's role in "the crusade against godless atheism."

At the moment Phil was dressed casually, seated in the backyard where the gathering had overflowed the house. He had ceded a few valuable minutes to a Palm Beach newspaper reporter, who asked for "the real lowdown" on the war. "You know, the Word," the man had intoned, winking conspiratorially.

Rogers's response was a blank stare. Sitting on the grass beside him was his nine-year-old nephew Johnny Bennett, his sister Marge's boy, who obviously worshiped the warrior he could not remember meeting before. "I don't know what you mean," Phil slowly replied. "I'm just a senior-grade lieutenant."

Disappointed at his inability to wrest strategic secrets from the naval officer, the reporter tried another tack. "Well, tell me something about the plane you fly," he prompted.

"I flew SBDs at Midway and Guadalcanal. Then, in late '42, I transferred to an escort carrier squadron with TBFs."

Now it was the journalist's turn to go blank. He looked down at Johnny, as if seeking help. "The Douglas Dauntless and Grumman Avenger!" the boy exclaimed, delighted to impart such fundamental data to the ignorant wretch. Johnny was also primed to contribute his not-inconsiderable knowledge of his uncle Ray's airplane, the sleek Martin B-26 Marauder. Rogers grinned and mussed his nephew's hair in appreciation.

Eventually Rogers hit upon a strategy. He decided to give only terse answers in hopes of ending the interview. Asked, "Are the Japs pretty tough?" he replied, "Yeah, plenty tough."

"Well, are their planes and pilots as good as ours?"

"No."

"Well . . . Would you say we're winning in the Pacific?"

"Sure."

The reporter finally tumbled to the stratagem and posed more complex queries. "Lieutenant, tell me about your citation at the Battle of Midway."

But Rogers invoked national security. "Oh, that's still classified," he said with a straight face. Rogers's Navy Cross citation had been published, as the reporter well knew. Shortly he went away to write a fluff piece extolling the virtues of "West Palm's own air hero, the quiet and self-effacing Lieut. Philip Rogers."

By midafternoon the crowd had dwindled to a few diehards. Rogers quietly appreciated the depleted stacks of cookies and doughnuts—not to mention a large cake—all of which must have required piles of sugar ration cards.

He was explaining some of the fine points of dive-bombing to a rapt Johnny Bennett when he heard a soft voice purring behind him. "There you are, sweetheart!"

Rogers turned to find himself staring at Audrey Bonzagni—all five feet ten of her. His heart fluttered as it slow-rolled off the top of a loop.

Since his return he had been the beneficiary of dozens of kisses—familial, friendly, even a few blatantly romantic. But Audrey clamped herself onto Phil Rogers like a female octopus and delivered a delicious, toe-curling kiss that could only be interpreted as predatory. Taking in the arcane ritual, Johnny sulked away in search of something more to eat.

When they came up for air, Audrey's tiger eyes were inches from Rogers's face. He gulped, trying to think of something to say. "Well, Audrey . . . Long time no see!"

She slid her arms from around him and uttered a deep, throaty laugh. "Oh, Phil, you can do better than that! After all, we went steady almost two years." Her red lips curled into the dimples that he had always admired in high school.

Audrey Bonzagni was not beautiful by most standards. *But God, is she sexy!* With his previous relationship in limbo, his mind raced, sorting out options, priorities, commitments.

"Well, I didn't expect to see you here, is all. What a surprise!"

Audrey took his arm and pulled him down next to her on a bench. "Your mother called a bunch of us. She's so nice. I just came from the music store with Julie Nottke."

Rogers recalled that the two girls, now young women his own age, had been best friends in school. Audrey, who had a wonderful singing voice, had been hired by Julie's father several years ago. "Well, I'll look forward to seeing her again." He moved to get up but Audrey's athletic grip pinned him. The expression on her face held a message that was clear. *I know what I want, Buster. Like Uncle Sam—I want you!*

Later that evening, Kathleen Rogers was mildly surprised when her son rolled up his sleeves and dived in to help wash a small mountain of dishes. He hummed a little tune as he concentrated on his work and she watched him in a series of sideways glances. He definitely looked older—at least, more mature—but there was something else. Something she had not seen in a long time.

"Philip, you seem awfully happy tonight. Did you enjoy the get-together after all?"

When he looked up from the sink there was a male gleam in his eyes. "I sure did, Mom. It was swell!" He leaned over and kissed her cheek.

Returning to his dishes, Phil Rogers resumed his mental calculations. *To Audrey or not to Audrey, that is the question.* He shook his head. *Rogers, you're dopey.* Still, it was nice to have a choice. Yes, that was it: having options was the best part of being alive.

SUNDAY, 12 MARCH
MCDILL ARMY AIR FIELD

Phil Rogers couldn't help looking up as a flight of four Marauders passed overhead. *We just have to watch airplanes,* he told himself, *no matter how often we see them.* With a professional eye he judged their formation as good, even by Navy standards, and he appreciated the matchless sound of eight Pratt & Whitney radial engines. Their combined sixteen thousand horsepower throbbed in the moist air with a pulsing authority that he found irresistible.

Feeling conspicuous in his Navy uniform, rumpled from a six-hour train ride, Rogers presented himself at the east gate and returned the sergeant's salute. "I'm Lieutenant Phil Rogers," he explained, "here to see my brother. Lieutenant Ray Rogers."

The noncom pulled a clipboard from the sentry's shed. "Ah, yes, sir, you're expected. I'll call him for you. Meanwhile, you can wait in the visitors' office across the street."

Almost twenty minutes later Phil heard his brother's voice around the corner. "Security alert! A Navy pilot has infiltrated the base! He's leaving seaweed in his tracks—and he's right here!" A khaki shape descended on the blue uniform, spoiling its creases, pulling Phil's visored hat off his head, and mussing his hair.

Four years older and two inches taller, the Navy officer fended off the air corps second lieutenant. "Cripes a'mighty! Don't they teach you Army weenies respect for senior officers?" Phil's "railroad track" bars proclaimed him two ranks superior to his brother.

"Hell, yes," Ray exclaimed. "But nobody here will admit that a Navy pilot is superior to anybody in the Army Air Forces! And if you think I'm gonna salute you, forget it!"

Phil made a halfhearted effort at rearranging his hair and replaced his hat. "You may note, mister, that the United States Navy does not produce mere 'pilots.' It produces by-God *aviators,* so let's have some respect."

Ray's blue-gray eyes went to his brother's gold wings, then to his own silver bombardier wings. Instantly Phil knew the meaning of the look, and regretted his innocent jibe. Ray's one letter on the subject had only hinted at his heartbreak in not making pilot training.

Alone in a corner of the officer's club the brothers quickly dispensed with preliminaries. They skimmed over the subject of their parents and sister and caught up on mutual friends. Phil was surprised to learn that one of Ray's schoolmates had been killed in Italy and another had lost a leg in a North Carolina jeep accident. After dissecting the state of the war, Ray got down to business. He leaned forward over his beer and said, "Tell me about combat flying."

Phil smiled at the recollection of a former squadron mate. "I had a pal in Bombing Three, Bernie Burnett. Great guy, good pilot, now somewhere on the East Coast. He said that breaking into combat is just like getting laid the first time. Lots of wondering and talk and speculation, but all of a sudden you're there and it's over before you realize it. After a little experience you know what to expect."

Ray chuckled politely, unwilling to admit that he knew as little of sex as he did of war. "But you've had a lot of experience." He looked again at Phil's ribbons: Navy Cross, Distinguished Flying Cross, Air Medal, and Purple Heart. "How did you get used to it?"

Phil put down his mug and leveled his gaze at his younger brother. "Ray, what you're asking me isn't really what you want to know. You're looking for a way to handle the fear. Well, I can say that you shouldn't worry about it too much. Before Midway, I was a lot more scared of screwing up than of getting killed. But later I realized everybody felt that way. You just concentrate on what you're trained to do and the rest will take care of itself."

MONDAY, 13 MARCH
MCDILL ARMY AIR FIELD

Ray Rogers imagined that he knew how matchmakers must feel, as he oozed pride in showing off his certified hero brother, but fretted that his fellow B-26 crew members somehow would fall short in Phil's estimation. Ray needn't have worried.

First Lieutenant Walter Lyman, pilot of the seven-man crew, was properly respectful. He even saluted—a gesture that Phil casually waved away. Then Rogers shook hands with each of the other men: copilot, navigator, flight engineer, and turret and tail gunners. Ray was especially pleased when his brother took pains with the enlisted men. "I take my hat off to you fellows. My radio man in Bombing Three saved my bacon a couple of times—at Midway and Guadalcanal." The sergeants beamed.

Lyman led a walkaround inspection of the B-26. It wasn't assigned to the crew yet—the fliers probably would not receive a "personal" airplane until they reported to a combat unit. "I'm sorry you can't fly this hop with us—" he began.

Phil waved again. "Oh, don't worry about it, Lieutenant. I'm just glad to meet Ray's crew." Phil did not say that he knew Ray had struck out with the base operations officer, a martinet concerned about a junior birdman's Navy brother flying in an Army aircraft.

"This is a B model," Lyman continued. "It has a wider span than the early '26s, which had some problems. High wing loading—"

"And high landing speed," Phil interjected.

Lyman cocked his head in curiosity. "Right . . ." The Army pilot shot a glance at Ray, whose look projected innocence.

"A Pensacola classmate of mine was on Midway," Phil replied. "He said four of these arrived just before the battle and he talked to one of the crews. They made an unescorted daylight torpedo attack on the Jap carriers. Two of 'em got back."

Phil had not thought of his Marine Corps friend Jim Carpenter lately. "Sunny Jim" would be a captain by now, probably back in the States after his second tour in the Solomon Islands.

"But the Navy didn't do a lot better," Phil continued. "There were six Avengers land-based at Midway, too; only one of them returned. Torpedo attacks aren't a very good career move, in *any* airplane."

"We heard about Torpedo Eight," Ray exclaimed. "They lost the whole outfit, right?"

Phil nodded. "All but one pilot from the *Hornet,* though the land-based TBFs also belonged to Torpedo Eight. People forget that." He fell silent for a moment, remembering that Torpedo 3 had flown away from *Yorktown* and never returned. Nobody talked about Lieutenant Commander Lance Massey's squadron.

"I suspect we'll go to Europe, so we probably won't have to worry about torpedo drops," Lyman offered. "But what can you tell us about the job?"

Phil shrugged. "Low and fast, in and out. With your speed you should be okay as long as you've some kind of escort. But after I rotated out of dive-bombers, my new outfit with TBFs did quite a bit of torpedo work—mostly practice 'fish' but a few with live warheads."

"How'd it go, sir?" asked McDonald, the copilot.

Phil snorted. "I guess we dropped a couple dozen all told, and I doubt if six ran hot, straight, and normal. Anyway, I hardly got a chance at Jap ships after Guadalcanal so we usually flew with four five hundred–pound bombs."

"Mr. Rogers, what about the Jap torpedoes?" McDonald seemed genuinely interested.

"Oh, that's easy," Phil deadpanned. "They work just fine."

"What about the Japs themselves," Lyman asked. "Just how tough are they?"

"Well, you must get intelligence briefings pretty much like we do. I've heard a lecture by a former naval attaché to Tokyo. He says they're a warlike race to start with, and they came a hell of a long way in a short time to catch up with us."

Ray interjected. "Actually, we don't hear much of that stuff. We're too busy just learning how to use the airplane."

Phil scanned the crew. He saw reflected in those seven faces his own prewar anxiety. He imagined how much he would have given for this chance—to talk with someone who had been places and done things he was going to have to do. He chose his words carefully.

"Fellows, I can tell you this much: The Japs aren't unbeatable. My Marine buddy, Carpenter, got clobbered at Midway, then he bagged six or eight planes at Guadalcanal. But Zeros killed two of the crews from my squadron and wiped out most of three torpedo outfits at Midway before we sank their carriers. Jap subs put me ashore three times in eight months—twice on the *Saratoga* and again when the *Yorktown* was sunk."

"But that was two years ago," Ray insisted. "Haven't things improved a lot since then?"

Phil turned toward his brother and gave him a long look. "Well, you guys don't need a Navy pilot to tell you the score. I read something about General Kenney, running the Army Air Force in the Southwest Pacific. You know what he says about the Japs?" Vacant expressions and shaking heads greeted the question.

"He says you take on Notre Dame every time you play."

Moments later Phil shoehorned himself into the copilot's seat while Lyman sat to his left. "It's all pretty routine," Lyman began explaining to his guest. The B-26 pilot touched each item in turn: "Throttle quadrant here between us, engine gauges grouped together, flight instruments on both sides." Rogers recognized everything, though he noted that the Army's air-speed indicators were calibrated in statute miles per hour rather than nautical miles per hour, as he was used to.

"The main thing my copilot does is watch the tachs during takeoff," Lyman explained. He touched the tachometer for both engines. "If we get a runaway prop, or if one of 'em goes into flat pitch, we're in big trouble. You have to act damned fast to save the airplane."

Rogers looked across the console at his host. "I didn't know you still had that problem. Hasn't the factory solved it yet?"

Lyman's face was set in a grim mask. "Not yet. We have Curtiss Electric propellers on this airplane, and as far as I'm concerned they're its only drawback. The high wing loading and 130 mile per hour approach speed are really no sweat as long as you pay attention. But if you lose an engine or get a runaway prop on takeoff—well, I've seen it happen." He extended his right hand, palm down, then abruptly flipped it over.

"So what do you do? Shut down right away?"

Lyman gave a tight-lipped grin. "No, sir. You shut it down *instantly!* Otherwise the torque on the operating engine just rolls you over. Both pilots can stand on the opposite rudder and put full aileron against the roll, but nobody can hold it long enough to save the ship. The power's got to come off like that." He snapped his fingers.

"That's what they mean by one a day in Tampa Bay?"

"Oh, Ray told you that one, did he?" Lyman was smiling now.

"Hell, no. He said you call this the 'flying prostitute'—no visible means of support." Rogers chuckled, jabbing a thumb toward the Marauder's thin, high-speed wing. Then he lowered his voice. "Tell me, Lieutenant. How's my brother doing? Holding up his end?"

Lyman leaned forward on the control yoke. "You bet. He's doing fine—now. When we formed the crew, he was still blue about not being selected for pilot training. But he realizes that the rest of us are here just to put him over the target."

Both men felt and heard the movement of someone entering the aircraft through the nosewheel well. Baranek, the navigator, appeared at the gap between the rudder pedals. "Walt, we've got our clearance. Ready to go."

Rogers levered himself out of the copilot's seat. "Guess that's my cue," he said, smiling at the man whose head and hands were responsible for Ray Rogers's life—and five others'. They shook hands in parting, then Phil eased himself along the walkway and swung down to the ground. The copilot gave a thumbs-up and climbed aboard, leaving the brothers alone.

"You've got a good crew, Ray. I mean it. Lyman knows his business, and I feel better knowing you'll be flying with him."

Ray shifted his weight to one foot—a petulant signal that Phil knew well. "Yeah. As long as I can't be flying myself."

Phil's trigger finger was under Ray's nose. "You listen to me, little brother. You take that out someplace and tie a can to it. Your pilot just told me that this whole crew's job is to put you over the target. Don't you let them down—or me, either." Phil remembered to unzip the smile he always used to leaven his temper.

And it still worked. For the third or fourth time in their lives, they spontaneously hugged and patted each other's backs. Then Phil abruptly turned and strode away in long, purposeful steps. He kept up the pace until he heard Lyman starting the left engine. When he looked over his shoulder, the Marauder was blurred in a haze of blue smoke and tears.

WEDNESDAY, 15 MARCH
OITA BASE, KYUSHU ISLAND

Sakaida sat on the grass in front of the operations office, surrounded by the seven pilots assigned to him for training. The second flight leader, a petty officer named Kikuchi, had survived the recent Rabaul battles, but all the others were rookies. Dressed in full flight gear, their fur-lined ear flaps turned up the better to hear their instructor, most of them still looked far too young to be budding aerial warriors. He decided to begin with the basics.

"I have learned from Lieutenant Commander Yoshimura that we will employ the two-plane pair, the *buntai*," Sakaida began. He explained that that meant two *buntai* to each *shotai,* and so on.

One of Sakaida's own pilots, Flight Petty Officer Ichiro Nakaya, leaned forward on his knees. Looking around, he said, "Sakaida-san, we have been accustomed to flying six-plane divisions with two pair of three. Why the change?"

Sakaida wondered if Nakaya had succumbed to the traditional Japanese superstition about the number four. But the boy had asked a sensible question and deserved a reply. "Combat experience has proved the superiority of the two-plane element," Sakaida began. "Nearly all our fighter units changed last summer, while I was still in the Solomons." He looked at Kikuchi, a slight nod urging him to comment.

"That is correct," Kikuchi said. "The Americans always met us over Rabaul in fours. We had to change in order to survive."

Nakaya licked his lips, obviously uncertain of his ground. One simply did not question doctrine in the Imperial Navy—especially when one had never seen combat. Sensing the boy's doubts, Sakaida interjected. "I know your thoughts, Nakaya. Look here." Reaching into a pocket, he tore a report form into several pieces and laid three in a triangular pattern on the grass. Then he arranged four more in the pattern of extended fingertips.

"These are the basic elements of combat units, our old three-plane section and the Americans' four. The difference is apparent, is it not? Four against three."

Nakaya was unconvinced. "Beg pardon, Sakaida-san. This does not seem a fair comparison. Shouldn't it be our three against the Yankee's two? Those are the basic elements, are they not?"

"Only in theory. When you meet the enemy, you will always meet him in fours. It is not possible to keep a six-plane *shotai* together in battle. The two wingmen in each three-plane element are too busy keeping formation on their leader, or they get separated and become vulnerable: one against two opponents or one against four. And that one always loses."

"It's true," Kikuchi snapped. The impatience in his voice was enough to overwhelm Nakaya's uncertainty. "I have seen it happen. One of our aces—a man undefeated in the air since 1941—lost support of his two wingmen while chasing a Vought fighter. The American's wingman crossed over and exploded our man." Kikuchi glared at the youngster. "You listen to your superiors, boy, and you might live longer."

Nakaya's pudgy face reddened under the rebuke. At a loss for words, he bowed his head and awkwardly muttered an apology. Sakaida felt certain the new flier would never again question anything, but that was not the aim. "All of you can learn something here," he began in a soft voice. "It is well to ask questions, for how else can you learn? Do not fear to clarify what you do not understand."

Sakaida's wingman, Flight Petty Officer Yoshio Yamamoto, tentatively raised a hand. "Why was the three-plane *shotai* used originally if four is superior?"

It was another logical question that Sakaida wanted to treat carefully. Not even flight chief petty officers could criticize the system with impunity. "I suspect it was because three is a natural number—a leader and two wingmen. It looks good at air displays and allows easy formation aerobatics. But in battle, it is as Kikuchi says. Keeping formation on the leader causes the wingmen to lose some vigilance." He scanned his audience for emphasis. "And that can be fatal."

Rogers walked up the steps to his parents' home and plopped into the porch swing. He leaned back and closed his eyes, remembering other evenings on that porch and that swing—a delightful few of them had been shared with Audrey. He listened to the night, savoring the once-familiar scents and sounds that meant Home.

"Oh, there you are, son. I didn't hear you come up." His father's voice caught Phil by surprise, coming from behind the screen door.

"I just got back, Dad." He turned toward his left, looking at the back-lighted form in the doorway. The familiar flag hung in the window next to the door, sporting two blue stars for the household's sons in the armed forces.

"It must be like old times with you and Audrey," Stephen said in his precise accountant's voice. Phil thought he detected a touch of humor in his father's voice. Or was it irony?

"Well, I guess nothing can ever really be the same." He looked up at his father, who swatted at a firefly. "Especially during wartime." Stephen said nothing, prompting Phil to continue. "You know we were pretty serious in high school, but we sort of lost touch when I left for college."

"You know we've always been fond of Audrey. Do you think she wants to take up where you left off?"

Phil stretched his arms and faked a yawn. It wasn't very late—barely past ten—and the father recognized the son's body language: embarrassment bordering on nervousness. *He wonders if I'm stringing Audrey along,* Phil thought. Well, the thought certainly had occurred to him; nothing could come of it in the short time left.

Phil was thankful when the elder Rogers changed the subject. "You got a phone call from a Lieutenant Burnett at the Fourth Naval District in Philadelphia. I wrote it down and said you would call back tomorrow."

"That's Bernie!" Phil exclaimed, eager for news of his former squadron mate. "He's at the Naval Aircraft Factory. Did he say what it's about?"

Stephen took a step closer, as if to scrutinize his son's expression in the dim light. "Something about a couple of speeches to war production plants."

Phil smiled to himself. *Good ol' Bernie. Who's he got in his pocket to get me on the traveling hero circuit?* Ordinarily Phil would have volunteered for multiengine transports before he would dream of making any more speeches, but now he seriously pondered the offer. He turned to his

father. "I'll have to think about it, but I sure would like to see Bernie again."
He wondered whether to unlimber his emotional heavy artillery, then fired
a salvo. "I really don't think I can turn him down, of all people, Dad."

Stephen Rogers knew a lot about Lieutenant Burnett: the Bombing-3
pilot who had led a wounded Phil Rogers back to *Yorktown* after the attack
on a Japanese cruiser at Midway. The cheerful, extroverted Bernie of so
many of Phil's early-war letters. "No, I don't suppose you could refuse him,
son." He turned and slowly walked back inside.

Actually, Phil's mind was made up, partly because the constant attention was wearing on him. He had seen many of his childhood friends
and he had sailed, orated, visited and hobnobbed enough. He had attended
church with his mother and gone fishing with his dad at Riviera Beach. But
mainly he needed to get away from Audrey, who had her emotional hooks
into him.

There was only one thing to do: get the hell out of town.

TUESDAY, 21 MARCH

Neither Phil Rogers nor Bernie Burnett had ever given much thought to
where bombs came from. But the Pennsylvania steel country was dotted
with ordnance factories working three shifts per day, five days per week.
Each was a Vulcan's forge of frantic activity amid gas furnaces, molten
steel, noxious fumes, and searing heat.

It was an informative evening for everyone. The aviators were fascinated to see where their ordnance originated, and the workers who produced
the weapons were enthralled to meet two young warriors who had delivered those bombs to the ultimate recipients.

"I'm sorry we don't have proper facilities for you gentlemen to speak
from," apologized the assistant plant manager, hosting the visitors in the
cafeteria. "But we just don't have room for big assemblies like some other
war plants." His name was Ferris Pyzdrowski, a medium-height, medium-
weight, medium-looking man apparently of medium age.

"Don't worry about it," Burnett responded. "We didn't expect the
red-carpet treatment."

In truth, Rogers was disappointed at the arrangements. He had envisioned a large stage hung with bunting and an auditorium with a loudspeaker
system, crammed with hundreds of eager war workers. But he realized that
such accommodations were limited to facilities like aircraft factories, which
needed open areas. He and Burnett had agreed to split the handshake tours
during the swing and graveyard shifts, respectively.

"We really do appreciate it," Pyzdrowski said. "You're practically the first fighting men we've seen here. I can't tell you what it means to our soldiers to talk to fellows like you."

The fliers exchanged wry glances. After two days of touring armament factories, Burnett and Rogers had caught on to some of the terminology. Several plants designated their employees "soldiers" or "fighters in the war of production" to enhance solidarity with the troops. But Rogers thought the situation was best described by a short, balding welder. "Before Pearl Harbor we was defense workers," he had explained between chomps of tobacco. "An' now we're war workers but th' goddamn job don't change none, and th' goddamn pay changes damn little."

Like most combatants, Burnett and Rogers had little sympathy with complaining civilians. Though the Office of War Production had placed a 10-percent ceiling on corporate profits, individual workers were eligible for almost unlimited overtime. It was a situation guaranteed to elicit at least a low grumble from Burnett, whose father was a onetime Ford executive now helping manage B-24 Liberator production at Willow Run.

As the swing shift came off and the graveyard shift arrived, the naval aviators were a magnet for curious and occasionally adoring workers. The cafeteria filled with as odd an assortment of humanity as Rogers had ever seen: teenagers to grandparents; boys and men, women and girls. Burnett had cited government statistics for 1943 showing five million more women in war production, and had hastily calculated the odds of a decidedly unromantic relationship with some of them.

Rogers noticed that many of the swing shift workers showed the genetic influence of Eastern Europeans only a generation or two removed from what now was an unwilling part of the Third Reich. Most were grimy; all were intrigued.

"Fellow soldiers," began Pyzdrowski, "I'm pleased to introduce to you some special guests this evening. Lieutenants Burnett and Rogers are Navy dive-bomber pilots who sank some Jap ships in the Midway and Guadalcanal battles. They're here to tell us how our bombs put those ships in Davy Jones's locker!"

Burnett nudged Rogers and chided him with a knowing smile. Neither was solely responsible for sinking any ships—that hardly ever happened—and in fact Burnett had never gained a confirmed hit. He patted his friend on the back. "Go get 'em, Buck!"

Rogers cleared his throat and took a step forward. "Well, I'm sure glad to get a chance to talk to you folks," he began. Gesturing behind himself, he added, "Bernie and I are like a lot of bomber pilots, I guess. We just took it for granted that when we manned our planes on the flight deck every morning that the bombs would be hanging in the racks. We really didn't wonder where they came from or who made them.

"But now that we've been here and talked to some of you, I'm not going to take that for granted again. I've seen how hard you work, and I'm going to tell my pals what a swell job you're doing." He scanned the faces, seeking an indication of how his words were being received. Finding none, he recalled his father's long-ago advice: A short speech is a popular speech. "So you keep turning 'em out and we'll see they get delivered!"

He took a step back, smiling sheepishly at the applause. It began in the front row as a polite ripple, then gathered momentum. Some of the younger workers emitted shrill whistles and others shouted, "You tell 'em, Lieutenant!" Rogers was embarrassed at the response.

Pyzdrowski waved for quiet and the noise abated. "Now I'm sure some of you soldiers have some questions for our fliers." He looked around, then pointed to a raised hand.

A man in the front row took a hesitant half step forward. He wore heavy work clothes and his face was a roadmap of a lifetime's toil and worry. "Well, ah, I do wonder 'bout somethin'," he began. "My oldest boy, he's in th' Air Corps. I jus' wonder why you boys'd wanta do a durn-fool thing like landing airplanes on a durn ship!" The question brought giggles from some of the women; chuckles from several men.

"Well, sir, I'm from Florida, on the Atlantic coast," Rogers replied. "I guess you'd say there's saltwater in my veins. Besides, I had a direct ancestor on the *Mayflower* so ships just come naturally to me." He looked expectantly at Burnett.

Bernie, who had been playing visual patty-cake with a short, cute brunette, straightened himself. "Well, I can't brag about my pedigree like Buck here," he said earnestly. "In fact, I'm just a lazy son of a gun. See, when I walked into the recruiting station in Detroit, the Navy office was closest to the door. The Air Corps was clear down the hall!" Even Rogers, who knew the story was an outrageous lie, was moved to laughter.

"I'd sure like to hear about some of the ships you fellers sank," a fortyish man called. "How 'bout it?" Another worker endorsed the sentiment, and more applause swept the room.

Rogers inhaled and pressed ahead. "Well, to tell you the truth, I dropped my first bomb about a hundred eighty miles short of the target." Burnett chortled at his side, gently shaking his head at the memory of Bombing 3's gremlins at Midway. Rogers ignored him and hastened to explain. "Our squadron had new Dauntlesses with electrical arming switches. But just when we cleared our task force and we flipped the switches, mine

and three others fell in the ocean!" His admission brought a mixture of surprised gasps and sympathetic chuckles.

"Fortunately, the rest of our squadron did a four-oh job and sank a Jap
carrier. That evening we went back and sank the last flattop in the Jap force."

"What about your other raids," Pyzdrowski urged.

"Well, in SBDs I dropped four bombs on Jap ships—a five
hundred–pounder and three half-tonners. I got two hits and a near miss,
though the first hit was on a cruiser that was nearly dead in the water." He
eyed Burnett, standing smugly on the sidelines, obviously enjoying his
friend's discomfiture. "But even that's a better record than anybody else in
this room!"

Caught by surprise, Burnett mugged a who-me? expression, searching the cafeteria for another SBD pilot. The audience loved it.

Later, Rogers accepted an invitation for a close-up look at the production line while Burnett regaled the graveyard shift. Rogers was introduced to a stout, thirtyish woman named Alma Hollis, whom Pyzdrowski
introduced as "one of our best soldiers." In fact, Alma Hollis was a bomb
spinner.

Hollis took considerable pride in showing her spinning machine, which
turned pipelike lengths of heated steel into bomb forgings. Rogers inferred
that very few women attained the position of bomb spinner, and it was apparent that Alma Hollis was good at her job. At her console behind a steel-
mesh screen, she deftly manipulated a set of controls that to Rogers looked
more complex than those for an aircraft's elevators, rudder, and ailerons.

With the heated forging locked into her spinner, Hollis activated one
handle that began rotating the object at high speed. "This winds up to about
two thousand r.p.m.," she shouted over the whine. "Then I pull this lever
and the torches close in on the nose." Rogers saw acetylene torches apply
their superheated flame to the end of the forging to prevent it from cooling.

"Now comes the hard part," Hollis yelled. She pulled a third control
arm that pressed a hardened steel roller against the heated end of the object. Instantly a fiery stream of sparks and tiny slivers showered the area,
and Rogers instinctively flinched. But Hollis paid no attention. The combat veteran recovered his poise and admired the concentration evident in
the woman's visored face as she shaped a perfectly-contoured nose to the
future bomb. In less than sixty seconds she was finished. Two burly men
removed the casing from the machine and sent it down the line, where the
next worker would shape the tail.

"That's quite a deal," Rogers commented. "How many bombs do you
turn out a day?"

"Oh, let's see . . ." Hollis feigned calculating in her head. "Close to five hundred or so." She smiled widely, showing stained teeth in a pudgy face. As her helpers shoved another forging into the spinner, Alma Hollis raised her visor, reached out, and kissed Phil Rogers—hard. "You sink more of them bastards for me," she shouted before turning back to her machine.

Walking away, Rogers said, "That Hollis is some dame. Are there many like her?"

"Not enough, if you ask me," the Pyzdrowski replied. "Our production director attended a conference a few months ago; said there were eight million new jobs nationwide. But even with all these women, some war industries are still short of workers. You've seen for yourself—we're hiring old people, Negroes, even some with physical handicaps."

Rogers absorbed that information. "Sounds like a good deal for everybody, as long as the damn war lasts."

Pyzdrowski grinned self-consciously. "You're right there, Lieutenant. Corporate profits this year will probably be twice what they were in '41."

"Well, what's that mean to your workers?"

"Oh, I'd say our better men earn about forty-five dollars a week. Alma and the other gal who work as spinners are paid a little less, but they produce just as many bombs so they're more efficient from a financial viewpoint."

Staring at the manager, Rogers asked, "That's not quite fair, is it?"

Pyzdrowski shrugged. "There's a war on, Lieutenant."

Rogers walked past a spinner roasting wieners over a red-hot bomb casing while millwrights cleaned and oiled his machine. "That's what everybody says, sir."

April 1944

MONDAY, 3 APRIL
NAVAL AIR STATION SAN DIEGO, CALIFORNIA

Rogers and Burnett were five minutes early for their appointment with Captain Arnold Edwards, the personnel officer of ComFair—Commander, Fleet Air—West Coast. They knew that requests for particular assignments were rarely granted, and had also heard dire predictions of the fate awaiting junior officers who kept Captain Edwards waiting. Reportedly a lieutenant commander who had committed that offense now was the "windsock officer" at scenic Adak, Alaska.

"I hear they call Edwards the Coronado Cobra," Burnett said, removing his visored hat as they entered the domed cement building. The air station sat upon North Island, jutting into San Diego Bay and adjoining the city of Coronado. It was conveniently near the fabled "Hotel Del," scene of some memorable parties over the past twenty years.

"Maybe he'll be sympathetic to old shipmates," Rogers offered. "Remember, he was on Admiral Fletcher's staff on the *Yorktown*."

"Ummm," Burnett replied noncommittally. As they climbed the stairs to the second floor, Rogers reflected that Annapolis graduates were not always sympathetic to reservists. But he knew that the U.S. Navy could not hope to conduct a world war without the reserves; there were simply too few regulars.

Entering the wood-paneled office, Bernie took the lead as senior of the two aviators. "Lieutenants Burnett and Rogers reporting as directed by Captain Edwards," he told the chief petty officer at the outer desk.

The chief buzzed the inner sanctum, spoke into the squawk box, and got a clipped reply. "You may go in, gentlemen," he announced. Rogers thought the man's demeanor a mixture of concern leavened with pity. Burnett rapped a regulation two times on the door and heard a snarled "Come!"

The two aviators marched into the office, crashed to attention two paces from the desk, and riveted their gaze over the head of Captain Arnold Edwards. They were slightly surprised to find themselves focusing on a large framed photo of USS *Yorktown* (CV-5), sunk twenty-two months before, off Midway.

Edwards took a minute to finish reading a personnel file, then plopped it onto his desk. He looked up at the lieutenants, noted that the taller one's wings were about 15 degrees low to port, and allowed the men to suffer a bit longer. Then his metallic voice grated, "Stand at ease, gentlemen."

Rogers lowered his gaze to the ComFair Personnel, the individual responsible for aviation detailing on the West Coast. If anything, Rogers thought that Captain Edwards looked younger than two years before. He had been a commander then, a lean forty-one with a face tanned and lined from a career spent at sea and in open-cockpit aircraft. *But the eyes are the same,* Rogers thought. Still that cold pale blue that turned ensigns' guts to icewater.

"So you want to fly together again," Edwards began. His tone carried a hint of accusation.

"Yes, sir," Burnett began. "We—"

Edwards cut off the reply like honed steel. "And who is who here? You have not extended me the courtesy of a proper introduction." If these had been two nuggets—fresh-caught aviators—he would have sent them out and required a proper entry. But they had been shot at in this war and he was prepared to cut them some slack.

"I'm Burnett, sir." Bernie instinctively snapped back to attention, his gaze welded to the bulkhead again.

"I see." Edwards shifted his gaze to the tall one. "Mr. Rogers, do you customarily wear your wings askew?"

Rogers risked a glance down and detected no error, but thought better of protesting the charge. "No, sir!" He emulated Bernie's rigid brace, thinking that if either flier offered an apology the Coronado Cobra would coil and strike at any sign of weakness.

Edwards sat back a moment, briefly enjoying the boys' discomfort. *Damn it,* he thought. *What I'd give to be in their place, bound for combat in a hot airplane.* He felt himself melt a little inside. "Very well. Now that we understand each other, pull up a chair."

Burnett and Rogers exchanged puzzled glances, then hurried to comply. They scooted up close to the desk, eager with anticipation. As they did so, Edwards buzzed the outer office and ordered some coffee brought in. When all three were settled with their cups, Edwards got down to business.

"I remember you from Bombing Three," he began. "Now, that cannot be a factor in where you are assigned, but it's nice to see old shipmates for a change."

Rogers almost dropped his cup, regulation white with a small blue anchor. *I'll be go to hell. He does remember us!*

"Yes, sir," Burnett replied. "We were with Commander Leslie on the *Saratoga* before we joined you in the old *Yorktown*. Then we went back out again under Mr. Shumway when the Sara was patched up for Guadalcanal."

Edwards touched the personnel folders. "So I see. Max Leslie was three years behind me at Annapolis. Fine officer. Last I heard, he was in command of an operational training base on the East Coast." He set down his cup after only two sips. "Now, it seems to me that you both would be in line for a job like that. I expect to have two slots for dive-bomber instructors at Los Alamitos . . ." He let the offer dangle, even though no such openings existed. *Let's see how eager these boys really are.*

Burnett leaned forward. "Oh, excuse me, sir. We've talked it over. Phil and me . . . er, I . . . would like to get back to carriers. We're sort of a team."

Edwards swiveled his reptilean gaze to Rogers. "Is that right, Lieutenant? I can understand Mr. Burnett, who's been at NAF Philadelphia for almost nine months. But you've been in combat almost constantly."

Rogers fidgeted in his chair. He had not expected this kind of grilling. "Captain, it would be more accurate to say that I've been in the Pacific Theater almost constantly. Frankly, sir, I felt I was spinning my wheels in the *Alazon Bay*. Besides a few strikes in the Solomons, it was mostly steaming back and forth, flying antisub patrols that never turned up anything." He leaned forward, stressing his earnestness. "Sir, I'll take whatever you've got, bombers or fighters. But Lieutenant Burnett and I sure would like to fly together again."

ComFair Personnel sat back, regarding the two friends. Again his sympathy for combat veterans short-circuited his usual reaction to aviators seeking preferential treatment—especially those who loudly moaned, "If only I could get to combat!" but gladly remained Stateside. *After all,* he mused, *pilots with far less background than these lads have been pulling for training command duty to pass along their "vast experience."*

"All right," Edwards decided. "There's a new air group forming at Pasco, Washington. I can't guarantee that you'll both go to the same squadron, but it's a fair guess that you'll be able to sink more Japs together. Will that suit you?"

The two smiles seemed to light up the room. "Yes, sir!" Burnett exclaimed. He and Rogers stood up to leave. "Thank you, Captain," Bernie added.

Edwards extended a hand to each flier and clenched two rock-hard grips. "I may not be doing you any favors, you know."

Rogers decided to ignore the implied warning. "We'll try to earn our keep, sir."

"One more thing!" Edwards exclaimed, freezing both men at the door. "This is a direct order. When you put another Jap ship on the bottom or shoot down a Zero, you *will* inform this office!"

"Aye, aye, sir!" The responses rang in happy unison.

FRIDAY, 7 APRIL

OVER SAEKI BAY

"Falcon Twenty-six just crashed in the water!"

Aloft in his Zero, Sakaida almost groaned aloud. *Not again!* He glanced north, the direction the panicky radio call had come from. He knew that *Junyo*'s Zero Model 32s were scheduled for bombing practice today while he led eight Zero Model 52s on an air combat training mission. Haze in the direction of Bungo Strait prevented any view of the area where towed target sleds were servicing the fledgling fighter-bombers of *Hikotai* 321.

Sakaida turned in his seat to check on his own rookie pilots, no more experienced than the youngster who had just flown into the channel between Kyushu and Shikoku.

The attrition was only increasing, and Sakaida knew that some of it was inevitable. There had been deck crashes by new pilots trying to land aboard *Junyo,* even in as simple a plane as the Zero. But the deadly litany accelerated: collisions and stall-spins by fighters in mock dogfights, target fixation by fighter-bombers and dive-bombers like the boy who had just died. Sakaida knew that there were already plans to limit the fighter-bombers to 35-degree gliding runs; not as effective as the high, steep diving attack, but more easily accomplished by inexperienced pilots.

Sakaida waggled his wings in a join-up signal and watched his wingmen close into acceptable echelon. The second flight took position to port, slightly higher. He briefly considered returning to Oita Base, but he shook off the urge. *These boys need all the training they can get,* he told himself.

And even that probably will not be enough. He signaled for another setup, allowing the second flight to attack his leading quartet.

The four Model 52s angled up and away—echeloned, streamlined shapes reminding Sakaida of a school of aerial sharks. But he watched them with a sense of melancholy foreboding. For he knew that there existed bigger predators in the airy ocean of the sky.

MONDAY, 10 APRIL

NAVAL AIR STATION PASCO, WASHINGTON

One by one the Hellcats dropped out of the darkening sky, descending across the river with the twilight behind them. Wheels down, flaps down, running lights strobing from their backs, the big Grumman fighters screeched onto the pavement in three-point landings twenty seconds apart.

Fighting Squadron 59 was home to roost.

Phil Rogers turned away from the flight line and walked back toward the maintenance shack. He did not have to be there, but he wanted to get a feel for his new unit and its surroundings. From experience in two other squadrons he knew that the leading chief was likely the best-informed man around, and everyone said that Chief Andersen of Fighting 59 never got far from the hangar.

Stepping into the small, brightly lit office, Rogers found a yeoman updating aircraft maintenance records. The "writer" looked about fourteen years old, and was so absorbed in his work that he failed to notice the officer enter. Rogers waited a few seconds, then scuffed the floor with one shoe.

The look on the kid's face was worth the wait. Curly hair, freckles, and a gap-toothed smile momentarily froze into an imitation of military bearing. "Excuse me, sir! I didn't see you, sir!" The sound of scraping chair legs on a cement floor and—could it be?—clicking heels accompanied the outburst.

Rogers hastened to put the quivering statue at ease. With a wave of one hand he said, "As you were, please." The yeoman relaxed almost visibly and the aviator smiled. "You're working kind of late, aren't you?"

"Yes, sir. We've been kinda busy, gettin' new airplanes an' all. Sir!"

"I'm Lieutenant Rogers. I just reported aboard today and wanted to look over the setup." He jerked a thumb toward the Pratt & Whitney growls outside the window. "Didn't expect the squadron to be so far along in the syllabus."

The yeoman glanced toward the flight line. "Oh, shucks, Lieutenant. That's the skipper, Lieutenant Commander Connell. We're still gettin' airplanes and he likes to have every one flown by himself or a senior pilot before anybody else takes 'em off the ground. That's why these four were out at dusk."

Rogers approved. Though it probably wasn't necessary, the procedure made sense. Grumman was delivering hundreds of Hellcats a month, and even the firm's superb reputation for reliability couldn't guarantee against a gremlin or two remaining hidden somewhere. Though factory and Navy acceptance pilots flight-checked the systems, there was the chance that intermediate maintenance could alter or leave out something. *Looks like I've got a flying skipper,* Rogers thought. He stepped outside to meet Mr. Connell.

ComFitRon 59 was easy to spot. The tallest of the men in the squadron, he exuded confidence and authority as he strode toward the line shack. Rogers heard one of the ensigns address him as "Skip," presumably short for skipper. Connell stopped and braced the offender, though Rogers could tell the CO was smiling. "Mr. Fielding, you may address me as 'sir,' or 'Skipper' or 'Captain' because this is a sea-going command. But if you ever use that Hollywood slang again, you will become laundry and morale officer in Snake Navel, Idaho." The ensign backed away, "sir-ring" himself to pieces while wondering if there really was an NAS Snake Navel. He certainly did not wish to find out.

Then Connell noticed the new officer walking out the door and diverted 30 degrees port to intercept him. Returning Rogers's salute, the CO said, "Good evening, Lieutenant."

"I'm Rogers, sir. Just got in today and was processed through the personnel office."

Connell's gaze went to the leaping panther insignia on Rogers's well-used flight jacket. The CO's face brightened in recognition as he shifted his parachute harness to one shoulder with his left hand and extended his right. "Oh, hell yes! Rogers, from Bombing Three. Welcome aboard." He pumped Phil's hand enthusiastically.

"You didn't have to look me up tonight, you know," Connell added. "I'd have met you with the other arrivals tomorrow morning."

"Well, sir, I'm afraid there's just me. I came up from North Island with Lieutenant Burnett and two others, but they all wound up in the bomber and torpedo outfits. Besides, I wanted to look at your setup as soon as possible."

Connell's face looked as if a cloud had crossed the moon, then the disappointment was gone. "Well, Rogers, if you're that eager, you came to the right place. If I have my way, we're going to fly thirty percent more hours than the bombers and torpeckers combined. We'll get more pilots in due time, but meanwhile I can sure use your experience."

Rogers reckoned Gordon Connell to be an up-front leader, probably the kind who did not mind bending rules in order to get results. "Skipper, if I may, I'd like to recommend Bernie Burnett. We were together in Bombing Three, and ComFair personnel sort of did us a favor by sending us both here. Any chance you might get him assigned to us?"

The CO peered into Rogers's face, but in the dark Phil could not tell the color of the man's eyes. After a pause, Connell intoned, "Well, I can try, but I doubt it'll do any good. Pat Clarey runs a real tight ship in VB-59, and he's almost as short of pilots as I am right now." He thought for a moment. "I'm a few numbers senior to him, though. I'll see what I can do." He tapped Rogers on the arm. "I'm headed home to dinner. Maybe you'd care to join me and Mrs. Connell some evening."

Rogers brightened at the invitation. "Why, thank you, sir." They exchanged farewell salutes, and Rogers's hand was still at visor level when Connell steamed off, hailing officers and enlisted men by name, even in the dark.

Watching the CO leave, Rogers felt better than he had in months. *If the rest of the outfit is anything like him, we're going to have one hell of a squadron.*

WEDNESDAY, 12 APRIL

OITA BASE

"Why cannot we get more flight time?" Petty Officer Nakaya asked. A second-class flight petty officer would not dare use that tone of voice to most chief petty officers, but Sakaida sympathized with the sentiment. He decided to be patient.

"We still do not have our full complement of aircraft," he explained. "The *hikotai* operations officer said that as of last week our air group still had less than one third of its allotted strength." Sakaida was quick to point out the silver lining in the gloom. "At least we and the fighter-bombers are better off than the carrier bomber and attack units. They only had four Type Ninety-nines at that time."

Nakaya shook his head slowly, and Sakaida wondered if the element leader was going to break into tears. Sakaida knew him as a conscientious individual who probably felt that the sacred bond of trust between leaders and followers was being broken.

"Sakaida-san, I know you state only the truth. But even the fighters

we have are outmoded!" Nakaya waved toward the flight line where ob-
solescent Zero Model 21s outnumbered the newer Model 52s by more than
two to one.

Enough of this, Sakaida decided. "Petty Officer Nakaya! Don't you
suppose that the newest aircraft go where the need is greatest? What right
have you to complain when our men on the battle fronts often lack for spare
parts?"

From ingrained reflex, Ichiro Nakaya braced himself at the unaccustomed display of martial authority. He knew that Sakaida's point was in-
disputable—units training in home waters had to take second best to combat
squadrons.

Privately, Sakaida berated himself for the outburst. His words had the
sound of self-importance and indignity. He resisted glancing left and right
to see who might have overheard him. The difficulties of operating at the
end of a long supply line were well known and widely understood—anyone who had been to a combat theater would acknowledge that fact. But
officially there were no shortages for the emperor's armed forces.

Sakaida had heard the hushed rumors, seen the furtive glances when
people discussed such things. It was said that the *kempaitai*—the military
police—had informants everywhere. He wondered whether its acolytes
would spirit away an experienced aviator who voiced such heresy. He
doubted it, but still . . .

With a brisk nod at a chastened Nakaya, Sakaida turned on his heel
and walked away.

THURSDAY, 13 APRIL
NAS PASCO, WASHINGTON

The Grumman F6F-3 was a big airplane for a carrier fighter—bigger even
than the Vought F4U-1A that Rogers's Pensacola classmate Jim Carpenter was flying. But sitting in the Hellcat marked 59-F-12, Rogers felt immediately at home: It had the same sort of roomy cockpit he had known in
the TBF-1 aboard escort carrier *Alazon Bay,* the same wing-folding mechanism that Roy Grumman reportedly had designed with a bent paper clip
stuck into a rubber eraser.

Rogers had scanned the pilot's handbook and experienced no difficulty
passing the blindfold test, thanks to the similiarity of the Hellcat's cockpit
to the Avenger's. Now he was ready to start the engine and go fly the airplane.

The squadron operations officer, Lieutenant Ron Harkin, stood on the
port wing coaching Rogers through the procedure. Rogers thought the op-

erations officer talked a good game, but something did not ring true. In their initial meeting Harkin had been at pains to mention his "first tour" in a combat zone, inferring that there had been a second. *Maybe he's got an inferiority complex around a combat SBD pilot,* Phil mused.

Rogers would have let it go, but Harkin added, "I know you're a red-hot bomber, Rogers, but you need to get sharp on gunnery. We're going to shoot down bags of Japs before this war is over." The following day, checking the squadron training syllabus, Rogers had noted that Mr. Harkin had yet to fly a gunnery hop.

However, Rogers admitted that Harkin did know how to conduct a checkout. As two mechanics turned the Hamilton-Standard propeller through five blades, Harkin leaned inside the cockpit and said, "It's pretty standard. Throttle one fifth open, leave your mixture at idle-cutoff, supercharger in neutral." He pointed to the electrical panel on the right side, below the canopy handle. "Turn your battery switch on, then the auxiliary fuel pump."

Rogers flipped the switches, heard the faint humming sounds, and depressed the primer switch for a five-count. With his left hand he rotated the magneto switch to "On both." Then he leaned outside the cockpit, checked that both mechs were safely away, and shouted, "Clear!" He engaged the starter and heard the familiar high-pitched whine as eighteen cylinders reluctantly kicked into motion, turning the three-blade prop.

A haze of oil-rich blue smoke swirled from the exhaust stacks, accompanied by a series of abrupt coughs from the Pratt & Whitney R-2800 engine. The loud, hollow barks clattered into a staccato rumble as the engine fired. Rogers depressed the latch on the red-knobbed mixture handle and, palm up, advanced it to "Auto rich." His experienced eyes swept over the gauges and he nodded to Harkin, who tapped him on the shoulder and slid off the wing.

Rogers kept a close check on the instruments. *Let's see . . . tach shows eight hundred r.p.m., oil pressure climbing to forty p.s.i. Looking good.* He nudged the throttle up to a thousand r.p.m. with his propeller control in low pitch and double-checked that his cowl flaps were fully open. As the cylinder-head temperature reached 40 degrees centigrade he cycled the propeller several times and tested the blower in neutral, low, and high, looking for any changes in oil pressure or r.p.m. Then he tested both magnetos. *Left mag—fifty r.p.m. drop. Right—maybe seventy-five.* He flipped the handle back to "Both," checked his generator output at twenty-eight volts, turned on his VHF radio, and prepared to taxi.

Picking up the microphone, Rogers called, "Pasco Tower, this is"— he remembered to look at the Bureau of Aeronautics serial number stamped on a placard below the turn-and-bank indicator—"Navy eight-six-five." He needed only the last three digits. "On the north ramp, ready to taxi for take-off."

The feminine voice shot back. "Roger, eight-six-five. You are cleared to taxi. Wind is two-eight-zero at twelve. Altimeter two-nine-nine-five. You are number three for takeoff." Rogers mentally sneered at the cute acronym for Navy females: Women Accepted for Voluntary Enlistment. He was about to replace the mike in its bracket when the WAVE added, "Have a good flight, sir." Rogers merely clicked the button in reply while thinking, *Hmmm. She does sound kind of cute. Wonder if Bernie's introduced himself yet.*

Taxiing behind two Helldivers, Rogers reached the downwind position and ran through his takeoff checklist. It wasn't much different from the Avenger's: seventeen items, beginning with wings locked and ending with trim tabs—rudder two notches nose right; ailerons and elevators at neutral.

As the Helldivers reached flying speed and lifted off, Rogers released tension on the big rudder pedals' toe brakes and smoothly advanced the throttle, keeping neutral stick pressure with his right hand. He felt seven tons accelerate into the westerly wind, drawn forward by two thousand horsepower. As the tires left the concrete mat, he immediately reached forward with his left hand, lifted the landing-gear lever, and felt the main-mounts begin their awkward routine. They unlocked downward, turned 90 degrees into the slipstream, and under fourteen hundred pounds of hydraulic pressure retracted into the wheel wells.

Rogers eased back on the throttle to maintain best climb: fifty-two inches of manifold pressure yielding 130 knots indicated airspeed. A quick look at his engine gauges convinced him that he was piloting a healthy airplane. He swiveled his head, cleared himself for a port turn, and eased into a 30-degree bank. If the Hellcat had had a rearview mirror, Phil Rogers would have seen a small grin on his face. Instead, he cranked the canopy closed and self-consciously patted the instrument panel next to the gunsight. "Hello, Hellcat," he said.

SUNDAY, 23 APRIL

NAS PASCO, WASHINGTON

Juanita Connell opened the icebox and handed another long-necked bottle to the guest.

"Thanks, ma'am," Rogers said. "Three ought to be my limit."

"Nonsense," the skipper's wife replied. "And *please,* don't call me 'ma'am' or even 'Mrs. Connell.' That's for official functions. And if we're lucky there won't be many of those!"

Rogers glanced across the folding kitchen table at Gordon Connell. The squadron commander winked and took a long pull from his own beer, his second of the evening.

Rogers still did not know what to make of the Connells; he had expected Juanita to be more like her husband: tall, athletic, handsome. Instead, she was of medium height, slightly heavy, with average blonde looks. *They must be in love,* Rogers mused. *No other way to explain it.* What she did share was Gordon's extroverted personality.

Dinner at the squadron commander's home was a new experience for Phil Rogers. Even when "home" was a tiny apartment in an eastern Washington railroad community that had found new importance with an air station and a nearby defense plant, being invited there was a most welcome diversion. Rogers relaxed in his straight-backed chair, which had one leg slightly shorter than the others. "Well, it's sure good of you folks to have me to dinner. I never got to do this in Bombing Three because we were deployed or in Hawaii from eight December on."

Connell asked, "What about Composite Squadron Fifty-four? I heard that Garrett's family lived in the islands."

"Yes . . ." Rogers almost said "sir." He gathered his thoughts, wondering how much to relate about one of Connell's fellow Annapolis alumni. "Commander Garrett was married to Admiral Purleigh's daughter, and they had a nice place near Ewa. But to tell you the truth, Skipper, VC-54 wasn't a very happy gang."

Connell absorbed that information with a noncommittal grunt. Finally he said, "Well, Stinky Garrett didn't get his nickname for nothing." There was no mirth in the CO's voice, and Rogers assumed that Commander Harold L. Garrett had not been a benevolent upperclassman.

"Which reminds me," Connell continued. "I checked with Clarey for you. He said he'd only swap Burnett if we can trade two pilots with similar experience. That isn't likely."

Rogers tried not to let his disappointment show, but Connell sensed it. "You know, Phil, so far you're the only really combat-experienced pilot I have. Ralph Platco, my exec, is still en route from the Great Lakes, where he's been with the carrier-qualification unit. Holly Hollister is a pretty sharp jaygee who came to the Navy via the Royal Canadian Air Force, but he'll tell you he only flew a few missions in Europe before he transferred to the U.S. armed forces. Then we're supposed to get an ex-enlisted pilot named Mancross who has some Japs to his credit, but he hasn't arrived yet."

"That's odd. I got the impression that the ops officer had seen some action."

Connell set down his beer and sighed wearily. "Well, it depends on how you cut it. Ron Harkin was two years behind me at the academy. He went to SOCs right out of Pensacola, and he's been a floatplane pilot all his life. He was aboard a cruiser up around the Aleutians last year, and I guess he got shot at. He pulled some strings to get into fighters, and I took him on because he was so damned eager." The CO paused to choose his words. "He handles the F6 all right, but he needs to get up to speed in fighter tactics." Rogers was grateful for the information. He felt that first impressions usually proved accurate, and his suspicions about Mr. Harkin had just been confirmed.

Juanita set a plate of fried chicken and a bowl of mashed potatoes on the table and sat down. "Dig in," she beamed. Her husband seemed to take a subtle cue. "Juanita's famous in the Atlantic Fleet," he said as Rogers forked a drumstick and a breast. "We used to have squadron parties built around her chicken recipe."

"What squadron was that?" Rogers asked.

"Oh, Fighting Seventy-one. I guess you hadn't heard."

Rogers perked up. "Gosh, no. I've never met anybody from the *Wasp*." He recalled that September afternoon when the word came off Guadalcanal. "Were you aboard when—"

"Yeah." Connell helped himself to more mashed potatoes. "We'd just recovered some SBDs when the torpedoes hit. The fires got out of control and we had to abandon."

Rogers thought he sensed a faint shiver in Juanita's frame. "We had such good friends in that ship," she offered. "We hardly know where any of them are anymore."

"Well, that's not quite true, honey." Connell swallowed another mouthful. "I still hear about Wally Beakley, Court Shands, and some of those fellows. Dave McCampbell has a squadron now, Fighting Fifteen, I think." Connell's attention focused on Rogers. "In fact, he's from your neck of the woods. Palm Beach, Florida, isn't it?"

"West Palm, actually. But I don't think I know him."

"Well, he's one hell of a fighter pilot and he was a hell of an LSO. In early '42 the *Wasp* made two ferry runs in the Mediterranean, delivering RAF fighters to Malta. Remember when Churchill asked, 'Who says a wasp can't sting twice?' On the second trip one of the Spitfires lost its belly tank on takeoff and Dave got him aboard on the third try."

Rogers gaped at Connell. "Without a tailhook?"

"Yeah, a swell Canadian kid named Smith. He stood on the brakes and stopped about six feet from the forward deck edge. That night we threw the kid a party with a cake and everything. Douglas Fairbanks, Jr., was in ship's company and presented him with a pair of Navy wings for his first carrier landing!" Connell laughed aloud at the memory, his voice filling the small kitchen. He decided not to mention that Pilot Officer Jerry Smith had disappeared chasing Luftwaffe bombers several months later.

Juanita merely smiled. It was apparent that she had heard this sea story before. She said, "That's one thing I really miss about the Navy, you know? The sense of family." She thought for a moment. "It's not the same at Hanford, where I work. Too many people—you really don't get to know each other."

Rogers waited for elaboration, but sensed there would be none. He did not wish to appear too inquisitive, but he wondered about the mysterious Hanford facility—the large government reservation northwest of Pasco. "I've only heard about the place," he ventured. "Evidently we're not supposed to fly over it."

Connell laughed again, touching his wife's arm. "Good luck, Phil. Juanita won't even tell me what she does there!"

"Oh, that's not true," she said. Addressing Rogers, she continued, "Because my husband is a naval officer I got quick clearance for secretarial work. That's why I joined Gordon at this garden spot. Otherwise I'd have stayed in Norfolk."

Rogers felt foolish, probing for information from the CO's wife. "Well, Mrs. . . . . ah, Juanita, if it isn't too sensitive . . ."

"It's some hush-hush war plant," Connell interjected. He leaned close, lowering his voice to a loud whisper. "There are two theories as to what goes on at Hanford. Republicans say it's a factory making Roosevelt campaign buttons. But informed rumor says they make the front ends of horses. . . ."

"And ship them to Washington, D.C., for final assembly!" Juanita completed the standing joke with a sardonic grin.

Rogers laughed with his hosts, savoring their company. Sixteen months would pass before the world learned about Hanford and something called the Manhattan Project.

SATURDAY, 29 APRIL
OITA BASE

The Emperor's forty-third birthday was a time of celebration and unification between the All-Highest and his devoted subjects. Standing in the ranks, impeccable in his starched dress whites, Sakaida reflected that the seventeenth year of Hirohito's divine reign saw the empire encompassing far more than the sixty-nine million native-born Japanese. There were lower orders as well: Okinawans, Formosans, Manchurians, and Koreans, all absorbed into the empire between 1874 and 1910—not to mention untold millions of conquered Chinese. Since 1941 Filipinos, Burmese, Siamese, Malays, and Javanese had been enfolded in the embrace of the Greater East Asia Co-Prosperity Sphere. That almost none of those people desired to partake of the blessings visited upon them was of little or no import.

Like most Japanese, Sakaida had never seen the Emperor nor even heard his voice. In fact, what the populace knew of the man-god was a curious mixture of fact and myth. Born Michinomiya Hirohito, according to tradition he was the 124th direct descendant of Jimmu, the legendary first Emperor of the land of Yamato. Hirohito was reportedly an authority on marine biology—which Sakaida regarded as only fitting for the ruler of an island nation—and had written numerous books on the subject. Hiroyoshi Sakaida, never an avid reader of anything, had not bothered to search them out.

Upon the death of his father, Emperor Taisho, the twenty-five-year-old prince regent had succeeded to the throne on the Christian holiday in December 1926. For his reign he chose the designation *Showa,* "Bright Peace," which Sakaida privately—very privately, in fact—regarded as highly ironic, considering that the era had featured continuous warfare on the Asian mainland and in the Pacific since 1931.

Hirohito's actual role in directing the current war to liberate all peoples of color from colonialism seemed uncertain. Sakaida inferred that, although the constitution granted him supreme authority, the Emperor largely ratified actions taken or recommended by his ministers. Not that it mattered much. Sakaida was merely an airplane pilot and would do what he was ordered, as would any imperial warrior.

Then his pride stung his consciousness. *No,* he told himself. *I am more than an airplane pilot. I am a carrier pilot!*

That thought was cut off by a guttural bark from the naval base commander, who turned toward Tokyo, removed his hat, and bowed low at the waist. The white-clad throng of devout subjects did likewise, and as Sakaida stared at his polished shoes, it seemed that only one thing was certain between this imperial birthday and the next: The war would continue.

F O U R

May 1944

FRIDAY, 5 MAY
NAVAL AIR STATION PASCO, WASHINGTON

The officer's club swarmed with tanned, obviously healthy young officers wearing dress blues. A cheerful din filled the confined spaces and barkeepers sweated as the three squadrons of Carrier Air Group 59 assembled for the first time. Rogers was on the third leg of his expanding-box search when he spotted Burnett astride a stool with a glass in each hand.

Bernie lit up with a wide grin and nudged his companion. "Hey, Buck! Drop anchor and sit a spell." He made the introductions. "Phil Rogers, Carl Sacco, and vice versa."

Rogers shook hands with the junior-grade lieutenant, a dark-complected flier now apparently Burnett's wingman in Bombing 59. Rogers pointed at his friend's port hand. "You hoarding, Burnett, or just getting a head start?"

"Hell, Rogers, you know me. Always plan ahead."

"What's your poison?"

Burnett shrugged expansively in the gesture Rogers knew so well. "Doggone if I know." He pointedly sniffed at the glass. "It's . . . uh, wet!"

Rogers shot a glance down the bar, where a long blue line had formed with much shouting and waving of dollar bills. He decided it would be a tedious wait so he relieved Burnett of half his liquid refreshment. Hoisting the glass with an evil grin, he said, "Happy days." Sacco chuckled.

Burnett exclaimed, "I'll get even with you, Rogers. I'm gonna write Sallyann that you're a hundred twenty miles away and haven't even called." While Rogers winced, Burnett motioned confidentially to Sacco. "Buck here's the intellectual type. Like librarians." The latter word was accompanied with suggestively raised eyebrows.

"No kidding, Lieutenant?" Sacco's voice carried a nasal East Coast quality. "My old man would agree with you. Mom's a librarian back in Camden."

So that's it, Rogers thought. *New Jersey.* Burnett merely hung his head in defeat. "Doomed. I'm doomed. Surrounded by the Pasco Literary Society."

Sacco's brown eyes were drawn to the ribbons below Rogers's wings of gold. Rogers instantly knew the meaning. *These kids are all the same— want their own Navy Crosses and DFCs.* "Mr. Rogers, ah, Bernie tells me that you used to fly together."

"Well, yeah. If you cut his heroism in half and multiply mine by three you'll be in the ballpark." He sipped his drink, which he couldn't identify. He knew what the youngster was leading up to—what's it like out there? "Actually, Sacco, I don't know what I can tell you that Bernie hasn't. After Bombing Three I did an incredibly dumb thing—actually volunteered for antisub duty on an escort aircraft carrier—and bored holes in the sky for about a year. I just don't know much about what's going on now."

Burnett interjected. "Our skipper, Mr. Clarey, says he wants to get action reports direct from fleet squadrons. He's put in a request through channels on the basis that it'll help our training, but we haven't heard anything. How 'bout you?"

Rogers shook his head. "No joy. But my CO's a real sharp cookie— Gordon Connell. He was on the *Wasp* while we were riding the Sara back from Guadalcanal."

Sacco relished the company of two combat veterans—men who wore the same uniform, the same wings, spoke the same jargon as he did, but who had Been There. The chasm between them was immense. He could barely restrain himself from asking what it had been like at Midway and Guadalcanal, but decided to bide his time. He knew he would learn more by listening than talking.

"Hey," Rogers continued, "guess who I heard from?" Burnett was forming a wisecrack when his friend continued. "Jim Carpenter! He's at El Toro, back from the Solomons after his second tour. Says he'll grab a Corsair and come see us."

"That'd be swell," Burnett replied. Turning to Sacco he said, "That's another thing about Rogers, here. He's a known companion of Marines, so you gotta be careful around him."

Sacco emitted a low whistle. "Corsairs—they're not carrier-qualified yet, are they?"

Rogers shrugged. "I don't know—Jim could probably tell you. Last I heard, VF-17 was bounced off the *Bunker Hill* and put ashore in the Solomons, and VF-12 had converted to Hellcats. If there's any other Navy Corsair squadrons, I haven't heard of 'em."

"Actually, there are two others," a voice said from behind Rogers. He turned, sensing that Burnett and Sacco were sliding off their stools. "I'm Tom Albertson," the intruder said, shifting his glass and extending his hand. "You must be Rogers."

Rogers was taken aback at the air group commander's informality. "Yes, sir. It's good to meet you." He remembered to shake hands with CAG-59.

Tom Albertson was a compact, not-quite-thirty aviator with three stripes on his sleeves and one row of ribbons on his dress blues. "I saw your file from ComFairWest," he explained. "I was tempted to put you in the bombers with Burnett, but I think we'll see more fighters in each air group. It might be useful to have dive-bombing experience in our fighter squadron."

Rogers relaxed, feeling grateful for the assignment. "Well, sir, the F6 is a fine airplane—if anything it's even easier to land than the SBD. I'm looking forward to carrier quals."

"That'll be awhile, but you gentlemen may be interested to know that F4Us already are embarked in fast carriers. Chick Harmer has a night-fighter squadron with Task Force Fifty-eight, not to mention Gus Widhelm's outfit in the Solomons."

Feeling bold, Sacco ventured an opinion. "Excuse me, sir, but that's pretty remarkable—flying Corsairs at night when they haven't been used on carriers in daylight!"

Albertson sized up the boy, one of nearly seventy ensigns and jaygees now assigned to the air group. "Well, mister, that's the kind of deluxe aviators we have in this Navy. I already mentioned Gus Widhelm. I knew him aboard the *Ranger* back around '39. He'd been away from the fleet for a couple of years but he asked to qualify in carrier landings, bombing, and gunnery—all on the same day!"

The CAG was warming to his subject, and Rogers wondered if the double scotch had lubricated his tongue. "Well, the captain was doubtful because it'd probably never been done before. But ol' Gus says, 'Sir, you are talking to Widhelm.' So he manned up and launched off in his SB2U, made six straight landings, then proceeded to make expert scores in bombing and gunnery!

"Now, somebody mentioned Fighting Twelve—Joe Clifton's squadron. His exec was Bob Dosé, and if there's a better aviator than ol' Bob, I don't know who it is. When we were in an escort squadron at Astoria, he landed an F4F on *the* slickest, iciest runway you ever saw. Nobody else was even flying that day, and even Bob nearly lost it. But when he taxied in and shut down, he said he had considered ground-looping the damn thing, sliding tail first and stopping by using the prop as an air brake!" Albertson shook his head in admiration. "That is heads-up flying."

By the time Commander Albertson finished his tale, other fliers had gathered at the end of the bar. Rogers listened as each related with respect or humor an episode he had witnessed or heard of—or otherwise swore was true. Rogers shot a glance at the air group commander, who seemed satisfied to nurse the double scotch and keep the conversation going. Then Rogers realized what Albertson was doing. *He's got us together like this to swap sea stories and learn something that might someday save a plane or a life.*

The camaraderie that was growing in Air Group 59 gave Phil Rogers a sense of belonging that he realized he had not known in more than a year, since leaving unhappy USS *Alazon Bay.*

THURSDAY, 11 MAY
IJNS *JUNYO*

Sakaida heard the strains of "Kumigayo" die away, watching Japan sink beneath the horizon. He almost shuddered at the symbolism. Leaning on the rail overlooking the carrier's wake, sensing the two-shaft geared turbines through the soles of his shoes, he felt an eerie ambivalence. He was glad to be under way, headed for whatever battle front Carrier Division 2 had drawn. But he felt a gnawing dread at what awaited the air group's green fliers. *We are not ready for combat,* he acknowledged with professional detachment. *We need more time, more training. More everything.*

When Kyushu's purple-blue landmass disappeared into the Pacific, he turned away and paced toward the chief petty officer aircrew spaces, two decks down. Like all noncommissioned berthing on Imperial Navy warships, the compartment was crowded but it was far more habitable than the enlisted men's quarters. There, the hammocks slung side by side had always reminded Sakaida of sardines crammed into a tin. At least he had an individual room that he shared with five other aviation NCOs.

Sorting out his clothes, Sakaida bumped another pilot. They muttered perfunctory apologies and introduced themselves. It was cultural as much as institutional, since all Japanese were constantly accommodating themselves to cramped living. Navy life only amplified the situation. The aviators hadn't met before, which Sakaida considered just another sign of the cobbled-up nature of *Junyo*'s air group and CarDiv Two generally. "I am Minami," the flier said, "second *shotai* leader in the fighter-bomber squadron."

Sakaida sized up the man—midtwenties and stout—and judged him probably to be capable of leading four new Zero Model 52s against the American carriers. Sakaida comforted himself with the thought, *At least we now have a full complement of aircraft.* But whether the other three members of Minami's section could do any good was beyond discussion at this point. Even an extrovert like Sakaida felt obliged to observe the properties with newly acquainted equals. "What do you make of our ship?" he asked. It was a polite way of trying to determine a pilot's previous carrier experience.

Minami shrugged his burly shoulders. "I graduated in the Otsu Twelfth Class and have been land-based until recently."

Quickly cycling that information, Sakaida determined that his roommate had finished high school in 1938 or '39. Minami would have entered the *Yoka Renshu-sei,* or Flight Reserve Enlisted program, and probably got his wings in early 1943. He had obviously done well to make chief petty officer this soon, as Sakaida was at least five years senior to him. *But there has been much attrition,* Sakaida recalled.

Stowing his sea bag, Sakaida straightened up. "Well then, we can learn more about our 'Soaring Falcon' together!"

Minami beamed his pleasure. "I would enjoy that. You realize, I have only been aboard during our carrier-qualification periods."

Sakaida nodded in sympathy. "The same for me." He glanced left and right as if fearing someone would overhear. "I came to carriers from cruiser floatplanes and sea fighters!" With that, the two aviators began exploring their new world.

Most Imperial Navy pilots had first heard of *Junyo* and her sister *Hiyo* before the war. Originally laid down as luxury liners for the NYK line in 1939, their design had anticipated a need for conversion to carriers. Fourteen months before Pearl Harbor, *Kashiwara Maru* had begun her evolution into *Junyo.* She was built with a double hull for torpedo protection and extra height between decks, and space was even allocated for aircraft elevators. Both carriers had been completed in the disastrous summer of 1942, and now each could operate fifty-three fighters, bombers, and attack planes.

Many of the fixtures in *Junyo* were familiar to Sakaida from elsewhere in the Imperial Navy and had a comforting similarity with other ships, from the berthing compartments and mess spaces to the Emperor's portrait and the Buddhist shrine. She appeared to be a well-built vessel, fully capable of fulfilling her mission.

But in touring the hangar bay crowded with Zero fighters, Aichi and Yokosuka carrier bombers, and Nakajima attack planes, Sakaida felt a vague uneasiness. The ship and her planes were only half the equation. Too many men—boys, actually—had a tentative, uncertain aura about them. That some were obviously still gaining their sea legs was to be expected among more than twelve hundred sailors and aviators, but the proportion was far too high.

Sakaida glanced at Minami, hailing another fighter-bomber pilot portside forward. It all came back to the same inescapable fact. *We need much more time to prepare for battle.*

SUNDAY, 14 MAY
NAS PASCO

Rogers fine-tuned his propeller pitch and r.p.m., then allowed himself to enjoy the scenery. He did not mind flying on the Sabbath—in fact, he welcomed it. From ten thousand feet he took in the eastern Washington landscape: the juncture of the Columbia and Snake rivers, the Horse Heaven Hills to the north, the Blue Mountains beyond Walla Walla to the east.

To newcomers like him, the area at first seemed remote and barren. But the very remoteness was one of the reasons the Navy had purchased the land and built the air station. While taxiing out Rogers had been obliged to wait for the beautiful Staggerwing Beech—officially a GB-2 liaison aircraft—belonging to the air station commander. Captain B. B. Smith's family reputedly had sold the property to the government, and part of the deal was that "B. B." would get command of the facility. Whether it was true or not, Rogers admired any four-striper who was so devoted to flying.

The old-timers said that Pasco had been one of the original air mail stops when civilian contractors took over from the federal government in 1926 in long-distance mail hauling. Varney Airline's Swallow and Stearman biplanes had pioneered Contract Air Mail Route Five between Spokane, Washington, and Elko, Nevada. Rogers tried to think back that far. *Hmmm . . . Nineteen twenty-six was a year before Lindbergh flew the Atlantic. I was eight.* He could place no specific event in that year, though he vaguely recalled his parents' reaction at finding him and his sister setting five-year-old Ray in motion aboard a Radio Flyer wagon—into on-coming traffic.

Rogers squirmed himself into a more comfortable position atop his seat-pack parachute, forcing his attention back to the present. He swiveled his head through the horizontal and vertical, checking that he was alone in the cloud-flecked sky. Then he set about learning more of what his plane could do for him and how much he could ask of it.

He had already explored the limits of the F6F's low-speed control, the flight regime in which carrier landings were made. He had not been disappointed. At 90 knots indicated, the Hellcat had been rock-steady with wheels and flaps down. In fact, Connell had proclaimed the big fighter to be "a baby buggy of a carrier plane," allowing precise control all the way to touchdown. Rogers, always something of a spot-landing devotee, took pride in putting his main wheels within six feet of a chosen mark on each landing. If he missed, and traffic permitted, he would add power, go round and try again.

But that was only an end to a means. As the squadron's newly appointed gunnery officer, Rogers was responsible for knowing the F6F's weapons and how they would effect the plane's airframe under combat loads. He had hoped that Connell would appoint him flight officer instead of Harkin, but the former floatplane pilot was slightly senior and now stood third in the squadron hierarchy. Though disappointed, Rogers harbored a theory that Harkin's lack of experience with aviation ordnance had been a factor in the CO's decision. Meanwhile, Rogers applied himself to learning as much as possible.

Toward that end, he had sat down with the ordnance chief and devised a series of questions not always answered in the manuals. How did external stores effect speed and fuel consumption? How would the F6F maneuver with a bomb or rockets attached? With those topics listed on his kneepad, he began a series of tests to establish a baseline of comparison. With full fuel and no belly tank or underwing ordnance, he methodically ran through the routine: power-on and power-off stalls; time-and-distance runs to establish cruise and maximum speeds in level flight; rate of climb to various altitudes; rough calculations for roll rate and turn radius, vertical performance, and more.

Some of the tests were interesting, even exciting, but many were tedious. However, Rogers acknowledged that some dark evening in the not-too-distant future, when fuel was running low and time was the most precious commodity in his world, the knowledge he gained might save one or more planes—one or more lives. He did not know if other squadrons were conducting similar tests, but he surmised that most of the good ones were. At least, those with skippers as industrious as Gordon Connell.

When done, Rogers would repeat the experiments with another Hellcat and average the results. Then he and his "ordies" would load drop tanks and varying combinations of bombs and the new aerial rockets—ARs—and he would fly the profiles again. In the end, he would know everything that was worth knowing about the Hellcat as a weapon platform.

Recognizing that he was approaching the southeastern edge of the forbidden Hanford zone, Rogers checked his altimeter. *Eight thousand feet— plenty good.* He briefly wondered what Juanita Connell was doing, then cleared his mind. He booted left rudder, popped the stick over and back, and bobbled slightly as he recovered from a half-snap roll. Looking at the horizon while hanging in his shoulder harness, he then pulled the stick into his lap and felt the onset of four times normal gravity as he completed a near-perfect split-S. He allowed his compass to settle down and noted he had recovered within 5 degrees of the reciprocal of his previous heading.

Rogers sang an off-key rendition of "Chattanooga Choo-Choo" all the way back into the traffic pattern. He calculated that he would be just in time to meet the CO at the skeet range.

TUESDAY, 16 MAY

TAWI-TAWI, SULU ARCHIPELAGO

There was good news and there was bad news. Carrier Division 2 had arrived intact after a five-day journey from home waters, and there had even been time for flight quarters en route. But when *Junyo* and the other eight carriers of the Mobile Fleet dropped anchor in the Sulu Archipelago, southwest of the Philippines, their squadrons remained aboard. Sakaida intuitively sensed problems, and his suspicions were soon confirmed.

"We were told that we would have a completed airfield here," Lieutenant Commander Yoshimura told his aviators assembled on the flight deck, "but it is still under construction." He allowed the fliers to absorb the information before continuing. "That means we will have little opportunity for combat tactics training, or even for proficiency flying," he explained.

An audible groan coursed through the assembly—more than two hundred angry, disappointed young men.

Sakaida ripped off his soft hat, barely containing the urge to fling it onto the wooden-plank deck. He looked around, saw that nobody had observed his unmilitary conduct—or cared—and snugged it back onto his close-cropped head.

Yoshimura shifted his feet uneasily and held up his hands, palms outward. "I know this is a disappointment to all of you," he said in a voice tinged with sympathy. "No one is more concerned than I am about a lack of flying here at Tawi-Tawi. But we will just have to make what we can of our time."

The attack aircraft *buntaicho* caught the senior squadron leader's attention. "Sir, is there any chance that the airfield may be completed before we depart?"

Yoshimura eyed his torpedo squadron *hikotaicho* and became grim-faced. "That is unlikely. However, the carrier division commander says we should be able to conduct periodic air operations at sea." Yoshimura did not sound optimistic, and his news hung suspended in the warm, moist air.

Sakaida wondered what ComCarDiv Two, Rear Admiral Takaji Joshima, thought of the tradeoff. *Surely he realizes that a few days per month at sea are poor compensation for regularly scheduled training ashore.*

With weary resignation, Sakaida did what sailors have always done—he resolved to stop worrying about what was beyond his power to change. Joshima certainly knew the sorry state of Air Group 652; the admiral flew his flag in *Junyo*. Not even the First Mobile Fleet commander, Vice Admiral Ozawa in *Taiho* with CarDiv One, could affect the situation.

When the men broke ranks, Sakaida sat on the deck edge, feet dangling in the catwalk. As if for the first time he studied Tawi-Tawi's volcanic mountains, imagining he could identify tobacco and sugarcane fields among the coconut palms. He wondered what the native Samals were like—Muslims, according to rumor. In all his travels Hiroyoshi Sakaida had never met any Muslims. He wondered what sort of liquor they drank.

SATURDAY, 20 MAY

NAS PASCO

The distinctive whistle in the traffic pattern caused everyone on the flight line to look up. "That's got to be Sunny Jim," Rogers said, adjusting his aviator sunglasses. He glanced at his watch. "And he's six minutes early." Burnett said nothing as the inverted gull-winged F4U flown by their Marine Corps friend Jim Carpenter swung into a 360-degree overhead approach, gear and flaps becoming visible.

In a descending left-hand turn, the Corsair seemed to drag its port wingtip on the concrete mat before the pilot rolled wings-level and flared in a nice three-point landing. "Show-off," muttered Burnett, but his tone expressed admiration. Everyone knew that forward visibility from the F4U's cockpit—fifteen feet behind the propeller, called for a well-honed sense of height.

Rogers and Burnett walked toward the spot on the transit flight line where the Marine visitor would park. As the tricolor Corsair swung around and they heard the R-2800 engine begin to die as the mixture was cut, Burnett nudged Rogers. "Man, take a look at those meatballs!" Forward of the cockpit, beneath a stenciled CAPT. J. E. CARPENTER, were twelve Rising Sun flags: two vertical rows of five and the start of a third row. "Now there's a real sunsetter," Rogers replied.

Pulling off his khaki helmet, the blond pilot beamed a smile at his two friends. Rogers thought, *Still the same old Sunny Jim,* and waved. In moments Carpenter alighted from the cockpit, ignoring the crowd of sailors and fliers who had never seen an F4U up close. He reached out for his old classmate. "Buck! My god, how long has it been?"

"Too damn long, buddy." The two friends stood grinning foolishly at each other before Burnett interjected. "Gosh, sir, I've never met an ace. Can I have your autograph?"

Carpenter laughed and his teeth flashed in the sun. "Burnett, you sure haven't changed."

They shook hands and Bernie pointed at the war paint. "C'mon, Carpenter, level with us. You bribed some poor bastard to put all those meatballs on your plane, right?"

"Hell, no, I didn't bribe anybody. I didn't have to." He was not about to admit that he had asked one of his squadron mechanics to do a hurry-up job the day before because it would intimidate his Navy friends.

While Burnett scaled the height of the Corsair's wing and fuselage to sit in the cockpit, Rogers and Carpenter caught up on almost a year's activities. "I'm still with VMF-226," the Marine began. "Like I said in my letter, we got back from the Solomons about three months ago. We'll go out again late this year, from what I hear. I'm flight officer but I could be exec by then."

Rogers choked back his envy. "You're doing better than me. We have the makings of a real fine squadron but I'm fourth in seniority behind three Academy types."

Carpenter folded his arms, leaning slightly forward. "That's kind of unusual, isn't it? Who's your CO?"

"Name's Gordon Connell—a hell of a good guy. He's about the flyingest skipper I've ever known, and that's saying something. You'll probably meet him while you're here."

"Well, tell me all about your love life," Carpenter prompted. "You still in touch with Sallyann?"

Rogers felt a faint flush beneath the skin. *Will you guys please leave it alone?* He looked up at Bernie, busily familiarizing himself with the roomy cockpit. "Negat. We sorta lost touch after she left Hawaii. How about you?"

The tall Californian raised both hands, palms up, in a gesture of futility. "Not much to tell. I hear from Elaine now and then but haven't really met anyone."

Rogers recalled Elaine Crowl, the cool, slim blonde Carpenter had met after Midway. Sallyann had considered them the perfect couple: both tall, blond, and beautiful. They had been involved in a riotous fistfight along with Phil, Bernie, and some other naval aviators in a Honolulu dinner club when some Army fliers had goaded them. Now it seemed a juvenile thing to have done—and long, long ago.

Gordon Connell's voice parted the crowd around the pilots. "Oh, there you are, Mr. Rogers. Hobnobbing with the Marines, I see!"

Rogers made the introductions and Connell responded warmly. "Good to meet you, Carpenter. My younger brother's a Marine. He was in the scout-snipers at Tarawa."

Rogers was astonished. *Jeez, I didn't know that!* The casualties of the Second Marine Division during three days last November had stunned the nation out of any complacency about the Pacific War.

Burnett reappeared at Carpenter's side, looking more than a head shorter. "Jim, I'll trade you straight across—your Corsair for my Helldiver. It's a fair deal, honest! They cost the same. I saw the figures in Philadelphia." Burnett was right: The big, two-seat Helldiver and the single-seat Corsair each cost the taxpayers $108,000.

"Go 'way, boy. Ya bother me." Carpenter did a fair impersonation of W. C. Fields.

Connell interjected almost apologetically. "Mr. Carpenter, I don't want to take up your limited time with your friends. But if you could spare us a half hour or so, I'd really appreciate anything you can tell us about current Jap fighter tactics."

Carpenter nodded decisively. "No sweat, Commander." He paused to organize his thoughts. "The biggest difference is that they've finally dropped their old three-plane formation. Now they're flying four-plane divisions just like we are.

"They still have some sharp pilots, but the overall quality is way down. One Zero shot the bejesus out of me at Midway," Carpenter added, touching a faint scar on his left cheek. "And I got several arrows in my hide at

Guadalcanal. But this last tour, I bagged six of them without a scratch. I think our squadron only lost two planes to Jap fighters. The weather was our biggest problem, just god-awful . . ."

"One moment," Connell interrupted. "I didn't mean to impose upon you while we stand here on a hot ramp. Gentlemen, I propose that we adjourn to the O-club."

The four men turned in unison toward the CO's jeep, hands waving animatedly in the universal language of aviators.

MONDAY, 22 MAY
OVERHEAD, CARRIER DIVISION TWO

It was good to be off the ship, and even better to be airborne again. Sakaida rolled his port wingtip downward, affording himself a better view of *Junyo, Hiyo,* and *Ryuho* two thousand meters below. He knew that Carrier Division 3 also was exercising today, taking advantage of the limited opportunity to give aircrews refresher training in carrier procedures.

Centering his controls again, Sakaida checked the spacing of his wingmen. Flight Seaman First Class Ikahika Doi was lagging slightly, but otherwise the four-plane *shotai* looked fairly good.

Sakaida's gaze turned northward, where the Tawi-Tawi Group of islands guarded the Sibatu passage between the Celebes and Sulu seas. Only forty miles east of the Borneo coast, thirty-mile-long Tawi-Tawi Island with its craggy 580-meter mountains seemed greenly remote from its esoteric purpose as an Imperial Navy base. *Indeed,* Sakaida reflected, *if not for its anchorage this place would be of no interest to us at all.* There wasn't even a town worthy of the title; the largest settlement had the alliterative name, Bato-Bato, like so many Pacific localities.

Outbound from the ship disposition, Sakaida led his Zeros fifteen miles, then reversed course. With a fishtailing motion—booting the rudder bar alternately left and right—he ordered Nakaya and Doi to position themselves well to starboard, slightly stepped up on the lead element. The leadership of *Hikotai* 321 took the pragmatic view that complexity was counterproductive, hence only a few basic formations were employed.

Sakaida raised one hand, making a circular motion while turning his head in exaggerated fashion. Yamamoto caught the gesture and repeated it for Nakaya and Doi. They understood at once: Keep a sharp lookout all around. Double-checking his watch, Sakaida confirmed that he was on time for the afternoon exercise.

What little knowledge Sakaida possessed about radar had been gained by his own effort. He knew that radio direction finding worked, though so far in this war it seemed to work a damn sight better for the Americans than for Japan. He recalled again that long search mission near Midway two years before, when the Grumman had found his floatplane even in a cloud layer and had given his three-man crew a nasty scare.

Now, as part of a fleet-defense problem, Sakaida hoped to see first hand how Japanese ship-based radar performed. If all went well, some of Lieutenant Commander Yoshimura's Model 52s would intercept the four- and eight-plane flights approaching from three quadrants. Sakaida fidgeted in his seat, scanned his engine gauges, and returned his gaze to the sea and sky. He would rather have used this rare opportunity to exercise his *shotai* in air-combat tactics, but orders were orders. If only—

Nakoya's voice came over the radio: "Contact! Low and right, Falcon Thirteen!"

Glancing down, Sakaida spotted them—four Zeros climbing toward him. Nakaya's vision was good; with more experience he could develop into a really proficient fighter pilot. Unable to resist the temptation, Sakaida waggled his wings in the prepare-to-attack signal, then shoved his stick forward. For the next few minutes he thoroughly enjoyed himself in a series of wrapped-up turning contests with Yoshimura's *shotai*. Sakaida concentrated on remembering what he did and how his wingmen performed. He judged the dogfight approximately even by the time the officer ordered both *shotai* to return to base.

Descending toward the carrier landing pattern, Sakaida sensed that his men were shaping up—but he felt a gnawing uncertainty. *If he had been an American leading a flight of Grummans, Yoshimura would have been caught at a serious disadvantage.* Sakaida wondered whether *Junyo*'s inexperienced radar operators or uncalibrated equipment was responsible for directing the interceptors to a position below the "enemy" instead of above. It always came down to the same thing: *We need more time.*

Sakaida's booted feet had hardly touched the flight deck when he saw Yoshimura take a running leap into the starboard catwalk and sprint aft toward the control station. "What is the commander's hurry?" Sakaida asked a plane director.

"They did not tell you?" the petty officer replied.

Sakaida lifted both earflaps of his flying helmet and shook his head. "We heard nothing. We hardly use our radios."

"It's all over the ship," the sailor said in wide-eyed amazement. He was an oysterman's son from Hokkaido, still imbued with the certainty that aviators conversed with the gods. "The carrier *Chiyoda* has been hit by torpedoes but they failed to explode. It was only a few minutes ago. One of our bomber crews saw it happen!"

Turning toward his three pilots, Sakaida wondered if his own face looked like theirs. He tried to think of some explanation, but nothing occurred to him. The fact that a CarDiv Three ship had been ambushed did little to relieve the shock. Embarrassed, he turned and led the way to the ladder leading to the hangar deck and below.

Submarines! he raged. One of the radiomen with whom Sakaida gambled had mentioned at least two enemy submarine contacts in the past week. Then only two days ago the First Mobile Fleet had been placed on six-hour notice in response to American carrier raids on Marcus and Wake islands. Nothing had come of the alert, but CarDiv and Fleet officers were decidedly nervous these days.

Obviously, the U.S. Navy now knew that Tawi-Tawi was the Mobile Fleet base. Almost certainly the submarine threat would severely curtail training operations. Reaching his bunk, Sakaida shed his helmet and flung his life preserver against the bulkhead. Mizuno, recently landed with his own fighter-bomber *shotai,* took one look at his normally affable roommate and decided to go elsewhere for a while.

WEDNESDAY, 24 MAY

NAS PASCO

Rogers settled into his front-row chair as the all-officers meeting convened. Actually, "all officers" meant all pilots, though the three nonflying officers were also present: the lieutenant responsible for aircraft engineering, and two junior-grade lieutenants, the bespectacled air combat intelligence officer, and the ordnance officer. The three were products of the Quonset Point school, "ninety-day wonders" who were commissioned as reserve officers under the aviation volunteer specialists program. Rogers knew some uncharitable regulars who insisted that the letters AV(S) meant "After victory, scram."

Gordon Connell stood at the head of the room, with a diagram of the squadron's new tactical organization displayed on the blackboard. "Gentlemen," he began as usual, "this meeting will acquaint you with our current division compositions. We now nearly have our full complement of pilots, and we'll probably receive some more. We have about six months left in our work-up syllabus, so there's plenty to do before we make the final cuts." The last comment caused some nervous stirring in the audience, especially among the ensigns. Connell knew that most of these boys—the good ones, anyway—literally would rather die than fail to make the grade. *No doubt some of them will,* Connell thought.

The CO took a moment to scan the four dozen young men under his command. Their average age was twenty-three, the youngest being nineteen-year-old Ensign Kenny Diskowski and the oldest being the matériel officer, thirty-one-year-old Lieutenant Don Mancross. Connell was particularly glad to have Mancross, a late arrival. Originally an enlisted pilot, he had flown F4Fs from the old *Lexington* and *Enterprise* in the 1942 battles before being commissioned late that year. He was two years older than the skipper, an exceptionally fine aviator, and he seemed to fit in.

"First things first, though," Connell continued. "Some of you have suggested that this squadron needs a name—something besides VF-59. Well, there have been several suggestions, ranging from 'Connell's Killers' to the 'Zoot-Suiters.' " There was a titter of laughter in the room, mixed with hoots of derision. The skipper raised his hands for silence, smiling broadly. "Personally, I prefer something like the 'Sunsetters.' But in fairness, I've considered all proposals and arrived at a compromise: We'll do it my way."

The officers laughed appreciatively at Connell's wry humor as he explained his choice. "The name fits us," he continued. "Our job will take us all the way west to Tokyo. And along the way we'll make sure that a lot of Japanese suns are permanently set. I'll see about getting a squadron patch designed and made." Rogers couldn't be sure, but he thought that the skipper winked at him, pointedly gazing at the old VB-3 patch on Rogers's jacket.

Turning to the blackboard, Connell ticked off each four-plane division, beginning with his own. "I'll lead Team One with Gilfrey on my wing, Holmberg as section lead, and Fry as number four." Lieutenant (junior grade) Horace "Horse" Holmberg was, not surprisingly, a lumberjack from Minnesota, and Jerry Gilfrey and Les Fry were twenty-two-year-old ensigns. "At least for starters, our divisions will shape up this way," Connell added. "A lieutenant or jaygee as leader with ensigns as wingmen. But I want to stress one thing." He held up a finger for emphasis. "This squadron will not stand on seniority alone—except where I'm concerned." His grin and tone of voice elicited laughter.

"I ran into Hugh Winters at ComFair recently," Connell explained. "He's working up Fighting Nineteen at Los Alamitos. We got to comparing notes, and he said something I agree with: 'It really took a war to get rid of all this crap from twenty-three years of peace.' " More appreciative chuckles arose from the pilots of VF-59. "So I want all of you to remember, if an ensign shows the most promise as a section or even a division leader, he'll get a shot at it. You old fuds wearing silver bars will just have to take your chances."

Kenny Diskowski was first out of his chair, stamping his feet and leading a chorus of "Hooray for the captain!" from the squadron's EPBA—the

Ensigns' Protective and Benevolent Association. Phil Rogers, onetime "bull ensign" of Bombing 3, clapped his hands in sympathy. He stole a glance at his seniors—the executive officer, Lieutenant Commander Ralph Platco, and Lieutenant Ron Harkin. Platco was grinning; Harkin was not.

"All right, back in your cages," Connell shouted. He resumed his description of the division composition. "Mr. Platco, as you know, is new to us, but he's sharp on carrier technique and procedures. He'll lead Team Two." As the skipper ran down the line, Rogers pondered the exec. *A difficult man to know—hard to get a handle on him. But he seems to know his business.* So far, Rogers had only spoken with Platco three times, and it occurred to him that perhaps Platco only seemed diffident in comparison to Connell, one of the finest leaders Rogers had known.

It was increasingly apparent to Rogers that combat leadership would fall upon the skipper and three relatively junior pilots—himself, Don Mancross, and "Holly" Hollister. He resolved to get better acquainted with the others, because if anything should happen to Connell . . .

Rogers vaguely heard something about Harkin, then realized the skipper was saying, "Lieutenant Rogers has Team Four with Diskowski, Fairfield, and Sossaman." Glancing over his shoulder, Rogers took in the three ensigns. He had only flown two or three hops with any of them, but he felt that Eddie Fairfield would be strongest of the trio.

The three nugget aviators returned Rogers's gaze, acknowledging the assignment. Rogers winked at them and received a thumbs-up from Fairfield and smiles from Kenny Diskowski and Brian Sossaman. A bond had been formed—a contract, really. The terms and provisions were both explicit and implicit, but they came down to just one thing: *Let's watch out for each other—and bring everybody home.*

SUNDAY, 28 MAY

IJNS *JUNYO*

Sitting at the narrow, cramped table in the chief petty officer's mess, Sakaida listened to the shoptalk while keeping his own council. The second *shotai* leader, Minami, seemed almost as well connected as Sakaida's gambling partner in the communications division. Their rumors, which enhanced limited hard information, were similar.

Minami was saying, "If it's true that the Americans have captured Biak, surely we'll sortie." The news had come late yesterday—enemy landings at Biak, on New Guinea's north coast. Sakaida felt that he knew just enough grand strategy to make himself dangerous, but if the New Guinea theater was being rolled up by the enemy, then Minami's prediction made sense. It was common knowledge that Imperial Navy doctrine was based upon the single decisive battle. Midway had been the premise for that strategy, and even noncommissioned officers now knew—or at least suspected—how *that* had worked out.

Sakaida sipped his hot tea and decided that he would carefully question Minami after the meal. The decisive battle for this phase of the war probably would be sought near Palau, within land-based air range of the Philippines. A look at the map indicated as much.

"But does this division have the experience for a fleet engagement with the Americans?"

Looking down the table, Sakaida identified the questioner as one of *Hikokitai* 652's torpedo-plane pilots who flew the fast Nakajima *Tenzan*. "We have not flown at all since the American submarine attack on *Chiyoda*," the man lamented.

Though nobody voiced an opinion, Sakaida considered the silence answer enough. The damned engineers ashore still had not completed Tawi-Tawi's airfield, so the carriers confined to the harbor merely swung around their anchors while their flight crews remained idle. *We are rusting even faster than our ships,* Sakaida mused.

If there was any cause for cheer, it was the fact that 652 at least stood at near full strength. Of the 144 aircraft allowed the group, Carrier Division 2's three carriers possessed 135, or 94 percent of the paper allotment. The old Zero Model 21 and 32 fighter-bombers had been replaced with current-production Model 52s before the division had left Japan, and *Junyo* herself owned 27 between the fighter and fighter-bomber units. Her carrier bomber squadron had nine new Yokosukas and nine old fixed-gear Aichis, while the torpedo squadron owned nine Nakajima *Tenzans*.

Still, Sakaida, and apparently most of his mess mates, realized that the ancient philosophy held true: Far better a sharp, old blade than a rusted new one.

June 1944

WEDNESDAY, 7 JUNE
NAS PASCO

The talk in the ready room was about D-Day and the future of the war in Europe. Rogers, just down from an evening formation flight with his division, allowed himself a brief thought. *Maybe Ray won't have to go to England after all.* But he had more urgent business in mind. He unzipped his flight jacket and poured himself a cup of coffee. Then he motioned for Kenny Diskowski, Eddie Fairfield, and Brian Sossaman to join him at the blackboard for a postflight chalk-talk.

"First," Rogers began, "you guys don't seem to have any problems with twilight join-ups, and that's fine. But remember, we're easing into this night-flying business. When you launch from a carrier before sunup, and for damn sure when you try to land aboard after dark, it's a whole new ball game."

Secretly, Rogers was pleased with his team's performance. The dusk takeoff, followed by an hour's navigation exercise and night landings, had gone reasonably well. He drew four crosses on the slate board, each representing a Hellcat, and looked at Diskowski.

"Ken, just one thing. When we enter the pattern to break up for a night landing, give me plenty of room, at least for now. In daylight we'll continue working on a tight interval—around twenty seconds—because that's how we'll operate at sea. Now, Commander Albertson says we'll be a night-qualified air group; remember, we'll need more time to get aboard in the dark."

Diskowski shifted his weight and looked chastened by the mild criticism. "Sir, I just didn't want to lose sight of you."

"That's understandable. But remember, you can usually spot another plane by its exhaust at night. The flames are always there—they just don't show in daylight."

Rogers assessed the emotions behind the three faces before him. Kenny Diskowski, the baby of the squadron, was a good young pilot, eager to please and earn acceptance. Eddie Fairfield, Rogers's section leader, showed cool competence; he would have a team of his own eventually. His wingman, Brian Sossaman, had hung in there. *All these guys need is experience,* Rogers thought. Others had not done as well; Harkin's division had become separated during an early night flight and the two sections had to return independently.

Rogers decided to offer some encouragement. "You fellows just remember: We haven't had as many night hours as some teams. The skipper's practically been feeding his guys carrot juice lately."

"Why is Team One doing so much night work?" Sossaman asked.

Rogers shrugged. "My guess is that Captain Connell figures the CO should lead all the rough ones, and his division needs to be ready for anything."

Fairfield's voice carried a trace of wistfulness. "The CAG ops officer says that night air groups are being formed. Man, I'm all for that. Let *them* hoot with the owls."

"Well, some guys actually like night flying, like Bill Martin in Air Group Ten. He wrote the first manual for night carrier operations two years ago. His middle initial is I—they say it stands for 'instrument'!"

An abrupt wailing noise pierced the atmosphere. Diskowski flinched as the siren increased in pitch and Sossaman paced to the window. He turned back, a vacant expression on his face. "I can't see anything. Wonder if it's some kind of drill . . ."

Other pilots crowded around the second-story windows, trying to glimpse something. Rogers turned and saw Ralph Platco pick up the phone, wait impatiently for something, then disappear out the door. Until Gordon Connell landed, the exec was in charge. Rogers had a thought. He walked to the scheduling board at the back of the room and saw that Teams 1, 3 and 5 were slated in overlapping time blocks for this period. *Connell, Harkin, and Mancross,* Rogers thought. He poured another cup of coffee and sat down to wait.

Eddie Fairfield looked up to see Platco enter the room. "Jesus, what's wrong with the exec?" Rogers turned in his seat to find a pasty-faced Platco shuffling toward the blackboard. He trailed gloom and silence in his wake.

Rogers heard somebody hiss "Pipe down!" to some kibitzers in the corner. Then Platco turned to face the two dozen pilots. He opened his mouth but no words came. Finally, he croaked, "I just talked to the tower. An F6F has crashed on the field. There's no radio contact with Commander Connell, or Gilfrey, either."

A dead silence fell over the room, but Rogers felt more irritated than concerned at the moment. "What about Holmberg and Fry? They're the captain's second section. They must know something." His tone was more critical than he intended: Right now Fighting 59 needed reassurance that somebody was in charge, and Phil Rogers saw that Ralph Platco was not providing it.

"I . . . I don't know," the exec stuttered. "Maybe they'll—"

Rogers stood up and paced to the squadron duty officer's desk, intending to call the control tower himself. The duty officer, Ensign Morgan Fielding, was on the phone again, speaking slowly. "Yes, that's right . . . You're sure?" The youngster listened intently as Rogers leaned over him. "What about the other one?" More anxious waiting tested Rogers's patience. "All right, I've got it. Thank you, sir."

Fielding looked up at Rogers. "That was base operations. The fire crew says that Gilfrey crashed at the eastern boundary of the field. He's in bad shape, headed for the dispensary. Another F6 went in about a half mile away."

"For Christ's sake, who's in that one?"

"They don't know yet, Lieutenant. The ops officer said he'd call when—"

A commotion erupted at the door as Horse Holmberg appeared, shedding flight gear. Instantly surrounded by a khaki swarm emitting a babble of questions, he elbowed his way toward Platco. The exec shouted down the junior officers, allowing Holmberg to speak.

"The skipper and Gilfrey are both down, sir. They must've run together in the pattern."

"Yes, we just heard that Gilfrey's headed for sick bay. Where's Fry?"

"Soon's we shut down he jumped in the follow-me jeep and headed for th' farthest crash. I figured I'd best report in."

"All right." Platco thought for a moment. "Any idea why they collided?"

Holmberg's big shoulders shrugged. "No, sir. I didn't see anything until I turned base and there was this fire on the ground, oh, maybe a mile short of the perimeter. The tower called and—"

The phone's shrill ring cut off Holmberg's account. Rogers, still standing by the desk, could tell more from Fielding's face than from his words. *It's bad,* Phil thought, feeling eerily detached. At length the duty officer said, "Thank you, sir."

Replacing the phone, Ensign Fielding looked up at his friends. "The skipper is dead."

THURSDAY, 8 JUNE

PASCO, WASHINGTON

Rogers stood motionless under the naked light bulb over the apartment door. He inhaled the cool night air and braced himself for what he was about to do. Glancing at his watch, he reflected that it was bad enough having to tell a loving wife that her husband was now an unrecognizable 180-pound corpse. Doing so at two A.M. was even worse.

In the final seconds before he shattered Juanita Connell's life, Rogers counted his pitiful blessings. *At least I convinced Platco to let me come first.* He would have half an hour or more alone with the new widow before Platco and the base chaplain arrived, but it seemed best. Relatively new to the squadron, Platco hardly knew Juanita, and Rogers was certain she had never met the padre at all.

At first Platco had considered waiting until dawn, and Rogers had agreed, if for no other reason than to obtain confirmation of the crash. But when Fry returned around midnight with the warrant officer from the crash crew, all doubt had been removed. Ensign Lester Fry, who almost certainly had lost a friend or acquaintance in flight training, had never seen the result of violent death up close.

In the last seconds of Juanita Connell's peaceful sleep, Rogers decided the direct approach was best. He would simply say, "I'm terribly, terribly sorry. There's been an accident and I've got to tell you . . . ." The other words would come, he was certain.

He rapped loudly, purposefully, repeatedly on the door. Then he waited. Minutes later the inside light snapped on and Juanita's face appeared at the window. Her hair was mussed and she appeared half in shadow. When she opened the door Rogers sought an indication of her mental state but he could not make out her eyes. He started to speak, conscious of a racing heart. His arms felt leaden. When his voice failed him, Philip Rogers could only place a cold hand over Juanita Connell's blanket-warm fingers. He winced as her scream shattered the night.

TUESDAY, 13 JUNE
IJNS *JUNYO*

Junyo was a turmoil of rumor and speculation as CarDiv Two and the rest of the Mobile Fleet departed Tawi-Tawi. Assembled on the flight deck with other *Hikokitai* 652 aviators, Sakaida overheard snatches of conversation and paid particular attention to officers and senior noncommissioned pilots like himself. He had been in the Imperial Navy long enough to know that most such "information" was outdated or simply wrong, but he had also learned to recognize what made sense.

Sakaida noticed Mizuno, his bunkmate from the fighter-bomber squadron, swapping theories with another petty officer. The one thing that seemed certain was that any hope of surprise had been lost. *The Americans must know we are at sea,* Sakaida gloomed. *How could they not by now?*

The enemy submarine attacks the previous month, resulting in periods of curtailed operations, had been bad enough. But only last week the Mobile Fleet had sustained two additional losses: the ammunition and supply ships *Takasaki* and *Ashizuri*. Officially the news was classified, but Tawi-Tawi was far too small an area for such information to remain secret. Each of those vessels could supply two carriers with ordnance and fuel, and even had extra aircrew quarters and aircraft repair facilities. Sakaida wondered how their loss would affect the Mobile Fleet's ability to perform its imminent mission.

A palpable tension ran through the ranks as somebody called "Attention!" More than two hundred men snapped into line as Lieutenant Commander Yoshimura mounted a platform, then motioned for his aviators to close around him. Sakaida strode forward with the others, consciously avoiding a place up front with the junior officers.

Yoshimura stood with hands on his hips, leaning slightly as *Junyo* increased speed. He wore a serious expression that Sakaida thought a bit too theatrical: *His war face,* the chief petty officer surmised, *for the benefit of the new men.*

"You are all aware that the fleet commander has ordered us to sortie on short notice," Yoshimura began. "We have been disappointed before, but this time the alarm is genuine."

A low, muttered sound of agreement coursed through the brown-clad airmen, dressed in flight suits and life vests. Operation Kon, the relief of Biak, had been an on again, off again affair. Reputedly some battleships and cruisers had sailed on that business, but nobody could say for sure.

Yoshimura continued. "Two days ago the Americans began bombardment of Guam and Saipan with capital ships and carrier aircraft. Yesterday evening, Naval General Headquarters determined that this is a genuine attack, not a diversion." The air group leader paused dramatically. "Therefore, the First Mobile Fleet is sailing to engage the enemy in a decisive battle! Operation A-Go will proceed!"

Sakaida glanced around as jubilant young warriors shouted their approval. Amid a chorus of *Banzai!*—"Ten thousand years, forever!"—Sakaida sought a like-minded soul. He locked eyes with Minami, who instantly looked away.

As the elation surged about him, eager young bodies jostling his own, Hiroyoshi Sakaida felt like the loneliest man in the world.

FRIDAY, 16 JUNE
NAS PASCO, WASHINGTON

"Pull!"

Rogers heard the clay pigeon take wing from the high house at position one to his left, instantly shouldered his shotgun, and tracked the target. In a crossing shot, left to right, he swung the 12-gauge's bead sight ahead of the bird and thought, *There!*

The trigger slap came a fraction late. But the pattern allowed two or three pellets to connect, tumbling the clay to earth. Rogers paid it no mind. Instead, he swung right, acquired the bird from position seven's low house and gained a quick sight picture. *Gotta hurry.* He knew it would be close. As he felt the second round fire, he was rewarded with a small black cloud when he powdered the target.

Rogers broke open the gun's action, ejecting the empty hulls. He shot a lethal grin at Burnett. "Twenty-one to nineteen. Like they say in tennis: game, set, match." They turned back toward the range master's building, where other shooters waited.

Burnett tried to appear unruffled. "Hey, Buck, that last one was damn near overhead. You almost lost it."

"Mr. Burnett, history is full of instances of 'almost.' But what is more pertinent, you owe me dinner."

Bernie cradled his borrowed weapon and squinted behind his amber lenses. "Uh, I think the bet was for first round of drinks, not dinner."

Rogers gave an exaggerated shrug. "Oh, yeah. Must've got carried away." Laughing contentedly, he stood his gun against the rack and draped his ammo vest around the barrel.

Don Mancross, awaiting his turn, beamed at his squadron mate. "Nice shooting, Phil. You still drinking courtesy of the bombers?"

Standing in the late-afternoon light, Rogers felt pleased with himself.

"Not regularly. Relatively few of them are gluttons for punishment like Burnett here."

Bernie spread his hands in a gesture of frustration. "Hey, can I help it if I'm practically the only bomber or torpecker who lets himself get beat up on?"

"Well, I wish the rest of your guys would follow your lead," Mancross replied. His normal speaking voice was so low it was almost hushed. "I hope you'll keep at it. Never know when some deflection shooting might save one of us. With your two twenty-millimeters, you could torch a Zero no sweat."

"Thanks," Burnett said. "But if you do your job, we won't have to shoot meatballs."

Rogers intervened. "Don, I guess you didn't know that Connell tried to get Bernie assigned to us. But Clarey wouldn't budge—said he's short of experienced pilots like everybody else."

"Well, I can't argue with that," Mancross whispered. He dropped his gaze to the pea gravel under his feet. "Doggone, Gordon was a damn fine CO."

Burnett swiveled his head, concerned an outsider might overhear. "How're things going in VF-59?" He felt comfortable asking the question in Rogers's presence, and judged Mancross "a good Joe."

The two fighter pilots exchanged glances. Rogers broke the silence. "I'd say we're doing okay for now. Platco's never going to be the leader that Connell was, but Don and I agree—he's got the squadron's interest at heart."

Encouraged by the response, Burnett pressed a bit. "That makes Harkin your exec, doesn't it?"

Rogers merely nodded. He was tempted to relate some of Harkin's ready-room boasts but decided not to. "I'm the new flight officer; Don's moved up to gunnery."

A nervous silence hung in the evening air. Burnett decided to change the subject. "Uh, how'd Mrs. Connell take it?"

"Not so good," Rogers said. He caught a sympathetic gaze from Mancross, who knew most of the story. It had been the worst half hour of Rogers's life, sitting on the worn sofa in that tiny apartment, absorbing the sobbing grief of a woman who must have loved her husband beyond reckoning. He did not want to discuss it.

"The investigation showed that Gilfrey's prop cut off most of Connell's tail. The skipper went in nose-first and was dead on impact." Rogers sighed. "At least it was quick."

Rogers and Mancross had seen the aircraft carcass. It had lain near the perimeter fence, dismembered the way Hellcats so often were. The airframe had broken at the manufacturing junction immediately aft of the cockpit. Deprived of its rigidity, the severed fuselage had lain like a partially inflated oblong balloon.

Rogers tapped Mancross on one arm. "Good shooting, Don. See you later." Walking toward the jeep en route to the club, Phil Rogers found he had lost some of his appetite.

MONDAY, 19 JUNE
IJNS *JUNYO*, 0830

The fighter squadron ready room was a cramped steel space filled with eager-nervous young fliers and growing tension. Seated in the third row with his *shotai,* Sakaida tried to keep an eye on the other pilots as well as the developing situation.

Of the three men in Sakaida's section, the second-class petty officer, Nakaya, seemed the most composed. That was to be expected, of course, since he was the most experienced. Sakaida's wingman, Yamamoto, was visibly edgy, while Seaman Ikuhiko Doi feigned sleep.

At the head of the room was a large-scale chart of the Central Pacific, at its center the Marianas Islands. The First Mobile Fleet was plotted some six hundred miles west-southwest of Saipan, where U.S. Marines—always their God-accursed Marines!—had stormed ashore three days ago. Sakaida noted the overlay showing the morning's search patterns, which had been launched almost four hours previously, ninety minutes before sunrise over the Philippine Sea.

From a sense of professional curiosity Sakaida had asked about the composition of the scouting flights. Remembering his own role in that capacity off Midway, two years ago this month, he was pleased to note a greater emphasis on reconnaissance. Sixteen cruiser-based floatplanes from CarDiv Three had been reinforced by nearly thirty more searchers by 0530. And they had found their quarry two hours later.

As a former scout pilot himself, Sakaida felt confident of the information being provided the Mobile Fleet. He compared yesterday's plots with this morning's and concluded that they were consistent. The three contacts from yesterday afternoon still showed on the chart with American carrier groups at grid coordinates U12CHI, URA4E and URA1A. That put U.S. Task Force 58 roughly centered at latitude 14 degrees 12 minutes north, longitude 141 degrees 55 minutes east last evening: two hundred miles west of Saipan.

The morning's most recent plot was designated 7I, some 160 miles west of Saipan. Sakaida took a sense of pride in that the discovery had come from an Aichi E13A, a cruiser-based scout identical to the one he had flown from cruiser *Tone* at Midway. On that occasion Sakaida had discovered the original USS *Yorktown* and tracked her on and off for three days before a submarine finished the work that carrier bombers had begun. It had been a chilling experience: He could imagine how the Aichi pilot felt today, facing a far larger force.

The exact composition of the enemy was unknown, but the 7I contact indicated two or more task groups, and yesterday's scouts had reported three. The Mobile Fleet's strength amounted to nine carriers. The Americans easily could have fifteen fleet carriers and many more small escort types. Sakaida kept his own counsel. But he knew that Midway could seem a tea ceremony in comparison to this battle.

IJNS *JUNYO*, 0915

Sakaida nudged Yamamoto out of a fitful nap as Lieutenant Commander Yoshimura entered the ready room. The air group commander had everyone's attention as he consulted some notes, then stood arms akimbo and surveyed the room.

"The battle has begun," Yoshimura announced. "Carrier Division Three launched sixty-nine airplanes commencing at 0830, and Division One followed with 130 more in the past quarter hour."

An excited buzz flitted through the ready room, sparking an electric response wherever it alit. Though Sakaida prided himself on his self-control, he felt a growing impatience. One of the squadron's *chutai* leaders felt bold enough to ask the question on everyone's mind. "Honorable commander, when will we be committed to the battle?"

"This division is being held in reserve," Yoshimura replied evenly. If he felt any irritation at the question, he concealed it well. "The air staff has ordered us to contribute to a strike group totaling nearly fifty aircraft. The scheduling is proceeding as of now . . ."

A bustling at the entrance to the ready room distracted Yoshimura. He looked to his right, saw a staff communications officer gesturing, and strode impatiently to the man. Sakaida craned his neck for a better view of the proceedings, but in a moment Yoshimura returned. His demeanor had changed.

"Some bad news from Carrier Division One," he said. "The flagship has been hit by a submarine torpedo. The number one elevator is jammed but apparently there is no danger of sinking." Yoshimura scanned his fighter pilots with an expressionless gaze. "Stand ready to man aircraft in thirty minutes."

The air group commander's exit left more questions than answers in his wake. Sakaida felt Yamamoto leaning close. "If *Taiho* has been torpedoed, then the Americans know our position as well as we know theirs."

Sakaida bit down the rancor he felt. His wingman's assessment merely stated the obvious, contributing nothing. Sakaida forced himself to be civil—after all, he might never see Yamamoto again. "I am more concerned about command of the Mobile Fleet. If Vice Admiral Ozawa is forced off *Taiho,* we do not know if he can retain command." His successor undoubtedly would be the leader of CarDiv Two or Three—either Rear Admiral Joshima or Rear Admiral Obayashi. Sakaida had only seen Takaji Joshima a few times and knew almost nothing of the man's qualifications. He was in command of the division and, in the strict hierarchy of the Imperial Navy, that was enough. Obayashi was even more of a cipher.

What leadership was evident had come from on high, from Naval General Headquarters in Tokyo. Admiral Soemu Toyoda's message to the fleet was inscribed on a blackboard in the ready room. Though four days old, it harkened back to the dawn of the Imperial Navy's emergence on the world stage. Admiral Togo's words before he crushed the Czar's Baltic Fleet at Tsushima Strait in 1905 still seemed applicable: "The rise and fall of Imperial Japan depends on this one battle. Every man shall do his utmost."

Sakaida sat back in his narrow seat, feeling that more than inspiration he needed relief. For the first time in five hours, he noticed that his kapok life preserver was pinching his kidneys.

OVERHEAD CARDIV TWO, 1020

Nothing ever goes according to plan, Sakaida told himself. The euphoria of his first combat launch had quickly worn off. Emotionally it had felt no different from his catapult shots off *Tone* before Pearl Harbor or Midway, nor even from taking off in his Type 2 float fighter for Guadalcanal. The visual images remained in his mind: the jet of steam from the bow showing the wind straight down the flight deck, the air officer's white flag ordering the launch to commence. But gone already was the elation he had felt gunning his Zero Model 52 down *Junyo*'s deck, canopy open so that he could almost hear the sailors' encouraging shouts. Waving their summer-weight caps over their heads, they had cheered each plane in turn, apparently certain of a grand victory in the making.

Sakaida swiveled his head: He was satisfied that his own flight was formed up, but assembling forty-seven planes from three carriers was taking too long. He glanced down, saw *Chiyoda* and *Zuiho* steaming into the wind with *Junyo,* and concluded that the Mobile Fleet's third attack group of the day was lagging badly. Merely getting the planes in the air was one thing; organizing them into tactical disposition was another.

Thus far only the fifteen Zero fighters had joined formation; only gradually did the twenty-five fighter-bombers and seven Nakajima B6N1 torpedo planes arrive in the holding pattern. The enemy was reported to be at least 320 nautical miles away, but Sakaida had little concern about his fuel situation—he was an experienced over-water pilot. The newer men, however, may have problems with fuel management. He did not even want to think about their navigation problems if they had to return alone.

OVER THE PHILIPPINE SEA, 1035

Sakaida's heart beat a concerted tattoo in his chest. *How can we be missing seventeen planes?* He looked over at Yamamoto, and twirled a finger, ordering a thorough search.

Sakaida pulled his chart from the leg pocket of his flight suit and tried to figure it out. The belated contact report—that was the only plausible explanation. Somehow in the last five minutes, more than one third of the division's airborne strike had missed the radio call diverting them farther north. Consulting his map again, Sakaida laid off the distance from the 7I contact to the more recent one designated 3Ri. Comparing his fingers against the scale, he saw the difference amounted to an additional fifty miles.

Sakaida quickly computed the time-distance equation. If the new contact was accurate, it meant more than ninety minutes' flight to the target area. *Then allow more for a search,* he told himself. The American fleet would no more remain stationary than would Vice Admiral Ozawa, but carrier operations were slaves of the wind. Sakaida looked down at the water's dappled surface. The whitecaps told him that the morning breeze was still steady out of the southeast.

NORTH OF U.S. TASK GROUP 58.4, 1300

Sakaida had not been so frustrated since Midway. The sea was holding its secrets close today, and nothing was working as planned. He forced himself to bring his focus back in the cockpit for a moment and scanned his instruments. Cylinder-head temperature, fuel and oil pressure: *All in the normal operating range,* he noted. He cocked his head to listen to his Sakae engine's steady drone. On long over-water flights, pilots frequently heard sounds that weren't there—a knock, a ping, a missed beat. Sakaida's engine was purring smoothly.

He directed his attention out of the cockpit, even out of his body, which was beginning to protest being strapped in a small, uncomfortable seat for three hours. Sakaida had double-checked his navigation, backing up the formation leader—whoever that may be now—and he was confident. *We are beyond the 3Ri contact point,* he told himself. *But we have seen nothing since those two battleships.*

At least he thought they had been battleships. More and more he harbored the uneasy feeling that he simply did not know enough: not about the enemy's ships or his aircraft, and certainly not enough about the most crucial data of all: the enemy's location. The junior officer apparently leading the twenty Zeros had made the logical choice, however. Finding nothing beyond the large warships, the formation was heading back toward their position. Sakaida approved, as far as it went. *If we cannot find carriers, perhaps we can attack other ships.* But what a few Zeros with medium-sized bombs could accomplish remained to be seen.

To ease some of the tension, Sakaida took his hands off the stick and throttle and flexed his fingers. He shook his arms as much as possible in the small cockpit, then worked his neck muscles. Again looking around, he realized he could hardly hope for better search conditions. From five thousand meters he had a splendid view of the ocean, obscured only by occasional puffy cumulus clouds. But nothing appeared—not even the two large ships seen several minutes before.

Sakaida inhaled the rubbery scent of his oxygen mask and hoped that the rest of the strike group was having better luck. Turning his head, he thought, *Maybe they will yet find something at the 7I contact . . . Grummans overhead!*

He had meant to vocalize the latter thought, but he could not tell if he had depressed the microphone button. *No time for that now,* his brain told him. Already he was shoving throttle, prop, and mixture controls against the stops, checking that his reflector gunsight rheostat was turned up, and pulling a hard climbing turn into the voracious Hellcats.

There must be twenty, he assessed. If so, it meant even odds. Which meant the *Hikokitai* 652 pilots were caught at a severe disadvantage: technical, training, and tactical.

The twelve F6F-3s from Coal Base were backed up by four Hellcat night fighters from Ginger Base. Above the scattered clouds, three dozen high-performance radial engines shrieked an air-cooled chorus of fifty thousand horsepower as the pilots of Mitsubishis and Grummans fought gravity, inertia, and each other's intellects in a single-minded effort to destroy each other.

As his adrenaline spiked, Sakaida began thinking himself through the combat. He badly wanted to turn in his seat, checking whether his three pilots had stayed with him through that initial maneuver. But he dared not. He had two Grummans in sight, 40 degrees to port off his nose, and he willed himself to keep them in view.

The eerie thought occurred to him. *It is Truk all over again.* The Grummans, fighting in pairs and fours, exhibited the same air discipline that Sakaida had come to expect of Americans. The lead Hellcat snapped out a tentative burst at about three hundred meters, and Sakaida had the impression he was not the target. Judging his nose-high climb would begin decelerating as gravity won its inevitable triumph over aerodynamic lift, he held on as long as possible. Then he briskly booted full right rudder, snapped the stick hard over, and hoped the timing worked.

It almost did. As the horizon tilted crazily in his windscreen, Sakaida sensed as much as saw two more Grummans diving in above him. He had intended for a crossing snapshot at the first pair, but the second section was almost in range. Realizing he had to break off his predictable flight path, he laid the stick all the way to port, simultaneously reversing rudder and slewing his Zero awkwardly in midair.

Sakaida laid his head back, sweeping the upper air where other tricolor blue fighters surely lurked. Seeing none, he risked a look behind him, wondering if he could find any trace of Yamamoto. He got the surprise of his life. *Yoshio! How did you do it?* In an accelerated heartbeat, he knew: *Yamamoto is too terrified to get separated from me.*

Not far below, a greasy black-brown smudge hung in the air. Nearby, scattered debris twinkled faintly in the sunlight and Sakaida thought he glimpsed a parachute in his peripheral vision. He caught a movement behind his starboard wing root and decided it afforded an opportunity. Half rolling to inverted, he retarded the throttle, brought the stick back against the stop and fell out of the sky in a split-S, hoping that Yamamoto would follow.

The view through his windscreen progressed from dark-blue water to a blurry impression of clouds, to the horizon coming back to greet him. And there, perhaps six hundred meters ahead, was the same fighter he had glimpsed before. Sakaida banged the throttle forward and jockeyed stick and rudder to put the shape in his gunsight.

He thought it was a Grumman and told himself, *Unless it turns I will never catch it.* Then it banked left and Sakaida bit his lip in anticipation.

He was aware that something had just gone into the water and assumed the American had killed one of Sakaida's friends.

Allowing plenty of lead, Sakaida had a fair view of the Grumman over his cowling. He laid off two full rings of deflection and fired his 7.7s. Their rapid cadence was strangely soothing—it felt good to shoot back. Sakaida saw waterspouts geyser somewhere near the American fighter, then was aware of another source of noise. He looked right and saw Yamamoto's plane perhaps a hundred meters away, firing all guns.

Sakaida glimpsed more geysers erupt in front of him—far too close to be his wingman's bullets. The icewater prickling between his shoulder blades told him what it was even as the square-winged shape raced between his cockpit and the sun.

Damn it! Sakaida cursed. *Where there is one Grumman there are always two!* He saw the second F6F's white belly flash overhead, zoom-climbing far too fast for a shot. But Yamamoto, profligate with his ammunition, nosed up and tripped off another burst.

Sakaida waggled his wings, getting Yamamoto's attention. The two Zeros climbed steeply back toward the original scene of the action, seeking safety in altitude. Whether any of their friends remained to contribute safety in numbers remained to be seen.

The radio had been indecipherable for several minutes, and Sakaida had mentally tuned it out. But now he heard a voice—Minami's?—describing an attack on U.S. carriers. And there, well to the south, were ships. The sky around them was speckled with flak bursts.

Briefly Sakaida wondered if he should turn that way, perhaps lend some help. But logic and self-preservation argued convincingly. *I have no bombs, I am low on ammunition and Yamamoto must be nearly empty.* With a long look at his fuel gauges, Sakaida brought his nose around to the west—to home.

IJNS *JUNYO*, 1612

There were so many empty chairs.

It was uncomfortably warm in the ready room—the Imperial Navy still rated habitability low on its priorities for ship construction, so there was no air conditioning. But while Sakaida ignored the heat, he found it difficult to reconcile the light losses of his strike group against what he knew about the others. Only seven planes had failed to return from the 1000 launch, and there were reports of damage to an American carrier. Sakaida took a moment to reflect that he might have heard Minami's voice after all—the one claiming a hit—because the fighter-bomber pilot was among the missing.

But CarDiv Two's 1100 launch, reinforced by *Zuikaku* planes from Air Group 601, had come to grief. It was hard to believe: eighty-two planes took off and none returned. Commander Yoshimura had been one of the formation leaders, and now he was gone.

As if reading his leader's mind, Nakaya edged up to Sakaida at the front of the room. "Sakaida-san, is there still no word?"

The *shotai* leader slowly shook his head. "None."

"Maybe they landed ashore." Nakaya's gaze went to the Marianas, where elements of eight naval air groups were based on Saipan, Guam, and Tinian.

"It is possible," Sakaida replied. The tone of his voice said otherwise.

Glancing sideways at his second section leader, Sakaida considered the fact that all four of them had returned was more than anyone could have prayed for. Since the generally irreligious Hiroyoshi Sakaida had bowed his head momentarily at the ship's shrine before manning his aircraft, he was prepared to concede divine intervention. Though Doi's Zero had taken a few .50-caliber rounds, the short, sharp combat had generally been inconclusive. And Yamamoto, the optimistic young fool, had even claimed one victory each for Sakaida and himself. Sakaida had let the claim stand rather than spoil the boy's day.

Yamamoto's stubby finger went to the track chart of Carrier Division 1. "I heard a staff officer say that *Taiho* has been abandoned."

"Yes, it's that crude oil from Borneo. The fleet commander knew the risk, but he had no choice." Sakaida did not need to elaborate. Everybody in the Imperial Navy above seaman second class knew that the American submarine campaign was starving the fleet of fuel oil. Borneo's unrefined product was usable but highly volatile, and the lingering effects of the torpedo damage to *Taiho* had doomed the 29,000-ton ship. Until about an hour ago she had been the second-largest aircraft carrier afloat, next to USS *Saratoga.*

"Now only *Zuikaku* remains from Operation Hawaii," Sakaida added gloomily. He could remember the November day that *Kido Butai,* the carrier striking force, had sailed from Hitokappu Bay in the chilly Kuriles. Six fine carriers—four sunk at Midway, and now in one day *Shokaku* as well as *Taiho* had joined them on the bottom.

Yamamoto stood silent for a moment. "It is strange," he muttered. "We are engaged in a battle between aircraft carriers, but both our losses today have been from enemy submarines."

Seeking some reason for optimism, Sakaida turned to his wingman.

"Apparently we are still out of range of the American carriers. Admiral Ozawa has retaken command and will direct the battle from a cruiser, I am told. Now get some sleep. This battle is not over."

Making 18 knots, the First Mobile Fleet steamed into the setting sun.

TUESDAY, 20 JUNE,
IJNS *JUNYO*, 1558

"The enemy has found us again."

Commander Surayama, *Junyo*'s air operations officer, had a small but rapt audience. "Admiral Ozawa's division reports an American scout plane radioed our position about twenty minutes ago," he continued. "Therefore, we can expect an air attack on this force before sunset."

Sakaida absorbed that information as just the latest in a litany of gloom. Ozawa's search planes had been out since 0530 hours, and Carrier Division 3 scouts had encountered American planes more than two hundred miles to the east. Somehow, the reports were discounted, even though four of the scouts had failed to return.

Few commissioned fliers remained among *Junyo*'s aviators, and Sakaida now found himself functioning as the fighter *hikotai*'s de facto operations officer. He knew that the rank-conscious Imperial Navy never would formalize the situation, but the job still had to be done. He ventured a question. "Commander, is there an estimate of enemy strength? We will need to know how to prepare the combat air patrol."

Surayama gave a frosty glance at the impertinent chief petty officer. "Admiral Ozawa now is in *Zuikaku*. His staff believes that four or five American carriers and one battleship were sunk or heavily damaged yesterday."

Surayama is quick on his feet, I'll give him that, Sakaida conceded. Slumping in his chair, he realized that the operations officer had seemingly given a logical answer without saying much at all. Ozawa's estimate could only be based on aviator claims, and Hiroyoshi Sakaida knew first hand how unreliable such reports could be. Excited, frightened young men, nearly all new to battle, usually reported what they expected to see. Or, worse yet, what they wanted to see.

Sakaida did some mental gymnastics. *Let us assume the reports are correct—five enemy carriers have been knocked out or sunk. That still leaves about ten with nearly all their bombers and fighters.* It was not a cheery prospect; the Mobile Fleet's remaining seven carriers were still badly outnumbered.

Nakaya slid into the empty seat to Sakaida's right. Leaning close, he dared give voice to his concerns. "Hiroyoshi, can we really defend against a massed air attack? Will we get help from Guam?"

Sakaida merely shrugged. He was uncomfortable expressing an opinion contrary to the official line, especially in the confines of so small a room. But Nakaya had done well yesterday, bringing himself and Doi back from the aerial ambush. *He deserves an answer,* Sakaida told himself. "Listen," he whispered, "I do not know any more about the American fleet than anyone else—even Surayama. But I do not believe we disabled five carriers. We might not have sunk even one." He looked around and saw that nobody was listening. "As for help from our planes ashore—I doubt it. The Americans are between us and Guam."

The disappointment showed in Nakaya's dark eyes. It was common knowledge that Vice Admiral Ozawa had counted on a relay system between the Mobile Fleet and the Marianas—launching strikes from both directions. Reportedly there were still one hundred operational planes on Guam and Tinian, where the Americans had not yet gone ashore. But Sakaida thought back four months to Truk, and how quickly the U.S. carrier pilots had dominated that powerful fleet base. *No,* he thought. *We'll get no help from Guam. We are on our own.*

OVERHEAD CARDIV TWO, 1858

The war gods had set a spectacular stage, and Sakaida took a moment to engrave it in his memory. As he circled in Falcon 12 with his flight at four thousand meters, the darkening ocean below stood in contrast to the huge white cumulus to the northeast. Sakaida could not recall a more wonderful sight in all his years of flying above this greatest of oceans. The low sun behind him cast its red rays through the atmosphere, tinting the cloud wondrous shades of yellow and orange. It was an eerily beautiful arena for the impending combat, capped by the 4,600-meter-high cumulus.

Sakaida knew that on the far side of the cloud steamed CarDiv One, now reduced to *Zuikaku* and her escorts. Below and behind him, under a screen of thirty-eight Zeros, was his own CarDiv Two, still intact, as was CarDiv Three to the south. Though each force operated independently, all maintained a similar course and speed: northwesterly at 24 knots.

For the moment Sakaida marveled at his inner calm. The Americans were inbound, no doubt about it. While the bearings relayed by fleet radar operators were highly improbable—he doubted the enemy would approach from the southwest—there had been sightings within the past twenty-five minutes. "Enemy splitting into four attack groups to the east," had been the floatplane's report. Sakaida realized that the Americans had just assigned targets: one strike group to each of the carrier divisions and one to the oilers trailing the carriers. *Ozawa was right to cancel the refueling,* Sakaida realized. *Otherwise we would be caught at a hopeless disadvantage.*

Nakaya was waggling his wings for attention. When Sakaida caught the signal, he swiveled his head—and gasped. His previous calm melted in an adrenaline rush. Emerging from behind the large cloud was a swarm of ordered dots.

Sakaida would have been appalled at the overall numerical disparity the Mobile Fleet now faced. There was no way to get a count as sightings came with increasing frequency, and in moments the radio went spastic. Therefore, no defender knew that seventy-seven Japanese carrier planes—not all of them fighters—were airborne to oppose 220 attackers. That was bad enough, but the local odds were hardly better: thirty-eight Zeros against one hundred planes from six U.S. Navy air groups bent on sinking Carrier Division 2.

Bright-colored flak bursts pockmarked the air as shipboard gunners caught the danger. In that moment Hiroyoshi Sakaida knew he was about to die and consigned himself to his ultimate duty: to perish in the service of the Emperor. Sakaida hoped his mother would be proud and stoic when she received the news.

He glimpsed the now-familiar silhouettes overhead—angular, blunt Grumman shapes, distinctive with their external fuel tanks. Any second now they would descend on him, so there was no time to waste. His mind registered one thought above all: *Get to the bombers!*

Sakaida brought his *shotai* around in a steep bank to approach the enemy formation from the side. Somewhere in that turn Nakaya and Doi disappeared from his vision and thus, from his control as the Hellcats dropped down. Sakaida registered the optimistic thought that his second section might tie up the escorts, allowing him and Yamamoto a shot at the bombers. Then he was concentrating on his attack.

Orange-yellow sunlight filtered through cloud and haze, bathing his cockpit in a comforting glow. For an instant Sakaida felt suspended in space rather than diving at nearly 300 knots to shoot other airmen out of the sky. He began tracking the American formation from well out, judging them to be Curtiss dive-bombers. A glance to one side showed Yamamoto selecting his own approach, now slightly ahead and to port.

In the front seat of 41 Sniper, the twenty-seven-year-old squadron commander from Iowa had selected his target—the nearest carrier in the center group—and was setting up his attack. He heard a high-pitched call in his earphones, something about "Fighters overhead!" and briefly wondered if that meant his friend Killer or Japs. When he looked around, he saw a lone Zero close aboard, well inside gunnery range. But the hostile pulled up without shooting.

"No guts," thought the Iowan. Then he pushed over to line up *Junyo* in his sight.

In Falcon 19, Flight Petty Officer Yamamoto raged to the gods. He had not only failed in his duty, he had disgraced himself in the most appalling fashion. The most basic error of all—failing to arm his guns! A churning, bilious sensation roiled inside him. He told himself that if he could not atone for his lapse, he would be obliged to seek *jibaku*—death by self-exploding. By the time he pulled around for another pass, the bombers were into their steep dives and he could not easily follow. He decided to climb, hoping to stay above the Grummans bound to be hunting in the area.

Sakaida knew the range was longish, but he triggered an optimistic burst from his 7.7s. He got a good look at the last three-plane section just as the bombers entered their dives and realized he had not distracted them. *Something is odd,* he thought, *Something is wrong.*

Then it hit him: the tall, graceful tail; the long canopy similar to a Zero's. These were not Curtisses. They were . . . Douglas dive-bombers! The same ones that had killed Imperial Navy carriers at Coral Sea, Midway, and Guadalcanal. Sakaida devoted an instant to seeking the American name and pulled it up from the recesses of his memory: Dauntless.

They are an old design, a prewar type, he recalled. *They were to have been replaced by the Curtiss bomber long ago.* But the Zero under his hands and feet also was of prewar vintage, and Sakaida acknowledged that it, too, should have been replaced.

Abruptly the upper air was clear. Sakaida rolled into a tight left turn, seeking a sign of friend or enemy, and found himself alone. Drifting swirls of flak bursts entered his vision, but he seemed alone for the moment. He realized that when the Douglas squadron had dived, the combat had gone with it. *Where is Yamamoto?* he wondered. *And what should I do now?*

Belatedly Sakaida remembered to check his engine gauges. He throttled back to a fast cruise setting, then looked down. Through the low cloud layer he discerned frantic wakes on the blue-black water, saw the bursting flak and tendrils of tracer fire and realized the attack was not yet over.

The fighter channel still was a babble—there would be no help from that source. So Sakaida decided to turn back along the Americans' inbound track, hoping to find more targets. Nearing the large cloud, which now had lost some of its rosy tint, he discerned a lone aircraft circling below. *It could be an American looking for his squadron,* Sakaida thought. He nosed over, descended slightly and began stalking the stranger from six o'clock low. He was within two hundred meters when he recognized the silhouette of a Zero 52.

Approaching from starboard, Sakaida eased into formation with the fighter. He read the number 321-19 painted white on an olive-green tail—and felt the ambivalence of relief and disgust. He triggered a short burst from his 7.7s and laughed as Yoshio Yamamoto visibly flinched in his seat. Shaking his head in silent admonishment, Sakaida led his wingman in a descent toward the east.

EAST OF THE MOBILE FLEET, 1910

There they are. Sakaida congratulated himself on assessing the Americans' likely rendezvous spot. It was not difficult, really, knowing that their fleet lay well to the east. He guessed that most of them would be low on fuel and take a direct line home. *After all, that is what I would do.*

Several other Zero pilots had made similar educated guesses; Sakaida estimated there were eight, or enough for a full *chutai.* He waggled his wings, asserting command over the impromptu group, and went down on a formation low to the water.

Sakaida began tracking a three-plane group and realized they were Douglases. *This cannot be the same unit we attacked before,* he told himself. And he was right; this squadron of SBD-5s from Sapphire Base had just attacked *Hiyo.*

He was momentarily distracted by a radio cry that pierced the general babble. "Falcon fighter squadron, Grummans above and behind!"

Sakaida immediately abandoned his pass at the Douglases, pulling up and around to confront the threat. He had just enough time to see Yamamoto pressing a run on the lead trio, to register that his wingman had scored hits—and to note an abrupt, awkward movement of Yamamoto's Zero. Then he lost sight and began looking for the American fighters.

They seemed everywhere. Sakaida felt as alone as a human could, seemingly surrounded by a swarm of white-starred Grummans. He rolled out of his breakaway turn, sparred briefly with a Hellcat that refused to play his game, and accelerated away. Then another pair entered his vision, just above to port.

Seizing the opportunity, Sakaida stood on his rudder bar and skidded left. He saw his crosshairs skimming the darkening horizon toward the nearer Grumman and tripped both triggers. Fiery gouts of 7.7- and 20-millimeter tracer snapped out toward the big fighter and Sakaida thought he saw pieces fly.

Elated, he forgot his fear, even his resignation. He reversed his controls, rolling right to bring his sight to bear on the second American. Both Grummans pulled up, going for the perch, but Sakaida had a favorable angle momentarily. Shoving the throttle full forward for maximum boost, he heard the Sakae engine respond and held the sight picture long enough to hose off a long, scything burst. The Hellcat seemed to quiver, then it was gone from view. He had the ephemeral impression of one or two splashes off to starboard.

Sakaida rolled wings-level, accelerated toward a gray-white cloud, and prayed. Only when he entered the misty safety did he throttle back.

IJNS *JUNYO* 1938

The landing-system lights stared a blue welcome at Sakaida as he flew Falcon 12 into the fourth wire. The happy lurch of hook engagement convinced him that he had survived.

Taxiing forward, Sakaida noted that there was plenty of room to park. As he followed the plane director's wands, applied his toe brakes, and retarded the mixture control he realized that there had been severe losses. He switched off left and right, turned the fuel selector off, and sat for a moment on the darkening flight deck. Only then did it occur to him that he had done something unusual—made a seminocturnal carrier landing.

Sakaida refused help from a solicitous plane captain and unstrapped himself. He dropped heavily to the teak-planked deck, gathering his senses as he willed his knees to remain steady. *I am more tired than I knew,* his brain told him. He slumped against the fuselage, wondering where he could get a stiff drink.

Nakaya materialized from the gloom. "Sakaida-san, I—I—"

"What is it?" Sakaida sensed something awful, but how much worse could it be? He had already seen *Hiyo* aflame, the victim of a skillfully executed American torpedo attack. Sailors were saying that *Junyo* herself had sustained bomb damage, but obviously not enough to prevent flight operations.

"I have lost Doi," Nakaya blurted out. There were tears behind the words.

"And I lost Yamamoto," Sakaida croaked. "He shot down a Douglas carrier bomber but they killed him." Nakaya seemed not to hear and Sakaida realized that his section leader wanted to talk, not listen. "What happened?"

"We were chasing bombers when . . ." Nakaya stifled a sob, then inhaled. "The Grummans caught us. God, what demons! Doi, he just—exploded!"

Sakaida was tempted to ask Nakaya how he had escaped a similar fate, then thought better of it. A battle had been fought and lost, great ships had been sunk. Hundreds of men had been shot, burned, drowned, or crushed to death. What did one more matter?

Leading Nakaya down to the ready room, Sakaida told himself that it mattered because half of his *shotai* was dead. Yoshio Yamamoto and Ikuhiko Doi had spent barely twenty years in this life. Now both were free of it: the toil, the grief, the gnawing fear. Free of the heaven-imposed duty to die for Nippon.

And free of family and laughter and spring flowers and young women, Sakaida told himself. He decided that if he was getting philosophical, he might as well get drunk. As soon as he gave his report, he would look up that bosun's mate with the sake.

WEDNESDAY, 21 JUNE

NAS PASCO

Ensign Eddie Fairfield ordinarily was an unassuming young man with slicked-back hair and earnest blue eyes. As an officer in the United States Navy he was expected to combine impeccable behavior with individual initiative, but the proposal he laid before Lieutenant Phil Rogers brought those concepts into confrontation.

"It's like this," Fairfield said to Rogers. He kept his voice low, but the noise of the fuel pumps on the flight line insured confidentiality. "After yesterday's second hop I got talking with the first-class who runs this gas crew. He said that he could be persuaded to top off our tanks almost anytime, provided that he had some—uh, compensation." Fairfield's eyebrows wiggled meaningfully.

Rogers forced the corners of his mouth downward, against the impulse he felt. "Mr. Fairfield, if you are suggesting that commissioned officers enter into a business arrangement with enlisted personnel . . ."

"Well, gee, Lieutenant. You said you wished we could get more flight time but there's only so much fuel allotment."

Rogers inhaled, feigning indignation. "I was about to say, it would depend entirely upon nature of the . . . compensation."

Fairfield leaned close to his leader. "A fifth of booze a week an' no questions asked."

Is that all? Rogers thought. *Cheap wartime help. But they're making a pure profit, considering that they're selling what isn't really theirs.* He pinned Ensign Fairfield with what he hoped was a stern superior officer's gaze. "Well, okay. But tell him, no questions *answered,* either!" Rogers could no longer suppress the grin.

Fairfield winked and turned back toward the first-class petty officer atop the nearest F6F.

Rogers pulled off his cloth helmet and walked down the line. The tangy aroma of 100/130 octane fuel swirled around him, combining with the scent of hot rubber and hydraulic fluid that, taken together, meant *airplanes.*

Officially, of course, Lieutenant Rogers had just approved an unlawful arrangement: bribery and conspiracy to misappropriate government property. While it was unlikely that officialdom ever would know of the deal, Platco could make things unpleasant for all concerned if he heard about it. Rogers felt that Gordon Connell not only would have learned of any such arrangement, but privately would have condoned it—but Connell was gone. Now that Juanita had returned to Norfolk, all contact with the Sunsetters' first skipper was ended.

Despite those considerations, Rogers felt the small risk in Fairfield's enterprise was worth it. Most pilots were logging thirty-plus hours per month, which was ample. But Rogers intended Team Three—his division's new tag, to be more than adequate. "We're going to be so well trained that we can fly in our sleep," he had told his pilots. But it wasn't just practicing tactics and maneuvers and gunnery that he wanted to perfect. Rogers wanted each of his pilots to be capable of leading the team, to know everyone's best moves and weaknesses. You only achieved that degree of proficiency by flying together constantly.

Rogers wanted ten more hours per month—roughly two thousand extra gallons for his team every four weeks. If that meant one or two more hops on weekends, so be it; there was not much else to do at NAS Pasco, anyway. If any of his pilots complained, the wisdom of his actions would become apparent when the targets began shooting back.

THURSDAY, 22 JUNE
IJNS *JUNYO*

Any sort of gambling usually made Sakaida feel better, and winning the anchor pool took no effort at all. Of course, the pot was pitifully small with so few surviving aircrew to participate, but that was beside the point. Sitting in the petty officers' mess, counting his yen, was not the worst way to end the Mobile Fleet's deployment.

It occurred to him that he had beat far worse odds than the finite probability of when *Junyo*'s anchor would splash into Nakagusuku Bay on the east coast of Okinawa. Yes, it was good to be back in friendly waters. But the mortality figures came swimming up at him from the darkness of his mind.

In two days of battle the Mobile Fleet had lost 92 percent of its carrier aircraft and one third of its flight decks, amounting to 45 percent of its carrier tonnage. Most of the surviving carriers had taken damage, and *Junyo* was hardest hit: two bomb hits starboard near the stacks, with six near-misses. Sakaida mentally catalogued what he knew of the others: *Zuikaku* and *Chiyoda,* both hit; *Ryuho,* slight damage. Apparently only *Zuiho* and *Chitose* had escaped harm.

Those, of course, were merely the casualties in matériel. Sakaida already had begun to deal with the prospect that nearly every carrier airman he had ever known was dead. That was how it went in the Imperial Navy. Officially, nobody was considered missing in action, and certainly not a prisoner of war. A man either came back or he did not.

Stacking his winnings, Sakaida felt the onset of an unexpected sense of calm. None of his friends over the years would ever have described the old Sakaida as philosophical—not the fun-loving, rhumba-dancing clown he had shown the world, the one who used to emulate Carmen Miranda with fruit on his head. But his world had changed in the past two years: after Midway and Guadalcanal in 1942; after the greater Solomons campaign of '43; and now after the aerial executions he had survived over Truk and the Philippine Sea.

Hiroyoshi Sakaida realized that he had become a new person. With a sense of awed surprise, it occurred to him: *I am not going to die in this war. From now on, there is nothing to fear!*

SATURDAY, 24 JUNE
NAS PASCO

Three aviators crawled on their hands and knees, diligently examining a fifty-foot canvas resembling an oversized windsock. Rogers stood near them, recording their comments on a clipboard.

"Nineteen black holes," called Fairfield.

"Twenty-eight red," chirped Diskowski. "Nice going, sir!"

"Fifteen blue," Sossaman added.

Rogers noted the figures, then squatted with the others. "With nine yellow that's seventy-one hits out of four hundred, which is . . . about seventeen percent for our division," he stated. He looked at Ensign Sossaman, who had been shooting yellow-painted bullets that morning. "Brian, if you'd stop under-deflecting we'd be up around twenty percent."

There was no response so Rogers tapped the pilot on one arm. "Come here a minute." He led Sossaman back to the tail end of the target sleeve. Diskowski and Fairfield followed, adding to the tension.

Rogers knelt down and fingered one of the .50-caliber holes ringed with traces of yellow paint. "Look here. Seven of your hits are way aft on the sleeve. It's not hard to correct—you just have to allow more lead."

"Yes, sir, I know. It's just that I can't get used to aiming so close to the tow plane."

Rogers smiled, hoping to encourage the kid. "If that's what's bothering you, forget it. In a full-deflection shot you can't come close to the TBF or SB2C unless you put your gunsight pipper ahead of it. Remember, he's towing the sleeve on a long cable."

Sossaman nodded unconvincingly. "Look, Brian, we've been down to the skeet range several times now. You know about lead—I've seen you break fifteen out of twenty-five."

"But Lieutenant, what if I do hit the tow plane?"

Rogers decided that some remedial education was required. He held up his left hand and placed his other hand at right angles to it. "Here you are at full deflection and boresight range, a thousand feet. How much lead do you need?"

Sossaman knew the school answer: the two-thirds rule. "My lead in mils is two thirds the target speed in knots."

"Okay, how fast is the tow plane?"

"Well, about a hundred fifty knots."

Rogers nodded. "Right. So your lead is?"

Sossaman glanced down in embarrassment. "A hundred mils."

"Now then," Rogers continued. "You know that one mil equals one foot at a thousand-foot range. So you're aiming at a point only a hundred feet ahead of the sleeve." He moved his right hand well ahead of his left. "The tow plane is clear to hell out here when you shoot."

"Yes, sir. But when we're making forty-five-degree approaches the angle narrows, right? Our bullets come closer to the tug."

"Sure." Rogers was engaged in a mental wrestling match. This was proving harder than he expected. Rubbing his chin, he continued. "What's your muzzle velocity, mister?"

Sossaman was taken aback. "I think the .50-caliber is about twenty-five hundred feet per second."

"It's more like twenty-eight hundred foot-seconds. So how long until that bullet reaches a thousand feet?"

"Well, gosh, I don't—"

"Just about four tenths of a second," Rogers interjected, "allowing for deceleration. So you have to aim wherever the target's going to be less than half a second later. But we're not going to be shooting at 150-knot Japs, unless we're lucky enough to find a patrol plane. We'll have 300-knot targets. Now, at 300 knots a plane makes just over five hundred feet per second. So you need to move your aim point about two hundred feet in front of it."

Sossaman shook his head in doubt. "I know all that, sir. But at the narrower angles—"

"At the narrower angles you reduce your lead by the sine of the angle-off as deflection decreases." He grinned again. "I studied math at Florida State. All you need to remember are the rules of thumb. Full deflection at sixty degrees, three quarters at thirty, half at twenty, and one quarter down to almost zero deflection." He held up his hands. "Easy."

"Yes, sir," Sossaman gloomed.

Rogers motioned to Fairfield and walked a few paces away. "Get hold of that petty officer we're bribing. I'm scheduling a gunnery hop tomorrow—just Sossaman and me."

Fairfield replied, "Sure thing, sir. But how are you going to get a target and tow plane?"

Rogers's eyes gleamed. "I may know somebody who's used to getting shot at."

SUNDAY, 25 JUNE, 0730

NAS PASCO GUNNERY RANGE

Glancing over his shoulder at Sossaman's Hellcat, Rogers waggled his wings and rolled into a high-side pass on the sleeve from starboard at ten thousand feet. In the early-morning light the target took on a yellow tint, streaming behind the Helldiver.

Rogers looked at his Mark VIII gunsight reticle, with 50- and 100-mil rings surrounding the center pipper. The display, reflected on an angled glass, appeared superimposed upon infinity. Rogers smoothly flew his sight through the target, ignoring the Helldiver tow plane. When he estimated he had reached a thousand-foot distance he fired a short burst. Only two of his six guns were loaded, but it was enough for now. He pulled up to watch Sossaman.

"Give it plenty of lead, now," Rogers called. He watched the Hellcat slanting down from the opposite side of the target, saw the gunsmoke and caught the glitter of empty brass cases under the wing as Sossaman began shooting.

It looked fairly decent. As Sossaman joined on him, Rogers swung around for a pass from port. "Leader is in," he radioed to the tow plane. Wanting to conserve his ammunition, Rogers barely touched the trigger. The brief pounding of his guns came to him as he concentrated on his sight picture.

He reached for the microphone but decided not to coach Sossaman this time. *Let him make his own mistakes.* Rogers had ordered Sossaman's two guns loaded with two hundred rounds each to allow for repeat passes, thus maximizing the practice potential of the tug sortie.

Over the next fifteen minutes Rogers took his pupil through four more passes: two low-side quartering and two overheads. The latter was Rogers's favorite. He passed ahead of the target three thousand feet above it, rolled inverted, and watched the world spin upside down. Looking through the top of his canopy, hanging in his seat belt, he caught sight of the sleeve and pulled the stick back. Once vertical, he neutralized the controls and tracked the sleeve from directly overhead.

Rogers fired one burst in each pass, recovering in a four-G pullout below and behind the Helldiver. Regaining orientation, he then called Sossaman down.

The student almost flubbed the first overhead pass, getting too steep too quickly. He recovered soon enough to track the sleeve briefly and got off a quick burst. Rogers thought that most of the bullets had gone wide.

But on the last run, Sossaman's timing was excellent. Sensing a good setup, he clamped down on the trigger and fired out. Upon rejoining, Rogers led him alongside the Helldiver marked 59-B-9 and waved. The '2C pilot slid back his canopy, and Burnett made an obscene gesture before banking for home.

NAS PASCO, 0925

Rogers finished counting the holes and smiled. "Brian, you've got it. You did especially well on that last run. I make it a total of fifty-nine."

Sossaman gave a little yip and pranced on the toes of his shoes. "Wow! That's—"

"Just about fifteen percent." Rogers beamed. "Look here," he said, picking up part of the sleeve. "You raked the target front to back on that last run." Rogers noted a series of yellow-tinged holes that ran vertically through the target. He had long since learned how to "read a sleeve" by the angle of entry and exit holes.

Burnett wandered over, hands in his pockets and helmet shoved back on his head. "You boys through playing so we can eat?"

Rogers and Sossaman began dragging the target out of the way. "Almost done, Bernie." He stopped and looked at his friend. "And, hey, thanks a hell of a lot."

"Oh, it's nothing, really. If I get court-martialed I'll just plead temporary insanity." He thought for a moment. "Naw, I'll say it was female deprivation—not getting laid regular. They'll believe that!"

Rogers turned serious. "Like I said, if there's any trouble over an unauthorized flight, have your CO talk to me. I'm the flight officer in my squadron and I have the authority."

Burnett pretended to shrug off the offer. "Hey, they've got a swell new dish at the mess hall. Half a canteloupe with a scoop of ice cream. You heroes can buy me a couple."

Sossaman beamed. "It's on me, sir." Then he turned to Rogers. "Uh, Lieutenant? Do you think we could do that again?"

P A R T   I I

"During the war, we studied every day what we had learned and drew upon our experiences. . . . What I was most enthusiastic about was to be a truly good leader [who] could produce more good pilots, to take care of them. . . . I feel much more proud of myself when I think that I never lost a wingman in combat, than when I think about the number of my victories."

Lieutenant (j.g.) Saburo Sakai
Japanese Navy Ace

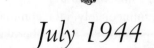

SIX

July 1944

The hangar was crowded but not excessively so, considering that the reformed *Hikokitai* 653 included the survivors of 652. Merely eleven aircraft had remained in CarDiv Three's three carriers, but Sakaida knew that even that lamentable figure surpassed the surviving aircraft of CarDiv Two.

As far as Sakaida knew, he and Nakaya were almost the only veterans of Air Group 652's fighter component. Now, with the Mobile Fleet reduced to four operational carriers, he knew the inevitable reorganization had begun. The assembled aviators waited patiently to learn their immediate fate.

It was not long coming. A lieutenant commander whom Sakaida had never seen before strode briskly to the front of the hangar and mounted the podium. He began speaking immediately, and Sakaida did not catch the man's name amid the shuffling feet and low hum of lingering conversation.

"Most of you know by now that Second Carrier Division has been disbanded," the officer was saying. Sakaida and Nakaya traded knowing glances—they had heard the rumors. It was not surprising, considering the beating the division had taken, but this was the first confirmation. "Therefore, *Hikokitai* 652 also has been disbanded. Most of you from that organization are being transferred to 653 and will be assigned accordingly."

The lieutenant commander turned toward an organizational chart behind him. "Carrier Division Three is now the strongest in the Mobile Fleet, with *Chitose, Chiyoda,* and *Zuiho.* Our *hikotai* within the *hikokitai* are Numbers 164 and 165 with fighters, Number 166 with fighter-bombers, and 263 flying carrier attack planes. The full allotment to each *hikotai* is forty-eight aircraft, but it will be some time before we are up to strength."

Nakaya leaned into Sakaida's shoulder and muttered, "Nothing changes." Sakaida emitted a noncommittal grunt.

"Training will begin immediately," the commander continued. "We expect to resume carrier operations in September with qualification landings in the Inland Sea." He looked at his brown-clad audience and knew that fewer than a quarter of the aviators had yet landed aboard a ship. "If we are fortunate, we will have time for some advanced combat training. But not until we can operate efficiently from our carriers." That somber message sank in as *hikotai* assignments were read off.

While waiting, Sakaida took in the animated conversations around him. It was always the same, he reflected—eager, excited young faces with that radiant glow of anticipation and dread. By now he knew the signs intimately. Such fine boys, all dedicated to dying for the Emperor if necessary and fearing nothing so much as disgrace or failure.

Sakaida absently began studying some of the nearer faces. *That one,* he thought, *and that one.* In fact, most of them had the indefinable aspect about them that Sakaida now thought of merely as The Look.

"What are you thinking, Sakaida-san?" Nakaya's question interrupted his musing. But Sakaida was at a loss. How did you explain that you had become able merely to look at a man and tell with near certainty that he was going to die?

THURSDAY, 13 JULY
NAS SAN DIEGO

Air Group 59 had taken over the North Island Officer's Club, spilling into the bar adjoining the anteroom within hours of their arrival from Pasco. Rogers and his team already had staked out a table for themselves, but made room when Don Mancross wandered in. The noise level continued to rise as Rogers overheard snatches of conversation.

"Who said Roosevelt wouldn't run for a fourth term?"

"Not me. The paper has an article where he says, 'I have as little right as a soldier to leave his position on the line.' "

"Balls," said a Republican. "Ain't nobody shooting at F.D.R. He's had three terms; I'm voting for Dewey and Bricker."

"Well, Tojo just resigned," cracked another flier. "Maybe he'll run in November."

"I heard on the radio that San Diego's population has doubled since '41. Do you realize that means twice as many women?"

At that moment the air group commander, Tom Albertson, arrived with his small staff.

"Hey, CAG!" hollered Brian Sossaman. "We got room over here. Uh, sir." His face reddened as Rogers and Mancross rolled their eyes at each other. Sossaman was on his third scotch and water, to the disgust of Kenny Diskowski, who was finishing his second Coca-Cola.

"You ought to take it easy, Brian," Diskowski said evenly. "You know, demon rum." He smiled but his tone was serious.

Sossaman pointedly shoved his glass away. "Hell, Dis, what do you know about booze? You can't buy a drink for another two years anyway."

"That's not so. It's only about fourteen months. My twentieth birthday's in September." He slurped his remaining Coke through a straw, then plucked the cherry out of the bottom.

Albertson slid into a chair and waved his thanks to his operations officer, who was standing in line at the bar with the CAG's order. "You fellows all settled in?" he asked.

"Yes, sir," Rogers replied. "But I've never seen the flight line so crowded. I wasn't sure we'd have space for the whole air group when we landed yesterday."

"It's not like the old days, that's for sure," Albertson mused. He regarded Rogers and Mancross, the only other prewar aviators at the table. "I can remember F3Fs and SBCs out there not so long ago. The biplane Navy!"

Mancross rattled his ice. "Yes, sir. I was in Fighting Two when we got the first F2As. Everybody thought the Brewsters were pretty hot stuff back then." He gave a self-deprecating snort. "We didn't know any better!"

"I remember that," Albertson replied. "Paul Ramsey must've been CO about then—1939?"

"Lieutenant Commander Duckworth, sir. Ramsey took over later. But we didn't get the Brewsters until late '40 because our first batch was diverted to Finland. We only got F4Fs a couple months before the Coral Sea."

Rogers looked at his superior. "Commander, speaking of carrier battles, did you have any luck with reports from the Philippine Sea?" He knew that CAG-59 placed high training value on recent information from the fleet.

"Negative. Too soon for any reports to trickle down. But I just talked to a pilot I used to know in the *Ranger* Air Group. He's on ComFair staff now, and the word is that on the first day, 19 June, we splashed maybe four hundred of 'em. Our losses were about thirty."

Eddie Fairfield squirmed in his padded chair. The body English was unmistakable: *Hot damn—wish we'd been there!*

The operations officer, a lieutenant commander named Robinson, set down a double scotch for Albertson. "Oh, thanks, Chuck." Albertson sipped his drink and wrinkled his nose. Pounding the tabletop, he shouted above the din, "Same damn thing in every port. Goddamn bartenders water down the drinks so's a sailor can't get an honest shot of booze!"

The three ensigns were wide-eyed at the commander's brazen humor. Rogers winked at Diskowski, who reveled in Commander Albertson's democratic behavior. The ensign ventured a question. "CAG, if they got that many Japs, do you think there'll be enough left when we get out there?"

Rogers and Mancross chortled at Diskowski's earnest tone; Albertson almost choked. When he recovered he said, "Mister . . ."

"Uh, Diskowski, sir."

"Oh, yeah. Well, Mr. Diskowski, don't you worry. There's plenty more where those came from—most of their nine carriers got away. Our subs sank two and we put another on the bottom the next evening. But it was a long-range strike—evidently about three hundred miles—and we lost a lot of planes in the water. They had to recover after dark, which tells me that our emphasis on night flying will pay off."

Rogers lowered his voice. "How bad was it, sir?"

Albertson paused for a moment. "Bad." He thought better of bar-room talk about the loss of nearly a hundred carrier planes—mostly to fuel exhaustion. "Our losses can be replaced but there's a real feud building over this. Shapes up as a blackshoe-brownshoe argument. Admiral Spruance is ComFifth Fleet, and he prevented Admiral Mitscher from pursuing the Jap carriers and finishing them off for good." Albertson shrugged and nervously tapped the floor with his polished aviator's brown shoes. "Midway all over again, they're saying."

Rogers leaned forward. "Sir, obviously I don't know much about this Saipan operation. But I was at Midway. True, Spruance is a blackshoe admiral, but our orders at Midway were to protect the island. We were in no shape to take on the Jap battleships."

"Point well taken, Rogers. No doubt Spruance was under orders to protect the Saipan landings. It's just a damn shame to let five or six Jap carriers off the hook." Albertson tasted his scotch again and looked around. "Are you fellows also drinking water tinged with alcohol?"

Mancross raised his glass. "Mine's fine, Commander."

Sossaman drained his remaining scotch. "This *is* kind of weak. Maybe Ensign Diskowski's onto something. He's on his second Coke, sir."

Albertson lanced Diskowski with a stare. "That so, mister?"

Diskowski looked down in embarrassment. "Yessir. I'm still nine-teen." Sossaman giggled louder than he intended.

Albertson took in the situation and stood up. "Well, no pilot in my air group is gonna drink Coca-Cola if he doesn't want to! You ever hear of a highball called the KO for Tokyo?"

Before Diskowski could reply, Albertson had him by the arm. "Come with me, Ensign. Your naval education is about to be broadened." The others watched in amazement as the commander led his charge behind the bar. The senior attendant, a first-class petty officer, was overwhelmed as the three-striper took over.

"All right," Albertson stated, setting a shaker on the bar. "Pour me two jiggers of bourbon." Diskowski searched the bottles and found what he needed. In quick succession CAG called for a jigger of rum, another of gin, and one each of French and Italian vermouth.

"I don't think we have the Italian kind, sir," Diskowski lamented.

"That's okay. Double up on the French stuff." When the ensign was finished pouring, Albertson had him blend the mixture in a shaker while he himself prepared a large highball glass with crushed ice and a lemon peel.

After Diskowski finished shaking, Albertson held up the glass and ordered, "Hit me, son." Diskowski poured and Albertson inhaled deeply, savoring the aroma with closed eyes. He took a sip, swallowed, and smacked his lips. "Purrfect," he intoned. He turned to the officers crowding the bar. "Gentlemen, I give you the KO for Tokyo. It's a sledgehammer of a drink, with a knockout punch. Guaranteed to overcome the resistance of the most reluctant female. Expertly mixed by our bartender here." He offered the glass to Diskowski, who didn't really want to drink but felt obliged. He managed to down a small amount of the lethal mixture without choking, then smiled sheepishly.

To the cheers of his fellow ensigns, Kenny Diskowski raised the glass in triumph. He caught Rogers's eye from the far table and returned the grin. Both fliers knew that from now on, Air Group 59 would follow Tom Albertson into the fires of hell.

SATURDAY, 15 JULY
OITA BASE, KYUSHU ISLAND

Sakaida milked the stick back and felt the Zero 52 pay off as the burble over the wing ran out of lift. The fighter stalled straight ahead, wings-level, and the tail wheel contacted the runway an instant before the mains. He tracked down the runway and easily made the turnoff leading back to the flight line.

Glancing to starboard, Sakaida was disappointed to see one of his apprentices float past the taxiway, still three meters high. *He flared too soon,* Sakaida realized. The boy managed a decent landing, but would have to take the long way around to reach the parking area.

The plane director met him with arms raised, and Sakaida nudged his left brake in response to the man's signals. A quick burst of throttle, an abrupt turn into line, cut the mixture and the flight was over. Sakaida saw two sailors scramble under the leading edge of his wings to chock the wheels, and momentarily he listened to the three-bladed prop whirling to a stop. Then he spotted trouble.

Damn—that prig Ono. Sakaida could guess what was going to happen. The *hikotai* leader, Lieutenant Ganji Ono, did not seem to fly very much but he seldom missed a chance to criticize the aerial faults of others. At least, those among his subordinates. Sakaida felt certain that he, a non-commissioned officer, was far and away the best aviator in the unit—his very survival had ensured that, if nothing else. Lieutenant Ono seemed merely to relish his authority; whether he could fly was secondary.

Sakaida scampered from his cockpit and stood to attention. He saluted as Ono approached, bracing himself for what was coming.

"*Joto Hiko Haiso* Sakaida! You are a flight chief petty officer. Don't you realize that carrier operations require precise timing? One of your *shotai* just missed his landing spot! He will impede taxiing aircraft for several minutes!"

Sakaida knew—and suspected that Ono knew—that the leading seaman's minor error would hardly affect flight-line operations. Quickly weighing the odds, Sakaida decided to push the matter as much as he dared. "Honored *Tai-i* Ono-san! I beg to observe that these pilots are rookies, unlike yourself." Sakaida's tongue was well in his cheek; he knew that Ono came from the thirty-eighth naval fighter pilot class and had graduated only ten months before. "They still have much to learn."

Ono's eyes widened in anger. "And it is your duty to teach them! See that you pay more attention to their training!" Ono spun on one heel and marched away before Sakaida could respond. But in that moment Sakaida got a satisfying jolt: He realized that Lieutenant Ono's face now had The Look.

MONDAY, 17 JULY

NAS SAN DIEGO

Tom Albertson addressed his pilots but spoke only long enough to introduce the two briefers. "Gentlemen. We've had a few days to practice the basics of close air support. Most of you are up to speed on bombing and gunnery, and I hope we'll fire some rockets before we leave. But now we're going to put what we've learned to use."

Turning toward the side of the platform, the air group commander continued speaking into the microphone. "We have two liaison officers from the Marine Corps with us . . ." Animated boos and hisses arose from the Navy men, but Albertson waved them down. "As I was saying, these two fine gentlemen are here to give us the benefit of their expertise. I present Major Tim Hayden from Camp Pendleton and Captain Jim Carpenter, visiting us from Mojave."

In the second row Rogers leaned over to Fairfield. "I'll be damned. I thought that looked like Sunny Jim. Couldn't tell behind the sunglasses at this distance."

"He's the F4U pilot who came to Pasco?" Rogers nodded, intent on the presentation.

"I'm here to help you aviators help us," Hayden began. He was another recruiting-poster Marine, tall and well built. "Most of you know that the Marine Corps pioneered air-ground support over the past two decades or so—especially during the Caribbean campaigns in the banana republics." He rocked back on his heels, awaiting the expected laughter. "Well, we did such a good job that other people began taking notice—like the *Luftwaffe*. That's right. Some of the *blitzkrieg* tactics that worked so well in Poland and France were copied from us, so we know they work!" He got a better response this time.

"We've learned a few things along the way," Hayden continued, "especially after Tarawa. We know that we can't always count on having Marine air, so it's been decided to increase air support training with Navy air groups. Now, a bit of background. In the early days we thought that any Marine officer with a map could identify enemy strongpoints or other targets and radio that information to his opposite number overhead. Well, there're just two things wrong with that." He held up one finger. "We learned that the only thing more dangerous than a monkey with a razor blade is a second lieutenant with a map."

The aviators hooted and hollered appreciatively. Hayden had gotten the audience's attention. Extending another finger, he added, "We also learned that it takes a flier to tell another pilot what to look for. An infantryman might think that a couple of tall trees makes a good reference point, but a pilot knows that from above, one tree looks like another. So we're putting specially trained pilots into infantry battalions to act as air controllers. Those are some of the officers you'll be working with in the next few days."

Hayden stepped aside as Carpenter stepped to the microphone. "Gentlemen, welcome to the Marine Corps. You're working for us now!" The groans and derisive hoots told Carpenter that he had scored so he pressed on. "You see, in the Marines everybody is a rifleman. Everybody, from the regimental commander on down to the cooks and bakers. Our doctrine is based on helping the rifleman with whatever supporting arms are available—including artillery and aviation. So it's important that we all speak the same language. My squadron, VMF-226, has been working on close air support up at Mojave and we think we do it pretty well. That's why my CO sent me here, to help pass along our information. I'll help you with the air liaison parties in a couple of battalions up the coast at Camp Pendleton."

Carpenter turned to the large-scale map behind him. It showed a wide coastal belt surrounding Camp Pendleton with its practice assault beaches and live-fire ranges. "We'll have companies and battalions ashore in these areas," Carpenter said, indicating the zones with a pointer. "The air liaison parties will be on a common radio frequency with your air group and squadron commanders, who will allot flights of four to eight planes to various strongpoints. Our platoon leaders and company commanders are trained to lay out orange panels immediately behind their lines to help you identify the farthest advance inland. We're assuming that everything east of those panels is hostile."

Turning back to the audience, Carpenter held the pointer at port arms. "The best way to attack a target near friendly troops is parallel to our main line of resistance. So if you're supporting a company front running north and south, that's usually the way the controller will ask you to make your run. Remember that in bombing, range errors usually exceed deflection, so we'd rather not attack from the beach because of the danger of short rounds. To some extent, your approach will be dictated by terrain, but remember: the idea is to kill Japs, not Marines."

After the briefing Carpenter found Rogers. "Looks like we'll be flying together again," the Marine said. "Like old times."

Rogers gave a grim smile. "I hope not. Last time we flew together was Guadalcanal!"

TUESDAY, 18 JULY
CAMP PENDLETON, CALIFORNIA

Rogers led his four Hellcats in an orbit midway between San Clemente and Oceanside. Behind him, almost obscured in the haze, was Santa Catalina Island, prewar vacation spot with the fabled resort of Avalon.

From eight thousand feet Rogers scrutinized the landing craft and amphibious tractors—amphtracks, the Marines called them—shuttling between the beach and an attack transport and two landing ship tanks offshore. The AP and LSTs apparently had put most of a rifle regiment on the beach, with Sherman tanks and a few light vehicles. Rogers inferred that the leading companies already were pushing inland across the San Diego–Los Angeles highway, securing "objectives" in their route.

Rogers had seen two genuine amphibious operations, but the exercise now underway seemed more professional, more polished. The Guadalcanal-Tulagi landings in August 1942 had gone well, considering they were not only the first in this war, but America's first wartime amphibious effort since 1898. However, they had been unopposed on the beaches. Newspaper reports indicated that the Saipan landings, and now the three-day-old Guam operation, were meeting resistance from the waterline inland.

Well, the taxpayers are getting their money's worth today, he reflected. *A full dress rehearsal for everybody, complete with battlefield smoke and live ordnance.* Looking inland he could see bomb bursts as some of Burnett's squadron dropped five hundred–pounders on "enemy" positions identified by the infantry.

The air-control radio circuit crackled again, requesting strafing on the right flank of a company "pinned down by automatic weapons." Knowing he was next up, Rogers checked his chart, saw that the coordinates indicated the southern part of the range, and turned his division southeasterly. Moments later Commander Albertson, the airborne strike leader, was on the radio. "Sunsetter Lead from Strike Lead. Your vector is one-three-zero. Contact the liaison party on C channel. Call sign Flintlock King Six."

"Roger, CAG. Sunsetter is crossing the beach now. We should be there in about eight minutes." Circling overland in his Avenger, Albertson acknowledged and turned his attention to other requests for assistance.

The terrain was relatively flat, with a few undulating hills in the target area. Rogers led his team east of the spot and took Diskowski down to identify the friendly unit. In the descent he switched his VHF radio to C channel and made the call. "Flintlock King Six from Sunset Three-One. Do you read?"

The response came back from the commander of King Company. What battalion or regiment he was dealing with, Rogers neither knew nor cared. "Three-One, this is King Six. I read you four by four. Do you have my position yet? Over."

Leveling out at eight hundred feet, Rogers flew parallel to the Marines' line of advance as he approached the grid coordinate. Diskowski came up on the radio, excitement in his voice. "Three-One, I see 'em! Two o'clock, low." *Well, of course they're low,* Rogers mused. He grinned to himself as he caught the orange panels laid out behind the company front.

"King Six, Sunset. I have four Hellcats with .50-caliber. Where do you want it? Over."

"Give me two runs west to east, on the military crest of that hill to my south. I'll correct as necessary. Over."

Rogers bent his Hellcat around in a port turn, adding power and climbing slightly. He radioed Fairfield, instructing the second section to await further orders. Then he rolled out of his turn, checking his gunsight and armament switches. Convinced that his guns were "hot," he waggled his wings and led Diskowski in a 30-degree descent toward the target.

From his vantage point at five thousand feet Rogers could not discern the actual military crest of the hill. So he estimated a point three quarters upslope and put his illuminated pipper on that spot. He began firing at a slant range of forty-five hundred feet and saw his bullets brew up a small cloud of dust and dirt. He corrected his aim upward slightly and triggered three more bursts before bottoming out at a thousand. *Lower than I should go into possible groundfire, but let's look good for the Marines.* He shoved up the power while climbing away and glanced back. Diskowski's bullets spread a pattern farther upslope, covering the area Rogers had missed. *Good job, kid,* he thought.

The infantry officer was keying his mike when Albertson's voice cut off everyone else. "All flights, all flights, this is Strike Leader. Cease fire, cease fire. We have casualties on the ground. Repeat, cease fire. Flight leaders acknowledge immediately and return to base."

Rogers waited his turn to call guns safe and outbound, then rejoined his second section. He was confident his own strafing had harmed no one, but the uncertainty gnawed at him all the way back to North Island.

WEDNESDAY, 19 JULY
OITA BASE

Sakaida was moderately surprised to find himself a new *chutai* leader—a step up in responsibility without commensurate promotion in rank. He suspected the impetus came from beyond the *hikotai* level, as Lieutenant Ono was hardly the sort to reward experience over seniority. But the *kokutai-cho,* Lieutenant Commander Nakamura, seemed genuinely concerned with his air group's development. Sakaida had only spoken with the man twice but perhaps there was a friend at court.

In any case, Sakaida had resolved to take advantage of his newfound latitude. With the seven new pilots seated around him near the *hikotai*'s line office, Sakaida debriefed them on their recent flight. He had a hard time finding anything to praise in their performance, but he also knew that un-relenting criticism could crush enthusiasm and initiative.

It's always the same, he thought. *So many new men and no time to train them adequately.* Beyond that, a growing shortage of aircraft and fuel had rendered realistic combat training almost impossible. Sakaida knew that *Hikokitai* 653 would be fortunate just to reach minimum proficiency in car-rier operations.

Therefore, he tried to impart some basic fighter philosophy to his pi-lots. There was no question of winning a battle against the Americans any-more. Now his objective was to keep some of these boys alive, and he knew where to start.

"I have learned three basic battle lessons," he began. *Keep it simple. Nothing fancy.* "If you follow these rules you might live to enjoy your girl-friends." His students laughed self-consciously but paid attention.

"First, never get too anxious for a shootdown," Sakaida continued. "Stay alive and learn. Then one day you'll have an enemy in your sights.

"Next, always keep the two *nige* in mind. The *nige-michi* is your es-cape route. Always think, 'What would I do if I were attacked right now? What would I do, where would I go?' Then there's the *nige-jike,* your time of escape. Know when *not* to attack.

"Finally, I try to stay nervous. Don't ever relax. Keep your head turn-ing and learn how to use your eyes rather than just looking into space. After all, if you see the enemy first, you are bound to emerge the winner!" *Well, maybe they'll believe it.*

Sakaida was about to ask for questions when he heard someone ap-proaching. He turned and saw the senior petty officer from the midmorn-ing watch. Looking up, Sakaida began to ask if something was wrong. The man's face told him.

"Beg pardon," the petty officer bowed by way of beginning. "Lieu-tenant Ono requests me to ask if you could remove your lecture to another area. The fire lane must be clear."

A derisive snort burst from Sakaida's nostrils. He did not care who heard him. *Ono never* asks *anything,* he thought. *And he damn certainly didn't phrase the "request" so politely.*

Feeling that Ono was watching from the office, Sakaida slowly rose to his feet, thinking, *The swine merely enjoys his authority.* Sakaida nod-ded curtly to the messenger and, without a word, led his men out of the warm sunlight into a shaded area of the building. The symbolism was all too ap-parent.

THURSDAY, 20 JULY
NAS SAN DIEGO

Rogers poured Carpenter a beer and leaned forward on the table. They had a corner to themselves in the officer's club, but everyone else there was discussing the same topic. "Jim, what the hell happened?"

The Marine took a pull at his brew but seemed not to taste it. "You probably know as much as I do by now, Buck. Some TBMs bombed an area that was supposed to be clear of troops, but there was a platoon in the vicinity. Two dead, six wounded."

Rogers bit his lip in concentration. "Yeah, that's what we heard. But we don't know how it happened. You talked to the mud Marines—how'd it go wrong?"

"Well, mixed signals, evidently. The platoon leader's fresh out of Basic School. He had his identification panels out, but he was farther inland than he thought. Actually, he must've been a couple hundred yards ahead of his company front."

Rogers thought of Major Culp's recent quip: *The only thing more dangerous than a monkey with a razor blade is a second lieutenant with a map.* "So what's likely to happen? Are they really going to hang Albertson out to dry?"

Carpenter averted his gaze, knowing what Albertson meant to Rogers and the air group. "I think so, Buck." Jim's voice was low in the room. "The division commander's mad enough to chew nails. Apparently he realizes the platoon leader was partly to blame, and I imagine that kid's prospects are lower than a snake's belly. But I'm hearing that our two-star is demanding the strike leader's ass."

Rogers placed his chin in his hands. "Damn it to hell . . . that means a new CAG." He looked at his friend. "We've already lost one fine leader in this air group—my skipper, Gordon Connell. I don't think the other COs are up to his level or Albertson's."

"Who's likely to take over?"

"Probably Clarey, the bomber skipper, unless somebody senior is brought in."

"What's he like?" Carpenter asked.

Rogers drummed his fingers on the tabletop. "I really don't know him. Bernie says he's competent enough—flies the airplane and hits the target. But my impression is that Clarey's too much of a number counter. I don't think he'd stick his neck out for anybody like Connell or Albertson would."

"I meant to ask how things are going with you guys. Is your new CO doing all right?"

"Yeah, all things considered. I mean, Platco was practically brand-new in the squadron as exec when Gordon got killed. He's getting on-the-job training as skipper, you might say." Rogers's voice drifted off and Carpenter noticed his friend's gaze had gone blank.

"Phil? Something wrong?"

"Oh, yeah. I was just thinking, Jim. I've seen the top and bottom of leadership, from my first skipper in Bombing Three to the composite squadron CO and the captain of the *Alazon Bay*. Well, I just hope that Platco stays healthy; he might grow into the job. But if anything happens to him, Ron Harkin's next in line. That son of a bitch is a glory hunter, and that makes him dangerous. He talks a good game, and he may fool some of the young guys. But he's nowhere as good as he thinks."

"Well, I guess we've all seen the type," Carpenter replied. "But I have to say, I've been damn lucky with COs. Nobody lasted long enough on Midway to make a difference, but Smitty built a hell of a good squadron by the time we got to Guadalcanal."

"You haven't mentioned your skipper in your own squadron."

Carpenter chuckled. "Red White—no kidding. Name's Charlie but he has a reddish tint to his hair. Good guy; no fireball but he knows what he's doing, and his people come first."

Rogers clinked glasses. "Some guys have all the luck."

TUESDAY, 25 JULY

OITA BASE, KYUSHU ISLAND

The inspection had not gone well. Lieutenant Commander Nakamura had been more thorough than inspecting officers were expected to be, and the previous week's tour of Attack *Hikotai* 263 had spurred dire predictions throughout Air Group 653. As the two cars with Nakamura's party departed the flight line, Sakaida bowed with the rest of the fighter unit and awaited the predictable reaction.

The second vehicle had barely turned down the street behind the hangar when Lieutenant Ganji Ono threw a tantrum. Grasping his officer's sword, he turned on Lieutenant (j.g.) Fukuoka, the maintenance officer. Nobody had given the order to disperse, so the spectacle was played out before dozens of witnesses.

"*Baka!* You fool!" Ono raged. "How *dare* you disgrace me . . . this unit . . . before the fighter group leader *and* the air group commander?" He half shoved, half punched Fukuoka in one shoulder, knocking the man off balance. That Ono had approved his squadron's preparations the day before clearly no longer mattered.

Even from fifteen meters, Sakaida could see that Ono's round face was purple with anger. The *hikotaicho* seemed to recover briefly, as if realizing that abusing another officer would get him dismissed. Instead, Ono stalked up to the maintenance chief petty officer who stoically stood his ground. "You! Did I not tell you to have the tool kits in order?"

The noncom played his role, knowing full well that there had been no mention of tool kits—only aircraft. Bowing deeply, he intoned, "Honorable Lieutenant, I beg to inform—"

"Silence, you idiot!" The chief resumed his brace, staring over Ono's shoulder. "You think to embarrass me and get me transferred! Is that it?" he shrieked.

Everyone knew it was an unanswerable question—everyone but Ono, who now was near tears. "Answer me!" When no reply came, he backhanded the noncom with a vicious swipe to the face. The NCO braced himself, knowing that prison was the price of resistance.

The two men stood inches apart, face to face, before Ono spun on one heel and stalked off. A deadly silence lingered behind him as men gradually drifted off. Sakaida found Flight Petty Officer Nakaya leaning against the wing of a Zero, breathing deeply. Now a *shotai* leader, Nakaya was visibly upset. Sakaida placed a hand on his shoulder. "He is terrified, Ichiro. I think he knows he is going to die."

"And he will take all of us to Hades with him." Nakaya's voice was a croak.

A violent lightning flashed in Sakaida's mind. *Unless Ono dies before then.*

WEDNESDAY, 26 JULY
NAS SAN DIEGO

"I relieve you, sir." The onshore breeze ruffled the orders as Lieutenant Commander Patrick Clarey saluted Commander Thomas Albertson, who returned the gesture. Air Group 59 had a new commander.

The change-of-command ceremony had been brief and informal, as Albertson wanted. There was much to be done; the air group was due back at Pasco the next day. But most of the pilots and many of the enlisted men insisted on speaking to their former leader one last time.

Awaiting his turn, Rogers noted that Ron Harkin was not bothering with any such sentiment. In fact, the fighter exec had injected himself into a conversation with Clarey. An uncharitable thought crossed Rogers's mind. *Harkin would probably leave his CO floating in the ocean if it would result in a promotion.*

"Phil." Albertson's voice was warm with recognition. They shook hands for long moments before Rogers could manage, "Goddamn, CAG. I'm sorry as I can be—"

"Don't let it get in the way, Phil. Officially this isn't a demotion, you know. I'm being kicked upstairs to staff. The ops officer was due to rotate out, anyway. Besides, I still might get another air group when this dies down."

"Unsat, Skipper." Rogers could not keep the venom from his voice. "This is a lynching. Everybody knows it."

Albertson gripped Rogers's shoulder so hard that it hurt. "Listen, Phil. You, Mancross, Potter, and Burnett and a few other combat veterans are even more important than before. This is a good air group. Hell, it's a superb air group—I built it!" He smiled grimly. "I want your promise that you'll support Pat as well as you did me. That's an order."

Rogers's head bobbed weakly. "Aye, aye, sir." Then he took one step back and delivered a salute so crisp that it seemed to leave a vacuum in the air.

Tom Albertson returned the respectful gesture slowly and with precision. In a low, hollow voice he pleaded, "Bring 'em home, Phil. Bring 'em all home." His lips quivered slightly before he turned and walked away at a pace that would tolerate no more farewells.

SATURDAY, 29 JULY
OITA BASE, KYUSHU ISLAND

Sitting in his steaming tub, Sakaida relaxed and plotted the assassination of his commanding officer. The peaceful surroundings of the bathhouse allowed him to concentrate on the problem without interruption; he had even told the pretty bath attendant that he did not wish to be disturbed.

This will require careful handling, Sakaida told himself. Next week's schedule was an opportunity too rare to miss. Ono flew so seldom with Sakaida's *chutai* that another chance might not arise before the air group began carrier qualifications. True, there was the hope that the lieutenant would conveniently kill himself in a deck-landing attempt, but Sakaida had learned never to rely upon Providence.

Yes, it was a ticklish business, ridding oneself of a dangerously incompetent officer. Even if you slid behind him and blew him out of the sky, there might be squeamish witnesses. So this way was better; it afforded deniability.

Like any hunter, Sakaida had studied his quarry and felt that he knew the best way to slay the beast. Ono's temper obviously was based on feelings of inadequacy as an aviator, and inferiority mixed with vanity could be a lethal concoction. "They outrank me but they cannot outfly me," Sakaida often said of most officers. It was a common sentiment in the Imperial Navy, where the finest fliers usually were noncommissioned pilots. In the Solomons and at Rabaul, the noncoms tended to look out for the enlightened leaders and sometimes just weren't there when the other kind needed help.

Sakaida had decided to bait his prey with an irresistible lure. He would allow Ono to gain the advantage in a mock dogfight, then spring the trap. It was possible that Ono could be driven to destruction from behind, but that was less likely to succeed than leading him to attempt something stupid. Besides, the elegance of the plan appealed to Sakaida's sense of poetic justice—the sheer artistry of execution. Ganji Ono would die in such a manner that nobody could accuse Hiroyoshi Sakaida of malfeasance.

Before he called for Michiko to join him in the bath, Sakaida had his plan locked up tight.

August 1944

MONDAY, 1 AUGUST
NAS PASCO

Pat Clarey stubbed out his cigarette and exhaled the last smoke from his Chesterfield. The small CAG operations office was a haze of blue-gray smoke during the organizational meeting and Rogers earnestly wished for some fresh air. He estimated that two thirds of the men he knew were smokers, and most of them used at least a pack a day.

"In case you're wondering," Clarey said in a flat voice, "it's official. Orders have been cut formalizing our current structure. Leo fleets up to bomber skipper and Bernie's the new exec for now." Lieutenant Commander Leo Hunziker, the new CO of Bombing 59, exchanged tight-lipped grins with Burnett. Neither wanted to appear overly grateful for his promotion, considering how they had come about.

"The rest of this month we'll follow the established syllabus," Clarey continued. "That means FCLP leading up to carrier qualifications."

Sitting with Platco and Harkin, Rogers was pleased at the news. He had been agitating for early field carrier landing practice, knowing that most of the air group's pilots were rusty in that crucial area.

Clarey consulted a clipboard with the air group schedule. "We're slated to go back to San Diego the twenty-seventh for about four days and bounce on an escort carrier. I hope we'll get a second session before we head to Hawaii.

"The rest of the time we'll devote to gunnery, including some detachments for the torpeckers to the Salton Sea. We'll also get up to speed on rocket firing." He turned toward Lieutenant Frank Overstreet, the air group ordnance officer. "More work for you, Frank. We didn't get as much time for that in San Diego as we wanted. Can we catch up?"

Overstreet sipped his coffee and caught a wink from Rogers. "Uh, yes, sir. We're getting three-fives next week. Besides, Phil here has been badgering me about it lately. But then I'd expect Buck Rogers to know all about rockets!" He chuckled at his own joke.

Barry Potter, the Torpedo 59 skipper, spoke up. "Pat, I'd like to clarify something. Do you want my Turkeys to shoot rockets? I'd rather concentrate on bombing and torpedoes."

Clarey seemed taken aback. New to air group command, he was unfamiliar with making doctrinal decisions. "Well, I don't know about that. I mean, why wouldn't you want to fire rockets?" He reached for another Chesterfield.

"While we were at North Island I talked to some ComFair people," Potter began. He thought better of mentioning Tom Albertson's passion for current fleet information. "Some of the squadrons at Saipan and Guam reported they took more losses in rocket attacks than the results justified. Against fixed defenses we're a big, slow target."

"I'll have to think about that," Clarey said while lighting up. "We could get a carrier skipper who wants maximum ordnance on target. We'd have to follow orders."

"Well, yes, if he ordered us to use aerial rockets. But I hope he would understand that F6Fs and '2Cs can bomb and fire rockets. Avengers can put torpedoes in the water; nobody else can."

"I'll get back to you, Barry." Carey sucked nervously on his cigarette, then looked at the fighter pilots. "One more thing. Ralph, I noticed some rising suns painted on a couple of your F6Fs."

Platco was taken by surprise. "Well, yeah. The plane captains put 'em on Mancross's and Rogers's airplanes. Why?"

"I'd like them taken off. It makes the bombers and torpedo planes look bad."

Before Platco could respond, Rogers jumped in. "Excuse me, sir. I don't care one way or another about meatballs on my airplane. In fact, my gunner in Bombing Three actually got both those Japs. But our mechanics are proud of those kills, and I think they're useful for morale." Seeing Clarey waver, he pressed the attack. "Besides, our line chief showed me a PacFleet authorization, dated last month."

Clarey thought for a moment. "Well, maybe you can repaint 'em when we get to a forward area."

Looking sideways at Rogers, Platco shrugged helplessly. "Yes, sir."

Rogers glanced at Burnett, who vainly tried to remain expressionless. The short exchange had confirmed Bernie's and Rogers's suspicion: *Clarey is never going to rock the boat.*

WEDNESDAY, 3 AUGUST
OVER THE INLAND SEA

Sakaida saw the canopy glint and knew what it meant. But he suppressed his professional instincts to turn into the threat and continued straight ahead at twenty-five hundred meters. He wondered when any of his wingmen would notice the sign of other aircraft above and behind them. *This will test their vigilance,* he told himself.

Flying with his head turned almost 180 degrees, Sakaida watched the glint begin a descent, then evolve into a dark dot as it approached. Close behind, he picked out the other three dots accompanying it, but he already had decided to ignore them. *Never mind,* he thought. *Ono is all that matters.*

By the time the lead attacker had sprouted visible wings, Sakaida was getting anxious. He risked a glance at his three *chutai* pilots, who were all blissfully flying straight and level. His wingman belatedly looked over, and waved. *Young idiot!* Sakaida raged. *There's a hostile fighter nearing gunnery range on you!* Sakaida swiveled his head and picked up the assailants again.

The leader—certainly Ono—was less than four hundred meters out. Sakaida's combative juices stirred inside him; he badly wanted to half-snap inverted and pull into a split-S. But he felt that Lieutenant Ono could not follow such a violent maneuver. Instead, with an effort of willpower, Sakaida rolled into a medium-banked turn to port.

Ganji Ono almost dropped the gift in his hands. He had not allowed for the momentum of his long dive and nearly overshot his intended victim. When Sakaida's Zero turned, the closure rate increased. Ono pondered what to do for one moment, then honked the stick back. He felt the onset of three Gs and zoom-climbed above Sakaida, sliding high and outside his turn.

Sakaida's wingmen scattered like a covey of quail. Glancing back, Sakaida noticed that they had lost any hope of mutual support. He made a mental note to berate them for sloppy flying, then turned his full attention to Ono.

Holding a constant-radius turn, Sakaida dropped his nose slightly. He pivoted right in his seat, reacquired Ono's fighter with the two fuselage stripes, and watched its black nose drop toward him again. *Good. Now follow me, Honorable Lieutenant.*

Sakaida rolled wings-level and continued his dive. Twice he turned 30 degrees either side of his heading in a semblance of evasion that Ono could follow. The relative angle off Sakaida's tail had narrowed as the *hikotai* commander bored in. Descending through one thousand meters altitude, Ono drove within two hundred meters of his adversary.

Sakaida talked himself through the upcoming maneuver. He had flown it repeatedly in his mind. *Not yet, just a bit longer.* He ignored his altimeter, estimating he was within two hundred meters of the water. Then he snapped the stick over to the right, roughly coordinating with rudder. Again his conditioned reflexes called for him to bury his nose but it was too soon.

Ono skidded past Sakaida's rudder, unable to follow the abrupt turn. Fishtailing badly, he overcorrected his reversal and visibly lost ground. But he retained the advantage, still behind Sakaida, who foolishly had eased off his rate of turn. Ono began to savor victory. He would drive the arrogant petty officer down to the wavetops until the oaf conceded defeat!

When Sakaida saw the whitecaps blowing from atop the gray crests, he knew he was where he wanted to be. With Ono 20 degrees behind him to port, he two-blocked the throttle, wrapped his Zero into a 70-degree bank, and nudged bottom rudder. When he was three wingspans off the waves, he adjusted with top rudder and neutralized his controls.

Ono had not caught the imperceptible skid toward the water. All he saw was Sakaida, being driven lower, holding a predictable flight path. He matched the degree of bank and retarded power slightly to maintain position, less than a hundred meters back. In a few more seconds his crosshairs would crawl up Sakaida's back. Triumph tickled the tip of his tongue. The taste was delicious.

Sakaida sensed as much as saw where Ono must be. They were down around eighty meters, airspeed bleeding off. Sakaida ventured a look behind, saw the near uptipped wings, the prop spinner not quite aligned with his rudder—and smiled.

Rolling vertical, Sakaida waited a handful of seconds, sucking Ono in deeper. Then he began a steady pull on the stick, maintaining a flipper turn. He felt his Zero begin to shudder, the stick vibrating in his hand. The excellent stall characteristics gave a good pilot plenty of warning, and Sakaida knew just how far he could let an incipient stall progress.

Ganji Ono did not. Though he felt the onset of buffet, he clung grimly to Sakaida's tail. *If he can do it, so can I!* But Sakaida had begun the turn at full power, affording him a few knots advantage over Ono, who had throttled back to avoid an embarrassing overshoot.

The irrevocable laws of aerodynamics permitted no amendments. When an airfoil ran out of continuous airflow over its curved surface, the wing no longer could sustain lift.

Ono felt the buffet and finally recognized the impending stall. With his stomach in his throat, he applied the school solution: level the wings, stuff the nose down and cram on full throttle. Close to the surface, out of airspeed, he was torque-rolled onto his back by the sudden power application. Impacting inverted, his canopy was crushed inward upon him and he died before the spray of his crash had begun to subside.

THURSDAY, 4 AUGUST
OITA BASE, KYUSHU ISLAND

Lieutenant Commander Nakamura allowed Sakaida to stand at attention throughout the investigation. As an air group commander, Nakamura could hardly be expected to ignore the death of one of his senior leaders, and there were procedures to be observed. Leaning forward over his austere desk, Nakamura reviewed the basic facts of the case. First: Flight Chief Petty Officer Sakaida's lead *shotai* had been engaged in battle practice against Lieutenant Ono's *shotai*. It was a scheduled event and no administrative irregularities had been discovered.

Second: The material condition of all aircraft was known to be satisfactory. No discrepancies were noted in the records of Ono's Zero Model 52.

Third: Sakaida was the only witness to the lieutenant's lamentable demise. Ordinarily that would be cause for suspicion, but as Sakaida had testified—and investigation had confirmed—the experience level of all other pilots was abysmally low. Consequently, the participants had been far too preoccupied to notice anything unusual after Ono's initial "surprise" pass at Sakaida's formation.

Fourth: Lieutenant Ono apparently had lost control of his aircraft while maneuvering at dangerously low altitude. That Sakaida had similarly been engaged in prohibited flight but returned safely could only be attributed to his greater experience. The report would in fact stress "experience" rather than "ability." It went without saying that commissioned officers in the Imperial Japanese Navy were fully competent in all their military duties.

Nakamura re-read the summary and signed it. While the accident investigator countersigned the report prepared by the committee secretary, Nakamura tapped his fingers on the desk, staring at Sakaida.

Fifth, the air group commander silently tallied, *Lieutenant Ganji Ono was an insufferable prig, a marginal aviator, and a counterproductive leader.* His sole positive attribute was his availability, and that led to his undoing.

"Sakaida, this committee finds you innocent of any offense in the unfortunate death of Lieutenant Ono." Nakamura chose his words for emphasis, as no charges had been leveled against Sakaida. But Nakamura had his suspicions. "You are hereby returned to your flying duties with responsibility for training your *chutai.* Dismissed."

Sakaida bowed from the waist, came to attention and did an about-face. As he marched toward the door he was brought up short by Nakamura's bark. "Sakaida!"

The noncom braced to attention. "I am going to watch you closely from now on."

"Hai!" With another bow, Sakaida eased himself out of the commander's presence, feeling a vast relief that he hoped did not show.

TUESDAY, 9 AUGUST

NAS PASCO

Lieutenant Frank Overstreet stood before a small crowd drawn from all three squadrons. As Air Group 59's ordnance expert, he would introduce the aircraft rocket to the officers and noncoms who would have to make the new weapon work in combat.

Standing upright beside him in the hangar was an opened five-foot-long shipping box. "This is our baby," Overstreet began, "a three-and-a-half-inch aerial rocket. I'm going to tell you everything I know about this thing, but frankly it isn't much, though I attended a crash course at Inyokern about this time last year. These babies weigh about fifty-five pounds fully assembled and reach 1,180 feet per second. They're proven in combat so we know they work."

He spent the next several minutes describing the components and how they fit together. The rocket motor, the largest part of the weapon, was a seamless steel tube containing the propellant. Four tailfins provided stability in flight, and two lug bands were topped with slots that slid onto the rails beneath the wing of an aircraft.

Overstreet then held up a streamlined shape resembling an oversized bullet. "This is the warhead," he explained. "It's three and a half inches in diameter and comes in several varieties. It can contain high explosive or smoke, and there's a solid version for use against submarines. That one will penetrate three inches of mild steel at one thousand yards."

The VB-59 ordnance chief raised a hand. "Sir, what about five-inch aircraft rockets?"

"Well, they're almost identical to this one except they mount a five-inch shell instead of the three-point-five warhead. Naturally, the bigger ones weigh more—up to eighty-five pounds—and they're a lot slower. There's also a five-inch high-velocity round, or HVAR. If you hit something with that, you get the same result as with a 5.38-caliber round. In other words, a plane firing six of these has the wallop of a destroyer's broadside." An appreciative murmur ran through the audience.

Overstreet pointed to a full-scale drawing showing the innards of an aerial rocket. "I'll try to explain a bit about what makes an AR work. Not that it's necessary, you understand, but you'll impress the hell out of any pilot who asks." The ordies laughed self-consciously in the presence of so many aviators. "The rocket propellant is a double-base powder called ballistite. It's similar to old-fashioned cordite but it burns a lot faster. I met some backroom boys from Cal Tech who helped develop ballistite; it's made to burn progressively rather than explode so you get rapid, even ignition."

The ordnance officer again pointed to his drawing. "When the firing circuit is closed, an electrical charge runs through the solenoid in the forward launch rail under the wing. The rocket's arming wires are retained there, allowing the small propeller to turn and arm the nose fuse. The rear launch rail has an outlet that you plug the electrical connector into. Then—bang."

Phil Rogers did not have to attend the lecture, but as VF-59's former gunnery officer he retained an interest. He raised his hand. "Frank, that's all very interesting and I'm sure I won't remember one bit of it by the time I'm likely to get captured." Ignoring the chuckles around him, he continued, "How accurate are they?"

"Glad you asked," Overstreet replied. "Just stick with me, okay? I already mentioned the 1,200-foot-per-second velocity of the three-point-five AR. But you have to add the aircraft's speed to that figure as well. Let's say a typical airspeed would be, oh, 250 knots. Roughly 150 foot-seconds, so the rocket's velocity is almost 1,350 feet per second, but that falls off pretty fast. Once the rocket motor burns out, it's just drag on the projectile. I have the ballistic tables and I'll show 'em to you later on.

"But to answer Lieutenant Rogers's question, tests show that the mean dispersion of these rockets at a slant range of a thousand yards runs between three and five mils—under ideal conditions." Overstreet shrugged eloquently. "I'd expect six to eight mils."

Mancross, who knew from experience that ideal conditions never exist in combat, did the simple arithmetic. "Hell, that's an eighteen to twenty-four-foot circle. That's fine for a ship or a building. What about other targets?"

"Good point," Overstreet replied. "The Bureau of Ordnance has found that the three-point-five warhead is no good on concrete or steel structures like bridges. But most warships are vulnerable, and so are relatively small targets like tanks that are hard to hit with bombs. It'll take practice to get proficient on pinpoint targets like that, but my gang will work with any of you squadron guys to get down a gunsight mil lead for realistic ranges."

Seeing no more hands raised, he gestured to the audience. "Come on up and take a look, gentlemen. Meet the future of aviation ordnance."

THURSDAY, 11 AUGUST
PASCO GUNNERY RANGE

"Here comes Buck Rogers in his 'rocket ship!' Watch out, Kane!" With that rare display of exuberance, Rogers replaced his microphone in its bracket and slanted Fox Nine into a 30-degree dive from five thousand feet. He knew the range officer would be ready to mark the impact of each 3.5-inch aerial rocket on a plotting board for pilot debriefing.

Rogers's armament switches were set: master arm on, bomb-rocket transfer switch selected for "Rocket." Diskowski allowed sufficient interval, then followed while Fairfield and Sossaman spaced themselves accordingly.

Settling into his approach, Rogers took time to crank in a little trim. He looked at the gunsight, checked that the ball was centered, then finessed the controls to place his pipper on the bull's-eye target scratched into the desert.

The only way to determine the range was to gauge how a given target appeared in the sight. Rogers knew that the bull was fifty feet across, which from three thousand feet measured nearly seventeen mils in the sight. But the Mark VIII gunsight had no such display—the minimum indication was fifty mil between the pipper and the inner ring. So he went by "seaman's eye" and, when the bull filled about one third of the fifty-mil circle, he pressed the button atop his stick.

His first impression was surprise. There was no recoil, no physical sensation except a slight vibration as the rocket left the port outboard rail. Three-point-two seconds later a sandy eruption burst well below the bull's-eye at the seven o'clock position. Rogers assumed that he had been slightly out of range. Keeping the same sight picture, he fired again. This time the hit came on the periphery of the bull at two o'clock.

Rogers added throttle and eased back on the stick. He reached for the microphone, called "Fox Nine is off," and safetied the master arm switch. Then he began a climbing port turn to rejoin the pattern as Diskowski's tenor voice came through: "Fox Ten in hot."

Two smoky tendrils streamed from beneath Diskowski's wings as Rogers reversed his turn. Each pilot would make three runs, firing six rockets apiece, but Rogers's reaction surprised him. He was reminded of his primary flight training days, when after a poor landing he wished he could reposition immediately at the threshold instead of going around the traffic pattern. *This is going to be fun,* he told himself. *After Connell and Albertson, we've earned it.*

Banking into another circuit, Rogers chuckled aloud. He could not wait to write Ray about the adventures of Buck Rogers in the twentieth century.

MONDAY, 15 AUGUST
OITA BASE, KYUSHU ISLAND

Sakaida examined the face of his new commanding officer and felt a sense of tentative relief. There was as yet no trace of The Look, though experience had shown that the ominous sign could emerge anytime. But during this initial meeting, Sakaida sensed that Lieutenant (j. g.) Shozo Uchida was a definite improvement over the late Lieutenant Ono—not that it was difficult to improve upon the previous squadron commander. True, Uchida showed the attitude toward noncommissioned personnel that was typical of graduates of the Eta Jima Naval Academy, but that was to be expected. His air of superiority was leavened with something approaching concern about the state of his pilots' training, and Sakaida considered that more than an even trade.

"There have been far too many accidents," Uchida was saying, "not only in our unit, but throughout the air group." Uchida paced before his desk while his *chutai* commanders stood at ease. Sakaida wasn't sure, but he thought the CO shot him a querying glance. Sakaida fidgeted uneasily. *What did Nakamura say about me?*

Uchida continued. "There is official concern in this matter of flying safety, and we are directed to limit battle practice in order to preserve aircraft. Most of our enlisted pilots come from the Flight Reserve Trainee Program, Classes 34 to 36, with a few Aviation Reserve Students. That means some of them only completed pilot training last month." He paused, hands behind his back, and scanned the leaders, of whom only Sakaida and Nakaya had combat experience at sea. "We will begin practicing carrier procedures this week. But until our men have more experience, we will *not* risk pilots foolishly in battle practice." This time Uchida looked directly at Sakaida. Then, glancing away, he intoned, "Carrier landings are dangerous enough."

TUESDAY, 29 AUGUST
NAVAL AUXILIARY AIR STATION REAM FIELD, SAN DIEGO

The air group brain trust sat in the crowded lobby of the bachelor officers' quarters, some sipping coffee, some smoking. Pat Clarey had a directive in hand and rattled the papers for attention. "Gentlemen, the reason I've called this meeting is this directive from ComAirPac. It's a hell of a time for this, in the middle of a carrier-qualification period, but it carries top priority. All Essex-class air groups are being reshuffled to provide for greater fighter protection. That means we have to cut back on the numbers of bombers."

He looked at Platco. "Ralph, effective immediately, your allocation is increased from thirty-six to fifty-four aircraft. In order to fill those eighteen extra seats you'll receive thirty pilots from VB-59. You'll have to get them checked out in F6Fs and fighter tactics, *fast.*"

Platco nodded slowly, glancing at Leo Hunziker, the bomber skipper, who asked, "Pat, what happens to us—and the TBMs? With that many fighters, something's got to give."

"My guess is that you'll keep twenty-four aircraft," the CAG responded, "and the Turkeys should remain at about twenty." He hastened to add, "It should be all right. The fighters can still bomb and there'll be enough TBMs to do a good job with torpedoes."

Hunziker slumped forward in his chair, knees on elbows, chin in hands. Rogers interpreted the body English. *Leo doesn't like it one damn bit—can't say I blame him.* "How do you want me to split up the squadron?" he asked.

Clarey fidgeted before answering. "Well, I think I should leave that up to you, Leo. You know your people. Consult with me when you draw up the list and I'll approve it."

Rogers glanced at Burnett and caught Bernie's disgusted grimace. *Hell, Clarey was the bomber skipper until a month ago,* Rogers realized. *He should know the setup as well as Leo. Guess he still doesn't want to make a hard decision.*

Hunziker picked up his cigarette from the ashtray, took a long pull, and squashed it. "Okay, you got it." The tone of his voice said, "Live with this, old buddy." Turning to Burnett, he asked, "Bernie, you still want to fly fighters?" Everyone knew he meant, "Do you still want to fly with Phil?"

Burnett sat upright, eyes wide. "Yes, sir! But if you need—"

The bomber CO interrupted. "No, we'll be all right. Vinnie has nearly as much experience as you do. So take your division and I'll assign five others plus some spares. I want to keep our teams together as much as possible." He managed a sad grin. "While you're learning to be fighter pilots maybe you can teach Ralph's bunch of Dilberts how to put a bomb on target."

Rogers was aware that Harkin was whispering to Platco, who nodded and turned to the CAG. "Pat, I am reminded that technically Mr. Burnett is senior to my exec. Ah, it might be . . . awkward, if you know what I mean. Could we suggest—"

"Hey, no problem, Ron!" Burnett leaned toward Harkin, beaming widely. "I don't want to be CNO. You stay as exec. Mr. Platco, just fit me in anywhere and my guys will haul the mail for you."

Clarey jumped at the offer. "That sounds reasonable. Is it okay with you, Ralph? Ron?"

Platco replied, "Sure, fine," and sipped some coffee. Harkin slid lower in his seat, folded his arms, and tried to avoid Burnett's disgustingly cheerful gaze. Rogers enjoyed watching as Lieutenant Ronald Harkin's face turned a beautiful beet red.

September 1944

The squadron spaces were almost deserted when Rogers walked in. He nodded to the duty officer and plopped into a chair near the window overlooking the flight line. His division was off for the afternoon, having completed its training syllabus early. *Those extracurricular flight hours really paid off,* he told himself. He wondered if Lieutenant Commander Platco had tumbled to the fuel subterfuge.

In one corner Fairfield and Sossaman swapped gossip with some other pilots. The topic of conversation alternated between girls and flying—*de rigueur* for aviators—and Rogers eavesdropped for a moment. Having been a "nugget" aviator himself three years ago, Phil appreciated their dilemma. *They know a lot more about aviation than about women,* he realized. *Like me.*

Fairfield spotted his team leader and hollered across the room. "Hey, Lieutenant. Maybe you can settle an argument."

Rogers looked over the top of a newspaper and grunted a noncommittal reply. Undeterred, Fairfield continued. "Fielding here says there's no way to get along with dames. But I say there's got to be a way. What do you think?"

Crumpling his paper, Rogers thought for a moment. His section leader was an accomplished young man. At twenty-four he owned an engineering degree and he'd been a varsity athlete at Northwestern. Rogers suspected that Fairfield had more knowledge of females than he allowed. "Well, I don't think it's so hard," Rogers began. "You just give 'em whatever they want."

Ensign Morgan Fielding, one of Don Mancross's pilots, replied. "Excuse me, sir. But what do women want?"

Rogers's lips flirted with a tight little smile. "Nobody knows." He disappeared behind his paper, humming a tune. He briefly thought of writing Audrey, then decided against it. *No point in it—better to concentrate on flying.* Phil Rogers knew the danger of mixing earthly emotion with airborne reality. He felt it could be a lethal brew.

He scanned the headlines. On the home front, American industry had resumed production of consumer goods, which had become more available in the past two months. Meanwhile, racetrack attendance continued to set records, while the juvenile delinquent rate was up 60 percent from 1941, and first-class machinists in shipyards now earned $2.75 per hour. Internationally, U.S. Marines had landed in the Palau Islands, only five hundred miles east of the Philippines. The European war was going well: American troops now were across the border into Belgium and had captured Lyon in the south. After heavy fighting, the British finally had seized Brussels and Antwerp.

A small cloud of concern crossed Phil's mind. *I haven't heard from Ray in a while.* Then the cloud was gone, scudding before the logical winds of reason. *He never does write very often.* Rogers turned to the comics.

Dick Tracy was staking out Gravel Gertie's shack while the real Buck Rogers searched for the Vault of Llore, and the steamy Miss Fury was taking a bath. Studying her nude back, Rogers failed to notice the officer standing beside him. "Phil."

Rogers looked up at the sound of a friend's voice. "Hi, Bernie. I didn't see you."

Burnett knelt at the side of the chair. A yellow telegram form dangled from one hand. Burnett's usual cheerfulness was absent and Rogers's mind went to general quarters. He heard himself ask, "What is it?"

Unspeaking, Burnett touched his friend's arm. In that moment Rogers catalogued the spectrum of possibilities. *Another crash in the squadron— maybe it's Harkin this time. Somebody from my Pensacola class. Mom or Dad.* Then he knew. "It's Ray."

Burnett nodded. He held up the telegram from West Palm Beach. Rogers grasped it and scanned the printed lines, taking in the few details. More than a week ago—parents notified day before yesterday. Takeoff accident in England. Letter following.

"Thanks, Bernie." With that, Rogers dropped the newspaper and slowly rose from the chair. Burnett watched as he walked from the room with the pained gait of a man grown old.

WEDNESDAY, 20 SEPTEMBER
OITA BASE, KYUSHU ISLAND

Lieutenant (j.g.) Shozo Uchida surveyed the warriors who would wield their new weapon; what he saw gave him little cause for optimism. *The names change constantly,* he thought, *but the faces only get younger.* He shrugged off the thought and proceeded.

"Most of you know that our *hikotai* will receive the latest Type Zero fighter," he began. "This is the Model 52B, which has not yet been issued fleetwide." He paced before the ordered ranks assembled beside the new fighter and gauged their reaction. The youngsters seemed pleased at the news, but most of the veterans, like Sakaida, realized there was only so much "stretch" in any airframe. Though faster than the Model 52A, his race-horse was being laden down like a draft animal.

"With this fighter you can dive at speeds of four hundred knots," Uchida continued. "The factory has strengthened the airframe in light of combat experience, and we will review our battle doctrine accordingly. You *shotai* and *chutai* leaders: Be sure that your men understand the advantages of increased diving speed." He decided not to dwell on the subject—at least not before the entire *hikotai*. Diving usually was an evasive maneuver against American fighters, and it had not worked terribly well.

"There are other improvements, too. As in the Model 52A, the wing cannons are new Mark Fours in place of the older Mark 99s. We now carry 125 rounds of twenty-millimeter ammunition per gun—belt-fed instead of the hundred-round drum. Additionally, one of the nose-mounted seven-point-seven machine guns has been replaced with a Type Three thirteen-millimeter for heavier armament."

Uchida pointed to the fuselage area behind the engine. "For the first time we have an automatic CO_2 fire-extinguisher system around the fuel tank, and there is increased pilot protection as well. The windscreen has a fifty-millimeter panel that is considered bullet-resistant.

"We will have only limited time for absorbing these fighters," Uchida cautioned. "Most of Air Group 653 is being transferred to the Second Air Fleet. But our most experienced carrier pilots will likely go to Admiral Ozawa's four active ships."

As Uchida detailed the administrative aspects of familiarization in the

Model 52B, Sakaida stood in the second row and pondered the future. He looked around him, musing who would go and who would stay. It was an important consideration for the most basic of reasons. He realized that wherever the pilots were sent, *Those who go are bound to die.*

October 1944

TUESDAY, 3 OCTOBER
BREMERTON, WASHINGTON

"You beauty." Burnett stood dockside with Rogers and several other VF-59 pilots. Towering above them was the dazzle-painted island of USS *Reprisal,* the U.S. Navy's newest fleet carrier. "But not like the old Sara, is she, Buck?"

"No. These Essex-class ships are a little smaller and displace about six thousand tons less weight. But apparently they're built with combat experience in mind."

Burnett was pleased with the response—perhaps the longest sentence Phil Rogers had uttered since learning of his brother's death. *Maybe he's snapping out of it,* Burnett thought.

Carl Sacco, Burnett's section leader, offered a question. "Do you think these ships could survive what happened to the old *Lexington* or *Yorktown?*" He knew that Burnett and Rogers had been aboard *Yorktown* at Midway.

"I don't know much about the Lex," Burnett replied, "but Old Yorky took one hell of a beating—bombs and torpedoes. Even then, they almost saved her."

Rogers turned toward the others. "The point is, if we do our job right, this ship won't have to take bombs *or* aerial torpedoes. I'm going to see Commander Platco about a series of lectures with the ship's CIC officers so we know who we're working with." He swiveled his head, taking in the fighter pilots around him. "We can fly well and we can shoot straight. If the radar boys put us onto the Japs in time, we'll play merry hell with them."

Kenny Diskowski shuffled his feet and glanced around him. Like the others, VF-59's junior pilot had noticed an edge to Rogers that no one had seen before. Everybody knew what it was about and tacitly agreed to let it alone—for now. But Diskowski had a plan of his own. "Fellows, when we stop in Alameda I'm going to call my mom. She throws terrific parties. Maybe you'd like to attend."

There were noncommittal grunts from the fliers. Burnett rolled his eyes at the thought of a matronly gathering hosted by grand dames of San Francisco society. Sensing the reluctance, Diskowski added a salient fact. "Mother used to work for a modeling agency, and I think she can get the Top of the Mark for an air group sendoff. Would that be okay?"

Rogers felt the ice melting and nudged the boy. "You'll go far, Mr. Diskowski."

SATURDAY, 7 OCTOBER
MARK HOPKINS HOTEL, SAN FRANCISCO

Rogers, Burnett, Mancross, and a few others were standing in a corner discussing the crosstown World Series in St. Louis, when conversation in the room abruptly died. Instinctively, Rogers turned to investigate as Burnett broke the silence with "I saw her first."

Ken Diskowski stood in the doorway with the most beautiful woman Phil Rogers had ever seen or imagined. She was taller than her escort, elegantly dressed in a dark double-breasted suit with stylish hat and gloves. Her knee-length skirt revealed legs that Betty Grable would have envied. And her face . . . *My god!* Rogers thought. Reviewing his mental catalog for a comparison, the first name that clicked on the screen was Vivien Leigh.

Diskowski scanned left and right, oblivious to the attention focused on him. Then, spotting Rogers, he said something to the woman and led her toward Phil's group.

"Fellows," Diskowski began, "I'd like to present my mother."

Eddie Fairfield's glass slipped from his hand and fell to the carpet with a dull thud. Nobody noticed as Ken continued, "Mother, this is my division leader, Lieutenant Rogers."

Mrs. Diskowski graciously extended her hand, a smile of recognition on her beautiful red lips. "Well, Lieutenant. It's a genuine pleasure to meet you at last."

Rogers's second reaction was gratitude that she had not said anything as common as "I've heard so much about you." His first reaction—astonishment—had not worn off. He swallowed and managed, "Mrs. Diskowski, you are most welcome. May we offer you something to drink?"

"Please call me Eleanor," she purred. "And thank you, no. Ken and I are going to dinner shortly. But after I missed your trip down here last month I resolved I'd make it this time, regardless. I'm just sorry Ken's father couldn't attend."

Rogers remembered a comment Kenny had made months before—something about a family shipping business. Mr. Diskowski evidently was now with the Maritime Commission.

At that moment Ralph Platco edged through the crowd. His expression clearly said, *What gives, kid?* Diskowski hastened to make the introductions. "Sir, may I introduce my mother, Eleanor Diskowski. Mother, this is our skipper, Lieutenant Commander Platco."

Platco's face passed through a progression of visible emotions: uncertainty to confusion to astonishment. But his Annapolis background retrieved the situation. "Why, Mrs. Diskowski, I was confused for a moment. I thought our junior pilot had brought along a film star!" He laughed nervously.

Mrs. Diskowski put the CO at ease as they discovered a mutual acquaintance, a VB-11 lieutenant from San Francisco. Eleanor was heard to exclaim, "Oh my, yes. Everybody knows Big Ed."

While additional pleasantries were exchanged, an intense commiseration proceeded in the corner. "My god, how old do you suppose she is?" asked Burnett.

"I don't know," Rogers replied, "but Ken's twenty. She must be forty anyway."

Mancross found his voice. "I'd have said thirty, tops."

Fairfield gave a low whistle. "Who'd have guessed? I mean, Kenny's a good-looking kid. But—holy smokes!"

"You said it," commented Sossaman.

"And how!" Burnett added.

On the way out, Eleanor Diskowski slipped away from her son and diverted to Rogers, who met her halfway. Holding his hand in both of hers, she leveled a gaze at him. "Lieutenant, I'm glad of this opportunity before I leave." She glanced across the room at Kenny animatedly talking to his friends. "I wouldn't want Ken to think his mother was being . . . maternal," she began with an ironic smile. "But I do want to say one thing."

Rogers knew what was coming. He braced himself.

"Please take care of my boy, Philip. If that's unfair of me, so be it. He's our only child. The one consolation we have is his trust in you. He doesn't want to fly with anyone else."

"Mrs. . . . Ah, that means a lot to me. It's exactly what I said about my first commanding officer." Rogers fought for the words but his mind resisted. *She's asking for a guarantee that her boy will live, and there aren't any guarantees.* Finally he stammered, "Eleanor, Ken's a fine young aviator. We'll look out for each other. I can promise you that."

Still holding Rogers's hand, Eleanor Diskowski leaned forward and kissed Rogers on the mouth. "God bless you, Philip."

As the beautiful mother walked away with her only son, Burnett appeared at Rogers's side. "Wow. That's some—"

"C'mon," Rogers interrupted. Hardly trusting his voice, he said, "I need a drink."

WEDNESDAY, 11 OCTOBER
OITA BASE, KYUSHU ISLAND

Sakaida stood on the flight line with Nakaya and a few other pilots of his *chutai,* gloomily contemplating the sudden dearth of fighters for them to fly. In the past forty-eight hours the main strength of Air Group 653 had rushed south to Formosa, where strong American fleet units had appeared. Everybody was talking about it, anticipating another big success after the Marianas "victory."

Keeping his own counsel, Sakaida decided to fight his impulse to correct the official line. Looking at Nakaya, he wondered if the *shotai* leader felt similarly. By almost any standard Nakaya was still a rookie, but the three-dimensional Darwinism of aerial combat had ceded him the rare title of survivor. *It is best not to shake his confidence,* Sakaida decided. But the other pilots remaining at Oita had not even Nakaya's skewed perception of reality.

"Why are we left behind with so few airplanes to fly?" Superior Seaman Kurusu whined. "We are as well prepared as those who have gone to the battle front."

Sakaida choked down his ire and, once more, tried to put the prettiest face on an ugly picture. "Because we are the best trained in carrier operations," he replied evenly. "Most of the *hikotais* sent to Formosa could be spared because they lack our recent experience in deck landings and takeoffs." Sakaida stood erect, hands on his hips, hoping that he imparted confidence. "Besides, superior seaman, who are you to question the Naval General Staff?"

Kurusu studied the toes of his flying boots. Only one rung up the ladder from aircrews, he realized he had overstepped his bounds. Many noncoms in the Imperial Navy were fond of resorting to their fists at such brash infractions, and others were harsher still. Jiro Kurusu was still wet behind the ears but not so damp that he failed to recognize Sakaida's mild rebuke. He mumbled an apology and did not even glance up when a Zero lifted off the runway for an engine test.

Silently, Sakaida appreciated the boy's spirit. *They are all so eager for battle. The young fools.* But he knew beyond doubt that the 154 aircraft of Carrier Divisions 3 and 4 that must by now have reached Formosa were as good as lost. He suspected it from the day they had been assigned to Second Air Fleet, the Homeland base force. From Oita, Taipei was only 750 nautical miles, staging southwestward through Okinawa. But now the base force reserve had been halved, leaving barely enough semitrained pilots and aircraft to fill Admiral Ozawa's four carriers.

Sakaida pulled off his soft cap and rubbed his temples. He had noticed an increasing tendency toward headaches at odd intervals, and one was building now. With nothing else to do, he left Nakaya in charge and stalked off to harangue the operations office about scheduling a little more flight time for his *chutai*. Walking away, he heard the youngsters chattering among themselves, envious of their friends now participating in the great victory that Radio Tokyo was touting hourly.

Sakaida did not look back. He had already mentally erased five of his seven pilots who now had The Look.

FRIDAY, 13 OCTOBER
USS *REPRISAL*

The khaki and blue crowd on the flight deck was arrayed by squadrons and divisions, standing at parade rest. There was a murmur of nervous banter in the ranks as the 888-foot carrier slid beneath the Golden Gate Bridge while automobiles honked in salute. Rogers faintly caught the Morse code message as several motorists blared a rapid *beep-beep-beep-beeeep:* V for victory.

Kenny Diskowski heard the same go-get-'em sentiment and smiled self-consciously. "Man, I'm glad I'm not superstitious," he said to nobody in particular. "Imagine passing under a bridge on Friday the thirteenth!"

Brian Sossaman chuckled. "You dope—it's a ladder that's unlucky, not a bridge."

"Well, a bridge is sort of like a ladder laid on its side." Diskowski's face reddened slightly. But he appreciated Eddie Fairfield's sentiment when the section leader said, "Hey, if that sendoff your mom sprung for isn't good luck, I don't know what is. You can invite me to Diskowski Shipping anytime!"

Kenny smiled in gratitude. "If I know my dad, it'll show up as a business expense."

On the bridge, two hundred feet above the flight deck, automobiles had slowed or stopped. Conscious of the spectacle, *Reprisal's* Captain John McEwen called the air group and ship's company to attention as the band struck up "I'll Be Seeing You." Burnett, curious about Rogers's state of mind, sneaked a sideways glance. But Rogers was staring straight ahead, unblinking in the relative wind as Air Group 59 left Alameda behind and sailed to war.

FRIDAY, 20 OCTOBER
IJNS *ZUIKAKU*

The sun had already descended behind the Japanese landmass as the Mobile Fleet sortied from the Inland Sea. In the growing darkness Sakaida sensed more than saw the remnants of Japan's carrier fleet—once the most powerful on earth. Besides *Zuikaku,* Admiral Ozawa possessed three light carriers, two hermaphrodite battleships boasting aft-end flight decks, three light cruisers, and eight destroyers.

The blue-clad sailors and airmen were dismissed from their leaving-port stations after singing "Going Out to Sea." Sakaida merely mouthed the words, though he saw misty eyes and even tears on several young faces. The ancient words affected some men that way:

"If I go away to sea, I shall return a corpse awash.
If Duty calls me to the mountain, a verdant sward will be my pall;
For the sake of the Emperor I will not die peacefully at home."

It is different for them, leaving for battle the first time, he told himself. Pacing forward on the teak deck, he realized with an electric jolt, *They still think we can win.*

As a senior petty officer, and arguably the most combat-experienced pilot in the *hikotai,* Sakaida had learned a few things about the "fleet's" destination. The Americans were raising their sights from Formosa to the Philippines—that much was beyond doubt. Though he lacked full details, Sakaida was aware that Ozawa's force would approach from the north on October 25, X-Day for the coordinated attack upon the U.S. fleet. Powerful surface units—Japan still possessed the largest battleships ever built—

would strike like a pincer and crush the enemy's amphibious shipping in Leyte Gulf. *At least that is the plan,* he mused.

His reverie was interrupted by Nakaya and Kurusu. "Sakaida-san, this is a propitious moment," Kurusu offered. "Will we really fight the Americans so soon?"

"Yes," Sakaida responded evenly. His voice seemed to float above the flight deck in the dark. "In five days' time."

"Then we may expect another fine victory!" Kurusu gushed. Nakaya was silent—he had already survived one victory. But Kurusu either failed to notice his superiors' attitude or chose to ignore it. "The radio broadcasts say that we sank nineteen Yankee carriers and four battleships off Formosa."

Not even Nakaya could let that pass. "You idiot! If the Americans had lost that many ships, how could they hope to attack the Philippines?"

Sakaida chortled in the dark. "That's true. You would think the propaganda bureau would be more careful with its victory claims." Suddenly he felt giddy. *I don't care who hears me. What can they do—send me to a battle zone?*

Then the faint pulsing was back inside Sakaida's skull. *Another damned headache.* He realized the attacks were more frequent whenever he had to deal with the groundless optimism of ignorant young aviators. *How often can I lie to them, or merely not tell the complete truth?* But he found another reason for false optimism.

"Remember one thing, Kurusu. This is a very lucky ship. I saw it first in the Hawaii Operation, and it has never been hit by a bomb or torpedo." Sakaida ticked off the engagements *Zuikaku* had fought: Coral Sea, Eastern Solomons, Santa Cruz, the Marianas—four of the war's five carrier battles. But Sakaida omitted a vital statistic: Since June the "Flying Crane" had been the sole survivor of the six carriers that had attacked Pearl Harbor.

SATURDAY, 21 OCTOBER
OVERHEAD, NAVAL AIR STATION KANEOHE

Rogers rolled port-wing-low in Crystal 12, one of VF-59's new F6F-5s, for a better look at the air station on Oahu's northeast coast. *I'd almost forgotten how damn beautiful it is,* he marveled. Even after his previous tours in Hawaii, the perfect splendor of the Mokapu Peninsula jutting into Kaneohe Bay still held the power to enchant him.

After the five-day transit from Alameda and getting settled, it was good to fly again. Rogers had told his team of Hawaii's wild beauty, and the young aviators were not disappointed. They marveled at Molokai's 1,500-foot cliffs falling straight into the sea. They gawked at waterfalls streaming vertically down from the clouds. And they would come to know the turbulence around Diamond Head that could cause planes to experience sudden hundred-foot altitude changes.

They had also scouted the high-class watering holes. Everybody talked about the Royal Hawaiian Hotel, but it was largely reserved for submariners. Reportedly the Moana was more fun; it cost more, but hosted some great parties.

Rogers raised his gaze from the cobalt-azure beauty and looked inland, over Oahu toward the western horizon. White-topped clouds stood sentinel, as if welcoming him back.

WEDNESDAY, 25 OCTOBER
IJNS *ZUIKAKU*, 0720

Sakaida could not tell how the battle was going. As a senior aviator, he had studied the situation map showing Vice Admiral Ozawa's grand strategy for the Philippines, but information was sketchy thus far. Looking at the three-pronged scheme, he only hoped that it was not like so many other Japanese Navy plans—overly complex with wide dispersal of ships and aircraft.

Yesterday, Vice Admiral Kurita's powerful Center Force had been mauled in the Sibuyan Sea by American carrier aircraft overflying the Philippines from the east. IJNS *Musashi,* one of the world's two largest battleships, had been sunk, and a cruiser had been turned back with damage. But Kurita's thirty-seven remaining ships, temporarily routed, were expected to reverse course and emerge into Leyte Gulf this morning to destroy the American troop transports.

Vice Admiral Nishimura's Southern Force—seven ships in all—had been subjected to air attack in the Sulu Sea but continued eastward via Surigao Strait. Apparently they had not fared well against enemy surface units, as little had been heard from them.

Sakaida's scan turned toward the top of the map. There, 250 miles off Cape Engano on the tip of Luzon, was the Main Body. It was rumored that, with only 116 aircraft in his four carriers, Ozawa was willing to sacrifice half of Japan's remaining flattops if only the American admiral, Halsey, would divert his own task forces northward—away from Kurita.

Lieutenant (j.g.) Uchida moved to Sakaida's side, dressed in flight gear. Always cautious with officers, Sakaida came to attention and bowed, but the *hikotaicho* paid little attention. As if reading Sakaida's mind, he offered, "We still have little solid intelligence today. But the air staff places great faith in the six hundred aircraft ashore."

Sakaida grunted acknowledgement. *Ozawa placed great faith in our land-based planes in the Marianas,* he recalled. *They did us no good at all.*

Uchida looked at the noncom. "Sakaida, how are your men? How is their spirit?"

It was an unexpected question. Most Imperial Navy officers assumed that all hands thirsted for battle and trusted implicitly in ultimate victory. "Their spirit seems excellent, honorable lieutenant." Sakaida thought for a heartbeat. "But I wish they had more training."

Sakaida caught Uchida's sideways glance toward the others behind him in the ready room. "I wish the same thing," the officer remarked. It was as close to dissent as he would voice. "And you, Sakaida? How do you feel on our day of battle?"

"I am . . . confident, sir." The two men's eyes locked for a moment. Sakaida knew that he could never explain his personal conviction—his absolute knowledge. *I have nothing to fear, Lieutenant Uchida, for I know I am not going to die today. But you—*He bit off the thought.

Fortunately, Uchida did not press the matter. He turned back to the theater map. "Make certain that your pilots know the airfields ashore in case we are . . . diverted there."

"Hai!" Sakaida acknowledged. The implied message was easy to read: Lieutenant (j.g.) Uchida knew this force was about to be sacrificed.

OVERHEAD, THE MOBILE FLEET, 0825

In Happy Crane 120, Sakaida orbited beneath the overcast and waited for the Grummans bearing dark-blue death. Still not privy to the overall picture, he inferred from the hasty briefing that Kurita's massive surface unit had in fact penetrated into Leyte Gulf and evidently was engaging enemy carriers and transports. If so, a momentous victory was in the making. The Philippines would be saved even if the Mobile Fleet was about to be sunk. What might happen later was beyond his immediate concern.

Sakaida's scan went to the lower right portion of his instrument panel. Fuel and oil pressure, manifold pressure and cylinder-head temperature—all normal. But there were problems outside the plane. The combined assets of Air Groups 601 and 653 had been reduced by half in a fifty-six-plane strike against a U.S. carrier force to the south, and Sakaida was certain he would never see those aviators again. They would be shot down or forced to land ashore. As for what was left with the carriers, *We cannot hope to defend this force with thirty fighters,* he thought yet again.

He turned his attention outward and minutes later caught flashes of light in midair. Bright white blotches demanded his attention as he realized that shipboard gunners were firing phosphorous rounds toward the threat. He turned southward, checking that his three wingmen were following, and there saw repeated his worst nightmare.

For an instant, Hiroyoshi Sakaida lost some of his mystical confidence in his fate, as orderly formations of black dots filled the sky. It was the evening of 20 June all over again, when American carrier aircraft swarmed the atmosphere over the Mobile Fleet off Saipan. But after quickly calculating that the odds were similar—that is, appalling—he lost himself in the oddly comforting routine of prebattle procedure. Throttle, propeller control, and mixture against the stops. Double-check for machine guns and cannon armed. Gunsight turned on. He cast one last glance at Kurusu off his port wing, and then the Grummans were upon him.

Leading 180 Hellcats, Helldivers, and Avengers from the three fast carrier task groups was a thirty-four-year-old air group commander, call sign 99 Rebel. A Southerner out of the Annapolis class of '33, he was at the peak of his powers: The day before he had shot down nine Japanese aircraft in ninety minutes. Now he methodically assigned targets among the seventeen Japanese ships, beginning with the carriers.

Sakaida immediately saw there was no chance of intercepting any bombers. It would be a purely defensive battle for survival.

He waited for the first two Grummans to commit on him, then snapped into a wrapped-up, mind-blurring port turn. He began talking himself through the action as he had so many times before. *Keep back pressure on the stick, don't lose altitude.* The indefinite horizon troubled him as clouds melded with sea. But his instincts told him he was sustaining a level turn, cutting inside the Hellcats' radius. If the American wingman stayed in the fight for another full circle, his greater speed would force him outside and Sakaida would have a shot. *If another Grumman doesn't get me first!* He wondered about Kurusu, who should be somewhere off his left wingtip.

Partial glimpses of reality hammered themselves into Sakaida's consciousness. A brownish-black explosion nearby, tracers playing crazy-quilt patterns across his windscreen, the mild bump as he flew through somebody's slipstream.

He drew a bead on the second Hellcat, marveling that the pilot of a faster fighter would stay in here and mix it up like this. Sakaida began pulling deflection on the Grumman and his left hand unconsciously tickled the cannon trigger—an awkward arrangement resembling a bicycle brake handle on the throttle. Then the American abruptly shoved his blunt nose down, rolled away from the turn, and was gone.

The Hellcat leader went with him, crossing Sakaida's sights left to right. Sakaida compressed the 20-millimeter firing mechanism with his fingers and thumbed the nose-gun trigger. The machine-gun receivers before his face pounded away, filling his cockpit with sound and gunsmoke. He thought he glimpsed bullet strikes on the Grumman's blue fuselage, but there was no time for pursuit.

How long was I in that circle? Sakaida squirmed in his seat, not daring a look inside the cockpit. His body and his ears told him that he had depleted too much airspeed—the Zero was at the low end of minimum fighting speed. *Keep two hundred knots or you'll surely die.*

Sakaida rolled wings-level for a moment, scanned left and right, and found himself alone. He recalled the dark-colored explosion close by. *That was Kurusu.* The boy's combat career had lasted—what? Fifteen seconds, perhaps. The second section also had vanished.

Knowing better than to fly straight and level in a combat zone, Sakaida shoved forward on the stick and traded altitude for speed. He gave his abused engine a break, retarding the throttle two centimeters. Then he was back in perpetual motion, seeking something to shoot.

Four Hellcats crossed under his right wing and, with a glance backward, he followed. Just as he reached firing range—no more than three hundred meters—they saw him. Each pair turned hard toward each other. Sakaida recognized the setup: that damnable double-team tactic that U.S. Navy fliers did so well. He took a chance. Pulling up steeply, rolling to his right in the direction of his propeller's torque, he cut the corner vertically on the left-hand pair now turning starboard.

Timing was critical now. As he pulled through the top of his zoom-climb, the nearest Grumman looked huge from 250 meters overhead as Sakaida risked a quick shot. He laid off three rings of deflection—more than he probably needed—and fired all four guns. His tracers crossed the Hellcat's nose, and impacts twinkled along the square-tipped wings. He had a sense of the fighter lurching, then rolling right, apparently out of control.

Enough of that! Pull hard left—the others will be coming! Sakaida dived even steeper as he reversed his turn. Just in time. The second section had rolled into a pass that would have caught Sakaida in an aerial hammer and anvil. But the Americans had no clear shot—they had never seen anyone use the vertical to negate the Thach Weave. The last they saw of the olive-green Zero, it was diving near vertically past them, far too close to line up their sights.

With his head turned over his left shoulder, Sakaida could hardly believe what he had just done. *Why didn't I think of that before?* He marveled that the offensive countermove had come to him when he needed it most—when he had a handful of seconds to live.

Diving southwest, he urged his Model 52B toward its redline speed of 395 knots. The last glance he had at the Mobile Fleet, one carrier already was dead in the water.

Behind him, down on the frenzied surface of the Philippine Sea, IJNS *Chitose* was sinking. The "Flying Crane," already torpedoed, was marked for further attention as American strike leaders changed hands. Ninety-nine Rebel turned over to a thirty-one-year-old who had been two years his junior at the Academy. The new strike coordinator, 99 Mohawk, competently directed the destruction of the remainder of the Mobile Fleet's precious carriers.

SATURDAY, 29 OCTOBER
CLARK AIRFIELD, LUZON

Wheels down, flaps down, mixture rich, propeller in low pitch. Sakaida completed his landing checklist as he flew the downwind leg of the traffic pattern. He was tired, bone-tired in a way he had never been, and he wanted only to sleep.

This patrol had been a wasted sortie; he had made no contact with the enemy. After flying ashore to Aparri following the fleet air battle, he had been reassigned to Batangas and then moved again to this fine complex built by the Americans, and throughout there had been plenty of opportunities for contact: the patrol over Vice Admiral Kurita's routed force, two interceptions of U.S. Army and Navy planes, constant alerts and frequent false alarms. Sakaida reckoned he had shot down two more enemy aircraft, but any success by the remnants of Ozawa's air groups hardly mattered anymore.

He banked into his base leg turn and judged he was a bit high. Easing off the throttle, he allowed the Zero to settle a little. Now Sakaida heard an odd noise—a low, rolling *caruuump*. He turned his head as the anti-aircraft guns on the ground began firing. His wingman, a *Chitose* pilot whose name Sakaida did not remember, was not there—just a dissipating fireball in the traffic pattern.

No longer tired, Sakaida pushed everything forward with his left hand. He sensed the geometry of the situation. American fighters had jumped his flight from above. Tracers sparkled over his canopy. *They killed my wingman because he was closest. But I am next.*

Sakaida's hands were a blur in the cockpit. Grasping the stick with his left, he moved his right to the landing gear and flap handles as he dived for the ground. It was his only chance. Low and slow, 180 meters above the runway, he needed speed. Now.

The assailants still had not entered his vision. *They must be above me and behind,* he realized. He shot a glance at the airfield and saw the two nearest hangars. Without thinking, he racked the Zero into a shallow, diving turn and crossed the runway at a nonregulation 40-degree angle. Leveling off at ten meters, he risked a look back.

The nearest enemy fighter's wings were alive with muzzle flashes. Sakaida felt impacts on his airframe, but the American had under-deflected from only 15 degrees angle-off. However, flying on the deck, aimed toward the hangars, Sakaida offered a predictable flight path. The nearest hangar loomed in his vision. In three seconds he would fly into the open door where aircraft were parked inside.

Eerily calm now, Sakaida nudged the stick back, got the altitude he needed, and popped the stick to the right. With abrupt precision he centered his controls, and, half a wingspan off the ground, through the top of his canopy, he saw the side of the hangar speed by at 125 knots.

Still in his vertically banked turn, he shot out behind the two hangars and felt as much as saw his pursuers' shadows pass over him. The Zero lacked enough airspeed just then to catch the Grummans, so Sakaida eased off his bank and skipped over the trees toward a nearby ravine. *The Americans will not stay long with our gunners firing at them,* he reasoned.

Circling low in the valley, keeping in shadow when possible, Sakaida kept thinking of what that Yankee pilot would tell his friends tonight. How he had destroyed one Zero in Clark's traffic pattern and had the leader dead to rights—and the amazing man just flew between two hangars! Sakaida chuckled to himself. Then he laughed aloud. In moments he was laughing so hard that tears streamed down his face.

When he landed, mechanics and other pilots wondered how even an expert like Sakaida could react that way to the death of yet another friend. True, the *Zuikaku* veteran had saved himself with some inspired flying, but the funeral pyre of the *Chitose* flier still smoldered at the end of the runway.

Between gasps for air in his laughing fit, Sakaida wondered whether he was going insane.

November 1944

Rogers dropped into the big carrier's landing pattern and smiled to himself. *Hello, old girl. It's been awhile.* The "reunion" was a pleasant surprise: while *Reprisal* began a yard period, Air Group 59 was using the time to do refresher CQ—carrier qualification.

Eight hundred feet below his Hellcat, United States Ship *Saratoga* (CV-3) steamed into the trade wind, flying the Charlie flag at her mast. Rogers took one glance to note the differences since he had last seen her a year before. *Jumpin' Joe Clifton was aboard with Air Group Twelve then,* he recalled. But even with a new paint job, more radar antennas and upgraded anti-aircraft armament, she was still "Sara," his first carrier. That had been in 1940—four years and a different world ago.

The aircraft were different as well. By now Rogers was adjusted to the Hellcat, which was slightly bigger, much faster, and 50 percent heavier than his old Dauntless. But both types were stable and well behaved in the landing pattern.

Rogers busied himself in the cockpit as he led his division up the carrier's starboard side. He slid back the canopy and locked it open, then ran down his checklist. Mixture in auto rich; propeller to 2,300 r.p.m.; supercharger in neutral. He half opened his cowl flaps for cooling, then the oil cooler and intercooler flaps. Next he extended his arresting hook, selected "landing gear down" and confirmed that the tail wheel was unlocked for a carrier landing. Finally, he lowered his landing flaps and felt the F6F-3 pitch slightly nose down. He retrimmed the big fighter, feeling solid and comfortable as he turned downwind.

Flying down *Saratoga*'s port side, Rogers looked to his right. Diskowski, Fairfield, and Sossaman were evenly spaced, guiding on him in preparation for the break. Somehow it was important to look sharp for Sara—*For old time's sake,* he thought. Looking back at Diskowski, Rogers blew his wingman a kiss and rolled smartly into an arcing, descending port turn. He knew that Kenny would wait twenty seconds before performing an identical maneuver, then the second section would follow.

Unlike a shore-based traffic pattern, Rogers flew his carrier approaches in a constant left-wing-low turn. He quickly picked up the landing signal officer and began flying by feel, no longer concerned with anything in the cockpit.

Looking good, Rogers talked himself into the approach. The LSO's paddles remained outstretched in the "Roger" position, indicating a satisfactory start. Rogers judged he was 150 to 200 feet off the water, on speed at 90 knots.

Nearing the deck, Rogers caught the first correction. The LSO leaned outboard, canting his body so that his paddles tilted perhaps 20 degrees. *Got to tighten up the turn,* Rogers realized. He coordinated stick and rudder, saw the LSO tilt sideways once more, then straighten up. Rogers neutralized his controls and two seconds later the orange-yellow paddles flashed smartly to the LSO's neck and belt buckle.

Rogers came back on the throttle and welded his gaze to the spot where experience told him he would hit the deck. Then the Grumman's nose blocked his view as he brought the stick back. He had the eerie sensation of dropping into something unseen.

The F6F contacted the deck tailwheel first, just as the arresting hook snagged the fourth wire. The mains dropped heavily, compressing the big landing-gear oleos, and bounced once. Rogers was tossed forward against his shoulder harness as seven tons of Hellcat were snagged to a stop in less than thirty feet. He remembered to keep his feet off the toe brakes while the aircraft rolled backward slightly and a teenage hook runner sprinted from the catwalk to disengage the tailhook.

The pilot got the signal to raise his hook; responding to the plane director's enthusiastic "come-on," Rogers advanced throttle and taxied forward over the lowered barriers. The plane director handed off Fox Nine to the next director up the deck, who pointed forward toward the parking area.

Rogers kept the R-2800 idling and unlocked his inertia-reel harness.

Leaning out of the cockpit, he craned his neck to see how Diskowski fared. *Looks good,* Rogers thought as the following fighter rolled over the seven-foot barriers lying flush with the deck. Fairfield's F6F appeared at the threshold, apparently ready for the cut signal.

Turning back forward, Rogers checked his instruments. *Everything in the green.* He was anxious to get going, to make his next five requalification landings and then maybe explore *Saratoga.* He had also scheduled Burnett's division to requal this morning, hoping to visit their old stateroom from Bombing 3 days.

He looked up at the distinctive funnel and island and felt a quiver of—what? Homesickness, perhaps. *Reprisal* was his new home, and a good one, judging from what he had seen thus far. She was getting last-minute upgrades from the Pacific Fleet Radar Center, and would have the most current electronics available when she joined the Fast Carrier Task Force. But to Philip Rogers and Bernard Burnett—who had been happy peacetime ensigns in *Saratoga,* who had been aboard both times she had felt enemy torpedoes, who had helped sink enemy warships from her deck—this would always be their first Navy home. It was good to be back, if only for a day.

MONDAY, 6 NOVEMBER
CLARK FIELD

"Sakaida, as nearly as we can determine, you are the senior surviving member of your *hikotai*," pronounced the army officer behind the desk. "Here are travel orders and passenger authorization for your flight to the Homeland. Good luck."

Sakaida saluted the major, then about-faced and paced from the personnel office. It felt odd, dealing with the Japanese Army Air Force, but after all, Clark was an army facility. On the way to the flight line to collect his ragtag group of carrier pilots, Sakaida briefly wondered what the officer had meant by "Good luck." *Or did it mean anything?*

Striding into the sunlight, Sakaida stopped on an impulse. He looked up into the cloud-flecked sky, closed his eyes, and inhaled. Green scents came to him on the humid breeze. *I want to remember this because I shall never be here again in this war.* When he opened his eyes again, the fluorescent-green landscape glared back at him.

Sakaida waved his papers at the collection of noncommissioned pilots. They fell in line behind him, talking animatedly about some recent event, but he paid little attention. He was more concerned with the capabilities of the army pilots who would fly the navy men home in Ki-48 II bombers. Sakaida knew little about the aircraft, other than they were manufactured by Kawasaki and cruised at about 175 knots. Approaching the twin-engine aircraft, he was heartened to see that both army crews were composed entirely of enlisted fliers.

As senior survivor, Sakaida went through the motions. He arrayed the dozen aviators in a row and called off their names. Only one other man was previously known to him—another piece of human flotsam washed ashore from *Zuikaku*. Satisfied that all were present, he exchanged salutes with the bomber pilots and directed his men to their respective planes.

Sakaida borrowed a seat cushion from one of the gunners and settled himself in the bomber's cramped fuselage. While the crew started engines, he paid more notice to the conversation around him. A third-class petty officer was excited. "It's true, Minomi. I saw the message myself. Nishizawa was killed less than two weeks ago."

"What's that?" Sakaida snapped. His voice was sharper than he intended.

The petty officer turned to his superior. In respectful tones, he said, "I beg to report. Warrant Officer Nishizawa of *Hikotai* 303 was killed in action late last month. He was a passenger in a transport aircraft shot down over Mindoro."

Sakaida leaned forward in concentration. As he fought to absorb that information, the expressions of the fliers around him gave the answer. *This must be how the Germans felt when their von Richthofen was killed,* Sakaida thought.

"At least he took dozens of the enemy with him," the second rating said.

Hiroyoshi Nishizawa was one of a handful of near-legendary naval fighter pilots. A twenty-four-year-old genius in a Zero, he was known as "The Devil" for his spectacular string of victory claims with the Tainan Wing at New Guinea. Since then his tally had climbed even higher, in the Solomons, and rumor—for what it was worth—said the figure had reached eighty- or ninety-plus. With the fabulous Sakai, who continued flying combat with one eye, Nishizawa had represented the epitome of the Zero fighter aces. *Now he is a cinder in a burned-out transport.* Sakaida looked around at the scratched, abused interior of the Ki-48. *Maybe that is what the major meant by "Good luck."*

As the bomber's twin Nakajima radial engines warmed, Sakaida sat back and pondered the rate of attrition. Lieutenant Nakagawa, nominal CO of Vice Admiral Ozawa's carrier fighters, had failed to return from the big raid against the American beachhead at Tacloban on November 3. Uchida and the others had been killed or had disappeared previously—mostly on October 25.

Taxiing to the downwind end of the runway, the Ki-48 hummed and lurched. But Hiroyoshi Sakaida ignored the inconvenience. He knew what his companions were thinking—if The Devil can die, certainly so can they. And though Sakaida was realist enough to rate himself below Nishizawa's eerie skill, he took comfort in one unassailable fact. *I am still safe. Nishizawa had a fatal flaw—he was unlucky.*

FRIDAY, 10 NOVEMBER
NAS KANEOHE

Burnett blinked at the afternoon sun as he bounded up the steps to the bachelor officers' quarters. He was a man in a hurry—he did not want to miss the 1500 event at the swimming pool. Checking his wristwatch, he nearly collided with Fairfield and Diskowski. "Hey, where are you guys going?" He realized they were dressed in flight suits and carried helmets, goggles, and oxygen masks.

"Ah, we're meeting Mr. Rogers in a half hour, sir," Fairfield replied. "He's got us scheduled for another tactics hop." The tone of Eddie's voice clearly hinted at disappointment bordering on resentment.

"You're gonna miss—"

"Yes, sir," Diskowski lamented. He could already envision the WAVES, civilian females, and assorted seminubile girls who would attend the air group swimming party. If Team 4 was lucky, some of the bathing beauties would still be on hand after the division landed, had been debriefed, and returned to BOQ. *In 1947,* the ensign thought to himself.

Burnett shook his head. "I don't get it. You guys already have more hours than any team in the squadron. What's special about this afternoon?"

Fairfield responded. "Mr. Rogers was able to schedule four new F6s with gyroscopic gunsights. He said that since our replacement planes are likely to have the new gadgets, we need to get up to speed with them. He even traded hops with Mr. Harkin's division. Can you believe it?" He raised his hands in a helpless gesture.

"Hell," Burnett exclaimed, "everybody's been briefed on the K-14 and -21."

"Yes, sir, but Mr. Rogers wants us to get more experience. We're going to fly gunnery patterns on each other and see what parameters are useful and what ones aren't. Apparently the gyro sights are best against steady, predictable targets like bombers. Phil wants to see how they'll handle a dogfight."

Burnett grinned. "That's my boy. Say, where is he right now?"

"Ah, he's been trying to see his Marine buddy over at Ewa, but I don't think they've linked up yet," Fairfield responded. He nodded toward Diskowski. "Kenny, Brian, and me have been trying to tell him that we'd like to do some socializing of our own, if you know what I mean." His eyebrows arched behind his sunglasses.

"Well, cheer up, mister. The squadron cookout is on the beach tomorrow. You can celebrate Armistice Day with the Sunsetters." An evil thought crossed his mind. "I'm sure one or two of the guys will let you talk to the gals they meet today."

Before Fairfield or Diskowski could respond, Burnett was up the steps and through the door, vocalizing, "I want a girl . . . just like the girl . . . that married Harry James!"

WEDNESDAY, 15 NOVEMBER
TOKYO

Sakaida stood in a sea of suppressed bereavement. The families waiting to receive their soldiers' ashes seemed to overflow the available space at Yasukuni Shrine, but he detected almost no outward show of emotion. *Why did I come here?* he asked himself. *What did I expect to find?*

Fresh off the train, with three hours to wait for the trip north, he had been drawn to Kudan Hill overlooking the city. Tokyo, he noted, was grayer, more somber than before. It might as well be a different city from the capital he had last seen in 1941. Most of the people were unusually quiet, seemingly focused inward, despite patriotic banners, loudspeaker exhortations, and absurdly optimistic radio reports from the various war fronts.

He had heard that among the casualties from Leyte Gulf was cruiser *Chikuma*. The name had sparked an involuntary reaction in him—a prickling between the shoulder blades—for she had been an intimate part of his navy life. As half of Cruiser Division Eight with his own *Tone* in 1941–42, *Chikuma* had been an everyday sight for then Flight Petty Officer Sakaida. Flying his Aichi reconnaissance floatplane, he had seen the twin sister ships from every angle in all types of weather. *So many of the famous old names are gone now,* he realized.

Sakaida wanted to ask of the officer he had overheard at the station, but knew better. The overtly curious were often detained by the *kempaitai*, the military police, who reportedly arrested ten thousand people annually. He wanted to steer clear of those bastards.

An elderly couple shuffled past Sakaida, and he stepped back to let them pass. The woman seemed bowed under the weight of her burden—a laquered white box that she carried in both hands. Her wrinkled face, long and drawn, showed none of the pride that Japan's parents were expected to hold for a son who had achieved the supreme honor. Sakaida looked at the husband and father, holding his wife's arm, and saw a quiver in the old gentleman's lower lip.

As the honored place for Japan's war dead, Yasukuni held special significance these days. Of the nation's 200,000 Buddhist and Shinto shrines, the only one rated higher was the Grand Shrine of Ise, home to the Sun Goddess founder of Nippon. More and more white boxes were returning from the empire's battle fronts, prompting repeats of this ceremony. Looking toward the temple, Sakaida saw armed officers handing the neatly labeled boxes to parents, wives or children in unwavering style: the name was read, there was a ritual exchange of bows, and the ash box was handed over.

Turning away from the shrine, Sakaida speculated on what proportion of all the war dead's remains ever made this journey. Sailors and naval aviators rarely featured in the rite, for dead ships and aircraft jealously guarded their drowned crews.

By the time he walked back toward the train station, another headache was building behind his eyes. It was not relieved by the latest broadcast from the Information Bureau, which announced, "We cannot reveal what further measures will be taken by the Japanese Fleet, but one thing now is clear: America has lost the war."

MONDAY, 19 NOVEMBER
YAMANUKI, HONSHU ISLAND

Sakaida did not know what to make of his plight. Walking through the streets of his home village, absorbing the mountainous winter beauty, he realized that he had already done everything there was to do. *And after barely three days,* he gloomed. *What am I going to do until Wednesday?*

The first twenty-four hours had been marvelous. Most of the townfolk had turned out to greet their returning war hero—he was by far the most prestigious citizen of the village on the Pilgrimage Road in the Japanese Alps. Despite several return trips to the Homeland, Hiroyoshi Sakaida had not been to Yamanuki since the autumn of 1941. He was wined and dined in splendor, introduced to relatives only dimly recalled, and received more invitations than he could possibly accept.

Yet after two days, reality forced itself upon him. He realized with a pang that much of the fare spread in his honor had been hoarded for weeks. There was enough food in the village, but almost none to spare. Few of his childhood friends remained, and the village honor roll contained an ap-

palling number of names either familiar or dear to him, including his two
best schoolmates: laughing Jiro Shinohara, killed in Burma, and the trick-
ster Goro Watanabe, presumably buried on Saipan.

Sakaida's father had died of tuberculosis at age forty in 1927. Barely
eleven, Hiroyoshi had taken on more responsibility than a child should bear,
but his mother had always been strong and supportive. Working seventy-
two-hour weeks to earn on average eight dollars per month, she had endured.
When her eldest son joined the navy as a way out of a life of unending physical labor, she never once complained. Now, stooped and used up at forty-
nine, at least she had some grandchildren from Hiroyoshi's brother and
sister.

A gust whipped snowflakes into Sakaida's face and he stuffed his
hands into his navy peacoat. Head bowed against the cold, he turned down
a side street and allowed the wind to propel him toward the communal bathhouse. If he was lucky, the Nakadate twins might be there. And Hiroyoshi
Sakaida was nothing if not lucky.

MONDAY, 27 NOVEMBER
USS *REPRISAL*

The new fleet carrier steamed west-southwest at 22 knots, escorted by a light
cruiser and two destroyers. Her flight and hangar decks were packed with
nearly ninety aircraft, including fifty-eight Hellcats. Most of the fighters
were new F6F-5s, their overall gloss blue paint contrasting with the older
tricolor schemes on the dash threes. Four of the F6Fs with bulbous hous-
ings on their starboard wings were radar-equipped night fighters being in-
tegrated into VF-59.

On the 02 level, in Ready Room One, Ralph Platco presided over a
meeting intended to ease integration of the fighter squadron into the ship's
operating routine.

Platco stood with a coffee cup in one hand while most of the other officers sat in padded, reclining chairs. More than half of them smoked cig-
arettes, though Burnett sported a rare cigar. Rogers, in the front row, had
stubbed out a partially consumed Lucky Strike. He was mildly irritated at
himself for indulging in the filthy habit that always left a foul aftertaste. He
remembered the night before Midway, trying to light one of Burnett's cig-
arettes and fumbling the attempt.

"We're going to be at least six days en route to Ulithi," Platco was saying. "So we may as well use the time to get sharp on our operating procedures. First, I want to deal with the night fighters. Mister McClung's crew
is new to most of you because they almost missed the boat." Platco pointed

his cup at Lieutenant (j.g.) Lon McClung, who tossed his head and laughed. The four "nighthawks" had landed aboard after the rest of the air group departed Kaneohe; their radar officer and enlisted men had followed in two TBFs.

"McClung's people will become Team Zero," Platco explained, "because I already lead Team One. They will presumably fly only dusk-to-dawn CAPs, but we may have to call on them during daylight if recent trends continue." He had received a short briefing on new Japanese aerial tactics during the Leyte Gulf battle, and the indications were frightening. But he decided to save that until later.

"Meanwhile, Lieutenant Lang has some new dope for us so I'll turn it over to him."

Lieutenant Henry Lang was a rail-thin stockbroker who had made a small fortune before the war, and his civilian success had marked him as a potential fighter director. Lang did not appreciate it at the time, but development of ship-based radar ranked second only to the Manhattan Project. Lang had made more than $10,000 in three consecutive years, and his managerial skills and astute judgment were duly noted. Thirty-three years old, he had gone directly from the three-month officer's training course at Quonset Point, Rhode Island, to the Fighter Direction School at St. Simon's Island, Georgia.

Standing before the aircraft status board, Lang spoke with a slow Northeastern twang. "First, I need to clear up some confusion about voice radio procedures. I have a PacFleet circular that refers us to the operation order given to each task group before we deploy for a combat operation. As you know, we'll likely alternate between Third and Fifth Fleets while we're out here, and the radio call signs usually change accordingly. But the *Reprisal* will remain Crystal Base for now, because that's our CIC identity. For TBS, the talk-between-ship frequency, we're 'Slugline,' but that doesn't concern air operations.

"What does concern us, for communication between CIC and airborne planes, is your individual call signs. Your aircraft side number, of course, changes almost every time you fly. Therefore, your team numbers will be used: Crystal One-One, One-Two, One-Three; or Two-One, Two-Two, et cetera. The exception is the air group commander, who is always Ninety-nine Crystal, regardless of what plane he's flying."

Lang stopped to gather his thoughts as he warmed to his subject. "Now, as you gentlemen may know, while in Hawaii this ship received some of the latest radar equipment available. I won't get too detailed, but it was time well spent, believe me.

"When we put this ship in commission this summer, she had five radars of four different types. But we learned that funnel exhaust and mutual interference caused problems that still have not been fully overcome. However, we've replaced the old rectangular SK antenna with the new circular SK-2 that gives us a tighter beam for long-range air search. It is particularly useful for night intercepts, where the closing range between fighter and bogey is critical.

"Also, the short-range SM set has been replaced by the SP, which is lighter and generally faster in acquiring a target. The new SR height-finder was unavailable to us in Pearl, so we're stuck with the SC-2 but it should meet our needs."

Aware that his audience showed little interest in radar nomenclature, Lang took a different tack. "My CIC team is pretty sharp. I admit that most of them hadn't heard of radar before I recruited them from the V-3 and V-4 divisions, but they're enthusiastic and they learn fast. I've talked to Lieutenant Commander Platco about some practice intercepts so we can recalibrate our sets. We didn't have much time after coming out of the yard in Pearl, but before we reach Ulithi I think you gentlemen and my team will know what each other can do." Lang felt awkward, all gangly in his creased khakis; he badly wanted to develop a rapport with the fighter pilots who would rely upon him. An idea crossed his mind. "That'll mean extra flying for you, but I trust you won't mind." Polite laughter skittered through the space and he felt better.

Lang saw a dark-haired aviator raise his hand in the front row. "Yes, Lieutenant."

"I'd like to volunteer Team Three for some calibration flights, Lieutenant." Rogers looked at Platco. "If that's all right with you, sir." *Extra flight time, more contact with the fighter director,* Rogers calculated. *Maybe a couple extra chances to kill Japs.*

Platco glanced at Ron Harkin, sitting across the aisle from Rogers. The squadron exec squirmed upright, as if compelled to speak. He shrugged at Platco, who nodded. "Okay by me, Rogers. As long as it doesn't interfere with other scheduled flights."

Harkin looked pointedly at Lang and said, "I trust you will treat everyone equally in giving vectors for intercepts, Mr. Lang. After all, the rest of us would like a chance to win some medals, too." He emitted a short, hollow laugh that deceived no one.

Lang's brown eyes darted back and forth between VF-59's exec and flight officer. *No love lost there,* he concluded. As a conservative businessman and Connecticut Republican, he would not draw hasty conclusions. But intuition told him that the leader of Team 3 was motivated by something far beyond glory.

E L E V E N

December 1944

SATURDAY, 2 DECEMBER
ULITHI ATOLL

Somebody called it "Murderers' Row," and the name had stuck. Standing on *Reprisal*'s flight deck with most of the other aviators, Rogers took in the spectacle and approved of the appellation. He surveyed the naval might of a maritime nation lying serenely at anchor beneath the bright Pacific sky—latent violence visible on the flight decks of thirteen fast carriers.

"Just look at that," Burnett exclaimed in a low voice. "I've never seen anything like it."

Rogers merely nodded, drinking in the kinetic energy of so much concentrated power. The big, handsome Essex-class ships seemed indistinguishable with their near-identical silhouettes and similar dazzle-pattern camouflage. But the sailors and airmen who served the twentieth-century men-of-war could recognize each ship at a glance.

The hull numbers were the giveaway, though each air group's geometric symbol painted on the planes' tails also yielded identities. And so they lay anchored in a line: *Essex, Ticonderoga, Hancock, Lexington, Yorktown, Wasp,* and *Hornet*—the last four names of other carriers sunk in this war. The light carriers, CVLs, also were well represented: *Independence, Cowpens, Monterey, Langley, Cabot,* and *San Jacinto.* But because ships have more personality than other man-made objects, most flattops bore affectionate nicknames: Big T, Hanna, Lady Lex, San Jac, and Mighty Moo.

"And that ain't all of 'em," Burnett offered. "I hear that four or five more carriers are on the West Coast or headed this way." He adjusted his sunglasses against the glare. Four hundred miles southwest of Guam, 10 degrees latitude above the equator, the Pacific sun baked the beautiful lagoon serving the Third Fleet—a 112-square-mile anchorage that could accommodate a thousand ships.

Rogers gave a noncommittal grunt to Burnett's remark. He did not want to voice what he felt—a secret little thrill somewhere deep inside; a fierce pride at being part of this. A quarter million tons of carriers itself was tremendously impressive, but add in battleships and other combatants, plus tankers, supply ships, and amphibious vessels: It was almost beyond reckoning.

Don Mancross's quiet voice drifted on the still air. "And to think every one of these ships was built after Pearl Harbor. . . ."

Rogers, Burnett, and the handful of others in the VF-59 crowd knew what he meant. That *was the thing about Mancross,* Rogers decided. *He doesn't say much, but when he talks he's on target.*

"You're right, Don," Burnett said. "When we covered the Guadalcanal landings with three carriers, we thought we were cooking with gas." He nudged Rogers, who merely smiled at the recollection.

So much had happened since Pearl Harbor, only three years ago. *Saratoga,* torpedoed twice. Sallyann. *Yorktown,* sunk at Midway.

A wasted year in *Alazon Bay*'s mediocre composite squadron. Rejoining Bernie in a fresh, new air group. Gordon Connell. Ray.

Rogers blinked behind his amber lenses and clinched his teeth behind tightly pressed lips. Finally, as the group dispersed, he remembered to unclench his fists.

MONDAY, 4 DECEMBER
TSUIKI BASE, KYUSHU

Sakaida's confidence had been badly shaken upon receiving his new orders. "You are joining the Special Attack Corps," the detailer had told him—not without some sympathy. "Pilots of your experience are much in demand."

For a moment, eight years of harsh discipline almost evaporated as Sakaida calculated the prospects of requesting another assignment. *Is it possible to decline this honor?* he wondered. He knew relatively little about the *kamikazes*—the "Divine Wind"—other than the fact that their "body-crashing" tactics were reported to be hugely successful. Aviators who dived their planes into enemy warships were being hailed as sky gods, but Hiroyoshi Sakaida was satisfied with remaining mortal. His inner confidence at surviving the war had been rocked to its post-Saipan foundation.

Now, standing in the personnel office of the Shinkai Unit, Sakaida awaited word from on high. From what little he had seen of the "sea-shaking" suicide unit, he was unimpressed. There were few aircraft—mostly old-model Zero fighters—and the facilities were run-down. Glancing at the other five new arrivals, Sakaida judged that none had half his flight time. Three seemed stoic enough, but one was visibly nervous and the other already had The Look.

"Attention!" screamed the chief petty officer at the desk. As the fliers braced themselves, Sakaida heard footsteps on the creaky floorboards behind him. His peripheral vision caught a completely bald officer with wrinkled skin. Then Sakaida realized the truth and his stomach churned.

The lieutenant standing before him smelled of antiseptic and something else—an ointment, Sakaida guessed. The skin around the man's eyes was relatively intact but he had almost no visible nostrils, and his mouth was a reddened slit set in taut, scarred flesh. Sakaida looked at the officer's hands, which were less deformed than his face.

"I am Lieutenant Kono, division officer of this unit," the man said. The voice was surprisingly harsh, and Sakaida's pulse jumped. His mind accepted what his senses denied: His friend, Ensign Yusuke Kono, shot down in flames near Guadalcanal more than two years ago, was alive, and now an officer. Sakaida recalled the appalling sight: Kono's blazing floatplane smashing into the waters of The Slot.

"You men are here as human bullets," Kono rasped. Sakaida realized that his friend's larynx must have suffered damage from the flames and smoke, since the voice was almost unrecognizable. "I am here to make certain that you die well, and kill many Americans with your sacrifice." He turned his eyes toward the senior NCO. "All but you, Sakaida. You will lead the fighter escort section being formed to protect the reconnaissance element and the *kamikazes* themselves."

Kono then swept from the room, limping slightly and leaving the stale-sweet scent of antiseptic in the air.

TUESDAY, 5 DECEMBER
ASOR ISLET, ULITHI ATOLL

The VF-59 delegation stood anxiously in the fleet air personnel office, eyeing representatives from several other Essex-class fighter squadrons. Though resenting Harkin's presence, Rogers understood why the skipper had brought the exec along. One more Annapolis man increased the chances of tapping into the old-boy network in the scramble for additional pilots.

While Platco was trying to charm the three-striper responsible for aircrew assignments, Rogers looked around. The quonset hut's screened doors and windows allowed infrequent breezes into the hot, cramped interior, where two or three electric fans fought a losing battle to make up the deficit. The commander's short-sleeve khakis bore perennial stains under the arms but Rogers considered the man's demeanor surprisingly pleasant.

"Look, Mr. Platco," the personnel officer repeated, "this directive is almost as much a surprise to me as it is to you. AirPac didn't have time to give us much notice—we're just lucky we have as many replacement pilots on hand as we do."

Platco ran his fingers through his sandy hair, already moist from the tropical atmosphere. "Very well, sir. We'll take what we can get today. But holy Christ—a seventy-three plane squadron! Where am I going to bunk a hundred officers and forty-nine enlisted?"

Harkin leaned on the counter, nodding at nothing. "We can thank Tokyo for this windfall, Skipper. If it wasn't for the suicide attacks, we wouldn't need to add nearly twenty fighters and their extra personnel."

"You gentlemen needn't be so aggrieved," the personnel officer interjected. "I've had two bomber COs and a CAG in here today, howling about their aircrew and plane reductions. The new air group allotment is fifteen each SB2Cs and TBMs—that means a loss of nine bombers and three torpedo planes."

Platco tried another approach. "Sir, we've only been here three days and we didn't get much information en route. Just how bad are things to force a change like this?"

The three-striper plopped his pencil on the counter. "Well, I guess it's no big secret anymore. Off Leyte in October the suicide planes sank a CVE and damaged several CVs. That's why the *Intrepid, Franklin,* and *Belleau Wood* aren't here right now." He grinned sardonically. "You arrived just in time."

"Suits me," Harkin said. "More Japs for us."

Rogers turned away in disgust. *The bastard never misses a chance to stick his foot in his mouth.* Turning to Platco, Phil said, "Excuse me, sir. I'll round up the new pilots while you finish here." Platco waved his approval and Rogers stepped outside.

As the screen door slammed behind him, Rogers slid on his cap and eyed a pilot coming toward him, carrying a folder. In addition to the man's gold wings and ensign's bar, there was something about his build, the way he walked. When the aviator glanced up, Rogers realized that he was look-ing into the Montana sky-blue eyes of William E. Barnes.

Barnes had just raised a hand to salute the taller officer's twin bars when the recognition became mutual. Salutes deteriorated into outstretched hands, heartfelt hugs, and a complete disregard for naval custom. "Bill! My god, it's good to see you. It must be two years?"

"Uh, yes, sir. We both left Bombing Three in November '42."

"That's right. You goldbrick, you never wrote me after you went to flight training. When did you get here?"

"I just rode an escort carrier with a bunch of other replacement pilots. AirPac is sending out five-man teams to fighter squadrons now, so we're grown from the ground up. My team is supposed to join VF-57 tomorrow."

Rogers shook his head. "Negative. I'm here as a talent scout. You're coming with me!"

Platco and Harkin appeared in the doorway and Barnes rendered them honors. Before he could speak, Rogers interjected. "Skipper, Mr. Harkin, this is Bill Barnes, my old gunner in Bombing Three. He kept the Zeros off my tail at Midway and Guadalcanal. I'm the one who recommended him for flight training."

Platco's eyebrows rose in appreciation. *He knows we can use an ex-perienced flier,* Rogers thought. "Sir, I'd like to suggest that Mr. Barnes's division might join . . ."

"Where are you assigned, mister?" Platco asked.

"Fighting 57 in the *Sharpsburg,* sir. But I'd sure like to fly with you."

Platco rubbed his chin. "Bobby Clement's outfit. He's a good type; he probably won't mind swapping straight across." The CO looked at Harkin. "Ron, if you and Rogers can fix it with the good commander in there, I'll approve it."

The exec uttered an unenthusiastic "Aye, aye, sir." But Phil Rogers and Bill Barnes hardly heard as they took the steps into the personnel of-fice.

FRIDAY, 8 DECEMBER
TSUIKI BASE, KYUSHU

Kono poured more sake for his guest and raised his own cup in salute. "Cel-ebrating three years of war," he sneered, adding the traditional healthful toast, *"Ogenki de!"*

"Here's to our certain victory!" Sakaida replied. Both men tossed back the rice wine, and Sakaida began feeling a pleasant buzz.

Abruptly Kono rasped, "You never told me about the Hawaii operation. What was it like over Pearl Harbor?"

Sakaida waved a deprecating hand. "I saw very little—too many clouds." It was his standard reply when asked about his reconnaissance mission ahead of the first 180 carrier planes. Few of his colleagues knew that then Flight Petty Officer Sakaida had scouted Pearl Harbor from cruiser *Tone* and that his officer observer had reported favorable conditions for surprise attack. True, the American carriers were absent, but all else had gone astonishingly well. Now Sakaida giggled inanely at the memory.

Kono, on the other hand, remained cold sober. "You always could hold your liquor," Sakaida slurred. "At least that much has not changed."

Kono's smile was a leer from a cadaverous skull. Obviously the man cared little for convention—the mere presence of a noncom in an officer's quarters was proof enough. "Everything else has changed, though." Kono's words were a bark in the room. "I cannot drink enough liquor to get drunk. Not after . . . this." He pointed a scarred finger at his head. And with mild shock, Sakaida saw the beginnings of tears in the eyes of the hardest man he had ever known. *The pain,* he realized, *must be agonizing.*

Sakaida decided to risk the unthinkable. "Kono-san, tell me about your surgery and your recovery. I only heard that you had been rescued— nothing after that."

The officer poured again and paused, staring at the bottle. He blinked away the moisture and finally spoke. "My goggles saved my eyes, and my gloves mostly protected my hands. The rest—well, I had twelve operations, Sakaida. Almost one a month after I returned to Japan. And every one was like the furies of hell. But I learned to walk again and to live with the pain and the smell and even with the people. The burn wards—they are . . ." His voice trailed off. As if embarrassed by his admission of human frailty, he changed the subject.

"I finally recovered enough to return to duty, but only as a flight instructor. When Admiral Onishi formed the Special Attack Corps, I volunteered." He lowered his voice. "Many of us 'broken gems' are considered expendable so I came here to help form this unit." He sipped his tea, savoring the taste. "But I have a promise from headquarters, Sakaida. When this unit is ready, I will lead the first attack. And you will get me to the target."

So that's it, Sakaida realized. *He got me transferred here just to help him achieve his own personal revenge.*

Kono leaned forward over the small table. "I want your promise, Sakaida. I want you to tell me that you will get me past the Grummans. Shoot them down, ram them, drive them into the ocean. Anything to get me above an American aircraft carrier. Then I will do the rest. I will repay them for—everything."

Enough of this, Sakaida decided. His buzz was turning into another headache. Rising to his feet, swaying slightly, Sakaida bowed carefully. "Honorable division officer, I swear it!"

"Thank you, Hiroyoshi." It was the first time since their reunion that Kono had used Sakaida's given name. As he closed the door behind him, Sakaida began to realize the power of revenge to drive good men insane with the lust to kill by dying.

WEDNESDAY, 13 DECEMBER
USS *REPRISAL*

Rogers sat at one end of a wardroom table, his four pilots seated around him. A new ensign, Wilmer Van Sley, had joined the team as the supernumerary, the spare pilot who would relieve one of the others as needed. Rogers had put the slender kid from Salt Lake on his wing for a CAP two days ago and judged him competent.

Shoving his coffee cup out of the way, Rogers leaned on the tablecloth. He had chosen his words carefully, and proceeded with what he hoped was a useful, heartfelt speech. "You fellows have all the dope you need for tomorrow's missions. We're on the morning CAP and the afternoon fighter sweep over Luzon, so we should have as good a shot at finding Japs as any other team." He looked around at the expectant faces and mentally catalogued them. Kenny Diskowski: disappointed at being displaced by Van Sley on the CAP but understanding that the new man would benefit from the experience. Eddie Fairfield: calm and composed. Brian Sossaman: perhaps a bit edgy, but eager. Wilmer Van Sley: already familiar as "Van," anxious and self-conscious.

"I want to tell you guys what you already know," Rogers continued. "You're ready for combat, and that includes you, Van." The new kid grinned and glanced around as if seeking approval. "The best advice I can give you is, get some sleep tonight. My first mission was Midway, and I hardly slept at all the night before. By afternoon I wished I'd been able to log more sack time."

Rogers felt he would never forget the night of 3 June 1942, aboard the old *Yorktown.* After chow he had wandered down to the hangar deck and found then radioman Barnes putting in unnecessary work on their dive-bomber. On the way to his room Rogers had swung by torpedo country and talked to Ensign Wayne Wik, a Pensacola classmate. Wik had never come back, nor had nine other VT-3 crews, and now Phil could not remember the last words he ever spoke to his friend.

"You'll be fine up there tomorrow," Rogers insisted. "All you have to do is remember your training. The rest will take care of itself once the shooting starts."

"Well, I'd be a whole lot happier if I knew *we* were going to be doing all the shooting," Fairfield quipped. His tone belied his words.

Rogers reached into a pocket and produced a length of surgical tubing. "I got this from the flight surgeon. Now, we *are* likely to get shot at tomorrow and one of us might even get hit. I wish I'd thought of this before Midway, because it would have saved me about a pint of blood. I took a piece of flak in one leg while bombing a cruiser and bled all the way back. Bernie over there led me to the *Enterprise* and helped get me aboard." All heads turned to the next table where Burnett was talking animatedly with his own division.

"I had to use my flight-suit belt as a tourniquet, and it wasn't very effective. So I got one of these for each of us. Keep 'em handy.

"One other thing. Take a shower tonight before water hours end, and wear clean skivvies tomorrow. That'll help reduce the chance of infection if you're wounded." Before anyone could respond to this potentially disheartening subject, Rogers pressed on. "I'm not trying to scare you guys— I'm just being realistic. But I'm not writing any last letters, either."

Burnett glanced around, took in the somber expressions, and intoned, "Hell, these buzzards probably can't write, anyway." He ambled over to Rogers's team and slid into a chair. The others took the hint, saying good night. When they had gone, Burnett turned serious. "Phil, I heard your little speech about Midway. I told my team pretty much the same thing. What do you think—we going to be okay?"

Rogers shrugged. "Why not? We're well trained with good equipment."

"That's not what I mean. Most of the new guys seem okay, and I'm damn glad to have Barnes with us. But . . . I'm still not impressed with Clarey as CAG, though Platco seems to be coming along."

"Well, for what it's worth, I agree with you, Bernie." Rogers leaned back, hands behind his head. "I think that Ralph has gotten better as we get closer to the shooting. But if anything happens to him, you and I may have to tackle Harkin head-on."

Now Burnett shrugged. "I never wanted to make admiral, anyway."

At 2200, Phil Rogers and Bernie Burnett were still talking when the loudspeaker announced the evening prayer. After a moment of silence, the ship's chaplain spoke what was foremost in three thousand minds.

"Merciful God, be with this ship as it faces its first battle morning. Steel the hearts of those who serve her in the cause of faith over paganism, of liberty over tyranny. Remember each of us, oh Lord; the few who have felt battle's sting and the many for whom war is still a mystery. We seek Thy blessing in securing our cherished four freedoms: freedom of speech, freedom of worship, freedom from want, and freedom from fear. This we ask in Thy name, oh Lord. Amen."

Burnett, usually embarrassed at such moments, was about to say that he especially wanted freedom from fear. He began to speak, but he stopped short when he saw Phil Rogers's eyes narrowed in concentration, staring at nothing. Nothing at all.

THURSDAY, 14 DECEMBER
CRYSTAL FOUR-ONE

Rogers leveled off at 14,500 feet, leading two fighter divisions armed with five hundred–pound bombs. He glanced up-sun in the midafternoon sky, squinting toward Don Mancross's team providing high escort. The strike group had formed up nicely after launch, and the base element of Leo Hunziker's SB2Cs already was outbound on 260 magnetic, bound for Vigan Airfield on northwestern Luzon. It was a respectable target for twenty-eight *Reprisal* aircraft: twelve bombers with eight Hellcat fighter-bombers and eight F6F escorts. If many Japanese aircraft intercepted, Rogers's two teams would jettison their bombs and help Teams 5 and 9 protect the bombers.

No such luck, Rogers told himself. While his division had bored holes in the sky on task group CAP, the day's first fighter sweep had turned up surprisingly little opposition. The only shootdown had been made by Harkin and his wingman, Ensign Gambini, who went into the squadron war diary as drawing first blood for the Sunsetters. Rogers had heard a quick postmortem from Barnes, flying in the exec's second division: how Harkin had broken off to flame a Betty bomber near San Nicolas even though the bandit had posed no threat.

Pushing the thought aside, Rogers swiveled his head to check the formation. He glimpsed the task group falling astern—white wakes on the dappled sea, now disappearing beneath low, puffy clouds. Kenny Diskowski was echeloned right, perhaps eighty yards away, while Fairfield and Sossaman flew combat spread to the left. Rogers pondered how his young pilots must feel at this moment, headed toward a hostile coast for the first time. If they had the jitters, it did not show. Diskowski even managed to appear casual with a laconic wave.

Rogers brought his attention back to the cockpit for a handful of seconds. His guns were armed, gunsight on, bomb-rocket transfer switch set for "Bomb," engine running typically Pratt & Whitney smooth. He looked back toward his wingman in time to see Diskowski's airplane vanish in a brownish-orange explosion.

In stop-frame motion, Rogers caught the tiny details: shreds of aluminum dangling in midair, fuel igniting in a 350-gallon fireball that flared into extinction, leaving windblown debris. Then reality returned as Rogers felt the concussion rock his Hellcat.

Phil was conscious of two emotions shrieking at him from different directions. *Bandits this far from shore? Unlikely.* But he forced his eyes to focus on the upper air where Japanese fighters might have ambushed the formation even as the other half of his brain registered that twenty-year-old Kenneth Diskowski had just died.

Rogers fumbled for his microphone, missed, and had to look at the bracket. His hand trembled slightly but he willed some control into his voice as he called on strike frequency. *To hell with radio silence.* "Crystal Leader from Four-One. Crystal Four-Two just exploded." He tried to focus his thinking. *What now?* He pressed the button again. "Must have been faulty ordnance. Shall we jettison? Over."

Seconds trailed past as Leo Hunziker pondered his reply. Rogers knew what the bomber skipper was thinking. The Helldivers carried their bombs internally but the Hellcats' bombs were exposed to the slipstream, where an unsafetied arming vane could turn in the wind and induce a premature explosion. It was unlikely that another bomb would malfunction, but still . . .

"Crystal Leader to Crystal chicks. Affirmative, Phil, drop 'em safe."

Why bother to drop safe? Rogers wondered. Then he knew. *Leo wants to see if any others explode.* Rogers checked his armament panel: master arm "On," bomb switch from "Fuse" to "Safe." He pressed the button and the Hellcat rose slightly as a quarter ton of weight separated; Rogers dropped into a circling descent to watch for detonations two and a half miles below. He waited an appropriate time—a long, long thirty seconds—and saw nothing. Then, climbing steeply in high blower, he began a tedious tailchase to catch the formation. He pushed the R-2800 hard: 2,550 r.p.m. at forty-nine inches manifold pressure. But Phil Rogers's mind and stomach churned in turmoil from more than his concern about fuel consumption and tactical cohesion. *God in heaven. What am I going to tell Eleanor Diskowski?*

SATURDAY, 16 DECEMBER
TSUIKI BASE

Hiroyoshi Sakaida was no more a sociologist than a physicist, but he realized that he was living in a laboratory of human stress analysis. After attending two *kamikaze* induction ceremonies, he had begun to realize that the human animal ran true to its infinite form. When volunteers were called for, there was usually a small pause—a moment suspended in time as young men considered what was being asked of them. Inevitably, one of the most fanatical or least mature would take the two steps forward. Then a handful of his friends or rivals would join him with an equal display of fervor. Finally, the others would succumb to the herd instinct and, regardless of their convictions, express their willingness to "body-crash" in the near future. Sakaida thought that perhaps he had arrived at an important insight: Humans—or at least young male humans—would rather die than appear lacking before their companions. With a tiny shock, he realized that the officers directing the *kamikaze* campaign were aware of this phenomenon and must be exploiting it.

Aside from the psychological concerns, Sakaida became fascinated with the technical aspects of aviation suicide. As the Shinkai Unit reached its allotted strength, Kono had begun tactical lectures for the future sky gods.

"This is your prime target," Kono began. He touched a recognition chart showing various classes of American aircraft carriers. "If you have a choice, always dive into one of these ships. Otherwise, try to identify a troop transport. These two types are the greatest threat to the empire." His ruined face swiveled across the room, and for once nobody looked away. "Is that understood?"

A hand rose tentatively in the third row and Kono nodded. "Beg pardon, honorable lieutenant. But should we not try to sink a battleship?" Flight Petty Officer Imura's voice was barely a whisper.

Sakaida thought he saw the ghost of a smile beneath Kono's scars. "No! Definitely not!" The red-scarred mask looked around the room again. "Who can tell me why?"

Flight Petty Officer Seno was on his feet. "Sir! A battleship is too heavily armored. We cannot hope to destroy such a ship even with a five hundred-kilogram bomb."

The officer nodded briskly and Seno sat down, obviously pleased with himself. "Correct," Kono stated. "And a battleship cannot seriously harm us. True, its big guns may bombard our coast, but no captain would risk his ship close to shore."

Sakaida thought for a moment and realized that Kono was right. As an island nation, most of Japan's population and industrial centers lay less than twenty miles inland, including Sasebo, Nagasaki, Hiroshima, Kobe, Osaka, Nagoya, Yokohama, and Tokyo itself. All lay within range of the Americans' sixteen-inch naval guns, but most were sheltered by harbors or bays.

Kono was speaking again in that brittle voice. "You must study all these silhouettes until you know them perfectly. You will be tested on your knowledge, because while carriers are easy to spot, transports are not. It is easy to confuse them with tankers, supply ships, and even hospital ships. But if we sink the transports, the Yankees cannot put an army ashore."

Kono waited for that information to sink into the teenage minds of his students. Then he turned to the main subject. "Now, what is the best way to sink an aircraft carrier?" He turned to Sakaida and pointed a talon finger.

Sakaida straightened his tunic, feeling oddly uncomfortable. It was one thing to watch the *kamikaze* hatchery at work; another to interact with it. But he was the expert—the only carrier pilot in the unit—and he pinned a scale drawing to the wall.

The carefully inked plan view of a generic aircraft carrier was surprisingly well done. Kono said that one of the trainees—a twenty-one-year-old former art student—had spent several evenings finishing the drawing. Sakaida suspected that the young man had been unable to sleep and preferred to lose himself in his work. Some of the pilots went to bed most evenings deadened by alcohol; some slept fitfully and some apparently not at all. Sakaida suspected that a handful shared their beds with each other: Two or three had "that look" about them—and his flesh crawled at the thought. But he assumed that if any of "those" sank a ship, the Shinto gods would be generous.

"A carrier is a floating ordnance depot with thin skin," he began. "It is stocked with aviation fuel, bombs, and ammunition beneath a wooden flight deck and a hull only about ten millimeters thick. If you penetrate either way with your plane and your bomb, you are almost certain to do great damage.

"This is the procedure I would recommend," he continued. Tracing a finger along the axis of the ship, he said, "It is best to dive from the stern, aiming for the center of the flight deck. That way, if you miss a little one way or another you still can strike a major blow. Assuming you have time, you should drop your bomb from low level and then . . . continue your dive into the deck. In this manner you inflict damage over a wider area."

Sakaida paused to swallow. He was surprised that his strain-induced headache had not returned by now, but he warmed to his subject. In a way, it was fascinating. "I admit that it is unlikely that one *kamikaze* can sink a big ship, but remember: You do not have to sink a carrier to put it out of action. If you start significant fires, the ship itself, its aircraft, and many of the crew will burn up. But every carrier has two or three highly vulnerable spots—these." He tapped the rectangular aircraft elevators outlined in red. "No carrier can operate for long with one or more elevators destroyed. Hit here, and you have denied the enemy the use of that ship."

Kono interrupted, his voice grating in the room. "You need to remember another thing. Do not dive too steeply or too fast. Maximum controllable airspeed is ideal, otherwise you might not be able to correct your aim at the last second. We will test the limits of our aircraft to determine the best angle and airspeed."

There is so much for these boys to remember, Sakaida thought. He was just wondering how much they could absorb, when Imura raised another question. "Honorable lieutenant, some pilots say it is best to close one's eyes at the instant before crashing in order to avoid a flinch that causes us to miss. What is best?"

"I don't know, boy. How much practice do you expect to get in crashing?"

Imura turned his reddening face away, and Sakaida expected a tirade to follow. But Kono surprised him. "Remember that a bee dies by stinging. You must not allow *anything* to deflect you from your aim," he said softly. "There is no way to predict your exact instant of impact, so keep your eyes wide open. Besides," he concluded, "I would not miss that last view for a throne in Hades."

MONDAY, 18 DECEMBER

USS *REPRISAL*

Rogers wanted to be alone, even on the wind-whipped signal platform. In worsening seas, it was one of the few places on the ship that did not smell of spilled food, coffee, or vomit. He did not mind the salt spray dousing his flight jacket and khaki pants as long as he could stand the damned wind.

In the four days since Diskowski's fiery death, the shock had worn off and some of the pain had begun to dull. But the team remained shaken—especially Brian Sossaman, who now regretted some of the unkind things he had said to Kenny over the past ten months. Rogers understood why his pilots leaned on him—for reassurance as much as leadership—but the emotional strain had taken a toll. Now he needed time to himself.

Standing two levels above the flight deck, Rogers grasped the railing and leaned against the ship's roll. He knew he should not be there, but neither would he be interrupted—not while most of the carrier's three thousand men were prone in their bunks or regurgitating the soles of their shoes.

Rogers shifted his weight and cursed the worsening weather. He felt that continued air operations would have helped his pilots recover quicker from Diskowski's senseless loss, as there would be no choice except to concentrate on the job at hand. But yesterday's fleet refueling had been canceled at noon: a difficult cross-swell and rising winds made the task all but impossible. Rogers knew that some of *Reprisal*'s officers were critically second-guessing Admiral Halsey's decision to steam northwest instead of east, away from Luzon and the storm. Don Mancross, who had served under Halsey in 1942, thought the old seadog wanted to remain within striking range of the Philippines, but now that option was gone.

The carrier's bow dug into a deep trough and Rogers lurched dangerously. As he lost his balance, his body was flung hard against the railing. For an instant his pulse peaked as he found himself looking at *Reprisal*'s storm-washed deck. He saw a tie-down chain loosened on a Hellcat secured near the deck edge and realized that the fighter probably would go overboard before long. He turned to undog the hatch behind him, intending to warn the flight deck officer.

Rogers did not know why, but as he opened the watertight door he glanced astern. The two trailing destroyers, one off each quarter, all but disappeared in the mountainous waves. The wind was accelerating drastically, and bow-taut lines on the mast shrieked an eerie dirge in the 90-knot cyclone. Rogers had not heard anything like it since Pensacola, when the stainless-steel flying wires of an N3N had howled in a steep dive.

More saltwater sprayed him, stinging his hands and cheeks. But Rogers was riveted in place, unable to take his eyes from the spectacle of the destroyers. They almost looked as though they were in flying formation, rolling hard over in near-perfect synchrony under the pounding wind and sea. *They're going to capsize,* he thought.

Both *Fletcher*-class destroyers lay almost on their starboard beams, stabilizing at 80 degrees. Rogers watched incredulously through water-blurred eyes as the ships weathered the roll, then slowly righted themselves. He noticed that the one off the port quarter, *M.M. Morrison,* had lost her mast with its radar antenna. The other, *Duke,* was still intact.

But the nautical pendulum continued to swing. Rogers bowed his head against the wind, almost losing his grip on the dog handle, as both rolled far, far to port. They seemed suspended there, two tiny gray shapes in a hostile mountain of gray-green water and pitiless wind beneath a slate sky. The sister ships remained uniformly balanced on a slippery razor's edge, vulnerable to the physical laws of moment and inertia. Rogers knew they both rode high in the water, dangerously low on fuel after two days' of canceled replenishment.

Duke's radar mast made the difference. The moment arm, extended at right angles to what would have been the surface of a calm sea, caught a wave. The air-search radar dish went under, pulling the rest of the mast with it. Rogers watched incredulously as two thousand tons of steel pivoted on its port rail, upended, and was gone. Only spume-flecked spray marked the spot where the ship had been. *Over 250 guys, just like that . . .* His teary eyes shifted to *Morrison,* which was painfully, ponderously righting herself.

His stomach reminded him that it was there. He stumbled inside, dogged the hatch, and slumped to the deck. Sailors scrambled around him in response to *Duke*'s demise, helpless to do anything but mark the spot and optimistically hurl lifebuoys or floater nets into the gale.

Rogers swallowed hard and felt something slide down his throat. He was sweating now, and the clammy perspiration beneath his clothes compounded his misery as he fought to retain his balance. In a sickening burst of realization, it came to him. He had thought that he knew his profession intimately after three years of war, but this was the distilled reality of combat: a churning mixture of nausea tinged with fear, and grief mated to an abiding anger—all completely beyond his power to control.

The ship began a roll to port, and Phil Rogers bit down the sob rising from his heart.

MONDAY, 25 DECEMBER
MOGMOG ISLAND, ULITHI ATOLL

"The things ya see when ya ain't got yer gun."

Lying in the sand beside two empty beer bottles, Rogers knew the voice and lifted the visor of his cap. He saw a pair of brown boondockers, white socks, khaki trousers, and little else. He pointedly lowered his cap over his face again and muttered, "Guess it's true. They really will let anybody on this island."

Jim Carpenter dropped a canvas bag and descended into a rifleman's sitting position, elbows braced on his knees. "I've been all over this sand heap. You avoiding me, buddy?"

Rogers sat up and punched his friend's shoulder. "Hell, Jim, I didn't even know you had left Hawaii. How'd you find me?"

"Ran into Burnett at the coconut-palm bar. We got here a couple days ago. We're in the *Sharpsburg* so I guess you and I'll be in the same task group. Just like old times." He smiled but did not relate Bernie's concern:

the strain of losing Diskowski, coupled with Halsey's questionable wisdom, had made Rogers visibly edgy, even distant. Loosen him up, get him drunk if you can, Burnett had said. Good advice.

Rogers took a long look at his flight-school classmate. It was hard to tell behind the sunglasses, but the impression was one of ill-disguised fatigue. *Like me,* he thought. "Jim, how the hell are you?"

"Well, Red White gave me a choice: Become his exec or take a staff job with FMFPac." He shrugged. "I went where I was needed the most."

Rogers sensed his friend's meaning. "It was news to me that Marines were going to carriers. Are you jarheads up to speed on carrier procedures?"

"We're really not, Phil. We've only averaged a dozen or so landings between here and San Diego. *Saratoga, Makassar Strait, Bataan*—all different types of ships without much consistency. We're supposed to get more landings before we leave, though." He looked out to the lagoon. "Things must be pretty damn rough to dump a couple of Marine squadrons into this situation."

Rogers folded his arms and leaned forward. "All I know is what I hear—more scuttlebutt than hard fact. But evidently the Japs began suicide tactics a couple months ago in the Philippines and that's why you're here. Say, it must be awful crowded in the *Sharpsburg*. Where are they putting all of you?"

Carpenter chuckled aloud. "They bounced the SB-Deuces off the ship to make room for us. I guess the bomber skipper was mad as hell, but there's nothing he could do about it. Besides, we can do a good job dive-bombing if we have to, and of course the TBMs can haul bombs or torpedoes."

No point avoiding it, Carpenter told himself. He said, "Burnett told me about the storm . . . and your wingman. I'm sure sorry, Buck. Any idea what happened?"

Rogers nudged a toe into the sand. "Our skipper investigated and found there'd been an accident on the hangar deck after the dawn launch. Some of the ordnancemen were distracted, and apparently Kenny's fuse wasn't fully safety-wired. But that doesn't excuse things. The ordnance chief and the plane captain both should have caught it."

"Well, I don't suppose it'll happen again."

"No. Guess not."

Carpenter turned away and brought up a canvas bag that clanked. "Hey, I brought you a Christmas present." He handed the bag to Rogers, who was surprised at its heft. Phil could also tell the contents were cold. He reached in and was astonished to feel ice cubes—real, honest-to-god ice cubes. There were also three bottles of cool beer.

The Marine laughed at his friend's expression. "Holy—" Rogers began. "Where'd you get ice on this frigging island?"

"I got influence. Besides, Marines are expected to show initiative."

"Go on, Carpenter. That means you stole it."

The Sunny Jim smile was back. "What do you care?"

"Not one damn bit." Carpenter produced a bottle opener and popped both caps off the Millers. The two aviators clanked the glass containers before tugging at the cool, delicious brew. "Merry Christmas, Jim."

"Merry Christmas, Buck."

P A R T   I I I

"The one thing that bothers me fifty years later is when people say that all those young guys 'gave their lives,' like my best friend Roger Boles. He didn't 'give' his life—it was torn from him at an early age. I never will forget that."

Lt. Cdr. Elvin L. Lindsay, USNR
Fighting Squadron 19, 1943–45

January 1945

Rogers could tell as he walked down the passageway that something had happened on the CAP off Formosa. High-pitched, rapid voices from the ready room were audible in the passageway. As he entered the low-ceilinged compartment hung with recognition models, charts, and flight gear, Rogers saw that Ron Harkin's face was crimson, his voice shrill.

Ensign Bill Barnes turned away from the crowd and saw Rogers in the entrance. For an instant the ex-aircrewman's gaze diverted to the deck. Then, seemingly laden with more than his Mae West and parachute harness, he trudged toward Rogers.

Rogers anticipated a squabble over victory credits after the reported aerial combat. He knew that Harkin did not want to split another kill with anyone. "What is it, Bill?"

Barnes pointed toward the entrance. "Let's talk outside." In the passageway, he spoke in low, forceful tones. "Harkin's division was vectored onto a couple of snoopers that were pretty cagey—Bettys or Frans, I guess—and apparently they split up. So my section was called in to help cut off one of the Japs. But Harkin went able-sugar, if you ask me. He was hollering on the radio, yelling for his wingman to break off so he could get a shot. It was confusing because we couldn't see the Japs or any of Harkin's people in the clouds."

Barnes swallowed hard and wiped his mouth on a sleeve. "I'd just got a new vector when I saw a parachute maybe two thousand feet off the water. An F6 pulled up past it, then did a wingover and made a pass. It was Harkin: He was in Crystal 21."

Rogers leaned forward, incredulous. "Are you hinting that—"

"Shit, no, I'm not *hinting*," Barnes spat out. "I'm *telling* you, Phil. Harkin gunned a parachute, and I think it was Gambini. He's missing."

Rogers tried to compose a response when Ralph Platco strode down the passageway. Barnes turned toward him. "Captain, I think—"

"Yes, I know, Barnes." Platco struck Rogers as eerily calm. "I was just in the radio shack. The *Andersen* picked up Gambini. He's badly wounded but he's alive . . ."

"What're you gonna do about it?" Barnes's voice carried an acid tone that Rogers had never heard.

Instantly Platco was all-Annapolis. "I am going to conduct an investigation as per regulations, Mr. Barnes. Starting as soon as you come to attention and address your commanding officer in accordance with those regulations." Rogers wanted to melt into the bulkhead. He risked a look at Platco and saw corded veins standing out in the CO's neck.

"Yes, *sir!*" Barnes shouted defiantly. He brought his heels together, braced himself and stared over Platco's shoulder.

Rogers sought to break the tension. "Sir, we're running back-to-back strikes and CAPs. We need to know if Mr. Harkin will continue on the flight schedule—"

Platco spun on his heels, turning to face Rogers. But this time the CO's voice was modulated. "As I said, there will be an investigation. I will not ruin an officer's career based on mere allegations." Then, shoulders slumped under an unseen burden, Ralph Platco stepped into the ready room.

"Career," Barnes sneered. "How does he suppose Paul Gambini feels about some ring-knocker's goddamn career?"

Rogers inhaled, then sighed aloud. "Don't worry, Bill. This is too serious to overlook. If Platco doesn't take action, there's still the CAG and the old man. You know Captain McEwen takes care of his people."

Barnes thought for a moment. "Well, I sure as hell hope so, because I'm telling you: I won't fly with that son of a bitch anymore. They can ground me, they can frigging court-martial me, but if I ever fly with Harkin again, he won't come back!"

Rogers watched his ex-gunner storm down the passageway, fists tight in frustrated rage.

THURSDAY, 4 JANUARY
TSUIKI BASE

Hiroyoshi Sakaida had never given much thought to aerodynamics as they applied to suicide. But after listening to one of Lieutenant Kono's lectures, he concluded that the Shinkai Unit must be one of the best-trained in the Third Special Attack Corps—probably in the entire command.

Sitting in the poorly heated classroom, it was almost possible to ignore the winter gale rattling the windows as wind swept off the bay on Kyushu's northeast coast. Sometimes it almost seemed as if Kono's ardor provided all the heat necessary.

"In a high-speed dive, even at the steepest angle, you still have lift on your wings," Kono explained with a typical aviator's gesture. "Remember your basic flying course?" he asked rhetorically. In truth, he and Sakaida doubted that flight instruction devoted much time to aerodynamics anymore. "You recall that in a ninety-degree dive your machine still has some forward motion. In order to achieve zero lift, you would have to push the stick forward so that your nose was actually past the vertical." He pointed one hand at the floor, then tilted the fingers slightly to illustrate his point.

Kono's obsidian eyes returned to his students. "But you do not want zero lift, do you?" he asked. Several close-cropped heads shook in the negative. "Tachibana, why not?"

Flight Superior Seaman Yoshio Tachibana had been one of those shaking his head. Now he earnestly wished he had kept still. "Ah, honorable division officer . . . I believe . . ."

"Yes, what do you believe?" Kono rasped. His ruined voice grated harder than usual when he was aroused. He waited two seconds. "You believe nothing, obviously." He sought another victim. "Seno!"

"Sir! At zero lift the wings . . . I mean, the controls, would not respond?" Seno instantly realized he had erred in replying with a question.

Oddly, Kono seemed satisfied. "Close enough, boy. At zero lift your aircraft is at maximum possible speed—what the engineers call terminal velocity. It cannot go any faster. That means difficulty in regaining control, so that your aim may be spoiled."

Sakaida, intrigued by the direction the conversation was taking, leaned forward. He ignored the not-distant moan of a coastal train whistle to concentrate on Kono's words.

"You want a medium-angle dive at maximum *controllable* airspeed," Kono repeated for perhaps the twelfth time. "But even then, at perhaps three hundred knots, you will experience tail heaviness as your nose wants to rise. Therefore, you must pay attention to your trim tabs. Set your elevator trim so that you can most easily work the stick for up-and-down motion: the pitch axis. Otherwise you may not be able to push your nose steeply downward to remain on target. Understood?"

Sakaida leaned back in appreciation of his friend's thoroughness. *Yes, it is quite simple,* he told himself. *You must not have to work too hard when it comes to body-crashing.*

SATURDAY, 6 JANUARY

USS *REPRISAL*

The wardroom was crowded to near-capacity with the hundred or so officers of VF-59. Most of the conversation centered on Ron Harkin's speedy departure following the intercept off Formosa. But Ralph Platco was only slightly less upset about losing a fighter to a Japanese bomber than having his former exec shoot a wingman's parachute. Some of the junior pilots concluded that Ensign Gambini was better off minus a leg than intact aboard *Reprisal.*

Rogers and Burnett sat up front, knowing the actual purpose of the meeting. Privately, Rogers was pleased with the turn of events. Not only was Harkin gone, but Barnes now had replaced Diskowski in Rogers's team. "You seem to have some influence with him," Platco had said after the scene in the passageway. "So teach him some respect."

Pat Clarey, the CAG and now a full commander, stood nearby in a last-minute conference with Platco, then called for attention. The buzz of conversation dropped into silence.

"Gentlemen," Clarey began. "AirPac has authorized air groups like ours to divide the fighters into two squadrons. The reason must be obvious to all of you: With seventy-three aircraft and over a hundred officers, the administrative load has become excessive.

"This decision is discretionary," Clarey explained. "Apparently, most of those air groups nearing the end of their tours have decided to remain with one F6F squadron. But because we have about five months to go, Mr. Platco and I think that the workload will be more evenly divided if we form a fighting-bombing squadron. We've discussed it with Captain McEwen, and he concurs." He nodded to Platco, who stepped forward.

Rogers thought that the CO appeared more relaxed than he had in seventy-two hours. *Well, Ralph's got rid of his main headache, and he has more to gain if he can split some of the paperwork,* Rogers reasoned. A tiny smile played around Platco's mouth as he began. "As you men know, we've been top-heavy with senior lieutenants for quite a while. Therefore, I'm pleased to announce that two former *bomber* pilots in this room"—Platco was interrupted by boos and hisses, then continued—"will buy the beer for all hands at the next wetting-down ceremony!"

At Clarey's urging, Rogers and Burnett stood and waved to the cheering pilots. Bernie clasped his hands over his head in the prizefighter's gesture of triumph before sitting again.

"Mr. Burnett is next-senior," Platco was explaining, "so he becomes the commanding officer of VBF-59. Mr. Rogers will be his exec." The skipper searched the crowd and found the plain, broad face he sought. "Mr. Mancross will fleet up to be my exec—at least until we see the next AlNav." Laughter tittered through the room; whatever the forthcoming promotion list said, Mancross was a popular choice and a logical one.

Burnett leaned close to whisper into Rogers's ear. "Damn glad to see that—I thought Clarey might insist on somebody more senior from another squadron."

Rogers glanced at the CO and CAG. "I don't think there was any question, Bernie. They sure don't want another Harkin in the job. Besides, Don's the best fighter pilot on this ship."

Burnett took on a pained expression. "You kidding me? Here I thought *I* was the best pilot on this ship. . . ."

Platco was calling for attention again. "I know that this reorganization will cause some questions, so let me hit the high spots. First, division organization. We'll pretty much split it down the middle. Teams One through Ten will remain with me, plus the night fighters of Team Zero. The other teams will go with Burnett, though we'll have to renumber some of them to fit the new organizational chart.

"Maintenance. We won't change anything there because both squadrons will fly the same aircraft without regard to side number. As far as mission assignments, if a special job arises for bombing, we may designate the VBFs for that purpose while the fighters provide escort. After all, we have two SBD hotshots leading that outfit." At this mention there were some groans from the higher-numbered teams whose pilots craved aerial combat.

Clarey had one last comment. "Gentlemen, you may have a chance to try your bombing against Japanese warships before long. This force is headed for the South China Sea in less than a week! Admiral Halsey believes that some battleships are holed up along the Indochina coast, where no Allied vessel has sailed since early 1942." He glanced from front to back, gauging the mood of his F6F pilots. "I think you can expect good hunting!"

As the meeting broke up, several aviators crowded around the new lieutenant commanders to offer congratulations. Finally Rogers looked at his friend and asked a fearful question. "Well, Bernie, how does it feel to be responsible for about fifty pilots and twenty enlisted?"

Burnett's reply came in a low, solemn voice. "It scares me shitless, old buddy."

SATURDAY, 13 JANUARY
USS *REPRISAL*

Rogers was scribbling at some unfinished paperwork in the crowded squadron spaces when Burnett sat down beside him. A subtle nod from the CO, and the yeoman disappeared into the passageway.

"Got some more bad news for you, Buck." Burnett knew that the direct route was best. "Seems I'm the one that always tells you these things." He locked eyes with his friend, willing himself not to glance away.

Rogers straightened in his metal chair. "Who is it, Bernie?"

"We just got a message from the *Sharpsburg.* Jim Carpenter was shot down at Tan Son Nhut yesterday afternoon." As the words sank in, Burnett added, "He's missing, Phil."

Rogers grasped the steel desk as the ship rolled slightly. "What do they know?"

Burnett raised the message sheet. "Word came from Carpenter's wingman. He saw him crash-land in a rice paddy and circled overhead but Jim didn't get out before his wingman, Lieutenant Keaton, had to leave. He might have been stunned from the crash, but at least the plane didn't burn."

"Was Jim wounded?"

"I guess not. Keaton says he radioed just before landing. Said to watch him set down . . . and to tell Rogers on Crystal Base."

Rogers clasped his hands behind his head and pressed his forearms against his face. Again he catalogued his flight-school classmates lost so far: the quiet Wayne Wik at Midway; fun-loving Bucky Peterson off Marcus Island in '43; combative Sean Mutagh in a midair at Jacksonville, and Hank Rodriguez, dead last year of pneumonia, of all things. Undoubtedly there were others. When he came up for air, his voice was hollow. "Thanks, Bernie. I guess we can only wait and hope for the best."

Burnett's hand rested on his friend's shoulder. "He could be with the French by now. That's a lot better than the Japs."

Rogers merely nodded, so Burnett changed the subject. Fingering Rogers's flight jacket, he said, "You know, I've been meaning to mention your old Bombing Three patch. Seems we ought to have a squadron emblem of our own. Any ideas?"

Phil glanced at the leaping panther on the dirty-white background. Burnett and Rogers both had left Bombing 3 in late 1942, but even through two other squadron tours, Phil had kept the patch: He disliked VC-54's cartoon emblem, and VF-59 still had not adopted one after Gordon Connell's death.

"Hell," Rogers said at last, "we don't even have a squadron nickname, do we?"

Burnett produced a scrap of paper from his pocket. "I've been collecting ideas. So far the suggestions lean toward something like Burnett's Blasters or a variation of Sunsetters, like Sunrisers or Sunbathers."

Rogers grimaced. "Sunbathers? What's that got to do with anything?"

"It's your boy Fairfield's idea," Burnett deadpanned. "He suggests a gorgeous broad, bare-ass naked on a beach blanket with a sunset in the background." He paused for a moment. "Actually, I'm giving it serious consideration."

Rogers tried hard not to smile, and failed. "You're the boss, *sir.* But I think I'll stick with my good old black panther."

TUESDAY, 16 JANUARY
CRYSTAL TWELVE-ONE

The radio channels were useless as a spastic babble erupted in response to the flak—Hong Kong's awesome, appalling flak. Air Group 59's carefully cultivated radio discipline had been shredded in the first fifteen seconds over the target.

Rogers thought that he had seen anti-aircraft fire in two and a half years. But not even yesterday's strikes elsewhere along the China coast prepared him for *this*. From fourteen thousand feet he could look down on almost any part of Kowloon's three square miles and see muzzle flashes, especially from the hills dominating the harbor.

Still, Pat Clarey was doing a decent job of holding things together. The leader of Strike Able had managed to designate targets before the anti-aircraft guns erupted in their full volcanic fury, and Leo Hunziker's SB2Cs were slanting into their dives against the big transports moored at the docks. Rogers sneaked a glance northeastward, where Kai Tak Airport jutted into the harbor. No enemy fighters had been seen thus far, and looking back at the flak-torn sky, Rogers conceded, *Can't blame 'em.*

Team 12—such was his division's identity now—had drawn flak suppression. Two five hundred–pounders slung under each Hellcat were intended to destroy or at least dissuade Japanese anti-aircraft gunners, but Rogers knew it was an impossible task. There were simply too many guns.

So he led Barnes down on a battery at the east end of the docks while Fairfield and Sossaman found a target of their own.

Looking through the reflector sight, Rogers was momentarily intrigued. The blackish-brown eruptions of pattern barrage fire did not bother him much, but the variety of tracers crisscrossing his vision was eerily enchanting. His F6F was jostled by a near-miss, but the big Grumman steadied up and he double-checked the ball in his sight. He nudged right rudder, centered the ball, and set the pipper on the center of a 25-millimeter position. Then he punched the red button and salvoed both bombs.

Intuitively, Rogers knew he had made a good drop. *They're done for.* He began a steady pull, bottoming out at 2,800 feet. As the Hellcat's blunt nose came up through the hills on the horizon, he glanced back and noted roiling smoke from the AA site. Then more scything tracers crossed his path and he bent the throttle, jinking erratically.

The strike frequency was becoming marginally useful as most of the attackers had pulled off-target. Rogers heard something about a TBM down in the bay but ignored it. *Can't do anything for them now.* He was moving constantly in the roomy cockpit, anxiously looking for his second section.

Barnes pulled abreast of him and rocked wings, indicating all was well. Then Rogers saw the other two Hellcats en route to the rendezvous and felt much better. *We got away with it!*

Most of the *Reprisal* aircraft passed Team 12, winging toward the rendezvous twenty miles offshore. By sections and divisions, they sorted themselves out and set course for the task force, though some *Sharpsburg* and *Crown Point* planes were mixed in. Rogers saw a Helldiver trailing smoke and knew the Beast probably would not make it, but cruiser floatplanes could pick up the crew if necessary.

"Any Crystal chick from Crystal Eleven-One. I'm kinda lonesome back here. Just clearing Tung Lung Island—shot up with a rough engine. Over."

Rogers's pulse spiked. *Bernie!* Then he heard Carl Sacco's voice, audibly concerned. "Crystal Eleven-One from Eleven-Two. I read you, Skipper. I'm orbiting at the rendezvous point, over."

Almost without realizing it, Rogers's thumb was on the mike button. "Belay that, Carl. This is Phil." *To hell with call signs.* "I'm closer; Bill and I'll meet Bernie. Everybody copy?"

He got a terse acknowledgment from Sacco and a breezy "Bless you, my son" from Burnett. Four minutes later the midwing silhouette of a Hellcat became visible in the morning sky. Rogers called, "I see an F6 dead ahead of me at 4,800 feet. No belly tank. That you, Bernie?"

"Ah, yeah. Thanks, Buck. I had to drop my tank when it caught fire."

Reversing course and allowing Burnett to pass beneath him, Rogers could see the condition of Eleven-One. There were visible 20-millimeter holes in the wings, and the Pratt & Whitney trailed a slowly worsening smoke plume. Rogers signaled Barnes to keep a lookout, especially above and behind, while sliding up on Burnett's wing.

Burnett slid back his canopy and leaned out. Flying slowly, making only about 140 knots, he wiped some oil off his windscreen. Then he patted the top of his head, pointing at Rogers: *You have the lead.* Rogers saluted in acknowledgment, grinning in anticipation. For the last two and a half years, Bernie had continually reminded him of the last day of the Midway battle, when Ensign Burnett led a wounded Ensign Rogers back to *Enterprise.* Now the kidding would come from the other direction.

The return flight was tedious but uneventful. Rogers discerned that Burnett's fighter cruised better at low power settings, so they remained at five thousand feet. Their low approach altitude largely negated the YE-ZB homing beacon, but Rogers was confident of his navigation. When the dots appeared on the horizon, he signaled Burnett and pointed ahead.

Burnett nodded and began his landing checklist; there might not be time as they neared the carriers. Then a gout of red-tinted smoke erupted from Burnett's exhaust. Rogers saw the cowling quiver under internal strain and suspected the R-2800 was about to throw a cylinder.

Burnett nosed down and chopped his throttle. There was no time for the daily recognition turns over the destroyer screen, only time for one terse call. "I'll have to ditch, Buck. Tell the smallboys to watch for me."

As the dying Hellcat established a favorable glide angle, Rogers looked at the ocean. He judged a Force 2 breeze from the southeast and watched Burnett turn into the wind. One of the screening destroyers was two miles away, almost straight ahead. *Good,* Rogers thought. *They'll be right there to pick him up.*

Rogers reached for his mike and called for Barnes to join up so they could perform the right-hand turns that indicated they were friendly. Then he switched channels to notify the task force fighter director, when the destroyer opened fire with radar-directed main batteries. The first salvo burst just ahead of Burnett. Rogers, two thousand feet above and behind, mashed the button. "Check fire, check fire! This is Crystal! Planes over the screen are friendly!"

The second salvo was the last. One of those four rounds—a proximity-fuzed 5.38-inch shell—detonated five feet from the crippled Grumman and severed Burnett's starboard wing. The destroyed Hellcat plunged into the water, bobbled slightly, and vanished.

THURSDAY, 18 JANUARY
USS *REPRISAL*

Rogers knocked on the door of the air group commander's office, and Pat Clarey looked up. "You wanted to see me, sir." The new VBF-59 skipper's voice was barely audible as the port catapult slammed an F6F off the deck. Operations would proceed, Rogers knew, regardless of losses.

"Sit down, Phil." Clarey moved aside to make room; he was being more solicitous than ever before. Rogers took a chair and leaned back, awaiting whatever was coming.

"I have a couple of things to discuss with you," Clarey began. "First, about Bernie. We got a reply to Captain McEwen's message, demanding to know what happened. The *Andersen* had a new gunnery officer who evidently wasn't up to speed with operating procedures. He knew there were three planes inbound, but only two had IFF. Without waiting, he concluded the one without radar identification was hostile and opened fire." Clarey flipped a paper. "According to this report, he thought you and Barnes were chasing a Jap."

Rogers's jaw tightened. "Godammit! If Bernie's IFF was out, it was because of battle damage. But Barnes made the recognition turns: starboard on even-numbered days. That tin can had no right to open fire without challenging us!"

Clarey nodded slowly. "That's right. And I suspect both the gunnery officer and the captain of that ship are due for reassignment at an unpleasant locale. Admiral Griggs runs a tight ship, you know."

Rogers made no comment. He knew that Rear Admiral Jacob Griggs, riding *Reprisal* as task group commander, would hold the guilty accountable. Even his call sign, Courthouse, indicated as much. *Fat lot of good it does Bernie, though,* Rogers thought.

The CAG leaned closer to Rogers. "Look, Phil, I know what Bernie meant to you. After all, he was my exec at one time. But you've got to snap out of it. Remember, we're hitting Formosa again in two days."

Rogers's eyes narrowed. "Snap out of what, Commander?"

"Come on, don't 'Commander' me. And don't play innocent. You've been brooding about Burnett and that's understandable, but you have fifty other pilots to look out for." Clarey's voice turned cool. "If you can't do that, I'll find someone who will."

The bastard means it, too, Rogers admitted. He locked eyes with Clarey. "Yes, sir. Message understood. I've just . . ." His voice trailed off and he feared he might blubber before the air group commander.

"All right, enough said. You'll remain as squadron CO, and I'm sure you can handle it."

Rogers almost smiled now. He and Clarey knew that every junior officer in the U.S. Navy was convinced that they could do at least as good a job as their skippers.

"But I want your recommendation for your new exec when we return to Ulithi. Brown's your flight officer, but does he have the ability and experience to be your permanent exec?"

Rogers shook his head. "Buster's a good man. He has the potential but not the experience. Not yet, anyway; he's a relatively junior lieutenant."

"Okay, then. I'll put in for an officer with a solid carrier background. Meanwhile, you run things as you see fit. Any questions, you know where to find me."

Phil rose as the catapult fired again. "Commander . . ."

Clarey looked up. "Yes?"

"You have nothing to worry about."

FRIDAY, 19 JANUARY
YOKOSUKA BASE, HONSHU, JAPAN

Sakaida climbed out of the aged Zero's cockpit and stood for a moment on the wing. Glancing around, he judged the Shinkai Unit fortunate in its new base—generally newer and certainly better maintained than the ramshackle facilities at Tsuiki.

Kono already was out of his fighter, talking to one of the base operations staff. For an instant Sakaida imagined that he could relate the conversation word for word. Lieutenant Kono, with his destroyed face, brittle voice and manner of a fleet admiral, certainly could intimidate ordinary mortals into almost anything. Sakaida felt that, if nothing else, Kono would demand the best possible billets for the future sky gods of the Shinkai Unit.

Inhaling the brisk winter air, Sakaida held his breath for a moment, then exhaled. Now that the unit had arrived at its operating base, the day was near when all the training would be put to use. Most of the pilots seemed to assume that they would be sent to a distant battle front: to destroy Yankee ships in Philippine or Formosan waters. But Kono had stated privately that he felt the American Navy soon must come to the very shores of Japan itself.

Whatever the location, Sakaida told himself, *it will be soon. And then Yusuke must die.*

MONDAY, 22 JANUARY
USS *REPRISAL*

Rogers had been trying to finish his letter for almost a week. He had started it twice but never got through the first page. Now, he risked giving the wrong impression—self-pity and a craving for revenge—and merely told his parents that he had lost his two best friends within four days of each other.

The weekend's Formosa strikes had been a qualified success: over one hundred enemy planes were thought to have been destroyed on the ground and ten tankers or cargo ships sunk. But during that Saturday noon hour the Japanese had come back in force. The reports trickled in by day's end: *Langley* hit by a bomb, *Ticonderoga* took two *kamikazes* that killed a reported 140, and a destroyer on radar picket duty also had been hit. As if that weren't bad enough, one of *Hancock*'s TBMs had accidentally dropped a bomb on the flight deck. Vice Admiral McCain, CTF-38, had been forced to return early to Ulithi in his stricken flagship.

Rogers set down his pen. He certainly could not write what he knew about Task Force 38 casualties, but that was beside the point, anyway. Instead, he tried to communicate the numbing sense of weariness growing inside him. First Kenny, last week Jim, then Bernie: the friends of his youth, dropping out of his life one at a time. And so often it was unnecessary, like Bernie's death and the fifty-odd men dead in *Hancock* from another horrible mistake unrelated to enemy action.

Rogers got up from his small writing table and paced the confines of the room he had shared with Burnett. Fuel oil whooshed through an overhead pipe, and Rogers listened to the sounds of the ship as 27,000 tons nosed through the Pacific swell. It occurred to him that this was all he knew anymore: living in cramped, sweltering carriers and waiting for the next stroke of bitter fate. He only felt reasonably at ease with himself when airborne. *No, that's not exactly right,* he told himself. *Maybe I'll feel better when we get to kill some Zeros.*

February 1945

The teleprinter in Ready Room 2 clattered a message across the screen and three dozen pilots of VBF-59 erupted into a bedlam of cheering. As if to convince any unbelievers, the printer added a confirming sentence: THIS TASK FORCE IS BOUND FOR TOKYO. STRIKES AGAINST JAPAN IN SIX DAYS.

Rogers almost smiled as he waved down the celebrants. While the aviators took their seats or crowded around the too-few chairs, the skipper allowed himself a moment's reflection. *Doggone, if only Bernie and Kenny had lived to see this.*

Rogers motioned to his new executive officer, Lieutenant Commander Hunter Diefendorf. The squadron still had not fully absorbed its replacements, but Rogers and most of the others quickly recognized the XO's worth. He spoke little, listened carefully, and flew an exemplary carrier pattern.

As the last excited chatter died away, Rogers began to speak. "Most of you have met Mr. Diefendorf, who's taken over Team Twelve now that my division is Team Eleven. He's been at this war longer than any of us, and I want you to hear a few things from a former Flying Tiger."

Diefendorf smiled shyly. He had not said much about his experiences with the American Volunteer Group, and the younger pilots especially badgered him for war stories. Rogers judged this to be a good opportunity to get past all that.

"Well, most people don't know it," Diefendorf began, "but the AVG was about sixty percent Navy and Marine pilots: Bob Neale, Tex Hill, Ken Jernstedt, Chuck Older. Lots of guys. Some of us were like Joe Rosbert and me—do damn near anything besides riding as third pilot on a PBY." Several ensigns hooted appreciatively but the exec pressed on. "When we arrived in Burma in '41, a lot of us had never seen a P-40, but Colonel Chennault said that didn't matter. What did matter was tactics and gunnery. We concentrated on that, and, well . . ." He shrugged. "You know the rest."

Most of the aviators thought they did know the rest: The Tigers received fabulous publicity at a time when Allied fortunes faced a low ebb. Besides combat success there was the allure of high adventure in exotic lands and the bonus of five hundred dollars for every Japanese plane destroyed.

"I've been asked why I didn't stay with the old man in China," Diefendorf continued. "Well, there's two reasons. First, when the AVG broke up in July '42, General Bissell told us that if we didn't volunteer for the Army we'd have to find our own way home, and he'd make sure our draft boards knew about us. That went over like a lead balloon.

"But mostly, after fighting the Japs for more than six months, I wanted to see this through. Wanted to finish the war by flying over Tokyo. I knew I couldn't do that in the Army Air Forces, so I came back to the Navy. Took me another two years to get back to the fleet, but here I am." He glanced around the room, obviously uneasy as an orator but the earnest focus of attention. "I'm no good at pep talks. Just wanted to say I'm really looking forward to flying with you fellows." As an afterthought he added, "The Japs are still tough but they can be beat. By the time we're done, they'll know we were there."

The response was more than polite applause. Rogers noticed that Burnett's division—especially Bernie's former wingman, Carl Sacco—clapped the hardest and whistled the loudest. *They're ready to take it out on the Japs,* Phil realized. *Good.*

"Thanks, Hunter." As Diefendorf sat down, Rogers added a word of explanation. "In case you fellows don't know it, Hunter's family are second-generation German Texas immigrants. He told me his mother's maiden name was Jaeger, and that's how he got the English name for it. That's appropriate, because I'm told we can expect excellent hunting. There are at least seven major military airfields in the Tokyo-Yokohama area, so it's open season—and there's no bag limit!"

More applause and foot stomping registered VBF-59's approval.

Rogers allowed that the braggadocio he expressed but did not feel was a legitimate leadership technique. *Most of these guys are eager, but a lot of them are scared,* he told himself. *Anything that boosts their confidence is worthwhile.*

"All right, here's the way things shape up. Admiral Spruance has returned as ComFifth Fleet, and Mitscher's running the carriers, so we're Task Force Fifty-eight this time. Our new call sign is Dagger Base; the op order shows the other changes. Briefly, the *Sharpsburg* is Granite, *Crown Point* is Lemon, and *Alliance* is Tartan. Altogether, the task force has sixteen carriers and a hundred escorts." Rogers paused for the exclamations he knew would follow. This would be the largest carrier force yet assembled, butting heads with the greatest concentration of land-based airpower in the Pacific.

"Most of the air groups are brand-new," Rogers continued. "Even newer than us. So remember that we're the lucky ones—we've got more experience than about three quarters of the groups going to Tokyo their first time out. I've talked to Commanders Clarey and Platco, and they promise that us fighter-bombers will get our fair share of chances at Japanese airplanes." Glancing at his own team, Rogers saw Eddie Fairfield grin and nudge Bill Barnes. Brian Sossaman and Van Sley traded concerned glances, and Rogers knew the meaning. *They both wonder if they'll be on the first fighter sweep. One of them has to stay behind.* Phil resolved not to worry about it. *After all,* he decided, *nobody said war is fair.*

THURSDAY, 15 FEBRUARY
YOKOSUKA BASE, TOKYO BAY

Kono was waiting on the flight line when the last members of Sakaida's *chutai* taxied into the parking area. Four of the enlisted pilots already were out of their fighters as the division officer approached, obviously on some urgency. Administration and tactics development increasingly kept Kono out of the cockpit—a situation that only made him more irritable.

Saluting in the crisp air, Sakaida bowed to his friend and superior. Kono snapped a return salute at the group but ignored the others. He motioned to Sakaida. "Walk with me."

Looking sideways, Sakaida noticed that Kono's scarred face had reddened even more in the blustery wind. The antiseptic scent was no longer detectable, and briefly Sakaida wondered if Kono had stopped using it. *The man lives in constant pain,* he reasoned. *So why should he care if others notice?*

After several paces, Kono asked, "How is battle practice progressing?"

The question caught Sakaida off guard. Previously, Kono had paid little attention to anything but the Shinkai Unit's primary mission: body-crashing. Sakaida had taken the commander's seeming indifference as a compliment—a mark of confidence in his escort leader. "Reasonably well, sir," Sakaida responded cautiously. "With a little more experience I believe that we can protect the special attack section properly."

Kono was pacing briskly again, looking at the concrete in front of him. "I have not had time to fly with you because of my primary obligation. But now that the *kamikazes* are through their training curriculum, I wish to measure your pilots' progress." He turned to Sakaida. "You will schedule me for an air combat training flight with one of your *shotai* tomorrow morning."

Sakaida nodded decisively. "*Hai!* It will be a pleasure, honorable division officer!"

Kono kept walking. "No it will not, Sakaida. I am going to twist your tails and see what you are made of."

The mutilated officer strode away before Sakaida could reply—besides, he could think of nothing to say.

FRIDAY, 16 FEBRUARY
DAGGER ELEVEN-ONE, 1130

Rogers knew that he would never forget his first view of Japan. Despite the marginal weather and bitter cold, despite the certainty of a hard time getting back aboard the ship, he was elated to see this sight—the enemy homeland. He wondered if his voyage across thirty-eight months and 5,400 nautical miles had been worth the wait. *Can't be too many pilots out here today who were at both Midway and Guadalcanal.*

Searching for landmarks, Rogers knew that Mount Fuji was hidden in the murk some sixty miles to the southwest. He had tracked the bombers' navigation since crossing the Chiba Peninsula, barely twenty minutes from the task force. Ahead lay Tokyo Bay, partially obscured by clouds, with the target on the near shore. Rogers glanced at his chart again and noted Kisarazu Airfield with its distinctive T-shaped runway pattern. Barry Potter would lead his TBMs and the SB2Cs southwesterly, following the Kisarazu–Chiba railway line into the target. Rogers approved of the plan: Attack from the north and continue southward over Uraga Strait, allowing minimal time over the target and a clear shot to the sea for any damaged aircraft.

Rogers glanced upward, noting Mancross's top-cover Hellcats just below the twelve thousand–foot overcast. The carrier planes sported white bands on their cowlings—extra recognition aids for this occasion—and

Rogers appreciated the effect, even in the gloom. Leading his own team on portside intermediate cover, Rogers was well positioned to bounce any interceptors that arose. He squirmed on his seat-pack parachute. *They've got to come. Platco said they were up in swarms for the first strike.* Rogers looked at his eight-day clock again. That was only two hours ago.

Then Don Mancross was calling on strike frequency. "Dagger chicks from Two-One. Bogeys, ten o'clock low."

SHINKAI THIRTEEN, 1132

Had he not needed both hands on the controls, Sakaida would have pounded a fist in frustration. Climbing southeasterly, he eased his *shotai* away from Kono's four Zero 52s, opening into battle formation. He quickly checked his instruments, then began searching for the Americans.

The entire morning had been a miserable cockup. Somehow the Yankees' dawn fighter sweep had gotten almost to the Honshu coast without being spotted, and they had quickly driven the defenders' fighters from the cloudy gray sky. Sakaida had been appalled to see dark-blue fighters streaking through the traffic pattern without so much as a flak burst to oppose them. Since then, he and Kono had tried without much success to obtain accurate information. So they did the next best thing. At first indication of more attacks, they had taken off and climbed at maximum speed over the bay.

Kono rocked his wings to attract attention, and Sakaida looked left, to the north. He barely made out Kono gesturing ahead, and tried to focus against the cloudy infinity. Finally he saw them. *Army fighters joining us. Good. We will need all the help we can get.*

Sakaida turned his attention back over his nose. Looking past his reflector gunsight, he once again saw his worst nightmare. The ordered black dots of Truk, the Marianas, and Leyte Gulf. Nothing else on earth resembled the professionalism of an American carrier air group. Sakaida tripped his machine-gun triggers to warn his friends and check his weapons.

Truk! The thought came to him from deep inside his subconscious. *The massacre at Truk—one year ago tomorrow.*

He turned his flight to intercept as the square-winged Grummans descended on him.

DAGGER ELEVEN-ONE, 1133

Rogers saw them now. From his perch four thousand feet above the bombers, he glimpsed a ragged formation of specks just crossing inland, southwest of the target. Knowing that the close cover would remain with the Avengers and Helldivers, he pulled his amber lenses over his eyes, glanced left and right, and shoved everything forward with his left hand.

In the final seconds before he opened fire, Rogers sorted his options. He was surprised—astonished, in fact—at how calm he felt. *Plenty of time to shoot, no time to miss.* He decided to press a high-side run on the second echelon of bandits, then pull up and roll in from the opposite quarter. *If we do it just right, we can keep above 'em til they're all dead.*

The nearest flight—a ragged line of four Zekes—passed under his nose. They were no threat; he knew that Eddie and Brian would handle them. He finessed stick and rudder, giving the nearest Zeke 150 mils deflection. *Don't need a full two hundred 'cause they're climbing. So . . . wait . . . right . . . there!*

Rogers pressed the trigger, felt more than heard the M-2s' authoritative bark, and flew his sight through the target. The Zeke fell apart, streaming aluminum and burning gasoline. Phil barely registered the kill before the dead Zeke's panicked wingman seemed to pivot in midair, swerving into a steeply banked port turn. Rogers made a quick decision. He retarded his throttle, stood on the right rudder pedal, checked the ball in its housing, and briskly centered it. *This is gonna be close.* He put his pipper on the wingroot and fired a two-second burst from barely a hundred yards astern.

The Zeke exploded before Rogers could get his finger off the trigger. He hopscotched the fireball, hearing pieces faintly banging against his airplane, then crammed on full power and climbed above the fight. He checked left and saw Barnes still with him, sliding into combat spread.

Recovering at six thousand feet, Rogers took time to assess the situation. Below him was a demonic furball of violently maneuvering fighters. He registered a mixture of Army and Navy types: Zekes, Oscars, Tojos, even some Vals. The two F6Fs cleared each other, then Rogers remembered to look around for his second section. He considered calling them but the circuit was jammed with shouts, warnings, yelps, and curses. *We'll find 'em later.* He nodded to Barnes, then dived back into the fight.

SHINKAI THIRTEEN, 1135

Hiroyoshi Sakaida considered himself a highly proficient fighter pilot, but the explosive deaths of his two *shotai* pilots had rocked his confidence. In the milling turmoil of the ensuing fight, his wingman had disappeared and Sakaida had tried to join anything with a *hinomaru,* but rising suns seemed outnumbered by white stars.

Glancing down, Sakaida recognized the Obitsu River leading north and east of Kisarazu. He decided to circle beneath the low clouds between the river and the airfield. *If the Yankees attack the field, I can intercept at least a few of them.*

He reduced power to his Sakae engine and forced himself to ease the grip on the stick.

DAGGER ELEVEN-ONE, 1140

Rogers skidded hard behind two Oscars—and executed the first from 250 yards. *No lookout doctrine,* he registered. He cut the corner on the second Nakajima, allowing one quarter deflection, and flamed it with three bursts. Turning away, he noted Barnes's second kill hit the ground, then glanced at the clock. It seemed incredible, but between them they had destroyed six bandits in as many minutes. The Army types, the Oscars, clearly were not as well flown as the Zekes. *Got to make a note of that for the debrief.*

A movement caught Rogers's attention to the north. He recognized the fat-bellied silhouettes of Potters's Avengers pulling off-target, leaving smoke and carnage on Kisarazu Airfield.

Rogers decided to swing north of the field and head off any bandits that tried to overtake the slow bombers. He estimated that three quarters of his ammunition was in the two Zekes and two Oscars that lay wrecked or burning on the ground, and gave the lead to Barnes.

One loop around here and we'll follow Potter, Rogers decided. For the first time since the shooting had started, he raised his goggles and wiped the sweat from his face. He looked back at Barnes in time to see a lone Zeke drop out of the clouds in a shallow, quartering run from port. *Oh God, no!*

Rogers turned toward Barnes, praying that Bill knew what it meant.

SHINKAI THIRTEEN, 1143

Sakaida still had most of his ammunition, and he did not need to conserve it. These two Grummans were making a nuisance of themselves, and if he could not get within range of the vulnerable bombers, he would kill one of the fighters before escaping into the low clouds. Raindrops streaked against his bulletproof windscreen as he lined up the leading American.

At three hundred meters, Sakaida squeezed with his throttle hand and thumbed down the machine-gun triggers.

DAGGER ELEVEN-TWO

Bill Barnes never saw the cannon and machine-gun tracers. Instead, he reacted according to the life-saving doctrine of Lieutenant Commander John S. Thach, late of Fighting 3.

When Rogers abruptly turned toward him, Barnes knew what it meant. The eerie sensation creeping up his spine was an ingrained reaction based on an unseen threat to his life, but he shoved throttle and prop full forward with his left hand while roughly coordinating stick and rudder into a maximum-rate starboard turn. He heard metallic *thunks* somewhere in his port wing, even as his vision bleached out to gray under the onset of G forces for which he was unprepared.

DAGGER ELEVEN-ONE

Rogers was glad to be flying a replacement F6F with a Mark 8 sight. The lead-computing K-21 was marvelous for tracking a predictable target, but the cut and thrust of dogfighting prevented the gyro from settling for a solution. *Doesn't matter,* Rogers thought, *if I can just force this Jap off Bill's tail.*

Ignoring his cultivated trigger control, Rogers clamped down and hosed a stream of heavy bullets ahead of the Zeke from 20 degrees off its nose. He was mildly surprised to see two or three white motes as armor-piercing incendiaries struck the olive-drab fuselage. Then the Zeke was gone, passing close aboard his starboard wingtip. Rogers glanced back and saw the insolent Japanese perform an elegant four-point roll while climbing into the overcast.

SHINKAI THIRTEEN

Sakaida held his climb, gingerly turning 30 degrees port while making the transition to instrument flight. His inner ear wobbled unsteadily after the impromptu air show, and for a moment his brash confidence was gone as he fought the onset of vertigo. He willed himself to concentrate on his artificial horizon, a mechanical connection with reality that finally won a difficult battle against his deceptive equilibrium.

Then he was on top, between cloud layers. He reduced throttle and r.p.m. to cruise settings and continued his heading toward Yokosuka. He was certain of only two things: Most of his carefully trained escort section was dead now, but he was alive. He slid back the canopy, inhaled the frigid air, and laughed most of the way back to base.

USS *REPRISAL*, 1255

Rogers and Barnes found Fairfield and Sossaman waiting for them in the ready room. Coherent conversation was nearly impossible as VBF-59 celebrated the best day in its six-week history. Pilots chattered incessantly, describing their first aerial victories with feigned casualness that deceived nobody.

Rogers overheard bits of conversation as he made his way to the head of the room.

"Colder'n a witch's tit up there."

"Fleming's guns froze just as he was lined up on a Nate."

"How'd you fellows do?" Rogers asked his wingmen.

"I got two, maybe three," Fairfield shouted. Leaning closer, where Rogers could smell the drying sweat on him, Fairfield added, "We'll have to see the film."

Rogers nodded, then looked at Sossaman, who grinned hugely while displaying two fingers. "How about you, Skipper?"

Rogers held up four fingers and Brian Sossaman's eyes widened in little-boy wonderment. "Hot damn, that's cookin' with gas," he enthused.

Rogers shrugged out of his parachute harness, trying to appear nonchalant. But, damn, it was good. A man felt that he could do anything after a day like this.

Diefendorf pressed his way through the crowd. "Phil, there's a debrief for all division leaders in the wardroom in fifteen minutes. Everybody wants to hear Mancross, including the admiral."

"Yeah? Why's that?"

"Hell, Don got six confirmed!"

Rogers merely shook his head, smiling inwardly at his own ego. *Four Japs in my first combat and I'm an also-ran!* He consoled himself with the knowledge that Mancross had been flying fighters since 1940 and already had two kills from 1942.

Barnes had unburdened himself, draping harness and Mae West over his seat. He was telling Fairfield of his close call, almost shouting in a hoarse, raspy voice. "If Phil hadn't seen him, I'd've been a dead duck." He stood as Rogers approached. "Sir, I haven't mentioned this before, but I have a nineteen-year-old sister. If you ever—"

Rogers's cackling laugh interrupted Barnes's earnest offer. The rest of the team joined in. It had been a long time since Lieutenant Commander Rogers had laughed that hard.

YOKOSUKA BASE, 1330

Lieutenant Kono surveyed the survivors of his fighter-escort *chutai,* who easily fit into his small office. Besides Sakaida and himself, only Flight Petty Officer Tachibana and Flight Superior Seaman Iwai had escaped the swarming Grummans during the forenoon combat. Though Kono had claimed a victory, and Tachibana a probable, everyone knew they counted for nothing.

"This was at least partly my fault," Kono began. "I should have paid more attention to battle practice for your *chutai,* Sakaida. But my orders were precise: Concentrate on the special attack portion of our training."

Shifting his feet, Sakaida considered his words. This was not the Yusuke Kono he knew. The man had never apologized for anything in his life—especially to noncommissioned personnel. "Honorable Division Officer, if I may respectfully differ. The odds were too great against us. This result was no different from Truk or the Marianas. The Americans have superior fighter aircraft with highly experienced pilots." He glanced sideways at the others. "We did well to save half our number."

Kono drummed his fingers on the desktop. "But this *was* different, Sakaida. Enemy aircraft penetrated the home islands' airspace, and that has not happened in almost three years. This time it was naval aircraft, which can come again and again—not a single mission, like the Army bombers in 1942." He looked up. "They will surely return. We must be ready."

Sakaida sensed the two junior pilots fidgeting beside him. They had both survived a nasty scare, and he knew that neither of them was anxious to repeat this morning's mission. "Sir, if I may make a suggestion." Kono nodded. "You saw for yourself what happened today. Our fighters, the Army's aircraft, all were operating in the same area, which only increased confusion in poor weather. I nearly collided with a Ki-43 in the clouds near Kisarazu. We should have designated operating areas to use our interceptors more efficiently."

Leaning back, Kono rubbed his scarred face. "Your suggestion has merit, and I am certain that Naval General Headquarters is taking such measures," he replied. "But my directive is to prepare for special attacks when the enemy carriers are found. We will stand by for attack orders today and tomorrow, if the weather clears. Meanwhile, keep as many escort fighters available as possible."

Sakaida bowed before leaving. He knew that the American fleet lurking out there had approached under cover of rain and clouds. Finding the enemy force would be difficult at best. As he left the building, he pulled up his collar against a sprinkling of wind-driven snow.

MONDAY, 19 FEBRUARY
USS *REPRISAL*

Rogers' assigned airplane, Crystal 33, was spotted well forward on the flight deck. In the cloud-dimmed early-morning light he found the kick step in the side of the fuselage and stretched himself for the athletic leg lift. Then, with an audible grunt, he pulled himself up to the wing, where nineteen-year-old Mickey Brompton already was standing. "Good morning, son."

"Morning, sir." The Iowa-earnest plane captain reached for Rogers's plotting board, which the teenager held until the pilot was seated in the cockpit. Then Rogers raised himself slightly while Brompton grasped the hefty snaps on the bottom of his parachute harness. A *click-click* told the aviator he was fastened to his seat-pack parachute. Rogers then inserted his plotting board on the rails beneath the instrument panel.

Once in an airplane, Rogers seldom indulged in small talk. It was part of his routine, a practiced method of focusing his attention. But he knew that Mickey Brompton would have mentioned any problems with Crystal 33, as the boy from Clear Lake already had warmed up the engine and had the wings locked. Rogers also knew that Brompton had completed the Hellcat's morning inspection, down to the 118th, and last, item—everything from checking the propeller for nicks and leaks to measuring the landing-gear struts for proper extension (4 7/16 inches) to inspecting the battery terminals for corrosion.

Rogers settled himself and nodded to Brompton, who dropped off the wing. Then the air officer's voice blared from the bullhorn, "Stand clear all props. Pilots, start engines." Rogers checked that he was feeding from starboard—the carburetor overflow returned to the right tank—and began the ritual. Almost without conscious effort, his experienced fingers danced through the procedures that were being duplicated in twenty-three other cockpits. In a few minutes *Reprisal*'s flight deck was a bedlam of engine noise and oil-rich haze, populated by agile sailors scrambling on all fours, duck-walking beneath wings while gauging propeller arcs.

With engine instruments climbing into the green, Crystal 33 was coaxed forward by the white-clad plane director. Nudging the throttle, Rogers deftly maneuvered the big fighter toward the port catapult, while Van Sley took the starboard. Given the crossed-arm stop signal, Rogers depressed his toe brakes and glimpsed two green-jerseyed men disappear beneath his wings. He knew they were affixing the catapult bridle to a pair of sturdy hooks either side of the 150-gallon drop tank. Meanwhile, at the rear of the airplane another sailor inserted the holdback hook into its fitting in the deck, rendering the F6F immobile even at full throttle.

Now the holdback man signaled the catapult operator in the catwalk to adjust the position of the shuttle until full tension was taken on the aircraft, and the "deck ape" then checked the tension ring and pulled its canvas shroud into place before giving a thumbs-up.

Rogers had turned his gyrocompass to the ship's heading and caged the instrument. When the catapult crewmen scampered aside, the launch officer demanded the pilot's attention.

Standing near the port wingtip, the launch director slowly twirled an upraised finger. Rogers advanced the throttle to thirty-five inches of mercury, yielding 2,100 r.p.m., checked his magnetos, and noted a sixty-rev drop in each mag. Satisfied, he nodded and received a two-finger turnup signal. Rogers ran throttle and prop control to the stop and, with his right hand, tightened the throttle friction lock. Then he grasped the stick again and braced his head against the rest.

One more glance at the instruments. *Everything's green.* He tensed his left arm against the throttle and prop handle as extra insurance, aware of the manic trembling through the Grumman airframe as 2,800 cubic inches of engine delivered more than two thousand horsepower to the twelve-foot propeller.

Strapped in as tightly as he could stand, assaulted by noise, Rogers wondered how much longer he could run a lashed-down engine. He did not see the launch officer slash down with his checkered flag, ordering the catapult operator in the catwalk to push a button.

Beneath the flight deck a blast of pressurized air flushed hydraulic fluid from its accumulating tank, forcing the fluid into a long cylinder parallel to the deck. As the fluid raged into the cylinder under intense pressure, a ram was advanced at high speed, driving a series of pulleys that slammed the bridle shuttle forward. Tons of inertia overcame the holdback, shattering the tension ring whose parts were contained within the shroud.

At the end of the stroke, the bridle was propelled forward and its loops fell away from the hooks beneath the wing. Grunting under the acceleration, Rogers's vision blurred at the vicious kick in the small of the back. But in two seconds he was making 70 knots.

The immense hydraulic power of the H-4B catapults was unlike anything else. Every cat shot was a brutal experience and Rogers was always glad that the worst part of the flight was behind him. He reached down, raised the landing-gear lever, and felt the Hellcat accelerate as the retraction killed 60 percent of his low-speed drag. Next he pulled up the flaps, adjusted power for cruise-climb, and watched Van Sley join off his starboard wing.

Iwo Jima lay sixty-five miles southeast.

OVER IWO JIMA, 0845

The rows of amphibious tractors swam toward the southern beaches like a swarm of well-ordered waterbugs. Rogers checked his watch and noticed that the landing appeared to be on schedule. H-Hour was 0900, and *Sharpsburg*'s strike under Red White had been shooting up the porkchop-shaped island since 0805 hours. Rogers, leading the second wave, would relieve the Corsairs on station. He switched to B channel on his VHF radio and contacted the CSA—commander of support aircraft.

"This is Dagger Eleven-One with twenty-four F6Fs, approaching your area. We have .50-caliber and rockets, over."

The CSA's response was immediate. "Roger, Dagger. Have you in sight. When gunfire lifts, concentrate on the high ground north of the beaches and the east slope of Suribachi. Over."

Rogers acknowledged and established his six divisions in a holding pattern: two parallel columns from which fighter-bombers could be called continually, maintaining constant pressure on the defenders. When his second hand ticked 0853, he rocked his wings and led Team 11 in a slanting descent toward Iwo's tortured shore. He had seven minutes to supervise his Hellcats in uninterrupted strafing.

In the descent from fifteen thousand feet, Rogers double-checked his armament switches and gunsight. The K-21 sight's "Christmas tree" reticle for air-ground delivery glowed at him while he tickled the trigger that would send his HVARs into the volcanic black ash. He recalled the briefing: six hundred–foot pullouts in deference to the naval bombardment, moving the racetrack pattern slightly inland on each pass.

Pulling up from his third run, Rogers rolled one wingtip down and looked at the amtracks as they approached the shore. He felt a little shiver of pride, recalling how far amphibious doctrine had come since Guadalcanal. This was the American way of war, he told himself: from the air and from the sea. He thought of Tom Albertson again. *Damn, I wish he could see this. He trained us for it. And so did Jim.*

The naval gunfire shifted two hundred yards inland as the first amtracks touched shore.

WEDNESDAY, 21 FEBRUARY
OVERHEAD USS *REPRISAL*

Dropping into the traffic pattern, Rogers glanced at the deck and immediately knew he would not get aboard anytime soon. *Bad barrier crash,* he thought. It looked as if an SB2C had bounced over the first steel barrier, probably had caught its wheels on the second, and flipped inverted into planes parked forward. There was a frenzy of activity around the upside-down Helldiver, which was perched on another '2C and two F6Fs. The mobile crane had not even begun to move into position, and darkness was only minutes away.

As he turned crosswind, Rogers noticed a light from the signal bridge. The blinker flicked off and on a few times before he began reading the message in mid-sequence: dash dot—dot dot—dash—dot. Then it repeated and Rogers mouthed the letters: George, Roger, Able, Nan, Item, Tare, Easy. *Granite. We're supposed to land on the* Sharpsburg *tonight.* Looking over his shoulder, he patted his head to Van Sley and turned out of the traffic circle, making for the gray-painted carrier a half mile away.

Then Rogers realized that this inconvenience held an advantage. It would give him a chance to talk to *Sharpsburg*'s Marines.

USS *SHARPSBURG*

Ready Room 2 had once belonged to Bombing 57, but that was months ago, before Red White's troops had arrived. As Rogers entered the cramped space, he felt simultaneously awkward and at home. This ready room was nearly identical to his own, except for the Marine Corps recruiting poster with a bulldog mascot wearing a World War I helmet.

The duty officer, a stocky second lieutenant, saw the Navy flier enter. "I'm Lieutenant Garrison, sir. May I help you?"

"Yes, you can. I'm Commander Rogers, the skipper of VBF-59 from the *Reprisal*. My team just landed because our deck's fouled. Looks like we'll be here overnight. I'd like to speak to your CO if he's available."

"Yes, sir. Please be seated and I'll call him. Would the commander like some coffee?"

Rogers unzipped his jacket, wondering why Marines always spoke in the third person. "Yeah, that'd be fine."

A few minutes later Garrison proffered a mug of coffee with some news. "Uh, Commander, I just wondered. Did you get a look at Task Group 58.5 before you landed?"

Rogers sipped the scalding liquid and looked up from his seat. "No. It's pretty low ceiling with decreasing visibility. That's the night-flying group, isn't it?"

"Yes, sir. Admiral Gardner with the *Enterprise* and *Saratoga*. Well, sir, we just got word. The Sara's burning. She took several hits from *kamikazes* and bombs."

"My god." Rogers's voice was barely audible. "When?"

Garrison shook his head. "Don't know for sure, Commander. Evidently two attacks."

Rogers's hand instinctively went to his jacket patch. He recalled his first cruise, when, as carefree ensigns in Bombing 3, he and Burnett had flown from *Saratoga.* He sensed a khaki shape approaching. "You Rogers?" the officer asked.

Setting down his mug, Rogers started to rise but was waved back. "Red White," the new lieutenant colonel said, extending his hand. Rogers shook as the Marine sat down beside him. "Air ops just said your division will be with us tonight. That'll give us a chance to compare notes. Were you on the fighter strike to Chichi Jima?"

"Yes, sir. We're supposed to prevent Jap planes from staging through there, but not a thing's moving. Just some flak."

White got to the point. "I guess you're wondering about Jim Carpenter, huh?"

Rogers nodded. "We were classmates at Pensacola."

"Yeah, I remember he mentioned that. Well, I'm afraid I can't help you very much, Mr. Rogers. We haven't heard a word about Jim since he went down. But I've asked his wingman to meet us for dinner. He can tell you more than anybody else."

Rogers stared at his mug for a moment. "Thank you, Colonel." He looked up at White. "What's your guess?"

The Marine studied Rogers before replying. *This guy's been around since '42. He's seen it all before.* "I hoped we'd hear something from the French by now, but it's hardly been a month." White rubbed his head and Rogers saw that the man's thinning hair did bear a trace of red. "The fact that he didn't get out of his plane before Keaton left . . . I don't know. Take a number. Thirty percent chance he's a prisoner."

Damn, Rogers thought. Then he realized he had spoken the word aloud.

White tapped the visitor's elbow. "If he's alive, he'll be okay. Jim's a tough cookie." White paused, wondering whether to explain the thought in his mind. He decided that a close friend was entitled. "You know, Rogers, he didn't have to make this cruise. He could have taken a cushy staff job in Hawaii."

"Yes, sir. Jim told me at Ulithi just after you guys arrived. But he said . . . he said he went where he was needed."

White sought to put a better face on a grim picture. "Well, there's one consolation. Maybe he's a prisoner of the French. It's the best we can hope for."

SUNDAY, 25 FEBRUARY
USS *REPRISAL*

The Marine orderly braced as he saw the aviator approaching the flag shelter, still wearing flight gear. "Lieutenant Commander Rogers, reporting to Admiral Griggs."

"Oh, there you are, son. Come on in here." The task group commander's voice rose above the sound of an F6F taking a wave-off in choppy seas. The forenoon recovery was not going well; Rogers knew that the LSO had been generous in giving him a cut high and in close.

"You wanted to see me, sir?"

"Yes. I have a hunch we're going to cancel further strikes against Tokyo. You just got back. What's it like out there?"

Rogers pulled off his helmet and leaned against the ship's roll. "Just miserable, Admiral. Visibility's way down—maybe three miles or so along the coast—and I think it's decreasing here. In addition, the deck must be rising and falling a good twenty feet."

Rear Admiral Jacob Griggs swiveled in his padded chair and rubbed his chin. He was a thickset trade-school product of the Class of '16. Rogers knew that Griggs had won his wings relatively early, in 1920, and had commanded an escort carrier two years ago. Now, at fifty-one, he was at the apex of his career.

"Did you see any airborne Japs, Mr. Rogers?"

"No, sir. But there was some combat on A channel—call sign Phantom, which must be in another task group. Apparently they were shooting up an airfield."

Griggs reached for a clipboard and flipped the pages of the task force operations order. "*Randolph,* in 58.4," he reported. "Raddy Radford's group. Hard to believe. We were classmates at the Academy and Pensacola, and now here we are with our own task groups off the Japanese coast. Mark my words, son. Art Radford is headed for the top."

Rogers mentally snapped at the sentiment. *Sure thing, Admiral. You and your college pals get your tickets punched while guys like Bernie and Kenny and Jim . . .* He caught himself. *No, that's not fair.* Rogers had seen films of USS *Langley,* America's first carrier. Her tiny flight deck was lined with dilapidated biplanes—more like flying machines than genuine aircraft. And Jake Griggs surely had lost youthful friends. Naval aviation always exacted a price in blood; even peacetime flying had its casualties, twenty-two years before.

Another F6F snagged the fourth wire, blowing a tire on impact with the deck. But the two officers on the bridge hardly noticed as Griggs returned to business. "With what you've told me, I'm not too concerned about any snoopers finding us in this weather. If they didn't find us before, it's unlikely they'll do so now." He gazed through the rain-specked glass behind Rogers's shoulder.

Uncertain whether the admiral expected a reply, Rogers ventured, "Well, sir, we sure could have used this weather at Iwo Jima."

Griggs shook his head abruptly. "Hell, yes. But there was never any doubt the Japs would come at us with everything possible. Iwo puts Tokyo in range of land-based fighters to escort the B-29s. Maybe we were lucky we weren't hurt any worse than we were. Though heaven knows, it was bad enough."

Rogers ventured a personal opinion. "I know, sir. The *Saratoga* was my first ship. Any word on casualties?"

Griggs turned to his flag lieutenant. "Mr. Eads, you have that?"

"Here, Admiral." The staff officer produced a message form.

Extending his arm to focus better, Griggs read the butcher's bill. "Damn, 123 dead or missing, almost 200 wounded. And the air group lost about half its planes." He put down the paper and looked around the bridge. "You realize, that's going to put a crimp in Matt Gardner's night-flying schedule. It leaves him only with the *Enterprise,* but that's a going concern. Bill Martin's Air Group Ninety, best in the business."

"Admiral, we heard about the *Bismarck Sea,*" Rogers ventured. "Any details available?"

"Yes, I think so . . . here. She was in Cal Durgin's escort group; he's another one of us from 1916. She was sunk by a *kamikaze* about the same time the *Saratoga* was hit. Over two hundred dead and missing." Griggs put down the paper again and looked directly at Rogers. "Tell me something, Commander. Can we do anything else to get a handle on these suiciders?"

Rogers thought for a long moment. No flag officer had previously asked his opinion on such matters. "Well, sir. I'd say we have to hit them where they live. Maybe use the night owls to cap them from dusk to dawn, then keep a couple of teams over the fields during daylight. That is, if we can find them."

Griggs leaned back, smiling slightly. "You and Jimmy Thach think alike. You probably don't know it, but that's just what he's suggesting to Admiral McCain in Third Fleet. They're calling it the big blue blanket. We'll try it the next time we operate over Japan."

Rogers gave a decisive nod, his chin thrust out. "My boys will do a good job for you, sir. They're still fired up after the first Tokyo strikes."

The admiral's gray eyebrows rose an inch. "Which reminds me, son.

Congratulations on your big day on the sixteenth. You showed fine leadership."

"Well, thank you, Admiral." Rogers went into his aw-shucks routine. "Actually, the Japs didn't maneuver very well so most of my shots were from astern. The Zeros were better flown than the Oscars or Tojos."

"Just the same, you'll do a lot of dining out on that story when you get back to San Diego." Griggs laughed.

A dim memory flickered in Rogers's mind. *San Diego—the office call with Bernie at North Island.* "Excuse me, sir. Do you know if Captain Edwards is still ComFair personnel officer? I forgot that I owe him a letter." Edwards's stern directive echoed in Rogers's brain: *When either of you sinks a ship or bags a Japanese plane, you* will *inform this office!*

Griggs laughed again. "Ha! The Coronado Cobra!" Then he shook his head. "No, I don't know offhand. I'm sure you can find out when we anchor at Ulithi in a week or so."

"Thank you, sir. I'd better get back to the ready room for the LSO debrief."

On his way down the ladder, Rogers tried composing a bittersweet message. *Dear Captain: As per your request, here's the dope: I got four Japs in one hop and Lieutenant Burnett got killed by our own frigging gunners. CO VBF-59 sends.*

March 1945

SATURDAY, 10 MARCH
YOKOSUKA BASE

The Shinkai Unit was an unlikely place to recruit fighter-pilot talent, but the message request amounted to exactly that. Kono slid the paper across his desk, where Sakaida stood at ease. "You may read it for yourself," Kono rasped. "Captain Umeda is seeking Class A combat pilots for his wing. You are qualified."

Sakaida picked up the message form and scanned it right to left. The essentials were all there: Captain Ganji Umeda, one of the more senior fighter pilots left in the Imperial Navy, was organizing a wing of four squadrons. Three would fly the new Kawanishi NIK2 *Shiden*. The fourth would fly reconnaissance missions. Only combat-experienced aviators were being sought at present. Sakaida recognized several prominent names among the division leaders. Mainly Etajima graduates, aces all.

"Well, what do you say?" Keno tried to keep a level tone in his voice, neither encouraging nor dissuading.

Sakaida returned the message form. "It is an honor to be asked, but I prefer to remain here until . . . er, for now." He berated himself for stumbling over those last words.

Kono inferred his meaning: *Until I have body-crashed an American aircraft carrier.* He nodded by way of dismissal, since Sakaida had the rest of the day off. Watching him exit, Yusuke Kono realized he had been paid a high compliment. Not many men would turn down a prestige assignment in favor of watching an old friend kill himself against an enemy ship.

FRIDAY, 16 MARCH
USS *REPRISAL*

"You know," Rogers said in a low voice, "I never get tired of watching this."

Barnes, Fairfield, Sacco, Van Sley, and a few others sat on the deck edge of the catwalk, watching the underway refueling. Two days out of Ulithi, Task Force 58 was under way again after nearly two weeks. It had been more than enough time: time to re-read letters, to catch up on the damned paperwork, to complete deferred aircraft maintenance. Worst of all, for some, too much time to think.

Fifty yards to starboard, the fleet oiler *Umatilla* kept station on *Reprisal.* Massive black hoses linked the two ships like external umbilicals as fuel oil and aviation gasoline were pumped into the carrier's massive bunkers. Rogers noted some of the fine points for the ensigns, who displayed a widespread lack of interest. "That's fine, Skipper, but what's it got to do with flying?" asked Van Sley.

Rogers felt his dander rise. This was part of the junior officers' professional education, but he remembered when he had felt much the same. Plowing a big, heavy ship through Pacific swells held not a candle to the joy and challenge of flying carrier aircraft. He modulated his voice. "Well, *mister,* if you think about it, you'll see it's got a lot in common with flying. Before Midway, when the old *Yorktown* was refueling out of Pearl, I was almost a boot ensign like you. But a real fine aviator from Bombing Five pointed out to me that keeping station like this is harder than formation flying."

Van Sley seemed only partly chastened. "How's that, sir?"

Rogers gestured. "Just look. You've got a tanker that must displace, oh, twenty-five thousand tons and handles like a barge. But that captain has perfectly matched speed and distance with us, at about twenty-seven thousand tons. He'll stay there forever if need be, keeping an even strain on the lines in almost any kind of sea state. You think you could do that?"

Van looked down in the perforated catwalk. "Ah, nosir."

Rogers traded winks with Bill Barnes. Though still wearing a gold bar himself, his expression said it all. *Ensigns!*

"Something else," Rogers added. "These fellows in the support force don't get much publicity. Hell, I don't think they get any. But ask yourself—how long could we stay out here without them? They keep us fueled and armed, and the transport CVEs keep us in airplanes and even replacement pilots. I checked *Jane's* in the library a few days ago. You realize that oilers have nearly tripled since Pearl Harbor and gasoline tankers have multiplied about twelve times?"

Van Sley summoned the courage to ask an impertinent question. "Sir, would you want to push one of those things around the ocean?"

Rogers stared at USS *Umatilla*. "Not on your life, Ensign."

MONDAY, 19 MARCH
SHINKAI THIRTEEN, 0748

After yesterday, Sakaida knew what today would hold, but that knowledge did nothing to alleviate the turmoil inside him. The Americans had blanketed forty-five Kyushu airfields with little to show for their effort, since Naval General Headquarters had withdrawn most planes from the area. True, the Yankees now were reported striking remaining battleships and carriers, but the fleet had nearly ceased to exist. Sakaida recalled that early this month the Imperial Navy's last two carrier divisions had been assigned to the Kure Naval District. But this morning, none of that mattered. What mattered was that Yusuke Kono was going to die.

Kono had left the Honshu coast, flying southwest toward the Yankees' operating area off Kyushu, obviously intent upon a professionally competent debut for the Shinkai Unit.

With only six fighter escorts, Sakaida knew he could not do much to protect the *kamikazes*. So he approved Kono's mission plan: remain in the low haze as much as possible to avoid the enemy combat air patrols, then attack the first carriers possible. *We cannot hide from radar,* he mused, *but if the Grummans cannot see us until we dive . . .*

Skirting two task groups, Sakaida glimpsed extremely satisfying results. Perhaps eight miles off his port wingtip, a fleet carrier spewed a moderately large fire that he guessed was being contained. Almost an equal distance to starboard he could tell only that a large ship was undergoing a conflagration that almost certainly would not be controlled. *Wonderful!* Sakaida exulted. *I've never seen such smoke and flames!*

Kono was waggling his wings for attention. Signaling a fast, shallow descent, he led the Shinkai Unit toward a third task group almost directly ahead.

USS *REPRISAL*, 0750

The barriers popped vertically into place behind Sossaman's fighter as the leading three F6Fs shut down their engines and sailors began folding wings.

Rogers was first out of his cockpit as he slid down the wing and hit the deck running. One of the plane handlers jogged alongside. "Excuse me, sir. We've heard that at least two carriers got tagged. Could you see anything?"

Rogers pulled up one flap of his helmet. The deckhand could see the perspiration on his forehead and smell the residue of adrenaline. "Hell, yes! We saw loads of *kamikazes*. Two carriers are burning—one each in 58.1 and 58.2." Rogers pointed generally west. "I think the call signs are Stinger and Clipper." Then he ran to consult with his team under the wing of Dagger Seventeen.

"I'm going to hustle up to the bridge and let the captain know what we saw. You guys get down to the ready rooms. Make sure that Ralph, Hunter, and the ACIO know that the Japs are coming out in small flights, staggered altitudes, and different headings. They've really wised up." He thought for a moment. He had splashed a bomb-laden Zeke and covered his second section while Fairfield and Sossaman bagged three more. "That was real good shooting, fellows. You hit everything you aimed at. Now get going." He patted Fairfield's elbow and turned toward the base of the island.

"All hands, take cover! Enemy aircraft on the port quarter." The flight-deck loudspeaker unnecessarily blared "Boots and Saddles," though the ship already was at general quarters.

Rogers stood riveted for a moment. He had never witnessed an air attack from the perspective of the target. *I can't do the captain any good right now. I'd only be in the way.* He sprinted toward the 40-millimeter mount aft of the island.

SHINKAI THIRTEEN, 0753
APPROACHING TASK FORCE 38

There! The circular disposition of a multicarrier task group appeared as though seen through thin gauze. Sakaida quickly recognized the four flight decks: two large, two small, as he had been briefed to expect. Kono rocked his wings again, looked over his shoulder at Sakaida—and waved goodbye. Then he dived toward the nearest flattop, three miles away.

Sakaida hardly had time to absorb the moment. He swiveled his head, checking for interceptors, and saw none. With that, he led his wingman in a slanting descent to cover Kono's attack section, marveling at the lack of opposition.

From long experience, the Japanese Navy knew how its enemy operated. When in range of hostile aircraft, individual American task groups usually remained within sight of one another to provide overlapping radar coverage for the entire task force. Similarly, ships' anti-aircraft guns formed a multilayered cone through which attacking planes must pass. Sakaida judged the time-distance equation. Three miles at about 330 knots—barely thirty seconds. He prayed to the war gods of Nihon that Yusuke Kono be granted that half minute of life to achieve divinity in death. Then the sky exploded.

USS REPRISAL

"They're going for the *Alliance!*"

Rogers was startled by the voice in his ear. Barnes, standing near enough to touch, read his mind. "Eddie and Brian got it covered, Phil. I wanted to see this, too."

Rogers gave a brisk nod, then turned his attention seaward. A thousand yards off the port quarter, the light carrier that was the target of the Shinkai Unit heeled in a hard starboard turn. Rogers grasped a handhold on the gun tub as Captain McEwen laid his own helm hard over to keep station. The Essex-class ship's tactical radius was being tested—a 765-yard circle inscribed on the surface of the sea at a pounding 30 knots. If he had had extra hands, Rogers would have clamped them hard over both ears. The gunfire was an incredible, unending pounding of sonic violence and reeling concussion. The quad-40 mount's rhythmic pounding was bad enough, but the din of the dual-mount five-inchers was appalling. The high chattering of the single-mount 20s hardly mattered.

Barnes was pointing now. Diving straight and fast, at perhaps a 30-degree angle, were two—no, three—dark shapes. Bursting flak and vari-colored tracers blocked their way. Rogers heard a shrill, atavistic shout: "Kill them, goddammit, kill them!" Then he realized the voice was his.

SHINKAI THIRTEEN

It looked good. Despite the horrific flak—worse than he had imagined—Sakaida controlled his emotions, urging Kono on. Occasionally jostled by near-misses, he concentrated on keeping position to shoot down—ram if necessary—any Yankee fighter that belatedly intervened.

They're getting our range now! His mental warning coincided with a brilliant spurt of fuel-fed flames from Kono's wingman. *Direct hit on Fukuoka. No time to think about it.* Kono easily adjusted to keep tracking the smaller carrier, which vainly tried to keep its stern to him. *Ten seconds,* Sakaida estimated. *Please . . .*

USS *REPRISAL*

Now the air was a dirty pox of flak bursts. White geysers of shells, bullets, and aircraft debris rose and fell in alabaster contrast to the black-brown eruptions in the hazy sky. Barnes was pounding Rogers's shoulder. "They got another one! They got another one!"

SHINKAI THIRTEEN, 0754

A rippling pattern of 40-millimeter fire burst across Kono's flight path. One of the big shells severed the outboard two feet of his port wing, inducing a left-hand roll. Kono began to correct when another hit slapped him inverted, torching his fuel tanks. High-speed aerodynamic forces tore his airframe apart. Debris and burning gasoline rained upon USS *Alliance.*

Sakaida froze at the controls. Almost belatedly he pulled out of his dive, already passing astern of the intended victim. In a handful of accelerated heartbeats, he realized with a numbing shock, *This was not to happen. Yusuke was to die by body-crashing.*

Twenty-millimeter tracers demanded his attention. With the speed gained in a six thousand–foot descent, Sakaida leveled off at two hundred feet and looked up. Another carrier—a much larger one—loomed in his windscreen. He popped the stick back, wondering what to do. And lacking standing orders, he went serenely insane.

USS *REPRISAL*

The gunners all were shouting at once. Mount captains pointed and swore hoarse profanities, demanding the impossible as the nearest Zero rocketed above and astern of the ship. Somehow, by luck or skill, this Japanese aviator had survived long enough to hold the fate of 3,385 Americans in his hands.

Rogers and Barnes watched, transfixed, as the Mitsubishi peaked in its zoom-climb, dropped a wing, and nosed over. Suddenly the two pilots felt very, very exposed on an 880-foot flight deck. Rogers glanced toward the catwalk and its dubious shelter. He glimpsed a stenciled sign on the rear of a 20-millimeter's shield: "Lead him, dammit, lead him!"

SHINKAI THIRTEEN

Even from five hundred meters, the ship looked huge. Peering through his gunsight, Sakaida noticed the operational details: aircraft parked forward, one elevator lowered—and dozens of muzzle flashes from the deck edges and stern. From reflex as much as anything, he tripped his triggers and saw his tracers enter the wood-plank deck.

USS *REPRISAL*

"Get down!" Barnes shoved Rogers prone onto the deck, hugging the edge of the quad-40 mount. Hands over his head, Phil involuntarily closed his eyes but felt as much as heard 20-millimeter rounds splintering the Douglas fir planks ten paces away. Then the moaning whine of a radial engine came and went. He looked up in time to see the olive-green fighter flash past. *Well, I'll be damned, he's not a suicider.*

Rogers got to his knees, grasping Barnes by the shoulders. The two friends traded ritual expressions of concern. "You okay?" Almost before they could reply, a gun captain screamed.

"Holy shit! I think he's coming back!"

SHINKAI THIRTEEN

The flak was not bad at all. In fact, this close to the ship, only the single 20-millimeter mounts could hope to track him. Sakaida emitted a shrill laugh that voiced a revelation. *The other ships will not fire at me for fear of hitting this one!* He rolled into a hard left turn—just about at pattern altitude, he judged—and went back for another try. Then something screamed at him to check his tail. And there was a Grumman, five hundred meters back.

USS *REPRISAL*, 0755

Rogers and Barnes sprinted across the deck for a better view. The Marines of the Eighth Division 20-millimeter mounts all were screaming and pointing forward, and Rogers saw why. "Bill, look! There's an F6F after him!"

The Americans watched with professional interest as the Zeke abruptly pulled up from its dive, climbing steeply into the low overcast. Seconds later the Hellcat, bearing the markings of *Alliance*'s VF-58, followed the intruder. Barnes shook his head. "Well, that's the last we'll see of that Jap. But God, what nerve!"

Rogers stood with his eyes locked on the low haze. "I'm not so sure. The Zeke can outclimb an F6 at low speed. This may not be over yet."

Barnes sat down on the deck and pulled off his sweat-stained cloth helmet. "You know, I was just thinking. We were on the *Saratoga* and *Yorktown* together, but we were never under air attack. This sort of—"

The Marine gunners were cheering again. *Just like a damn rooting section,* Rogers thought, as a fighter fell out of the overcast. Not burning but definitely out of control, it splashed into the ocean a half mile to port. More cheers, back pounding, and gutteral male barks erupted.

Moments later a parachute drifted downward. "Hell's fahr," exclaimed a 20-millimeter gunner. "Ah'll finish that ol' boy." He trained his Oerlikon on the defeated aviator and drew a bead.

Rogers reacted the only way he could. From the deck edge he aimed a hard kick at the back of the Marine's head, knocking off the gunner's helmet and sending him sprawling. "You jerk! That was an F6!"

"Look out!" someone yelled. "Here he comes again!"

SHINKAI THIRTEEN, 0756

Hiroyoshi Sakaida felt bullet-proof and invisible. It had been ridiculously easy to do a hammerhead-turn back on the foolish Grumman pilot and shoot him into the sea. Suspended nose high at low level, just above the haze layer, the Hellcat had run out of options. Sakaida's shells and bullets had pounded into the blunt cowling, destroying the huge radial engine. He had glimpsed the American go over the side at about three hundred meters.

Now back below the layer, Sakaida briefly pondered making another strafing pass from astern of the big carrier. The frenzied chemistry of his brain discarded that option as he lowered his nose in line with the port catwalk. *Not even their light weapons can shoot at me now,* he exulted as an idea lit in his mind.

It was marvelous how combat tension inspired innovation.

USS *REPRISAL*

Barnes saw what was coming as well as anyone else. He grasped Rogers's flight-suit leg and screamed, "Get down, Phil!"

Rogers ignored him. Standing calmly on the deck, arms folded, he watched the Zero 52 approach at perhaps three hundred feet. Beginning aft of the fantail, the Mitsubishi rolled wings vertical and hesitated. Fascinated, Rogers could see the pilot in his cockpit.

Amidships the Zeke inverted as several 20-millimeters tried to track it. Then beyond the bow the insane Japanese was wings-vertical again in the third point of his hesitation slow roll. A scything line of tracers clipped his rudder, shredding some fabric, as the wings leveled in the fourth point of the roll.

Then, clipping the waves in a fury of geysers, he was gone.

Barnes got to his feet. He opened his mouth but no words came. Rogers merely nodded. "You said it."

WEDNESDAY, 21 MARCH
YOKOSUKA BASE

Lieutenant Commander Takeo Watanabe had almost no naval expertise. But he held a master's degree in psychology from Tokyo University, and before the war he had specialized in stress tolerance. His analysis of earthquake victims had brought him to prominence, and since 1942, when he was called into the navy, he had expanded his studies.

The subject currently before him was one for the books. For the last two days Watanabe had studied Flight Chief Petty Officer Sakaida. The interviews had not gone well. The man giggled at odd intervals and had no explanation for his incredible actions over the enemy fleet. He became sullen and even resentful when questioned about his emotions.

It was too bad, Watanabe told himself. Sakaida had an excellent record: from Pearl Harbor to Midway and the Solomons, the Marianas and Philippines campaigns. Most recently assigned to a Special Attack unit, he had managed to penetrate to the core of an American task group and had indulged in wild aerobatics over one of the carriers—and had returned to tell the tale. *Amazing,* Watanabe concluded. If not for another escort pilot's confirmation, he would have dismissed the story as fanciful. But that was not the point. The question was elemental: Why had Sakaida not plunged himself into that ship?

Undoubtedly this Sakaida is a superb aviator, the psychologist concluded, *but what of his mental state?* There were indications of recurring headaches and erratic behavior: dancing with tropical fruit on his head—undoubtedly when intoxicated—and uncontrolled laughter at inappropriate times. Watanabe knew the school diagnosis: combat fatigue compounded by possible mental instability.

Watanabe picked up a form and re-read his verdict. *Subject noncommissioned officer requires rest and close examination. Recommend immediate grounding and commitment to Naval Hospital Yokosuka for psychiatric evaluation.*

FRIDAY, 23 MARCH
USS *REPRISAL*

Rear Admiral Jacob Griggs faced his brain trust, assembled in the wardroom. Two dozen aviators, staff officers, fighter directors, and communicators were assembled to hear "Courthouse" explain his plans for Operation Iceberg.

"Gentlemen," the task group commander began. "Some of you already know that the invasion of Okinawa begins in nine days. Love Day is one April, though the bombardment has already started. Beginning today, ten battleships and eighteen escort carriers will strike selected targets on Okinawa, so presumably there'll be less for us to do once we arrive."

Griggs turned to face a large-scale map of southern Japan, the Ryukyu Islands and Okinawa island itself. "Our main problem will be air defense, because the Japanese can funnel hundreds of planes down from the home islands." He traced a path from Kyushu southward. "The straight-line distance is only about three hundred fifty miles, and they have a good intermediate base here, at Amami-O-Shima." He tapped the largest island between Kyushu and Okinawa.

"Now, we've all seen what the Japs can do when they get a chance. The *Franklin* has as many as eight hundred dead, and Captain Gehres has her under way for the States. I doubt we'll see her again. And the *Wasp* lost more than a hundred killed from the same attacks day before yesterday." He looked around the room, knowing that he had everyone's full attention. Then Griggs turned to Lieutenant Lang. "Next we'll hear from our senior fighter director."

Henry Lang wiped his palms as he rose and stepped to the map. Public speaking was not his forte; he insisted that he was more comfortable speaking into a microphone. "Thank you, sir," he began. "Gentlemen, I think we've learned quite a lot about the way the Japs work. They've gotten more cagey of late, especially with the *kamikazes*. They know that, unlike when we're opposing conventional bombers, with the suiciders our defenses have to be nearly one hundred percent effective. The only way to stop the suicider is to kill him—shoot him down as far out as possible."

Lang began to pace. "On the eighteenth alone, we plotted fifty-one raids, from singles up to groups of eight or ten. During the attacks of the nineteenth, they came at us from different altitudes and headings, making good use of clouds and haze. Instead of concentrating their planes in large formations, they split up into smaller groups of perhaps three to six. That's bad enough. But the ones I really fear are the singles. They're dead meat for our fighters, but finding them can be awfully tough, especially at dawn or dusk."

Clearing his throat, the fighter director showed signs of nervousness. He knew he might be overstepping his bounds, but so be it. "Now, I've raised this next item with Admiral Griggs, and I think it fair to say that we agree on this point." Griggs nodded from the front row, so Lang took encouragement. "One of the reasons two carriers got tagged the other day was insufficient fighters. We sent a lot of F6Fs and F4Us up to Kure with strikes against the remaining fleet units, and it doesn't look like a good tradeoff. We now recognize that the Jap Navy is no longer a factor in this war. So from here on, we'll try to conserve our VF strength for fleet defense."

A murmur of agreement ran through the room. Then Lang heard some soft laughter and looked for the source. "Mr. Mancross, Mr. Rogers. Did you want to say something?"

As the more senior, Phil stood up. "Well, yes, actually. Don and I were just comparing notes. At the start of the war, eighteen F4Fs weren't enough. In '42 we had twenty-seven per ship and that didn't work. Now we're up to seventy-three fighters on the Essexes and even that still isn't enough. Nothing changes!"

Griggs turned in his seat. "You boys might like to know that it's been suggested we devote one carrier per task group exclusively to fighters. I don't think it will happen, but the fact that the suggestion has been made shows the emphasis on fleet defense. My God, when I think of the airshow that Zero put on the other day. If he'd been a *kamikaze* . . ." Griggs shook his gray head.

"Yes, sir," Lang interjected. "That's why we've developed our *kamikaze* doctrine. It's not just enough to intercept them and turn them back. We have to kill every one of them."

When the meeting broke up, Rogers went directly to the ready room. He found Barnes pouring coffee. "Bill, I've been thinking about that Jap the other day—the one who slow-rolled over our heads. Did you also see the Zeke that hit you over Chiba?"

"Hell, by the time I saw him he was almost gone. Why? Is there a connection?"

"Maybe. Just before he pulled up into the clouds he did a four-point roll."

Barnes's eyes widened. "You mean—"

"Well, I don't know. It just seems that would be a hell of a coincidence if two Japs both flew that way." Rogers stared at the deck, lost in thought. At length he said, "I'll tell you something, Bill. That guy is dangerous. If I ever see him again, I'm going to nail him. Before he nails one of us."

TUESDAY, 27 MARCH

YOKOSUKA BASE

Sakaida faced a dilemma. Though he chafed at the hospital regimentation and lack of flying, he found that he enjoyed sleeping in, walking the

grounds, and making friends with some of the staff. Most of his fellow patients in the noncommissioned psychiatric ward left something to be desired
as conversationalists.

More talkative was Dr. Fiume, who if anything was too chatty. Sakaida
took an instinctive dislike to the man who controlled the patients' fates: his
mousy appearance, prissy mannerisms, and especially his prying questions.
The initial interview did not go well.

"Tell me, Sakaida, why do you think you are here?" the doctor had
begun.

Sakaida made the mistake of answering honestly. "Basically, honorable doctor, I am here because I am alive."

Fiume's face registered as much comprehension as some of Sakaida's
roommates. "Of course you are alive, Sakaida! What kind of answer is
that?"

With studied patience, Sakaida had explained. "I returned to Yokosuka Base after escorting my division officer in a special attack on enemy
aircraft carriers. But because I returned alive I was sent here."

The doctor blinked behind his rimless glasses. "Well, if you were ordered to die in action with the enemy, why did you not do so? Your division officer died gloriously."

What do you know about dying gloriously, honorable doctor? Sakaida
adjusted his gown. Perhaps the worst thing about hospital life was the
clothing—a loose-fitting gown, sandals, and a ridiculous, visorless hat with
a red cross. "Honorable doctor, my division officer was not only ordered
to body-crash, he led the mission. My orders were to escort him to the target, observe the results, and report back."

"Yes, but you landed in a hysterical laughing fit. You were unable to
give a coherent report, and one of your squadron reported that you performed stunts over an enemy ship. The base commander says you should
have body-crashed instead of showing off your flying skills." Sakaida failed
to respond, so the doctor pressed him. "How do you explain this?"

Hiroyoshi Sakaida saw beyond the windowless room. His vision expanded to infinity, to a sky filled with nothing but bursting violence and
torching aircraft. At length he mumbled, "The headaches . . . I cannot always recall what happens."

"I see," Fiume said, scribbling a note for the patient's file. "Reevalu-
ate mental competence for flying. Possibly refer case to authorities regarding performance of duty."

April 1945

D-Day at Okinawa was called Love Day, and the fact that it fell on Easter Sunday as well as April Fool's Day seemed all the more incongruous. But Rogers looked down from his TarCAP station and marveled yet again at the magnitude of the enterprise. *Whatever they call it, this is the biggest damn operation I ever hope to see.* It dwarfed Iwo Jima and reduced the Guadalcanal landings to insignificance.

Lieutenant General Simon Bolivar Buckner's Tenth Army was ashore, apparently without meeting any opposition. Rogers recalled Rear Admiral Griggs's briefing in which he described the forces involved: well over half a million men embarked in nearly 1,500 ships, counting the British Pacific Fleet now striking the Sakashima Islands between Okinawa and Formosa. The landing force numbered 183,000 assault and support troops in four Army and three Marine divisions.

Of course, that many ships and the importance of Okinawa should produce a violent response. Yet the Japanese had been surprisingly inactive. *Reprisal*'s intelligence officers reported almost no opposition ashore, and TF-58 CAPs had splashed fewer than ten bandits.

Rogers noticed he was coming abreast of Purple Beach in the southern landing area as he stretched his orbit point offshore. Okinawa's west coast fronted on the East China Sea and afforded the invaders direct access to Kadena and Yontan airfields. Word had come that the 6th Marine Division had seized the latter facility by midday, which meant the Tactical Air Force soon could go ashore. *Suits me fine,* Rogers mused. *We'll be able to concentrate on the kamikazes.* He swiveled his head, searching the darkening sky. *No joy today, but they'll come. Sure as hell, they'll come.*

In the dimming sunlight he turned team Dagger Eleven toward the task force, overflying the continual back and forthing of landing craft. Rogers pondered the anomaly of Buckner, an Army general, leading one of the largest amphibious operations yet conducted. He shook his head at the irony. *What would Sunny Jim say? Hell,* he thought bitterly, *Jim may not even be alive.*

THURSDAY, 5 APRIL
YOKOSUKA BASE

"Chief Petty Officer Sakaida! Please report to the anteroom immediately. You have a visitor." The orderly added, "I suggest that you wear your uniform. This captain is no briefcase carrier."

Petty Officer Fujimoto, who bunked to Sakaida's right, rolled over and regarded the aviator with interest. "If you know a captain, you can get me transferred back to *Musashi!*"

Discarding his gown and pulling on his trousers, Sakaida merely shook his head. *It's either pitiful or laughable.* Fujimoto had been a signalman on IJNS *Musashi,* one of the two biggest battleships in the Imperial Navy— or any other, for that matter. Sunk nearly six months ago in the Philippines, she had lost most of her crew in multiple air attacks. Fujimoto, the damnable wretch, could not accept that fact.

"I do not know any captains," Sakaida said evenly. He buttoned his uniform blouse, tugged it straight, and hastened through the ward doors. Behind him Fujimoto screamed, "You can come with me, Sakaida! *Musashi* needs floatplane pilots!"

Entering the anteroom, Sakaida immediately picked out the visitor. *Kuwahara was right. This one is no briefcase carrier.* He snapped to attention, bowed low and announced, "Flight Chief Petty Officer Sakaida, reporting as ordered."

"I am Captain Umeda," the officer announced. At five feet ten he towered above Sakaida and most other Japanese, but his bearing overrode even his physical stature. Heavyset with a stern face, he invited equal doses of fear and respect. "I am here to obtain your release, but only if you wish to return to flying duty."

Sakaida's eyes widened in disbelief. "Honored Captain, I wish nothing else than to fly again—especially under your command!"

The officer regarded Sakaida closely. Since entering combat over China in 1938, Ganji Umeda had known all types of pilots. As one of the select few to introduce the Zero Model 11 to front-line service in 1940, his experience and reputation had grown, as had his tolerance for renegades. When he talked to Dr. Fiume, he had pointed out that his command currently included far worse cases than Sakaida: alcoholics, thieves, black marketeers, and at least one murderer. "Sakaida is merely eccentric or crazy. In either case, I can use him," Umeda had stated. Such bluntness was unsettling to Fiume, but it was effective. Umeda already had Sakaida's release papers.

"I command Air Group 342, the Mamoru Wing at Kanoya Base," Umeda explained. "In fact, I tried to obtain you once before."

Sakaida was taken aback. "*Hai!* Lieutenant Kono told me, sir. I felt that I was needed with the Shinkai Unit, but—"

"Yes, I know." Umeda's voice said that he knew a great deal more, and Sakaida wondered if the captain had known Kono in China. "You must understand one thing, Sakaida. I am short of Class A combat pilots. That's the only reason I'm here. We fly the *Shiden Kai*, which is not at all like the Zero fighter. You will fly the way I tell you, or I'll send you directly back here. Is that understood?"

Sakaida knew a good deal when he saw one. He bowed again, keeping his eyes on the deck. "Perfectly, Honorable Captain."

FRIDAY, 6 APRIL

USS *REPRISAL*

"Oh, hell!" The assistant fighter director immediately covered his lapse with a more regulation-type statement: "Raid Five, Raid Five. Ten-plus bearing three-four-zero. Ninety miles and closing."

The air conditioning was never quiet in Combat Information Center, but the cramped space seemed warm—the result of heated vacuum tubes and concerned humans in a sealed steel compartment.

Henry Lang absorbed the information. "Good thing we refueled day before yesterday," he murmured to himself. "That would've been a hellacious time for a raid." Grabbing the command phone off the bulkhead, he made the call. "Courthouse, Dagger Base. Raid Five now on our screen. Three-four-zero at ninety miles."

Lang listened a moment as Jacob Griggs asked a handful of astute questions. "Ah, yes, sir," the FDO replied. "We still have eight chicks overhead but they're due to recover in fifteen minutes." In response to another question, Lang answered, "They are ammo-plus, sir, but getting short on gas."

Finally Lang said, "Aye, aye, sir." He hung up and looked at his assistant, Lieutenant (j.g.) John Vermilya. "John, let's rotate the operators while we have time. I'll scramble the on-deck fighters and we'll tackle these new boys with a fresh team." He reached for his microphone and punched in A channel. "Lemon Three-One and Four-One, this is Dagger Base. Pancake Lemon Base."

While Lang recalled *Crown Point*'s airborne ForceCAP and ordered immediate launch of *Reprisal*'s two standby divisions, Vermilya hastened the thirty-minute rotation of radar operators. Experience had shown that most men developed eyestrain trying to concentrate on flickering radar scopes for more than half an hour. Consequently, the CIC team numbered six other officers and thirty-four enlisted men—radar operators, plotters, and talkers—to meet the requirements of a twenty-four-hour day.

Lang squirmed on his swivel chair and leaned forward on the plotting table with its repeater scope. He could select any of the six radar screens in the center for his own evaluation without leaving his seat or bothering one of the operators. He looked at the clock: 1015. Rubbing his temples, he calculated that he had been on duty almost five hours. He pulled off his earphones and stood up. "John, you take over. I'll stand by here."

Throughout the compartment, relief radar operators were brought up to date by the previous shift. Vermilya already knew the tactical situation, having watched as the last two raids were tracked and dispersed by the combat air patrol. He looked again at the Plexiglas plotting board, a spider's web of compass bearings out to a radius of one hundred nautical miles. Superimposed in crayon were antisub and fighter patrols as well as the Rad-CAPs, the radar CAPs over the picket destroyers.

Vermilya consulted his own scope, slaved to the SK air-search radar. He picked up the eight Hellcats just launched to relieve the duty CAP and called on A channel, "Dagger Eleven-One from Dagger Base. Over."

"Eleven-One to Dagger Base. Read you five by five."

Lang perked up. "That's Phil Rogers. This is shaping up like a good day for fighter skippers." During the day's second CAP, Lang had vectored Ralph Platco's team into an intercept that netted four splashes, but a lone suicider had survived to inflict slight damage on the battleship *Illinois*. Now it only seemed fair that the VBF skipper should get a chance.

Vermilya keyed his mike. "Eleven-One, Freddie is Dagger Base. Make your cockerel crow, over."

"Roger." There was a delay while Rogers, who now knew that *Reprisal* would control him, switched on his IFF transponder. Vermilya was rewarded with a strobe around the radar blips that indicated Rogers's two divisions.

Confirming the F6Fs' location by radar, Vermilya looked at the six-foot Plexiglas plotting board. The track of Raid Six, generally from the northwest, was traced in yellow by a seaman striker who had long ago mastered the arcane art of printing backward. He remained behind the transparent board providing up-to-date visual information without obscuring the data. When the raid was dispersed, the board would be photographed for debriefing analysis.

As Vermilya calculated the time/distance problem, Lang stepped back. From long practice he already knew what heading and airspeed he would assign the fighters. Vermilya took only slightly longer to act. "Dagger Eleven, Dagger Base. Vector three-five-five. Ten-plus at angels twelve, eighty miles. Buster, over."

Rogers acknowledged the orders: a fast-cruise power setting. Halfway to the intercept, Lang ordered Team 13 to orbit. It was not a popular directive, but the fighter-bomber pilots recognized the wisdom in it. Any hostiles that got past Rogers's division still would have to deal with another Hellcat quartet.

Several minutes passed as the CIC watch took note of the three-dimensional hunt being conducted beyond human vision. Inexorably, the two tracks neared one another as Raid Five converged on Dagger Eleven. Still the tutor, Lang forced himself to remain quiet, taking the measure of John Vermilya's esoteric talent.

"They ought to be in sight anytime now," Vermilya offered. By his reckoning, the two formations were less than ten miles from each other. He turned his head to address his boss. "Hank, if there's no contact in another minute I'm going to . . ."

"Dagger Eleven-One here. Tally ho! Twelve bandits, ten o'clock. I am attacking."

Before the fighter director could acknowledge, the channel was usurped by Rogers deploying his division. "Eddie, this is Buck. Hit 'em from this side. I'm taking Van to port and we'll bracket 'em."

"Gotcha, Cap'n."

The next two minutes were eerily quiet, interrupted only occasionally by calls from four young Americans trying to kill a dozen young Japanese. The radio and radar told the story, for those who could follow it. Hostile blips—those without transponder identifiers—began dropping off the scope.

"Splash one, Skipper."

"Stay with me, damn it."

"Lead him, Van, lead him . . . nice shooting!"

"Splash two more."

Finally: "Dagger Base, this is Eleven-One. Heads up. We are ammo-minus and there's several still headed your way. Out."

Vermilya acknowledged the transmission. He already had five sur-viving *kamikazes* on his scope, headed for Dagger 13. "Hank, Team Eleven's got less than half its ammo and Thirteen's going to be engaged. I think we ought to reinforce the CAP."

Lang already was on the horn. Checking the deck-indicator code, he saw that *Sharpsburg* had two more divisions standing by. He called the flag bridge to tell Griggs what he planned to do. "Courthouse, this is Dagger Base. Bandits are thinned out but still coming, down to about forty miles. With your permission, I'm going to scramble two Granite teams."

He hung up the phone. "Okay, we'll have eight more chicks in a few minutes."

Vermilya did not reply. He was concentrating on his radar picture and the second combat. It happened amazingly fast. In minutes Dagger Thirteen-One called, "Grand slam three rats and two fish. Request pancake ammo. One pancake hurt. Over."

Vermilya checked his scope, which showed no remaining hostile. "Dagger Thirteen, Clara. Stand by." He looked at Lang in the darkened room. "I think I'll bring back Thirteen so they can land their wounded man. I'd like to keep Eleven up there until the Granite chicks relieve them."

"Okay, John. But let's make it fast."

"Dagger Thirteen, pancake base. Steer one-three-zero, buster." He got an acknowledgement, then called Rogers. "Dagger Eleven, resume. Orbit until relieved."

"Eleven-One, roger."

Vermilya slumped in his chair. He realized that his lower back hurt from the strain, and rubbed one shoulder.

"Good job, John." Lang's voice came out of the darkness behind him. "We splashed them all this time. Looks like we've earned a rest for a little bit."

"Mr. Lang, you'd better give a listen to Bald Eagle, sir." The radioman second class monitoring the task force command net had one hand cupped to his earphones.

Scooping up a headset, Lang punched in the frequency and listened hard. His pupils, already dilated in the dim light, widened even more. "Oh, no. Copper Base on Picket Station Twelve."

Vermilya straightened in his chair. "What is it?"

"It's the *Books*—I worked an intercept with her just the other day. She's sinking, and another picket destroyer's taken two suiciders."

"Damn." Vermilya's gaze went to the picket stations around Okinawa. He looked at his boss again. "That's the third time today. Do you think—"

"Yeah. The Japs are trying to blind us by sinking the radar pickets."

SATURDAY, 7 APRIL

DAGGER ELEVEN-ONE

Rogers was tired: of the unrelenting flight schedule, of flying in marginal weather, of the demands of command, of unending losses. Yesterday had been terrible: Japanese fliers hit nineteen ships and sank six. But today he was tired of sitting on a hard seat-pack parachute for four hours at a stretch. The warm memory of the full-body rubdowns Sallyann used to give him was flooding his mind—then Pat Clarey's excited tones brought him back to where he was and what he was about to do.

It had been a long hunt. Following yesterday's submarine reports, this morning *Essex* search planes had found the largest Japanese fleet unit to sortie in months, and then PBM flying boats had taken over the tracking. The air group briefing had necessarily been short and incomplete, but it seemed that Vice Admiral Mitscher was about to put one over on the members of "the gun club," Rear Admiral Deyo's force of old battleships. Deyo had intended to tackle IJNS *Yamato* and her escorts, in the last surface engagement of the war, but the aviators had range, speed, and ambition on them.

Scud-running through low clouds, Rogers tried to concentrate on the job at hand. As yet he had seen none of the ten Japanese warships bound for Okinawa, but the anticipation of attacking *Yamato* stirred him. In three years of war he had never seen a Japanese battleship. Now he mused that he finally would get his chance—with one 500-pound bomb.

Descending below the broken clouds, Rogers found the rest of Air Group 59, echeloned in aerial stair-steps behind Clarey's CAG section. Squadrons from another task group were just completing their attack, and B channel was alive with electronic-filtered voices calling hits and misses, asking for directions, or merely sight-seeing. *They're not as well trained as we are,* Rogers realized. *Now they can watch some pros at work.*

Clarey had things in hand. On the assigned frequency he calmly allotted targets. "This is 99 Dagger to 89 Dagger. Barry, set up your torpeckers for an anvil attack on the BB and tell me when you're ready. Ralph, you'll cover them."

Potter and Platco acknowledged, then Clarey was back on the air. "Leo and Phil, take the cruiser to the southwest." Rogers ruefully accepted his task. *Hell, I've sunk a cruiser—I want a battleship!* Still, he admitted the wisdom of CAG's orders: Bombs of five hundred or a thousand pounds would not accomplish much against *Yamato*'s 64,000 tons. But against the cruiser was another matter.

From there on it was almost routine. Under clouds, Air Group 59 played out its professional choreography. Flak rippled the atmosphere and combined with some spectacular phosphorous rounds bursting in fiery white tentacles. Rogers briefly noted that the spectacle was more impressive than dangerous, then led eight fighter-bombers down on the *Agano*-class light cruiser. He was barely aware of the avengers setting up their low, straight torpedo runs on the huge *Yamato*.

"This is Barry. We're going in now."

"Roger, Barry, this is Ralph. We're in our strafing runs, fellow."

Rogers had his Mark 21 gunsight set for air-surface, with the Christmas-tree reticle showing mil values for high-velocity aerial rocket delivery. The cruiser was clearly damaged, throwing smoke but still under way. Rogers aimed at the forward turret and from a 30-degree dive began firing his five-inch rockets at 4,500 feet. Before the sixth HVAR shot off the rail, bombs began falling around the slim, gray shape as Leo Hunziker's Helldivers ran in from the starboard quarter. Rogers was pleased. *Good timing, this ought to work.* He thought he saw the bright flash of at least two five-inch warheads around the bridge.

Light-caliber anti-aircraft fire rippled across his vision, and Rogers was momentarily startled. He realized that his concentration had been spoiled, and he was now too low for accurate bombing. Cursing softly, he came up on the power, eased out of his dive, and pulled off to port. He considered calling for a rendezvous but decided against it. *The fellows know what to do.*

Climbing toward a new roll-in point abeam of the stricken cruiser, Rogers looked back. Barnes apparently had dropped his bomb and was joining up. Fairfield and Sossaman were farther behind. For a moment the drab colors of his world grasped Rogers's attention: a bleeding, gray ship on a spume-topped blue-gray sea beneath lowering gray clouds rent by brownish-black smoke bursts. More small-caliber stuff squirted ineffectually at the dark-blue airplanes mauling the cruiser. And for no reason at all, Phil Rogers was afraid.

His forearms felt heavy now, and he released his hands from the controls. Flexing his fingers, stomping his feet, he tried to settle down. Each second on this reciprocal heading took him another 265 feet from the target. He looked around. There was Barnes, closing up and looking at his leader. There were dozens of other planes in the air, and clearly the cruiser was done for. But Lieutenant Commander Rogers, ComBombFitRon 59, still had his damned bomb under the starboard wing, and it would not do to jettison the thing in the ocean. He grasped stick and throttle, inhaled deeply, and eased into a standard-rate turn back toward the target.

Apparently Bombing 59 had completed its attack. Residual water rings were subsiding on either side of the cruiser, which had lost headway. The flak had all but disappeared. *Do it now,* Rogers told himself. He flicked his rocket-bomb transfer switch to "Bomb," then slanted into a long, shallow approach from astern and began tracking the doomed ship.

A few more tracers crossed his reflector sight, port to starboard. And Rogers realized with an adrenaline rush: *It's the* Mikuma *attack all over!* The sixth of June '42: Midway again. Always Midway, that linchpin of his naval life. The destroyer's tracers, an ensign's breezy confidence ("They can't hit you at wide deflection"), the sudden searing pain in the leg.

I got a Navy Cross for that, Rogers reminded himself. *Said I'd have to earn the damn thing someday. Like now.*

At 2,500 feet, he was tracking smoothly. His gloved thumb went to the red button atop the stick. Satisfied with the sight picture, he pressed— hard—and felt a quarter-ton come off the airplane.

Low enough. Pull. Rogers's vision faded to fuzzy gray and he lost the horizon. Then he was nose-up and climbing. He felt the heavy pressure on the elevators and retrimmed for climb. Barnes's voice scratched at his earphones. "That's a hit, Skipper! You see it?"

Rogers rolled one wing down and saw only more smoke from the cruiser. He picked up the mike and replied, "No, Bill. Let's get the boys rounded up." Rogers circled south of the small suicide armada, regrouping his two divisions and considering options. With bombs and most of their rockets gone, the Hellcats could contribute little more than flak suppression against the remaining destroyers. Then, outbound twenty-two minutes after the 6,600-ton cruiser rolled over and sank, Rogers heard Fairfield's voice, oddly shrill: "Wahoo! Lookit that!" He added belatedly, "The battle wagon, off our starboard quarter."

Rogers craned his neck, looking back past his armor plate. *Yamato,* the largest battleship on Planet Earth, had disappeared under a boiling mushroom cloud. Three destroyers scurried nearby, leaving concerned gray-white wakes to mark their orbits as yet another air group arrived on station.

Rogers formed up Team 11 and set course for home. He felt he had finally earned his Navy Cross—not for damage to the enemy, but for reasons no one else would ever know.

WEDNESDAY, 11 APRIL

KANOYA BASE

Sakaida thought the new fighter just did not look right. Too big, too angular—too ugly.

The Kawanishi N1K2, officially titled *Shiden Kai* or "Violet Lightning" by some deskbound poet, sat upon a spindly looking landing gear. The bulbous nose housed 1,990 horsepower to swing a large four-blade propeller, lending the plane a brutish, businesslike appearance. Still the aircraft's name was appropriate to *Hikotai* 801, which called itself *Senden*—the Flashing Lightning Group.

Sakaida was surprised to learn that despite its apparent bulk the *Shiden* Model 21 was only marginally larger than the Zero Model 52. The main difference was wingspan, as the Kawanishi land-based interceptor measured twelve meters against the Model 52's eleven.

"Ah, there you are. What do you think of it?"

Sakaida turned toward the voice, his reverie broken. Warrant Officer Koichi Magoshi stood at the nose, resting against one of the prop blades. Magoshi oversaw each pilot's checkout in *Hikotai* 801, and Sakaida still did not know what to make of either the instructor or the airplane. Everything was so new—the base, the unit, the equipment. Everything.

"It isn't what I'm used to," Sakaida replied cautiously.

Magoshi shuffled around the nose of the fighter, studying his pupil. "That's right—you came from floatplanes, didn't you?"

For a moment Sakaida's temper flared. The fact that the two were former enlisted men allowed a give-and-take, though Sakaida reflected that a fistfight with his check pilot would not be an auspicious beginning. "That's not what I mean. I flew Zeros before, that's all." He kept the resentment from his voice.

The instructor was unperturbed. "You know, the *Shiden* was developed from the *Kyofu* floatplane. Fewer than a hundred of those were built."

Sakaida knew of the N1K *Kyofu*, the "Mighty Wind." It was a big step up from the Type 2 sea fighters he had flown in the Solomons and at Truk, but the very concept was now obsolete. He decided to change the subject. "This aircraft is so different. More like a battle ax than a fencing sword."

Magoshi's smile caught Sakaida by surprise. "That is exactly right!" he enthused. "The *Shiden* has power and speed to match the American

Grummans and Vought-Sikorskys. The days of dogfighting are behind us—we shall use speed and power."

Sakaida rested a hand on one of the four 20-millimeter cannons. "From what I have heard, the armament is the *Shiden*'s main advantage. Will it really do three hundred fifty knots?"

Sitting on the port tire, Magoshi tipped his visored cap back on his head. "No, it will not. The original design called for that, but the most I've seen is three-twenty at fifty-five hundred meters."

"Less than twenty knots better than a top-rated Zero Model 52," Sakaida muttered. "What about maneuverability and climb?"

"Well, of course nothing matches the Zero. This airplane turns better than the J2M2, but the *Raiden* is only being built in small numbers. As for climb, the *Shiden* is about twenty seconds slower than the Model 52 Zero to six thousand meters."

Sakaida shrugged. "Then what is the advantage in building this or the *Raiden*?" He had seen the Thunderbolt interceptor, Mitsubishi's successor to the Zero, but had not flown one.

"You said it yourself, Sakaida. A battle ax is more powerful than a sword. Our tactics are changing to keep up with the Americans." He looked at the *Shiden*'s beefy airframe. "With more firepower and a more durable design, we can engage the enemy with more chance of success. And survival," he added glumly.

A scarlet thread of anxiety wove its way into Sakaida's consciousness. Intellectually, he recognized the natural human resistance to change, even to progress. But the Zero had become part of him, emotionally and almost physically. He felt completely confident in his ability with it. Looking at the inelegant *Shiden,* he noticed the rough workmanship and wondered about his future. "Are more *kokutai* receiving this fighter?"

"Yes, as production allows." Magoshi glanced left and right, as if seeking confidentiality. "This airplane entered production more than two years ago," he explained. "Air Group Two-Zero-One took the first Model 11 *Shidens* to the Philippines and was nearly wiped out last fall. I am told that lack of spare parts and landing-gear problems were as troublesome as the Grummans." Sakaida knew better than to ask the source of Magoshi's information. "The Model 21 is getting better support and planning. Kawanishi has reduced component parts from over sixty thousand to barely forty thousand, but production is still slow."

Something isn't right, Sakaida realized. An aircraft that entered production in 1943 should be well along by now. He risked an impertinent question. "What's the delay?"

Magoshi rose and stood close to Sakaida, speaking in a low, modu-

lated voice. "Well, I guess you deserve a straight answer." He nodded toward the *Shiden*. "The Model 21 really is a different airplane than the original. Only the wings are the same. The rest of the airframe had to be
redesigned because of operational problems and to simplify construction
and maintenance. All that takes time." He shrugged in a frustrated, angry
gesture. "Then there's the Americans . . ."

Sakaida cut him off with a curt *"Hai!"* Some things simply were not
said on a Japanese Navy base in 1945, but the damned B-29s were cutting
into engine and airframe production.

Hiroyoshi Sakaida looked for a long moment into the face of Koichi
Magoshi and two imperial warriors found their own likeness reflected in
one other's eyes. The knowledge there was tacitly concrete.

Their country was going to lose the war.

FRIDAY, 13 APRIL
USS *REPRISAL*

As always, there was shoptalk in the wardroom. Rogers, Pat Clarey, Ralph
Platco, and Barry Potter discussed air group matters while the stewards
served dinner. There was a time when, dining with three Annapolis men,
Phil would have expected a generalized discussion. Tradition held that
naval officers did not discuss ladies, religion or business in the wardroom,
but pragmatism won out. Conversation turned on the upcoming Kyushu
strikes, though Potter was still excited about the *Yamato* hunt six days before.

"The boys really did a swell job," he enthused. "We lost Hardisty on
the run-in but since we've examined the photos we think we can claim six
hits."

Clarey leaned over as a Negro steward set a bowl of soup before him.
"All right, Barry, write it up and I'll endorse the citations." Potter grinned
in spite of himself, prompting a smile from Rogers. *Barry's a good guy,
but no stoneface. You can read him like a book.* It was no surprise that Potter was a big loser in the CO/XO poker games.

Platco stirred his soup. "Hey, remember the report about the Jap pilot
that was captured the other day? He said a big *kamikaze* raid was due yesterday. Turned out he was right."

Clarey nodded. "Yes. It's confirmed that the *Enterprise* and *Essex* both
were hit. Scuttlebutt has it the Big E will head for Pearl. Apparently the
Essex isn't badly hurt."

Rogers instinctively shifted in his chair as the carrier wallowed in a
long swell. Behind him he heard an angry voice. "Hey, watch it, boy!"

The modulated buzz of conversation dropped off. Rogers turned to find a young steward solicitously dabbing at an officer's shirt with a towel. "I— I'm awful sorry, suh. Th' ship jus' caught me off balance—"

"Oh, shut up." The lieutenant, whom Rogers recognized as a Bombing 59 pilot, grabbed the towel and tried to soak up the navy-bean soup stains. The steward made a hasty withdrawal.

Rogers scanned the room. Leo Hunziker was absent so Rogers turned to Clarey. "Sir, I don't think an officer should address anyone that way. Hunziker should talk to that . . . man."

Clarey shrugged noncommittally. "That's Carter—always was a hothead." Awaiting further comment, Rogers realized that none was forthcoming. *Of course,* Phil realized. *Carter's one of Clarey's bomber pilots.* He glanced at Platco, who seemed unconcerned, then at Potter, who looked embarrassed; the air group commander obviously considered the matter closed. *Pat's turned into a good CAG in the air, but he still won't rattle cages that need rattling.*

Rogers turned to his own soup, remembering other meals on other ships. The Navy relied on Negroes and Filipinos for its mess stewards, but they lived in a world apart. Rogers recalled the rumor aboard *Saratoga* after she was torpedoed in January '42—how two Filipino stewards had panicked and tried to undog a hatch that would have compromised water tight integrity. *If the rumors were true, they got what they deserved, but . . .*

No, it's not just the Navy, Rogers thought. *It's bigger than that.* He recalled the press reports about race riots in Detroit and New York two summers ago. And last spring Senator Maybank of South Carolina told the Senate that the South would not open polls to Negroes. Though a Floridian, Phil Rogers considered himself only peripherally a Southerner. Although he had no colored friends, that was largely because of his profession, but he did know a few aviators of Spanish ancestry. However, the Army Air Forces had Negro pilots. For a moment he toyed with the idea of Negro naval aviators. *Nah, we'll just as likely have women flying from carriers. Although, come to think of it . . .*

"This is the captain speaking." The loudspeaker interrupted thoughts and conversations. Like everyone else, Rogers instinctively turned toward the speaker on the bulkhead, wondering about the long pause.

Captain McEwen's baritone continued, audibly straining for control. "I have a dispatch that contains very sad news for all hands. Men, the Commander-in-Chief is dead. President Roosevelt died today in Warm Springs, Georgia."

Rogers turned to Barry Potter, who was sitting beside him. The torpedo skipper's face mirrored the bewilderment and disbelief on most of the others in the room. McEwen continued, "Vice President Truman has been sworn in, and the war effort will continue as before. But the Navy has lost a great leader, and whatever our individual politics, I know that Franklin Roosevelt will be sorely missed."

"My God," Platco stammered, "I can hardly believe it. F.D.R.'s been President more than twelve years." Everyone present knew what he meant: The younger airmen and sailors could hardly remember anyone else occupying that office.

Clarey sat back in his chair. "You know, the captain's right. Whatever anybody thinks of Roosevelt's politics, he was all for the Navy."

"Well, sure. He and Teddy were both Navy secretaries," Potter observed.

"No, more than that," Clarey argued. "One of my father's friends worked for Frank Knox in the Navy Department. He said that General Marshall got up in one meeting and said, 'Mr. President, I would appreciate it if you would stop referring to the Army as 'you' and the Navy as 'us.' "

While the others laughed, Rogers stirred uneasily. "You know, Truman was in the Army artillery in the last war. He may not be as sympathetic to the Navy."

"Maybe not," Clarey replied. "But the Pacific is still a Navy theater. MacArthur ran out of room two months ago when he recaptured Manila. King and Nimitz will call the shots at least until we invade Japan."

Potter leaned forward, his chin in one hand. "It just occurred to me—this is Friday the thirteenth. We've had enough bad luck without the President dying." He forgot that in America, across the International Date Line, it was Thursday the twelfth.

Rogers said, "You know, we left Alameda on Friday the thirteenth last October." He thought of the flight-deck banter between Diskowski and Sossaman. *Kenny was the superstitious one, and now he's dead.* Staring at the white tablecloth with the silver napkin rings, the incongruity got to him. He choked down the knot building in his throat.

Potter nudged him. "Phil? You say something?"

"No, I was just thinking—this is one goddamned long war."

SUNDAY, 15 APRIL
KANOYA BASE, 0822

"*Senden*, immediate takeoff! Enemy aircraft approaching the coast at Sata-Misaki!"

Like the rest of the Flashing Lightning *hikotai,* Sakaida reacted instinctively. His booted feet sprinted him through the door and fifty meters to the flight line before he remembered that he was not yet combat-qualified in the *Shiden Kai*. Nevertheless he grasped the knotted rope leading to the cockpit of the fighter marked C 342-18 and pulled himself up. By the time he swung into the cockpit and began buckling in, he felt no concern that he had first flown the *Shiden Kai* three days before.

He slid his feet into the rudder-bar stirrups, moved the elevators and ailerons through their full arcs, and was satisfied the control locks were removed. Then he forced himself to deal with the starting procedure: battery on; throttle cracked; mixture at idle-cutoff; magnetos to both; primer— *Where the hell? Oh, yes.* He heard other planes' engines bark into life on either side of him.

DAGGER ELEVEN-ONE, 0823

From eighteen thousand feet up the Kyushu coast lay like a three-dimensional map before *Reprisal*'s Strike Able. The hook of land called Sata-Misaki, Cape Safa, showed the way to the entrance to Kagoshima Bay, in the far south of the island, where the Japanese fleet used to have a major anchorage. But this was April 1945, and Rogers had seen the end of the Imperial Navy at sea. Warships were no longer a major concern. He glanced at the strip map on his kneeboard. Today Air Group 59 was hunting airfields, and southern Kyushu was full of them. He inhaled beneath his oxygen mask and tapped the major target areas: Kagoshima itself, Ibusuki, Miyazaki. And Kanoya.

KANOYA BASE, 0825

Sakaida willed himself to relax. His first two attempts to start the balky Nakajima engine had failed, and a squadron scramble was the absolute worst time for fumbling. Most of the other dozen *Shiden*s were taxing out, and Sakaida imagined the querulous looks their pilots must be directing toward him.

He flexed his fingers and fought to concentrate. *This has happened before,* he reminded himself. At Rekata Bay in 1942 he had sat helplessly in his A6M2-N sea fighter while American aircraft were reported inbound. Mechanics had worked to get him started while the other A6M2-Ns lifted off, water streaming from their floats. He had finally gotten airborne but had arrived too late to save Yusuke Kono from a fiery agony in New Georgia Sound.

Kono—he has been dead nearly a month. Don't think about that. Think about getting this God-cursed engine started! His fingers returned to the priming switch as the lead fighters left the runway, tucking their wheels into their wings.

DAGGER ELEVEN-ONE, 0826

Rogers added a little power, nudging on thirty-four inches of manifold pressure. Leading three divisions on a fighter-bomber sweep, he intended to leave one division as top cover while he worked over the facilities and aircraft. Then he would relieve Diefendorf, who would either finish the destruction or proceed to an alternate target.

Rogers glanced left and right, noting that other Hellcats were diverting to their own destinations. This was the Big Blue Blanket at work: smothering enemy airfields that harbored attack aircraft or *kamikazes*. Admiral Griggs had said, "If they won't come up and fight, we'll hammer them to pieces where they sit."

Fine with me, Admiral. Rogers had begun to realize that he usually felt better when he could shoot, bomb, or strafe something. Combat, he found, was an excellent cure for fatigue.

He turned 20 degrees to starboard and skirted the coast northeastward to Uchinoura before turning inland for the target, Kanoya Base.

KANOYA BASE, 0828

The Homare 21 radial engine's eighteen cylinders reluctantly kicked over in a loud, hollow cough. Sakaida gingerly handled throttle and mixture, allowing the engine to settle down to a steady rumble. He scanned the gauges and did not like what he saw: the oil pressure had not come up to the mark, but he told himself that could be a temporary situation or a faulty instrument.

Sakaida turned on his radio and tried to sort out the static. He never held much confidence in his nation's electronic products, and voice radio remained an unreliable means of aircraft communication. Unshielded ignitions played havoc with reception.

Turning in his seat, he beckoned to one of the mechanics, who scrambled onto the wing. "Have the division officer call operations," Sakaida shouted. "See if you can tell where the Americans are." The man nodded briskly and slid down the wing.

DAGGER ELEVEN-ONE, 0829

"Dagger Eleven flight, target at ten o'clock. Hunter, keep us in sight. I'll call you again when I see what's what."

"Roger, Phil." Diefendorf's calm voice crackled clearly on the VHF channel reserved for air-to-air communications.

Rogers had reached his run-in altitude at approximately the desired spot: fourteen thousand feet, six miles from Kanoya Base. He shifted to neutral blower, bringing the prop back to 2,300 r.p.m. Then he lowered his Hellcat's nose and led two divisions down to destroy something worthwhile.

SENDEN EIGHTEEN, 0830

The Homare 21 still wasn't developing maximum power, but Sakaida had made up his mind. He allowed the big fighter to accelerate longer than normal, then eased it off the ground. Immediately he reached down, retracted his wheels, and watched the airspeed rise through 110 knots. Satisfied that he had a working weapon in his hands, he adjusted power for a fast climb and rolled into a southeasterly turn. That was the direction last indicated for the Americans' approach, and he hoped to catch his squadron somewhere over the coast.

Climbing at 130 knots, Sakaida reached to his armament panel and tugged the four knobs. He felt the hydraulic chargers chamber 20-millimeter rounds in the two cannon in each wing, then turned on his reflector sight. He was ready to fight. *But where are the Americans?*

DAGGER ELEVEN-ONE, 0831

It looked like a good set-up: Make two fast passes, bombing and strafing, then head outbound ten miles to the coast. Rogers easily picked up the big air station and, marveling at the lack of opposition, keyed his mike. "Buzz, swing to the west. We'll split the defenses."

Lieutenant Buzz Berent, the skipper of Team 14, quickly acknowledged, leading his four F6Fs in a wide loop to the left. Rogers calculated that Team 14 would strike from the opposite quadrant shortly after his own Team 11 completed its first run.

Easing into his dive, Rogers searched for his briefed targets. Three large hangars stood out—his team would handle them. He saw the belated muzzle flashes from the ground and ignored the tracers. *They're underdeflecting—forget 'em.* He set his pipper on the middle hangar, steadied up the Hellcat, and pressed the button. *Four o'clock,* he thought, certain that the bomb would punch through the lower-right-hand corner of the roof. He still had time, so he switched to "Rocket" and pressed the trigger twice. The outboard HVARs sizzled away from him, converging on the hangar.

Rogers honked the stick back and rolled into a 40-degree port turn.

Don't give the gunners a straight path. His peripheral vision registered bomb and rocket strikes on two other hangars. It was going very well . . . Right up to the moment that Diefendorf called, "Dagger! Bandits overhead, to the southeast. Coming down now!"

SENDEN EIGHTEEN

The frequency was scratchy, but Sakaida made out the meaning well enough. The radio operator's voice sounded almost falsetto as he announced Grummans attacking Kanoya Base. For an instant Sakaida raged. Presumably Squadron 404 had been deployed to the east. *How did the Yankees get in without being seen?* Then he was shoving up the power, ruddering through a reversal, heading back the way he had come. But he already knew it was too late.

DAGGER ELEVEN-ONE, 0832

Rogers and Barnes smoothly executed a low-level weave with Fairfield and Sossaman, each section covering the other as they prepared to meet the threat. Rogers had the geometry of the situation in mind: Team 11 would climb to meet the interceptors, who would be sandwiched between himself and Diefendorf's Team 12. *Good deal. Buzz will get a shot at the field.*

There they were, several low-wing silhouettes nose-on at about two miles. For a moment Rogers thought they were Zekes, but as the range closed he realized they must be something else. *Whatever they are, we're outnumbered until Hunter arrives. Got to break 'em up.* On impulse, he put the leading bandits in his sight. He nosed up a bit and fired two HVARs. The big rockets streamed toward the first two *Shiden*s, which immediately split. He exulted. *You bastards never had rockets shot at you.*

Rogers tacked onto the right-hand fighter and firewalled everything. Pulling fifty-two inches, he closed to three hundred yards, tracked the bandit in his sight, and opened fire. *Hello there,* he thought—he was surprised when his tracers sparkled across the *Shiden*'s starboard wingtip. *This guy's smart—kicked left rudder to throw me off.* Rogers realized that he was up against better opponents than he had seen before.

But he was still in the saddle. He cut the corner, slid across the bandit's tail, and laid off a quarter-deflection shot from eight o'clock. The *Shiden* lit up as armor-piercing incendiaries sparkled over the fuselage. Rogers expected it to disintegrate, but it remained wings-level. *Damn! This guy's tough.* He bored in to two hundred yards, fired again, and watched the olive-green fighter come apart. *It's a George,* he realized. *A hot ship.* He passed overhead, checked for Barnes, found him abeam, and eased into a climbing turn. Diefendorf's team had descended on the other Georges, and the fight was degenerating into a low-altitude brawl. Rogers saw two more wrecks on the ground east of the airfield. He looked westward, where Team 14 must appear any second now.

SENDEN EIGHTEEN, 0833

Sakaida was appalled at the burning hangars. Then he discerned orange-white eruptions through the greasy smoke and realized the attack was still in progress. At twelve hundred meters he began a shallow descent, aiming for the southwest corner of the air station boundary, looking for a target. He decided that if he found nothing on his first pass he would cross the field, seeking combat over Kanoya East. Two gloss-blue shapes entered his vision. Grummans! Diving west to east. He realized they had either just bombed or just strafed the hangars and flight line, as planes were burning on the ramp. He checked overhead—he was up-sun in the afternoon sky— and saw no other Americans. He rolled into an intercept heading, indicating 300 knots.

DAGGER ELEVEN-ONE

Rogers heard the helpless agony in the call: "Buzz! There's Japs behind—" The abrupt end of O'Keefe's call told him more than he wanted to know. He looked for his second section, could not find Eddie Fairfield and Brian Sossaman, so decided to race westward. More cries on the radio now . . . something seriously wrong. Two Georges passed beneath him. *Everybody's all mixed up now. Let 'em go.* Team 14 needed help.

SENDEN EIGHTEEN

Sakaida was impressed. He had never seen the effect of four 20-millimeter cannons, but the way the tail-end Grumman had erupted at 250 meters pleased him immensely. *The Yankee was too busy looking at the ground to notice me.* Now he had latched on to its leader, and he needed to make quick work of it before other Grummans learned he was there.

This American seemed to know his business. Instead of the rookie's response of indulging in aerobatics or making a dash for safety, he pulled into a climbing turn. Sakaida recognized the move for what it was: an attempt to make him overshoot. But he was able to match the radius of the turn and, only three hundred meters over the center of the field, he laid off

30 degrees of deflection. With the Yankee fighter seemingly suspended nose-high, superimposed on a towering pillar of gray-black smoke, he pressed the firing handle on his throttle.

DAGGER ELEVEN-ONE, 0834

Rogers could see the fight, but he hardly believed what he saw. One F6 had gone right in, burning between the runways. Another was dueling with a well-flown George—and losing. Buzz Berent's lead section now was between Rogers and the combat, almost in range.

From less than a mile, Rogers saw the vulnerable Hellcat decelerate, nose over, and dive into the smoke. The George pilot seemed eerily unconcerned, apparently sure of a kill, because he briefly leveled his wings—and began flying aerobatics.

SENDEN EIGHTEEN

If anyone had asked him, Sakaida could not have said what prompted him to indulge in a prideful display of stunt flying. He simply felt—what? *I feel good, very good,* he exulted, *almost the way I did over the American carriers.* Barely above pattern altitude, he coordinated stick and rudder and stopped his *Shiden* with wings vertical to the ground. He held the attitude briefly, then repeated the motion, continuing the hesitation roll to the right. Hanging from his straps, he glanced through the top of the canopy as Kanoya's main runway appeared "above" him. The tingling sensation returned, and Sakaida laughed again, relishing his control over his aircraft while recognizing the onset of that old gleeful madness.

DAGGER ELEVEN-ONE

What are the odds? Rogers gaped, unbelieving, as the George completed the second and third points of a hesitation slow roll. *The same stunt that Zero pulled during the* kamikaze *attack.* He had heard of Japanese pilots indulging in combat aerobatics, but usually in an unsubtle attempt to lure American fighters away from their bombers. Overhead *Reprisal,* and now this time—it made no sense. Rogers acknowledged the shiver between his shoulder blades, conceded that somehow this might be the same Jap with a new plane, and began plotting to kill him.

Others had the same idea. Alerted by more AA fire, the George turned to face Berent and Canepa. Gunfire streaked between the antagonists, then the Kawanishi was past the Grummans, headed for Phil Rogers and Bill Barnes.

Rogers did not like the situation. *This guy's not afraid of us, he might do anything.* He called Barnes. "Bill, I'm going high and right. You pull up left." Rogers heard no response, but none was required. The Hellcats broke in opposite directions, much as the first two Georges had done, but there was method to the Americans' plan. In a few seconds, somebody was going to get gunfire through his airframe.

SENDEN EIGHTEEN, 0835

Sakaida's rapture drowned in adrenaline. *Two Grummans down already, and now here are more!* He felt himself growing giddy again—the same joyful hysteria. The medics thought it was dementia; he knew it was salvation. He went to his torque side, confronting the closest Grumman.

For the second time in two months Hiroyoshi Sakaida put William Barnes in his gunsight. The Hellcat loomed in Sakaida's reflector glass, descending on the *Shiden Kai* in a steeply banked, shallow dive. Instantly Sakaida knew he held a small advantage—the F6F's zoom-climb had carried it just beyond the radius of his own wrapped-up turn. He laid off a shallow deflection shot and pressed both triggers.

DAGGER ELEVEN-ONE

Half a mile away, Rogers topped out of his own pull-up and shoved the stick hard over. He half expected to see the George race for cover amid the flak guns rather than engage either prong of the vertical trap. Incredibly, the Japanese had nosed up for a shot at Barnes. The George was actually pressing the fight!

This guy really is crazy! The certainty registered in Rogers's mind as he saw the muzzle flashes from the George's cannon. Barnes, not quite aligned, had no chance to shoot. With 20-millimeter rounds snapping around him, he two-blocked the throttle and twisted into a tight spiral. Rogers, seeing the evasive maneuver, knew that one of only two things could happen. The Jap would pursue Barnes, giving Rogers a shot from dead astern. Or the Jap could reverse into Rogers, resulting in a momentary standoff before one of them killed the other.

SENDEN EIGHTEEN

I have him! Sakaida registered the first Grumman nosing down from twelve hundred meters, apparently out of control. He quit shooting when the Yankee dropped out of his sight, but there was no time to watch the expected crash. Nose-high, bleeding off airspeed, he pushed over while exulting, *Three down so far!* Then he remembered the other Grumman.

Sakaida did not know exactly where the first Hellcat was just now. But training and experience told him that the other American had to be somewhere above and behind him, almost certainly diving toward his tail at high speed. With a confidence born of fatalism, he kept the stick well back, allowing more knots to dissipate. At the incipient stall, he kicked right rudder, allowed the Kawanishi to drop off to starboard, and crammed on full throttle.

Outside his canopy, Sakaida's world rotated through 135 degrees as his nose came back toward the still-unseen threat. He laughed out loud again.

DAGGER ELEVEN-ONE

Rogers was taken by surprise. He had begun tracking the dark-green fighter, estimating that a 150-mil deflection would allow him to shoot earliest if it reversed course. But the abrupt, power-on stall-turn had caught him unprepared; he had never seen a Japanese use the vertical this way. And a tiny shiver of doubt clouded his mind. *Maybe this bastard knows something I don't.* Then a more disturbing thought crowded in: *Maybe he doesn't care if he lives or not.*

They met almost nose to nose, each bottoming out of their three-dimensional arabesque. Neither had time to line up the other, so neither fired. Rogers, already with throttle and prop firewalled, left them that way. Straining against his shoulder harness, trying to keep his enemy in sight, he realized he could not win by turning. That would cede his opponent a crucial altitude advantage. So he pulled up again.

SENDEN EIGHTEEN, 0836

Sakaida felt bullet-proof once more. Less than fifteen hundred meters over his home base, locked in single combat, he could imagine that the Greater East Asia Co-Prosperity Sphere was watching him. He conceded that this American was experienced and capable—there had been no desperate, ineffective gunfire in their brief passage—but time was on Sakaida's side. He twisted in his seat, moving his head enough to track the gloss-blue Grumman in its pitch-up, and wondered, *How long will this Yankee fight me here?* Sakaida realized that his own deficit was ammunition. He estimated that each Type 99 cannon retained about fifteen rounds, but that would be enough. He already knew what four 20-millimeters could do when he brought them to bear.

DAGGER ELEVEN-ONE

Rogers held his roller-coaster pull-up as long as he dared. The pattern was clear now—this combat could continue almost indefinitely. Though he was confident of winning, an enemy airfield was no place to hang around. *He's good, but how smart is he? This time I'll fox him,* Phil told himself. By holding his nose-over longer than before, he expected to upset the George's timing on the downside, giving an extra few seconds to acquire, track, and shoot.

"Dagger Lead! Phil, this is Buzz. I've got you covered!"

Rogers's spirit soared. *Damn! I forgot about Berent. His section was inbound a couple minutes ago.* Phil dared not look away from the George, but Berent and Canepa had to be overhead, watching the fight. An ephemeral concern for Barnes came and went. Rogers knew this combat was about to end: Kill this bird, then regroup and get the hell out of here. Squirming against his restraints, he saw the dark-green Kawanishi bobble slightly in its nose-high attitude, then reluctantly begin to nose over. This was a very talented aviator, but the odds against him had just tripled. Rogers grinned to himself. *Got him.*

SENDEN EIGHTEEN

The Homare engine faltered just slightly—barely enough for Sakaida to feel the difference. But it was enough to deprive him of the power he needed to remain level with the American. In this seesaw battle of timing, skill, and nerves, the abused engine had proven the chink in his armor. As he pushed the nose down he shot a glance at his opponent, even now diving in from the perch, and was appalled to see two more Grummans as well. Confidence melted and mysticism turned to reality as giddiness tightwalked the precipice of panic.

The flak gunners at the east edge of the field were astute enough to open fire. Sakaida almost welcomed the 25-millimeter tracers burning past him, hoping the gunfire would deter the three Americans. But he knew better. For a fiery instant he saw Kono in his mind's eye, deliberately diving himself into the water off Guadalcanal to quench the fire that was consuming him. The earth was more unyielding than the sea, but Sakaida knew he had no choice. *In ten seconds the Grummans will shoot me out of the sky.*

DAGGER ELEVEN-ONE, 0837

Rogers was calm now. The flak—light stuff, mostly—was ineffective. Pulling fifty inches and 2,550 r.p.m. from his engine, he hauled into range and put his pipper on the Kawanishi's rudder. Oddly, the Japanese had dived almost to ground level in the time it took Rogers to close for a decent shot. He fired a ranging burst at 5 degrees deflection and saw his armor-piercing incendiaries strike sparks where they struck. He fired again and—it was peculiar. The George hit flat, perhaps still doing 100 knots, and bounced twice. On the second impact it violently lurched sideways, spinning like a child's top. Then Rogers was past it, losing sight in the swirling dust. *That's odd,* he thought. It almost looked as if the Jap had deliberately forced his plane into the ground. *Well, no time to think about it.* He punched the mike button. "Dagger flights, this is Eleven-One. Head for the rendezvous. Acknowledge."

As Diefendorf's and Berent's surviving pilots checked in, Rogers was relieved to see Barnes rejoining. Two others were missing besides O'Keefe, whose wingman Herman was shot up, but Rogers accepted that. *It could have been worse.* He still marveled at the way that other George had taken on a skyful of F6s; the way it had impacted the ground. *He was a terrific pilot,* Rogers admitted. *For us, he's better off dead.*

MONDAY, 16 APRIL, 0630
USS *REPRISAL*

Diefendorf was scribbling a revised flight schedule when Rogers plopped into a seat beside him. "How's it going, Hunter?"

The exec hardly looked up. "So-so, Skipper. I had to scratch Team Fourteen from the air plan, so somebody else will have to double up."

Rogers nodded. Finally he asked, "Buzz still shook about losing O'Keefe and Wiltz?"

"Yeah. Well, that's just part of it. I checked on Wiltz in sick bay. Shrapnel in one leg and part of his back. Buzz is a good man, just worn out. A lot of the guys are." He noted the lines around Rogers's eyes. "Including you."

Rogers ignored the sentiment. "You know, the F6F in-commission rate is over ninety percent. We don't need more fighters, we need fighter pilots. I'm going to suggest to Clarey that we transition some bomber guys to F6s. It'd give some of our people a little rest. I discussed it with Ralph and he's for it, too."

Diefendorf set down his tablet. "Well, that might work. I could sure use some more sack time. That ever been done?"

"I don't know. Some air group commanders have done it, though. Emmett Riera went from Bombing Twenty to Air Group Eleven and checked out in an F6 at sea. No reason some of our guys can't do it."

"But you know, Phil, the bomber pilots won't know tactics, and I imagine they're rusty as hell at gunnery."

"I thought of that. But most CAPs are pretty dull. Leo's people are sharp, and that's what we need more than great shooters. Just a heads-up pilot who can fly wing and give one of our guys some rest."

Diefendorf leaned back and turned more toward Rogers. "Word is the *kamikaze* boys are coming out today. You want to stay on the second launch?"

Rogers tensed. "Hell, yes. Why wouldn't I?"

"You've been on all the big ones, Phil. The *Yamato* strike, most of the sweeps and your share of CAPs. Then that big fight yesterday. Just thought you might want a rest."

"Forget it. I'm okay." The words snapped more than Rogers intended, and he sought to change the subject. "But you're right. Those Japs yesterday were pros. We can't underestimate any of them."

Diefendorf yawned. "Maybe we'll get some easy meat today."

DAGGER ELEVEN-ONE, 1047

Rogers had allowed himself to think this might be an uneventful patrol. There had been combat over the radar pickets all morning, but so far no bandits had penetrated the ForceCAP, and Phil's two teams had been orbiting idly for almost an hour.

"Dagger Eleven from Dagger Base. Vector two-seven-zero. 'Gate.' Contact Joker Base on B channel. Acknowledge."

Holy smokes. Rogers depressed the mike switch on his throttle. "Dagger Base from Dagger Eleven. Am heading two-seven-zero at 'Gate.' Will call Joker on B channel. Out."

Rogers had never received a Gate order before: war emergency power for maximum speed with water injection. Obviously, there was a crisis at one of the radar picket stations. He eyed his two divisions, then nodded and rolled onto a westerly heading.

The Hellcat pilots now became exceedingly busy. Each checked the water gauge on the right of the main instrument panel and closed the water pump switch that purged the lines of air. Then, leaving the mixture in

"Auto-Lean," he switched his supercharger to "High Blower" and shoved the throttle through the "gate"—the limit stop on the quadrant.

The numbers came to Rogers like childhood multiplication tables. *Let's see . . . 2,700 r.p.m. and sixty inches. Oil pressure holding at sixty-five PSI.* The water-injection feature of the R-2800 engine allowed five minutes of maximum engine performance—no more. After that, the engine would begin to burn itself out.

Phil double-checked his IFF to identify himself electronically to the destroyers. The Hellcats began eating up the miles, pushing 360 knots in a shallow descent through the rarified atmosphere.

NEARING PICKET STATION NINETEEN, 1052

The water injection ran out just as Rogers switched to B channel and heard the action.

"Rattler Four-One, vector three-three-zero."

"Joker, Rattler. I'm empty, pardner. Have to leave you."

Jeez, Rogers realized, *their CAP is out of ammo.* He made the call and received a fervent reply. "Dagger, thank God. This is Joker. Have you at angels one-eight, twelve miles."

"Roger, Joker. What's the situation?"

"Dagger, they're crawling all over us. Flashlight Base is the one on fire. He will be your Snap controller. I want your second division overhead at angels ten. Acknowledge."

Rogers could see the smoking destroyer northeast of the controlling ship. It looked bad. "Roger, Joker. I am over to Snap. Dagger Thirteen will cap you."

The fighter director came back. "Look for F4Us outbound. They sure saved our bacon."

Rogers shook his head; he had never heard a fighter director so rattled. The unnecessary transmissions were proof enough. But when Rogers looked at Flashlight—whatever her real name was—it was obvious that the *kamikazes* had made an impression.

In a fast, steep descent, Rogers led his team toward the stricken destroyer. His "Snap" patrol would remain within visual distance of Flashlight, allowing close-in defense against raiders who penetrated the radar screen.

Reaching five thousand feet, Rogers waggled his wings to signal Eddie Fairfield. "Dagger Lead to Eleven-Three. Orbit northeast, Eddie. I'll stay about five miles northwest." Fairfield rogered, taking Sossaman with him.

"Snap, this is Dagger Eleven. Four chicks on station, angels five."

There was a delay that Rogers imagined was due to one of the ship's lookouts confirming his presence. When the response came, it carried heart-felt tones. "Roger, Dagger. Thank you. Use C channel for Snap control, over."

Rogers switched to the alternate frequency, leaving B channel for radar control of the second division. Just as he made the change, Flashlight was back on the air. "Dagger, heads up! Joker reports many more bogeys inbound at angels six to ten."

DAGGER ELEVEN-ONE, 1100

Things immediately turned to hash. Before Rogers eyeballed the bandits, Barnes was demanding his attention with violent wing rocking. Rogers turned his head toward his wingman, who was gesturing animatedly: tapping his earphones and shaking his head: *Oh, no. Not now.* Rogers depressed the mike button. "Bill, this is Buck. Do you read me?" There was no response; Barnes's radio was out.

Snap was back on the air. "Dagger One, your vector is three-five-zero. Raid count twenty-plus. Over."

Forcing the complications from his mind, Rogers went to military power. The last time he looked in the cockpit he saw fifty-two inches manifold pressure. Then he saw antique airplanes with fixed landing gear. Suddenly he felt better.

It was a curious oleo of Aichi dive-bombers and aged Mitsubishi fighters: pretty little open-cockpit airplanes with neat wheel spats. Rogers knew he would always remember the ragged formation silhouetted against the high, thin overcast.

Time was important. Eight Hellcats could ruin two dozen Vals and Nates, but it had to be quick execution. Rogers held his climb as long as he dared, then turned into the Japanese formation. He rolled into a low-side pass and rotated his throttle grip, setting up his Mark 21 sight. The reticle's ring of diamonds condensed around the lead dive-bomber, and for an instant Rogers was concerned when the pipper did not appear. Then he relaxed. *I'm tracking from way far out.* The pipper floated into view from the right, and Rogers tried a test burst.

Tracers sparkled toward the dive-bomber fifteen hundred feet away. It looked good. Still closing, controlling the reticle with his left hand, Rogers pressed the trigger again. Hits flashed all over the Aichi, which nosed down, shedding smoke and parts. Hardly registering the kill, Rogers switched targets. He was into boresight range on another Val. *Steady . . . there!* He fired again and saw hits, but already he was pulling up, hopping over the formation. He looked back and saw the second Val swerve away. *Call it a probable. No time to check.*

Barnes was with him, sliding across his tail to set up abeam for another pass. Rogers led the section back into the Japanese, who now broke formation. He latched on to another Val, not bothering with the gyro tracking sight. Instead, Rogers drove up the Aichi's tail, vaguely wondering at the lack of return fire from the gunner's cockpit. Phil steadied up, checked the ball in its housing, and fired. From two hundred yards he saw the big 709-grain bullets chop the bomber apart. A fuel tank ignited and the Val went down, a flamer.

Another bomber ahead at one o'clock. Rogers bent the throttle, hauled into gun range, and fired immediately. His tracers went wide. *Damn it to hell!* He realized he had fired from a slight skid. Regaining control, he leveled his wings, set the pipper on the wing root, and pressed the trigger twice. A roiling explosion engulfed the Val.

Rogers pulled up, looked for Barnes, and saw him engaged with a Nate. *Not worth it,* Rogers thought. He turned back toward the picket station, noting several burning wrecks on the water. Flashlight was obviously the focus of the attack, and her gunners apparently had splashed some *kamikazes*. But her smoke and flames drew suiciders like flies to honey. Rogers dived into the flak belt and said a brief prayer. *Please God, don't let the gunners kill me like they did Bernie. Please Mr. Pratt; please Mr. Whitney—keep this engine together.*

A plucky Nate had ignored the aerial carnage, boring down on the destroyer. Rogers felt he was out of range but held slightly high and fired. He thought he saw the little fighter wobble, but it straightened out. *Not much time left.* He pushed his Hellcat hard, reeling in the Nate, and fired again. There was no fire or explosion. It simply rolled over to starboard and dived into the water a half mile from Flashlight.

Multiple 40-millimeter bursts flashed across his nose. Rogers knew what that meant: He was in range of the shipboard gunners, who would shoot at anything. He wrapped the F6 into a four-G turn, vision going gray at the edges, then climbed back to the north.

The Snap fighter director was trying to call the threats, but there were too many to sort out. Rogers was surprised to see a retractable-gear fighter cross his nose and turned to track it, then recognized the distinctive Hellcat silhouette with its centerline tank. He turned to join and saw that it was Brian Sossaman. He swiveled his head. *Where's Eddie and Bill?*

A strange voice came on the circuit. "Flashlight, this is Checkerboard Two-One. Fifteen miles northwest with six F4Us."

Marines from Okinawa, Rogers realized. *Hope they hurry.*

With Sossaman in tow, Phil turned for his Snap station. He reduced power to the abused engine, noticing the cylinder-head temperature pushing 260 centigrade. *Can't worry about that.* But before they reached the patrol point, Flashlight was back on the air. "Any chick from Snap control. More bandits reported inbound low level, due north about five miles."

Rogers quickly appraised his situation. *Still enough fuel but ammo's getting low. But the Marine Corsairs aren't here yet.* He punched the button. "Snap, Dagger Eleven. We'll take it."

He was unprepared for what he found. Two Nates, skimming the waves, had no room to maneuver. Rogers split-essed down behind them from five o'clock and closed in. He began tracking the right-hand wingman, but curiosity stayed his finger. Rogers eased within fifty yards and found himself uncomfortable in recognizing another human being. He had never been this close to an enemy fighter.

The pilot was bare-headed behind his tiny windscreen, except for a white headband. He appeared to be wearing some sort of robe of scarlet that was whipped by the slipstream. Rogers flew formation for a few heartbeats, pondering whether the odd dress had religious significance. Then he eased back, slipped astern, and even retrimmed his fighter before pressing the trigger. Sossaman's Nate hit the water three seconds later.

Phil Rogers felt an eerie ambivalence at what he had done. This had been an execution, not a combat. Then he looked back at the stricken Benson-class destroyer in time to see two Vals plunge into her and explode amidships. He watched in frustrated rage as she rolled over and began to sink.

USS *REPRISAL*, 1320

Rogers nearly collided with his missing pilots at the base of the ladder leading to the 02 level. "Hey, Skipper. How'd you do out there?" Fairfield's voice betrayed his emotion, his concern at having gotten separated in the dogfight.

Rogers raised five fingers. "It doesn't matter how many we splashed. They still got through and sank that DD." Rogers was mildly angry with himself. *The best day I'll ever have in a fighter. I should be high as a kite, but I'm just so . . . tired.*

The debrief began immediately as the ACIO noted the highlights. A detailed account would be compiled later, but Rogers sat back and watched seven other elated aviators describe the execution of more than twenty Japanese. Then Henderson beckoned to Rogers. "Commander, I'd like to get your report if that's all right."

Rogers slumped in his seat, still wearing everything but his helmet and chute harness. "Three Vals and two Nates plus one Val probable."

Henderson's eyes widened. "That's worth a Navy Cross, sir."

"I've got a Navy Cross," Rogers replied without irony. "Besides, it didn't keep them from sinking Flashlight. Do you know who that was? The radar controller was Joker."

Henderson dug up an operations order and traced a finger down the mimeographed pages. "Here it is. Flashlight—the *Donovon.* And Joker is . . . um, *Ralls.*" He looked up at the CO. "Do you know somebody aboard those ships, Skipper?"

"No, I don't think so. Just seems I should remember . . ."

The squaw box behind Henderson buzzed. He turned and answered, "Ready Two, aye."

"This is the flag bridge. Is Commander Rogers there?"

Henderson depressed the switch. "Yes, sir. He just landed."

"Send him up. The admiral wants to talk to him."

Rogers raised himself from the comfortable seat. Still wearing his gun and Mae West, he waved to Henderson. "On the way."

USS *REPRISAL,* 1330

Admiral Jake Griggs met Rogers halfway across the bridge. "I just heard, son. You boys put up one hell of a fine fight." He shook Rogers's hand with more enthusiasm than Rogers felt.

"Thank you, sir. But we were too late. The *Donovon* was already burning when we arrived. Two Vals finished her off."

"Yes, I know." Griggs stood back and assessed the proud-tired young man before him. "But your fighters saved that other destroyer, which certainly would have sunk as well."

"I guess so." Rogers looked around. "Admiral, I need to sit down." Without awaiting permission he slid onto a swivel chair.

"I can see you're tired, Rogers, so I won't keep you. But I need to know a few things. First, what are the Japs doing? It sounds like they're swarming our radar pickets."

Rogers nodded slowly. "Yes, sir. When we arrived, there were twenty-plus inbound. I don't know how many attacked before we got there, but I'd say we fought about thirty before it was over. Mostly Vals and Nates flying pretty low. Under the radar, I guess."

Griggs lifted his helmet with one hand. The ship had been at general quarters most of the day. "Interesting. It means they're getting short of front-line types. Any fighter escorts?"

Rogers tried to concentrate. "I don't think so. At least I didn't see any. Maybe the Corsair top cover kept them away."

At that moment the loudspeaker blared. "Dagger, this is Mainbrace. Bandits off your port quarter!" *Montana*'s shrill announcement was accompanied by a crescendo of 20- and 40-millimeter gunfire. *Reprisal* heeled to starboard as Captain McEwen began a hard port turn, compounding the raiders' tracking.

Rogers pressed himself against the glass. Looking aft, he searched the flak-speckled sky for long moments before he saw them: two single-engine types, diving untouched through the AA bursts and tracers. The attackers' flight path told Rogers what he feared most. *They're* kamikazes; *they've got us boresighted.*

Belatedly the aft five-inchers pounded out a concussive salvo. Rogers was astonished to see the nearest suicider chopped in two, apparently by a direct hit. The wings and forward fuselage cartwheeled toward the water; Rogers noticed with disapproval that several tracer bursts followed it. *Target fixation,* he realized. *Gunners need more training.*

The second plane—now identifiable as a Judy—came straight in. It bobbled slightly from 20-millimeter hits but remained on course. *Just like he's on final,* Rogers thought. Somebody pulled him to the deck two seconds before impact.

Phil did not remember feeling the explosion, but he heard it clearly. It came as a long, rolling bellow that seemed unceasing. When Griggs's flag lieutenant eased off him, Rogers deciphered the odd noise. Flames were reflected in the bridge windows and he realized without looking that gasoline-fed fires were sweeping the flight deck.

Peering through the dense, roiling smoke, at the crinkling, melting wings and tails of Hellcats that were visible through the blaze, Rogers made a guess as to what had happened. The Judy had scored a near-perfect hit, smashing into the planes parked forward.

A commander on Griggs's staff reached for the phone to the navigation bridge. "Never mind that, Bert," the admiral said with surprising calm. "The captain's got his hands full."

"Do you want to vacate the bridge, sir?" Rogers did not see who had asked the question, but he already had backed away from the windows. The heat was becoming uncomfortable.

The task group CO seemed unperturbed. "Well, I guess we'd better for now, at least." He thought for a moment. "We'll move to the aft wardroom and stay out of the way."

Rogers turned to follow the staff, but he lingered for one more look at the battle below. Asbestos-suited firefighters had moved to the periphery of the blaze, wielding lengthy nozzles that smothered persistent flames with thick, aqueous foam. *We've learned a lot about fires on carriers,* he thought. *If only we'd had that gear on the old* Yorktown *in '42.*

READY ROOM TWO, 1340

Partway up, inside the island, Ready 2 was safe from the flight-deck fire, but the room was crowded with chattering, frightened aviators. Lieutenant Larry Drake, the duty officer, spotted Rogers immediately. "How bad is it?"

Rogers glanced around before answering. Most pilots were sitting in their assigned chairs, but some were gathering survival gear: Mae Wests, first-aid kits, canteens. Rogers was astonished to see two fliers on their knees, praying. One was Brian Sossaman.

Rogers smelled incipient panic in the room. He glared at Drake and snapped, "You mean, 'How bad is it, *sir!* ' "

Astonished, Drake stammered. "Well, I just mean, sir—"

"Goddammit, Drake! Diefendorf is up on CAP. That makes you senior in my absence. What's the matter with you?"

Drake's shoulders sagged as if he were a deflated balloon. "All right, Captain. All right." Drake turned to exert some control as Rogers strode to the head of the room. But Sossaman intercepted him. "Sir, I've got to make a confession."

Rogers was stymied for a heartbeat. "Well, not now, damn it. The chaplain's probably damn busy. Besides, I didn't know you were Catholic." *Hell, Brian, I didn't even know you were religious.*

Sossaman glanced around, almost furtively. "Oh, no, sir . . . not that kind of confession. It's just that I, ah, can't swim."

"What?"

Sossaman glanced at the deck, his face flushed in embarrassment. "See, at Corpus I took another fellow's Morse code test and he did my swim test. I just couldn't do that jump off the platform into a bunch of burning oil." He peered at Rogers through reddened eyes. "And now it looks like we might have to abandon ship."

"Who in hell said that?" Rogers's voice rose above the din.

"Well, I heard some damage-control crewmen in the passageway. Sir."

Ignoring him, Rogers turned toward the pilots. "Now hear this! Hey! Shut up, all of you!" In the front row, Barnes and Fairfield exchanged glances. They had never seen him this way: red-faced, snarling, outraged.

"Everybody sit down. That's an order! If you don't have a seat, park your ass on the deck." When calm returned, Rogers lowered his voice. "I don't give a goddamn what you've heard! I saw the hit from the flag bridge, and the hot papas are fighting the fire. We will damn well stay here until this fucking ship starts to sink!" He unsnapped the shoulder holster of his Victory Model .38. His vicious tone had more effect than his calculated words.

Only Bill Barnes, who had known Phil Rogers since 1941, recognized the irony. Looking at his old Bombing 3 pilot, Barnes realized: *That Jap suicider may have given Phil the rest he needs to avoid killing himself in this war.*

TUESDAY, 17 APRIL
KANOYA BASE

Captain Ganji Umeda stood on the flight line, a portable microphone system on the rostrum before him. The Mamoru Wing's pilots and nonflying officers were arrayed in dress uniforms, ordered by *hikotai,* trying to ignore some of the debris still littering the air station. Umeda had intended to hold this memorial ceremony in Hangar Two, but it had been half-destroyed in the air attack two days before.

The wing commander wasted no time. "Our unit now has been blooded in defense of the homeland," he began. "We have engaged the enemy in the very skies over our base, and though the initial combat came earlier than I preferred, your valor has been proven. High honor to *Kinsei,* to *Tenrai* and to *Senden*—each of which has taken its toll of the attackers!"

He allowed a ritual cheer from each *hikotai.* The wing had claimed twelve enemies shot down, mainly by *Tenrai*'s "Heavenly Thunder" pilots, who had also taken the heaviest losses.

When the shouts abated, Umeda allowed himself a few words of self-congratulation. "Our method of fighting has also proved itself. The scientific approach to air battle that this wing advocates has shown itself well suited to our aircraft. And though there were losses, we will learn from each new combat with the enemy." He knew the message would not be lost: dogfighting brought only marginal success. Use of speed, hit-and-run tactics, and the *Shiden*'s potent armament were the keys to victory.

Surveying the blue uniforms, Umeda nodded at the *hikotaicho* of the *Senden* unit. Lieutenant Hajime Homma about-faced and bawled, "Sakaida, three paces forward!"

Sakaida already felt conspicuous: His sprained left arm was in a sling and he wore a back brace under his uniform. He ached all over, but the N1K's rugged airframe had absorbed the worst of the impact. He stepped out of line with an awkward movement and braced to attention as Umeda approached, carrying a sword. Without preamble, Umeda announced, "I have had three of these swords made for special presentation. The first goes to the pilot who demonstrated exceptional skill and zest for battle over our own field. To Flight Chief Petty Officer Sakaida, this weapon is presented for demonstrating the spirit of the Mamoru Wing!"

Umeda held out the elegant sword and sheath with both hands to the astonished recipient. Sakaida realized the sentiment behind the gift: awards for noncommissioned personnel were virtually nonexistant in the Imperial Navy. This was Umeda's way of giving official recognition for a standout combat performance. He drew the sword from the inlaid scabbard to reveal the engraving on the blade. *Buko Batsugan:* "For conspicuous military valor."

Sakaida bowed slowly from the waist, wincing at the pain in his back. "I am deeply honored, sir. My gratitude is . . ." He ran out of words, and took the sword in one hand.

Umeda interjected, "No. I must thank you, Sakaida. You have proven my faith in you, and I am recommending you for promotion to warrant officer."

Sakaida flinched visibly, astonished as if by a slap. Then he remembered protocol. He bowed again and took three steps back. For the first time in at least three years, he felt as if he would burst the confines of his uniform blouse.

WEDNESDAY, 18 APRIL
USS *REPRISAL*

"It's still a mess, but a damn sight better than I'd have thought day before yesterday." Diefendorf's assessment was shared by the other aviators standing around the forward elevator well. The *kamikaze* hit and ensuing fire had jammed the elevator full down, and the cavernous square hole in the flight deck would remain all the way to Ulithi.

Rogers nudged some charred planking with his shoe. "I saw the captain yesterday. He said we were lucky they were striking planes below at the time. Otherwise, the elevator might have collapsed. Anyway, we'll probably have to go to Alameda for repairs."

"That wouldn't be hard to take," Don Mancross offered. Rogers was surprised at this sentiment from the VF exec. Looking carefully, he noticed lines in Mancross's wide-nosed face that had not been apparent before. "You know the *Intrepid* also got clobbered," Mancross added. "Doggone. Johnny Hyland's aboard with Air Group Ten. Sure hope he's okay."

Rogers turned and surveyed the fire-blackened area where sailors had jettisoned all debris around the Judy's impact. Fuel fires had consumed twenty-two aircraft, several of which were reduced merely to engines. The heat was so intense that even some propellers had melted. It was just as bad on the hangar deck, where the *kamikaze*'s bomb had exploded.

Eddie Fairfield walked up to the group of lieutenants and lieutenant commanders. He had seen the row of weighted canvas sacks on the hangar deck. He saluted Rogers and announced, "Skipper, I came by the exec's office like you asked. Looks like we lost fifteen killed and about sixty wounded. There'll be a burial at sea this afternoon."

Rogers did not care to dwell on losses, though VBF-59 had had its share. Two divisions had landed and parked forward, relieved on station by Diefendorf's CAP flight. Of the eight pilots, three had been killed and two injured. Rogers nudged Diefendorf. "Hunter, you guys were damn lucky. The Jap must have hit right after you launched."

"Yeah. We didn't see the hit, but we saw the fires start. Figured we'd have to land aboard the *Sharpsburg,* but we recovered four hours later." He shook his head. "Amazing what those damage-control guys can do."

Rogers scuffed a shoe on a warped tie-down. *Amazing what one fanatic can do.*

SATURDAY, 21 APRIL

USS *REPRISAL*

"Thirty-seven days at sea," Rogers calculated. "Brother, that's long enough."

The small procession entered Ulithi lagoon via the north passage. Steaming line astern, the battered carrier followed two destroyers and an Atlanta-class anti-aircraft cruiser into the anchorage. Three of the ships bore battle damage, though *Reprisal*'s was the most dramatic.

Rogers, Diefendorf, and a few other VBF-59 officers lined the gallery on the port side. "Any idea how long we'll be here, sir?" Buster Brown asked. It was the same question everyone had voiced during the four-day transit.

"Not yet. First we have to offload aircraft and ordnance. That'll take a day or so. But I heard the engineer reckons a couple of weeks if we don't go to Pearl."

"Hell," Diefendorf exclaimed. "I never expected to get home again this soon."

Rogers lost interest in the conversation. *I don't want to think about home—mine or anybody else's.* After completing the squadron paperwork and—worst of all—the letters to three families, he looked forward to nothing so much as sleep.

KANOYA BASE

Lieutenant Hajime Homma was not the worst *hikotaicho* Sakaida had served under. In fact, *Hikotai* 801 reflected the professionalism of the entire Mamoru Wing, bearing as it did the imprint of Captain Umeda's passion for "scientific fighting." But Homma's leadership approach contained almost juvenile aspects that Hiroyoshi Sakaida merely tolerated.

The signposts erected in the unit area were the most visible manifestation of Homma's attitude. Elitism, Sakaida knew, could be a double-edged sword. Carefully cultivated, it helped build morale; wielded carelessly, it bred snobbery or—worse—complacency. The latest marker proclaimed the *Senden* area the province of the "Flashing Lightning Elite Fighter Unit." All others were invited to stay clear.

There was also a tally board with a neatly stenciled row of American roundels. An arrow through the cockade represented a "confirmed" victory; a plain roundel denoted a "probable."

Sakaida was pacing by the board when a voice brought him up short. "Ah, there you are!" Homma's cheery voice forced the NCO to stop, about-face, and salute. "You look much better! Are you checking on our score-keeper, Sakaida?"

After nine years in the Imperial Navy, Sakaida harbored a suspicion of officers who were both cheerful *and* friendly. But this one seemed impressed with his ability, and Sakaida preferred the Hommas of the world to the Onos, hands down.

"No, Honorable *Hikotaicho*. I am going to the operations office to check if the Model 21 pilot manuals have arrived." It was one of the vagaries of centralized government that new equipment often was issued without instructions. Sometimes Sakaida wondered whether Japan's half dozen leading industrial families knew about such things—or even cared.

"Your industriousness is commendable, Sakaida." Homma fell alongside as they walked to the office. "Incidentally, your commission is being processed by wing headquarters. When you put on your new uniform, you will look splendid with that fine sword."

Sakaida's parting salute was crisp but silent. He had two theories about Homma. *Either the lieutenant sees me as a way to Umeda,* Sakaida reasoned, *or he is very lax in dealing with his men.* Either way, it meant trouble for Hiroyoshi Sakaida, holder of the sword for conspicuous military valor.

P A R T   I V

"I'll tell you a secret: I *loved* aerial combat. On the day the war ended, I sat down and cried, but not from relief that it was over."

World War II fighter ace, speaking in 1985

May 1945

Reveille meant general quarters, even en route to Hawaii. As Rogers slipped out of the lower bunk in his stateroom, he felt the oppressive heat building once more. *Another good day to spend in the ready room,* he decided. He shook Diefendorf in the upper rack, who pulled his pillow over his head. "C'mon, XO, you know the drill. Dawn GQ for all hands."

Diefendorf emerged from a tumble of sheets. "Damn it, what's the point of being in a rear area if you can't sack out?"

Rogers was pulling on a new set of khakis. "Remember, Ulithi's a rear area that's been attacked at least twice: miniature subs just before we arrived, and that long-range *kamikaze.*"

"Oh, hell, we left Ulithi five days ago. Besides, that zoot-suiter was a couple months ago." Diefendorf remembered the events of March 11, when a night-riding Fran bomber smashed into *Randolph.* The carrier had just finished showing movies; otherwise the toll would have been more than the twenty-seven killed on the hangar deck.

The scurrying scuffle had not yet abated in the passageway when the bosun's whistle shrilled over the public address system. "Attention, men. This is the captain speaking." Rogers and Diefendorf exchanged questioning glances. McEwen's tone said this was not bad news. "I have an important message. The war in Europe is over!"

If John McEwen paused for the cheering to abate, he needn't have waited. The news of VE-Day was met with a calm that bordered on indifference. "Makes no difference to us," a sailor told his buddy outside Rogers's compartment.

McEwen continued. "Last night, at a schoolhouse in Reims, France, Nazi Germany agreed to unconditional surrender to the Allied Powers. Cessation of hostilities on all fronts begins today at 2301 European time. Therefore, President Truman and Prime Minister Churchill have declared May eighth to be Victory in Europe: VE-Day.

"Men, as we know, this means the job is only half done but we can rejoice at what it means to our shipmates in the Atlantic. Meanwhile, we'll be there when they haul down the Rising Sun at Hirohito's palace, and at that time I'm going to spring for the biggest party this or any other ship has ever seen!"

Diefendorf's eyes went wide. "How 'bout it, Phil? Think we'll be on hand to see that?"

Rogers stared at the photographs on his small writing table. "All I know is that VE-Day came eight months too late for my kid brother."

SATURDAY, 12 MAY

KANOYA BASE

The alert had come just in time, and Sakaida numbly wondered how long it could continue. *Three straight days of enemy air attacks, and not even the night is safe.* He had seen one or two shooting stars in yesterday's predawn and knew without asking what they were. For over a year the American navy had used carrier-based, radar-guided night fighters, which extended their control of Japanese airspace. Now they were destroying planes taking off on early-morning search missions over Nippon itself.

At least this takeoff was a daylight event. And he relished being airborne instead of hunkering in slit trenches while enemy carrier planes insolently flew through Kanoya's traffic pattern, strafing at will. Now fighter-bombers were rampaging over Kagoshima Bay again, and as Sakaida led his four *Shidens* in a southwesterly climb, he hoped the second *chutai* would catch up.

Passing the bay's eastern shore, bound for Yamagawa on the opposite side, Sakaida discerned specks on his windscreen. The optical quality of the three-inch armored glass was not excellent, and Sakaida had been frightened more than once when nicks or oil spots had spiked his pulse. But these specks were changing elevation, and they grew inverted-gull wings as the range closed. Sakaida inhaled deeply, flexed his fingers, and focused his mind. He had never fought Corsairs before.

With an altitude advantage, Sakaida hoped for an overhead pass at the leading F4Us. He shoved throttle and prop to the stops, accelerating to over 300 knots. Captain Umeda's "scientific fighting" principles stressed speed, teamwork, and firepower to win the battle—turning the Americans' strengths against them.

Tracers lanced out toward the distinctive silhouettes four hundred meters ahead, and Sakaida realized that Mogashi was firing. The battle was developing almost too fast to comprehend.

Sakaida marveled at the Voughts' speed. The leading F4U abruptly rolled into a near-vertical bank with effortless grace and flashed through Sakaida's Type 99 gunsight before he could fire. He noted the Corsair's excellent rate of roll, and trusting Mogashi to watch his tail, he stood on the rudder bar and veered hard after it. Kagoshima Bay tilted crazily in his windscreen as gravity blurred his vision.

The American was almost out of range now, pirouetting above and behind him. Sakaida knew what was about to happen. The Corsair would drop its nose and initiate a high-side gunnery run from about five hundred meters' range. There was only one counter to that move: meet him nose to nose.

Rolling out of his pursuit turn, Sakaida centered his controls and raised his nose slightly. There was no way to practice head-on gunnery. Just put the crosshairs slightly above the target for the heavy 20-millimeter shells' ballistic drop, and start shooting. Sakaida clamped down on the trigger as he saw the American's muzzle flashes. There was too little time—the fighters were past each other in barely two seconds, clawing around for another pass. At the completion of the second evolution, Sakaida thrilled to a realization. *I can do this longer than he can! Soon he must break off and I will be on his tail.*

Starting his third pull-up into the American, Sakaida began to lose some of his confidence. He had never worked this hard. His body was clammy with sweat beneath his flight suit and his face had become flushed. He badly wanted to look to the opposite side to check on Magoshi, but he dared not take his eyes off the beautiful Vought fighter.

High-pitched pings screeched through the airframe somewhere behind his seat. Nothing else sounded like that. Sakaida knew what it meant. *Magoshi is dead—he would not be separated from me!* Without bothering to check behind, he stomped on the rudder bar and slashed the stick rearward and right in a violent half-snap roll. Then he sucked the stick back against the seat and, through graying vision, watched sky trade places with earth.

He knew that he was safe for the few seconds of his descent. But when he came nose-level at the bottom of the split-S he would be predictable to his pursuers. *What shall I do?*

For lack of another option, he dived within two hundred meters of the water and bent the throttle toward Kagoshima Bay's northern shore. *They will not want to follow me farther inland,* he reasoned. Flying with his head turned alternately over both shoulders, he saw medium-altitude specks but could not tell their types. Another thirty seconds and he knew he would live. The Americans evidently had thought him destroyed or they called off the chase.

Sakaida eased back to cruise power, checked his gauges, and slid back the canopy. He was powerfully thirsty, with a throbbing headache building in his temples. He felt dizzy and giddy; for a moment he wondered whether he would erupt in laughter again. Instead, he realized that he could still know fear. Appalled at that knowledge, he threw up his lunch.

WEDNESDAY, 16 MAY

USS *REPRISAL*

Leaving Pearl Harbor, the ship's band had blared out a lusty version of "California, Here I Come." Spirits were high in anticipation of possible leave in Alameda, where the carrier would undergo repair in the navy yard. It was a dream come true: *Reprisal*'s damage could not be handled at Pearl.

Most of the ship's department heads were fortunate in that their sailors' work continued much as normal. A, B, E, M and R divisions, which tended to auxiliary machinery, boilers, electrical, main propulsion, and hull concerns, could function normally; K and M divisions, communications and navigation, remained marginally active; while S Division was busy keeping more than three thousand men supplied and fed. Even the gunnery department's fire-control and first through eighth divisions could conduct maintenance and inspect weapons. But without aircraft to operate, the air group and the V-1 through V-5 divisions had almost nothing to do: no flying, no deck activity, no air plan to write, no bogeys to track, no ordnance to load. Rogers and the other squadron commanders struggled with three days of enforced idleness, trying to find useful things for their men to do. It was not easy.

Some physical-fitness enthusiasts organized medicine-ball or volleyball games, while a few hardy souls jogged up and down the flight deck. However, the forward three hundred feet were off limits to all but work parties, as the charred, warped planks impeded even casual running.

Most aviators congregated in the wardrooms or visited back and forth between ready rooms. Rogers catalogued the conversations, which predictably focused on four subjects.

"I keep telling you guys, an LSO should only give you one signal on each pass. Most pilots are consistent in their errors, and he gets to know 'em. But if you throw him a curve by doing something unexpected, you'll prob'ly get a wave-off. . . ."

"Yesterday I was talking to the flight surgeon, and he agrees with me. Some dames can fake it better than others, but they can't imitate increased pulse or perspiration. . . ."

"I wish Admiral Griggs had stayed aboard. I know they need task group commanders, but the chow hasn't been as good since we left Pearl. . . ."

"I'm saving for a house. Between us my wife and I can make a good down payment on a two-bedroom place that runs about $7,500. Although she sort of wants a bigger house for a larger family. You know, another room, a garage. Maybe twelve grand. . . ."

Rogers slumped into his seat at the head of the ready room. He had not given much thought to finances. Since joining the Navy he usually had more money than he could easily spend. After all, in 1942 an ensign had drawn $157.50 per month and Rogers got 50 percent extra for flight pay—a princely $236.25, plus allowances. Now, as a lieutenant commander, he earned $287.50 plus flight pay ($143.75) plus 10 percent overseas service ($28.75). With no dependents, he drew an additional $21.00 per month. That totalled $481, or $5,772 annually. *Hell, you can buy a decent house for barely one year's pay.*

Rogers heard muted giggling and turned around. Two rows back, Brian Sossaman and Carl Sacco were bent over a sleeping pilot. When the two pranksters stood up, they revealed a paper mustache taped to Wilmer Van Sley's upper lip. "Van's still only shaving about twice a week," Sossaman observed. "He'll hardly notice."

Rogers locked his commanding-officer gaze on Ensign Sossaman. Pointing to the vacant seat beside him, Phil said, "Sit down, mister. We are going to talk."

Sossaman's eyes were wide in concern and Rogers could read the expression. *Gosh, Captain, I haven't done anything.* "What is it, sir?"

"Your aquatic ability, I believe, leaves something to be desired."

One corner of Sossaman's mouth sagged. "Yes, sir. A lot to be desired, actually."

"Well, as soon as possible, I'm going to toss you in a pool. Sink or swim."

"But Skipper, I always wear a Mae West and I have my seat-pack raft." The aw-gee-whiz tone in Sossaman's voice was almost humorous.

"And what if your raft gets punctured and your Mae West won't inflate? Then you're on your own. No soap, Brian. You need to learn how to swim."

"Yes, sir." He sounded like a student forced to do homework on Saturday night.

Rogers pondered how to increase the boy's confidence. Then it came to him. "Hey, you remember our extracurricular gunnery hops at Pasco?" Sossaman nodded. "Well, it's no different. You were convinced you couldn't shoot and I knew all along that you could. When you started following directions, what happened?"

Sossaman knew when he was beat. "I started hitting the sleeve."

"Correct. Besides, you told me yourself, it wasn't swimming that bothered you. It was the jump off that tower into burning oil. You didn't want that part of the training."

"No, sir. I sure didn't."

"Well, there's other aspects as well, mister. For instance, if you're in the water and a Zero starts strafing you, what would you do?"

I'd frigging die, sir. "Try to duck under, I guess."

"Okay, as far as it goes. But how far down would you dive?"

Sossaman shook his head. "Does it matter? I mean, as long as he can't see me."

"It sure as hell does matter. If you'd attended the swim classes instead of having your buddy fill in while you took his code tests, you'd know something. With three feet of saltwater above, you're pretty safe even from .50 caliber."

"Well I'll be damned. Sir. I never heard that."

"In which case, I have made my point." Rogers was pleased with himself.

"Aye, aye, sir."

"Think nothing of it, Ensign. Nothing at all."

MONDAY, 21 MAY
KANOYA BASE

"Certain elements in the naval general staff wish to abandon Kyushu," Captain Ganji Umeda told his command. "They believe that we can no longer control the air in this part of the homeland. But I am not prepared to accept such a defeatist attitude."

Sitting in the front row with *Hikotai* 801's other officers, Sakaida was rocked on his emotional heels. For the wing commander to voice concepts such as abandonment was appalling. It was bad enough to admit that perhaps the Imperial Army and Navy air arms could not control the southernmost of Japan's home islands. But Kyushu, the cradle of Japanese civilization! Every school student learned that Mount Takachiho was where Prince Ninigi descended from his rainbow bridge to erect a palace and a dynasty that continued to the present, the 124th descendant, Emperor Hirohito.

Even discounting historical myth, Kyushu was the scene of the thirteenth-century *kamikaze,* the original divine wind that scattered Kublai Khan's invasion fleets. Seventeenth-century Nagasaki had become the trading center with European barbarians. Though born and raised on Honshu, Sakaida knew the facts and fables as well as anyone, and his superiors' admission of defeat tore at his fighting heart as much as at his national pride.

Then Umeda struck with the other fist. "Therefore, I am being recalled to Tokyo," he said in an even voice. "The air-defense committee wishes me to contribute the Mamoru Wing's knowledge to measures being planned." He motioned to his second in command. "Commander Miwa will assume command. I expect each of you to give him the loyalty and valor you have bestowed upon me."

Ganji Umeda brought his heels together and saluted crisply. Before Eichiro Miwa could spring to his feet with an order to render honors, Umeda's white-gloved hand sliced downward as he descended from the stage. Then, to everyone's surprise, he trooped the line, shaking hands with each pilot in turn. When he came to Sakaida he looked down at his newest warrant officer. "Take good care of that sword," the wing commander ventured. "You may have need of it before this war is over."

Sakaida could only salute; his voice failed him.

TUESDAY, 22 MAY
NAS ALAMEDA

Rogers lay on his bunk in the bachelor officers' quarters, hands behind his head in the darkened room. He heard radial engines throbbing through the twilight—TBMs, he thought, probably getting in some "pinky" field carrier landing practice.

Despite the efforts of Diefendorf, Fairfield, and some others, Rogers was in no mood for partying. While they patronized the officer's club, he preferred to be alone. It was difficult to explain, even to himself, but Rogers felt oddly distanced from reality. He knew that he should be delighted to be out of combat ahead of schedule, but—no, that was not quite true. *I should be glad to be back in Uncle Sugar,* he mused, and that was not the same thing.

As yet he did not know his next assignment—only that he was due for shore duty. Training Command was a likely prospect, and that could be good or bad. Operational training might be tolerable—at least it involved fleet aircraft—but Rogers dreaded the prospects of nurse-maiding some cadet in a Stearman or N3N.

May '45, he thought. *Three years ago I still hadn't flown combat. Now, after three squadron tours, I'm still not ready to be sidelined. This war isn't over yet.* Whatever the source, Rogers realized that he still possessed a reservoir of emotional stamina that could take him to the end. Mentally he tiptoed around the edge of the emotional abyss, careful not to peer too closely into the chasm for fear of what he might learn about himself.

By the time he got up for dinner, Phil Rogers was in a mood that could be eased only by spilling enemy blood. A plan began forming in his mind.

THURSDAY, 24 MAY
KANOYA BASE

Suddenly Lieutenant Homma had no time for small talk with warrant officers. At first Sakaida thought the *hikotaicho*'s new attitude was related to the inevitable readjustment following Captain Umeda's departure, but that theory now was disproved. Twice in the past two days Homma had walked briskly past him, exchanging salutes with barely a word.

Now here was Homma again, standing before *Hikotai* 801's office. Accompanying the new wing leader, Commander Miwa, he pointed out the Imperial Navy's motto over the doorway: "Fight when you see the enemy. Fight bravely and destroy the enemy."

As both officers stepped toward the entrance, Sakaida braced himself and stiffly saluted. Miwa passed almost without seeing him while Homma merely raised a hand in a halfhearted salute. Sakaida watched them disappear from his peripheral vision. *Miwa is capable, but no Umeda,* he reasoned. *And because I am not close to Miwa, Homma will waste no more time with me. Very well, Honorable Division Officer.*

The Mamoru Wing was readjusting to its new leader. That was to be expected; a shakedown period followed every command change. If Homma would leave him to his work, Sakaida would reckon that arrangement to be well worth the bargain.

SATURDAY, 26 MAY
NAS ALAMEDA

Rogers did not feel like socializing. However, the air group bash sponsored by Pat Clarey offered an excellent chance to pursue his plan. It was a poorly kept secret that Captain McEwen would attend to bid farewell to Air Group 59, and Rogers wanted to corner both officers. Timing would be important. *Let 'em both get a little loose, maybe a little sentimental, then spring the trap.* Then he realized, *We're detached from the* Reprisal. *McEwen's no longer in the loop!*

It was a good plan, shrewdly conceived, taking advantage of time and place. The officer's club, after all, was a logical venue. Lots of cheerful, boisterous young aviators would lend gaiety to the event and possibly deflect a superior officer's tendency to say no.

En route to the cloakroom, Rogers overheard the usual shoptalk. "I ran into Al Vraciu early this year," a fighter pilot was saying. "You remember—he got six Judies in about eight minutes at the Turkey Shoot. Well, he went back out with VF-20 and got bagged over Luzon. Some guerrillas picked him up, and the whole bunch was running from the Japs when this little guy jogs alongside Al. He says, 'Excuse me, sir, there are two things I want to know. Has Madeleine Carroll remarried, and does Deanna Durbin have a baby yet?' "

Two air station officers were swapping fleet information. "ComFair has the latest dope," offered a commander. "Apparently there were no *kamikaze* hits from early April to early this month. Then on the eleventh the *Bunker Hill* took a zoot-suiter. Bad fire and lots of casualties, especially in the air group."

"Damn!" A lieutenant commander rattled his ice cubes. "That's Air Group 84—Rog Hedrick's outfit. I knew him when he was Tom Blackburn's exec in VF-17."

"Well, about three days later another suicider tagged the *Enterprise.* Evidently went right down the forward elevator and blew it three hundred feet in the air. The ship's probably done in this war, but there were only about a dozen killed."

Rogers had barely tossed his hat onto the rack when Hunter Diefendorf flagged him. The squadron exec was fraternally looped. Rogers had never seen his natural reserve so dissipated. "You won't believe this," Diefendorf exulted, "but *the* most gorgeous female in San Francisco has been asking about you."

He's seeing pink elephants, Phil reasoned. "Hell, Dief, I don't know any women here." But Diefendorf seemed not to hear while leading him to a table. Approaching the corner, Rogers saw the back of a stylish brunette sitting with Ralph Platco and a graying civilian.

"I found him," Diefendorf exclaimed to the crowd. The woman turned in her seat and Rogers looked into the beautiful blue eyes of Eleanor Diskowski.

He almost turned around. His stomach churned as his brain shrieked. *I do not want to do this, I do* not *want to do this.* He was still trying to formulate a phrase when Kenny's mother rose and extended a hand. "Philip." He grasped her gloved hand and pressed harder than intended. "Mrs. Diskowski . . ."

"Eleanor, please." Her lips curled. "May I introduce my husband? Elliott."

Shaking hands with the tall, graying gentleman, Rogers could see Kenny reflected in the older man's face. "It's good to meet you, sir." *That's god-awful trite,* he thought.

"Thank you, Commander. I would like to say how much the letters from you and Commander Platco meant to us."

Rogers barely could remember what he had written. It had been only slightly less painful a task than rousing Juanita Connell at two in the morning. "It's not much consolation, I'm afraid. Ken was special."

The president of Diskowski Shipping slipped a bony hand around his wife's shoulders. The parents nodded as Rogers became aware of the beginning, middle, and end of every passing second. Looking down at Platco, Rogers's eyes begged *Help me!* Ralph interjected, "Oh, there's Fairfield and Sossaman. I'm sure you would like to talk to them." He attracted Rogers's wingmen, enabling him to slip away.

Platco caught up with Rogers at the bar. "I'm sorry about that, Phil. I didn't think to warn you. Diskowski heard we had returned and tracked me down the other day."

Rogers inhaled half a bourbon and water, carefully setting the glass on the bar. "It's okay," he croaked. "I'm just no good at . . . that." He looked around. "Is Clarey here yet?"

"Uh . . . yeah. Over there." Platco pointed to the end of the bar where the air group commander stood with Barry Potter, Leo Hunziker, and three or four other pilots.

"Hey, Phil, what're you drinking?" Potter asked.

He finished his drink and, abandoning his original plan to bide his time, plunged straight ahead.

"Just finished one," Rogers replied. Addressing Clarey, he said, "Commander, since the air group's staying here and the ship won't leave for another month or so, I'd like to request reassignment. Will you endorse my request to join a deployed squadron?"

Clarey regarded the fighter-bomber CO. "That's a damn fool thing to do. You've earned a rest, just like everyone else. Besides, I happen to know you've been requested for the replacement air group at Los Alamitos."

Aware that everyone was looking at him, Rogers controlled his voice. "I'm not quite ready for that, sir. Besides, we'll get a rest right here."

"Not much of one." He peered at Rogers as if seeing him under a microscope. "Are you sure about this?"

"Very sure."

Clarey inhaled, then sighed. "All right. Put it in writing and I'll forward it." He glanced around the small group, noting the querulous expressions.

"Thank you, sir." Rogers exited as quickly as possible, praying that the Diskowskis did not spot him. Taking his hat, he wondered whether the Coronado Cobra was still preying on careless junior officers at North Island.

June 1945

SUNDAY, 3 JUNE
OVER KAGOSHIMA BAY

Sakaida circled the splash and allowed himself to laugh aloud in the cockpit. True, this American had not been as skilled as the one over Kagoshima on the fourteenth, but he still flew reasonably well. And most notably, he had been mounted on a Vought. Sakaida relished the prestige of destroying one of the fast, tough opponents. He waggled his wings at the Yankee, who even now was climbing into an inflatable raft. *Perhaps I will meet him tonight,* Sakaida thought. *Yes, that would be delicious: to talk with a pilot one had shot down.*

He never saw the other *Shiden Kai* until far too late. Its high-speed shadow on the water entered his vision only a moment before 20-millimeter shells geysered around the yellow raft. Sakaida rolled out of his low orbit, cramming on combat power while wondering what he would do. He cut the corner of the strafer's turn and for a moment tracked him in his reflector sight. He had already decided not to shoot when he recognized the markings. Hajime Homma had progressed from sloganeer to murderer.

THURSDAY, 7 JUNE
NAS ALAMEDA

A loud, insistent knocking jarred the door to Rogers's BOQ room. "Come!" he barked. He was mildly angry at being interrupted while packing.

The door opened, seemingly to admit a small crowd. Barnes, Fairfield, Sossaman, and Van Sley entered the small room. Rogers straightened up from his bag. "Well, I didn't expect to see you fellows so soon."

"Yeah," Barnes replied. "You figured to slip out of town without so much as a good-bye to the guys that kept you healthy."

"Besides, I need to wet down my extra half stripe," Fairfield added. "Just got word, I'm on the list for jaygee. The new AlNav is out."

"Well, congratulations, Eddie." Rogers shook hands with his former section leader. "Too bad we don't have something to christen you with."

"Actually, we do, sir." Barnes produced a paper sack that gurgled when moved. "Van?"

While Wilmer Van Sley set out four paper cups, Barnes took the glass off Rogers's sink and poured something amber from the bag. As he added a token amount to the cups there was another knock on the door.

"Jiggers, the cops!" Sossaman exclaimed.

Rogers moved toward the knob. "For cryin' out loud, can't a guy even . . ."

Don Mancross's homely face appeared. "Hey, Phil, I just heard—"

"Join the party," Rogers said. "Everybody else is."

Van Sley handed yet another cup to Mancross, who sniffed appreciatively. "What are we celebrating? You guys getting liberty?"

"Yes, sir. But the skipper's leaving," Sossaman said. "Uh, I mean, we're not celebrating that. We're just sort of, ah, saying good-bye."

"And wetting down Eddie's half stripe." Rogers raised his glass to Fairfield.

The six aviators all took a sip. In the awkward silence, Rogers said, "You realize, gentlemen, that booze is not allowed in BOQ."

Mancross regarded Rogers. "Your secret is safe with me. I just heard the scuttlebutt, Phil. Didn't expect you'd ship out so soon."

Rogers inhaled. "Well, they said I could go to Air Group 98 at Los Al: operational training for fighter-bomber pilots. It's a good deal—close to Los Angeles and some fine people to work with: Gene Fairfax, Jig Dog Ramage, Tex Harris. But I've sort of got a second wind. I figure to go back and get in some more shooting."

"How'd you get orders so fast?" Mancross asked. "If you don't mind me asking."

Rogers took another sip. "I was surprised myself. I made the request less than two weeks ago. Anyway, I'm headed for Guam via Pearl. Leaving Monday morning."

Barnes looked at the tiled floor. *Something's wrong, something doesn't fit. Got to find out what's going on.* He decided to bide his time.

Rogers changed the subject. "But I'm going to miss you guys. You did a swell job for me—did everything I asked, and more."

Fairfield came over to Rogers. "Skipper, there were times when I was damn tired of flying those extra hops at Pasco. But it sure paid off. The Zeros hardly laid a glove on us." He chuckled like a kid. "I wonder if that first-class is still peddling bootleg gas."

"Hell," Rogers smiled, "he's probably a chief by now and owns the air station." The others laughed as he continued. "But it was a no-lose situation. If we ran into plenty of targets, we were ready. If not, it didn't matter."

Mancross agreed. "Luck of the draw," he muttered. "Lots of good pilots didn't even see a Jap." He looked around the room and felt it was time to leave. "Good luck, Phil. Next time, drinks are on me." He pressed Rogers's hand, then was gone.

The others made their exits with an embarrassing mixture of fondness, admiration, and gratitude. Young men who had survived carrier aviation and combat together were bound by more than shared experiences. And yet some words, some sentiments simply would not come. Rogers felt it an oddly unsatisfactory parting.

Finally only Barnes was left; he looked up from the bunk. "Phil, what's going on?"

A small storm rolled across Rogers's forehead. *You mean what's going on, sir?* But he knew there was no point putting on a senior-officer act with William E. Barnes, formerly radioman second class. "I just want to get back to the fleet for a while. Smell the ozone some more, add a few extra meatballs. Maybe even do some good."

That's only part of it, Barnes told himself. *But this isn't the time to push.* He thought for a moment. "Skipper, let me come with you." Before Rogers could reply, Barnes interjected. "Remember, I only joined you after your tour began. I'm still eligible for more combat."

"Aren't you still—"

"Hey, if Clarey cut you loose, he can sure afford to lose me. Far as he's concerned, I'm just another ensign." He arched his eyebrows expectantly. "Besides, you must know somebody at ComFair."

"What do you mean?"

Come on, Skipper! "Well, you logged a cross-country to North Island last week, right? Besides, I hear you're friendly with somebody in AirPac personnel."

Rogers locked eyes with his former gunner. *The guy knows me pretty well.* But Barnes might never learn of the markers that had been called in, the references cited without permission. Suffice it to say that a certain captain from the Annapolis Class of '23 and a rear admiral out of '16 had gone out of their way to accommodate a former aviation cadet whose blood was still up.

Rogers heard himself say, "I'll make a phone call."

SATURDAY, 9 JUNE
KANOYA BASE

Sakaida was quietly surprised that Commander Miwa continued virtually all of Captain Umeda's policies. That included a periodic review of combat lessons learned—something that Sakaida had never experienced before Umeda. Any such evaluation previously had been done informally, usually by pilots indulging in shoptalk. But Miwa had convened the current panel at wing headquarters specifically to air differing approaches to tactical problems.

The meeting room was small and sparsely furnished, but a dozen or so pilots squeezed in with folding chairs. Each *hikotai* was represented by its commanding officer and two or three senior men. Owing to losses, and his growing experience, Sakaida had been selected to represent his *chutai*.

"The Americans are deploying larger numbers of their Voughts," Miwa said from the head of the room. "We are encountering them more often, and I want better ways to fight them." He looked at the *Hikotai* 801 commander. "Lieutenant Homma, your unit fought the Voughts over Kagoshima Wan recently. What did you conclude?"

Homma twitched visibly, apparently unprepared for a direct question. "Sir, the Voughts are faster than our current fighters. We believe they have superior high-altitude performance, but our armament is heavier . . ." His voice trailed off.

Everybody in this room knows that, Sakaida mused. Miwa obviously concluded the same thing as he looked around. "I want more specific information. Come . . ." Miwa fastened on the warrant officer who seemed so competent. "Sakaida!"

Sakaida rose to his feet. "Yes, Honorable Commander!"

"You have shot down two or more Voughts recently. What did you learn?"

Feeling Homma's stony gaze, Sakaida pressed ahead. "Sir, the Vought is faster, as the *hikotaicho* says; as much as thirty knots faster. It accelerates better as well. Additionally, it has a greater roll rate than the *Shiden Kai,* and excellent zoom-climb characteristics."

Miwa blinked in surprise at the depth of the warrant officer's assessment. Sensing an advantage, Sakaida thought, *If I cannot get a fair hear-*

ing in the most professional flying unit in the navy, all my knowledge is wasted. "Beg the commander's pardon," he blurted. "If we could capture a Vought and its pilot, we could learn much."

Miwa blinked in surprise. "What are you suggesting?"

Sakaida's mind churned. "Sir, at the next opportunity, we should try to force down a Vought intact. Otherwise, we should ensure that enemy pilots who bail out are not killed."

Miwa began to pace. He thought for a long moment before replying. "Our duty is to destroy the enemy," he began cautiously. "But it is true: We may be losing opportunities to interrogate valuable prisoners." He stopped and took in the fliers' collective mood, then added, "From now on, no pilot of this wing will shoot at descending parachutes or strafe Americans on the ground." He looked at Homma. "Even if that has happened before."

Following further discussion, Miwa dismissed the meeting. "The *hiko-taichos* will remain to discuss this matter," he announced. "The rest of you are dismissed."

Filing out of the room, Sakaida did not have to look back. He could feel Hajime Homma's eyes burning a crosshair pattern into the nape of his neck.

TUESDAY, 12 JUNE
PEARL HARBOR

"Well smear my ears with jelly and stake me to an anthill. Is that Buck Rogers?" Rogers turned in the corridor of headquarters. Behind him was a tall, grinning lieutenant commander with outstretched hand. The face emerged from Rogers's memory as he shook. "Ben Nichols! I was just looking for you." He remembered to introduce Barnes, explaining, "Ben got me off the *Alazon Bay*. I guess I still owe you one, Ben."

Nichols's gray eyes shone. "Damn right. Besides, you almost missed me."

"You're not in aviation detailing anymore?"

"Not after Friday. I'm going to VC-70 at Puunene. Ain't gonna fly no goddamn TBM, neither. I'm already checked out in the FM-2. It beats the hell out of the old F4Fs we had on the *Saratoga* . . . what was it? Three, four years ago."

Rogers was pleased for his former shipmate. "That's swell, Ben. But I thought you'd wrangle a fast carrier slot."

"Hey, I jumped at the first seat that came along. Besides, there's some good folks in escort carriers. You heard that VC-10 was aboard the *Gam-*

bier Bay when she was sunk at Leyte? Well, Ed Huxtable is reforming them at Ventura and Bush Bringle's been damn near round the world with VOC-1. They're logging more hours per pilot than anybody I know of."

"Well," Rogers added, "that's sort of why we're here. Not much doing around Alameda so Bill and I came on out again." He handed over his travel orders.

Nichols stepped aside to let a captain and a WAVE lieutenant pass. Scanning the documents, he lowered his voice. "Phil, I gotta ask. What sort of horsepower do you have? Double-A air travel on less than two weeks' notice!" He gave a low whistle. "Somebody really wants you, pronto."

Play it down, Rogers thought. "When the *Reprisal* put into Alameda for repairs, I looked up Captain Edwards at North Island." He shrugged. "I guess he likes me."

"Guess so." Nichols leveled his gaze at Rogers. "Phil, I'm sorry about Burnett. I didn't know him very well, but I know you two went way back. I also heard about Gordon Connell. I guess he was one hell of a fine skipper."

Rogers shifted his feet, then asked, "What's doing out here? I've not heard much lately."

"Oh, lots doing in WestPac. Headquarters and the logistics support group at Leyte-Samar were ready in April, but the carriers will use Ulithi, Saipan, and Guam until sometime this month. I see that's where you're headed. A few days ago I'd have thought you'd go to one of the RAGs: Air Group 100 here at Barbers Point or 99 at Saipan. But apparently you're headed for the fleet again."

Barnes ventured a question. "Commander, is there any word on fleet operations?"

Nichols raised his hands expressively. "More of the same, mostly. I hear that Task Group 38.3 put into Leyte on the first after seventy-nine days of sustained operations. Apparently Sherman's boys were pooped. The other groups ran Kyushu strikes for a week or so, but not much doing. It looks like the Japs have just about given up there. Our fighters only made about twenty shootdowns in all that time."

Rogers shook his head. "Can you imagine us giving up the airspace over Florida or Texas? What's behind it, Ben? Building up their reserves?"

"Yeah, I'd say they're hoarding for the invasion. We've pretty much had a free rein over the southern part of Japan since late April. The Japs are doing about all they can. They're saving their strength until they need it most."

"It's still sort of hard to believe we'll have to invade," Rogers mused.

"I mean, of course the Japanese aren't big on surrendering, but they must know what it'll mean. Women, children . . . everybody. What kind of leaders would do that to their people?"

Nichols suppressed a snort. "C'mon, Phil, you know what they're like: China, the Philippines, the death march, *kamikazes.* Hell, on Saipan and Okinawa, Japanese *mothers* threw their kids off the cliffs and jumped after them. Their troops killed their own wounded, then committed suicide. Just imagine what it'll be like in the home islands." His voice rose an octave as he warmed to his subject. "I play bridge with a major on the staff of Third Amphibious Corps. He says that after they dope out supplies and logistics and shipping, there's just one question they discuss over chow, because it's the only one that matters."

"Yeah?"

"How do you kill seventy million people?"

FRIDAY, 15 JUNE

LEYTE-SAMAR ANCHORAGE

Rogers regretted leaving Barnes ashore, but as he scaled the ladder from the whale boat to *Sharpsburg*'s hangar deck, he recalled that his orders from the task group commander were to report to the flagship alone. Riding out to the ship, he had discussed the previous day's excitement with the boat crew. *Sharpsburg*'s sister ship, *Randolph,* bore visible scars where a flat-hatting P-38 pilot had cut it too close and clipped the flight deck. Tempers were running high: eleven men were dead and scuttlebutt held that Rear Admiral Frederick Sherman had ordered his gunners to fire on any Army aircraft overflying the anchorage.

Reaching the top of the ladder, Rogers saluted the flag at the stern, then returned the courtesy from the officer of the deck. "Lieutenant Commander Rogers, reporting to the task group commander as ordered."

The lieutenant checked his clipboard, then nodded. "Yes, sir, I believe he is expecting you. The admiral should be in his flag quarters. If you—"

"I know the way." Rogers had started to walk forward when it occurred to him that he lacked some important information. "Excuse me, lieutenant. I just got off the MATS flight from Guam. Who *is* the task group commander?"

"Why, Rear Admiral Griggs." The officer blinked as if to add, *Of course!*

"Oh, I didn't know. Last I saw him, he got off the *Reprisal* in Ulithi."

"He's been aboard for a couple of weeks. This is his flagship until further notice."

While trotting up the interior ladders in the island, Rogers began fitting pieces of his puzzle together. *If Griggs has been back here for two weeks, that could explain my priority travel orders. But what does he want? Well, there's one way to find out.* He announced himself to the Marine orderly, who opened the door. Rogers removed his hat, stepped inside, and was met by the flag lieutenant, a nonaviator who led him into the inner sanctum.

There, leaning over a chart, was Jake Griggs—with ex–CAG-59 Tom Albertson. Both men looked up and switched on little-boy smiles that shouted *Surprise!*

Rogers barely recovered enough to acknowledge the admiral while shaking Albertson's hand for thirty seconds. "Why, I had no idea . . ."

Griggs relished his little triumph. "Things must make more sense to you now, Rogers." The old man's eyes gleamed. "I convinced Tom to come out as my new operations officer. Didn't take much persuading, either."

"That's for sure," Albertson enthused. "I'd have done about anything after almost a year at ComFair." The blank expression on Rogers's face prompted an explanation. "I was in Scouting 41 when the admiral was air officer on the *Ranger.*"

Griggs sat down and motioned to Rogers. "Son, I'm sorry I won't be able to visit very long. I'm due at a conference on the *Shangri-La* at 1400." He looked at his watch. "There's been some big changes since April. Ted Sherman just turned over his group to Jerry Bogan, and Ted's begun planning the next series of Task Force Fifty-eight operations under Admiral Spruance. Vice Admiral Mitscher went to Washington as DCNO(Air)." Griggs smiled ironically. "I'm sure he considers it a demotion."

"No sir, I hadn't heard. In fact, when I stopped at Guam and got orders to report to the task group commander, nobody said it was you."

"Well, we'll be up to full strength fairly soon. The *King's Mountain* has joined us and the *Reprisal*'s due back with a new air group in a few weeks. But in the meantime we have another vacancy to fill." He looked at Albertson.

"That's right. Phil, once we learned you were coming back so soon, we figured maybe we'd stash you somewhere—probably in a replacement air group until something opened up. This next series of strikes goes against the home islands and we knew we'd find a slot for you. Well, several days ago a vacancy occurred. One of our CVL CAGs was killed and we need a combat-experienced replacement." Albertson looked at his former subordinate. "What do you say?"

Rogers gulped. "An air group! I wasn't even sure I'd get another squadron. I told Captain Edwards that I'd take an XO slot as long as I could get back to combat."

"Well, you've got your wish," Griggs interjected. "Son, I have to go. Tom will fill you in and we'll discuss it later. But I need your answer tonight. Fair enough?"

Rogers stood. "Yes, sir. Fair enough." As Griggs departed with his aide, Rogers and Albertson sat down again. Rogers expected a pleasant discussion about mutual friends, but Albertson pressed the issue. "It's like this, Phil. The *Crown Point* lost its air group commander and we need an immediate replacement. There are two men in line ahead of you, and they're both qualified. But you have more experience, and I think you have some special qualities that I'll come to. So, are you interested?"

Rogers spread his hands. "Well, sure. But what's the background?"

"The CAG was a dilbert called Fast Freddie Kelso. He killed himself in an F6 when he ignored a wave-off. Hit the deck and went in the drink." Albertson shook his head sadly. "The dumb jerk."

An unbelieving expression crossed Rogers's face. "Oh, don't get me wrong," Albertson hastened to add. "I knew the guy somewhat and I guess he was okay, but he had no business commanding an air group. He was a latecomer to aviation—got his wings as a lieutenant in '43 and only had the flight time of a new jaygee."

"Oh, a career opportunist."

"You got it." Albertson turned serious. "Freddie had stars in his eyes, Phil. Second-generation Academy, track man, top ten percent of his class, bound and determined to make chief of naval operations. Well, I guess there's nothing wrong with that, but Kelso was all for Kelso. He would never stand up for anybody against a brass hat."

Rogers stared at the bulkhead. "Then how did he get a slot like that?"

Albertson blinked. "Why, Mr. Rogers, I do believe you are naive."

"Okay, who did he know?"

"He was a Green Bowler. Word is they look out for each other where personnel assignments are concerned."

Rogers was aware of an Annapolis group that recruited promising midshipmen—mainly athletes—into a secret circle called the Green Bowl Society. Though its primary activity was illegal drinking parties, acceptance reportedly meant career-enhancing contacts. A scandal had erupted in 1942 when a Green Bowl roster had surfaced that showed some famous names.

"Don't think you're out in the cold," Albertson continued. "Remember, I'm a ring knocker and I didn't even hear about Green Bowl until three years ago."

Rogers was curious now. "What's the air group been like, after Kelso cashed in?"

"Not good. Frankly, we're doing you no favor with this job. The captain is Jerome Cheney Johnston IV, a good ship handler but a horse's ass. Uh, that's not for attribution, if you please." Albertson gave a confidential smile. "He had Kelso's goat; apparently he was not only commanding the carrier, but using Freddy as just a conduit to run the air group as well. Kelso lacked both the experience and the willingness to stand up to him. So you've got your work cut out for you."

"Jeez, Tom. What do you recommend?"

"Stick to your guns, damn it. If Johnston wants you to do something dumb—and he probably will—play it by the book. If you can't talk him out of something, make him put it in writing over your protest. Remember, he's ambitious and sure as hell doesn't want a miniature mutiny on his record."

Rogers sighed aloud. "Well, there goes my postwar career." He smiled.

Albertson leaned forward. "Phil, let me tell you something. You've got Admiral Griggs behind you. He's jumping you over a three-striper and a senior lieutenant commander because you've had more combat and we know you take care of your people. If we thought otherwise, you wouldn't be here."

"Well . . . I'll do what I can. What sort of help can I expect aboard?"

Albertson's head shook slowly. "Actually, I don't think you'll get much support from the wardroom. The exec says 'Aye, aye, sir' a lot and not much more. But the air officer's all right and the torpedo skipper's a nifty guy: Windy Wynn."

Rogers let out a long breath. "Okay. But how am I going to play with the big boys like the Green Bowlers?"

A deep, ironic laugh erupted from Tom Albertson. "Phil, you take the cake. Haven't you heard? Jake Griggs is a Green Bowler! Remember, just because a guy wears an Academy ring doesn't mean he's a gold-plated s.o.b."

Rogers tried to smile. "Keep reminding me, will you? Sir?"

SATURDAY, 16 JUNE
USS *CROWN POINT*

Rogers thought it was like meeting the girl on a blind date. *You want to look good, while not seeming too nervous.* He straightened his tie, tucked his hat under one arm, slicked back his hair, and rapped on the door marked "Capt. J. C. Johnston, USN."

"Enter," came the reply.

Rogers stepped into the cabin, entering the austere presence. Seated behind his desk, which bore a nameplate identical to the placard on the door, was the commanding officer of USS *Crown Point*. Rogers strode to the desk, braced to attention, and offered his personnel file. "Lieutenant Commander Rogers, sir. Reporting aboard as air group commander."

J. C. Johnston IV took the dossier and laid it on the desk. A heavyset man, balding prematurely at forty-one, he wore glasses for reading—a point upon which he was sensitive. "Yes, Rogers. I've been expecting you." He motioned to a chair, which Phil accepted, being careful to sit on the edge while holding his hat on his lap.

Johnston studied the specimen, applying the taxonomy of the military kingdom: phylum—Navy; class—officer; order—reservist; family—aviator; genus—carrier; species—fighter.

"I'm glad of this opportunity to get to know each other," Johnston began. "We probably won't sortie for a couple of weeks, and that should be more than enough time for you to get acquainted with our operating procedures."

"Yes, sir," Rogers replied. *And for you to get acquainted with mine.*

"You are replacing a good man, Rogers. Lieutenant Commander Kelso was a fine officer with a splendid record all the way back to the Academy. He was a gallant gentleman, and I believe he would have gone far in the Navy."

"I regret I didn't have the pleasure of knowing him, Captain." *Little white lie.*

Johnston leaned forward, folding his hands. "It is, ah, unusual for a reservist to hold such a command. You may not be aware of it, Rogers, but you came to this position ahead of two other officers—both of whom are Naval Academy men." He cleared his throat. "Obviously you possess some special talents which no doubt will soon become apparent."

Feeling his face redden, Rogers did a slow three-count. "Well, thank you, sir. I'll certainly do my best to live up to Admiral Griggs's confidence in me." *Take that, you brass-plated son of a bitch.*

Johnston coughed, which Rogers recognized as a nervous tic. "Yes, of course. You were aboard the *Reprisal* when she was the task group flagship."

"Yes, sir. Admiral Griggs is about the most people-oriented senior officer I have ever known. In fact, sir, the air group loved him. He not only spoke their language, he listened to them. I'm sure you know how much that means to junior officers, Captain."

Picking up the dossier, Johnston muttered something that Rogers interpreted as "Why, yes, of course." Then the captain intoned, "You will do me the pleasure of dining with me this evening, Rogers. Get to know one another better."

Phil got to his feet. "Certainly, sir. I shall look forward to it."

Halfway to the door, Rogers was brought up short. "Oh, by the way, Rogers. I see that you brought another officer with you from the *Reprisal*—an Ensign Barnes. That's rather unusual, isn't it?"

"Well, it may be unusual, Captain, but I think it's warranted. He was my wingman in VBF-59 and we served together long before then. I felt there would be a benefit in having somebody in my team who knows how I fly. The admiral agreed."

"Hmm. Quite so, quite so. I'm sure he's a good officer."

Rogers could not resist. "Oh, yes, sir. I find that former enlisted men make excellent officers." Before the captain could respond, Rogers got the hell out of the cabin, savoring the expression on Jerome Cheney Johnston IV's face.

Outside the door, Rogers pulled off his tie and stuffed it in a pocket. He stopped a moment to inspect the ship's heritage board. Named for a Revolutionary War battle in New York State, *Crown Point* was an *Independence*-class carrier laid down in Camden, New Jersey, in late 1942. Such was the efficiency of New York Shipbuilding Corporation that she had been commissioned only fourteen months later—two years ahead of schedule. Johnston was her second captain.

The new CAG went looking for the maintenance chief, and found his man on the hangar deck, supervising an engine change in an F6F. "Chief Rimmerman?"

Chief Aviation Machinist Mate Richard Rimmerman straightened up from the R-2800. "Here, sir." He was a burly man in his late thirties; Rogers evaluated him as a hands-on type of leader. A teacher more than a driver.

Rogers introduced himself and said, "If you can spare a moment, I'd like to talk." They walked to a secluded corner where Rogers came directly to the point. "Chief, I need some straight talk. What sort of shape are we in?"

Rimmerman's face betrayed his confusion. "Well, sir . . . ah, beggin' your pardon, Commander. Why ask me when you can talk to Lieutenant Wahl? He's the engineering officer. And Mr. Clark, one of th' Grumman tech-reps, will be aboard in a coupla days."

"Chief Rimmerman, I'm asking *you*." Rogers kept a sober expression.

Rimmerman's eyebrows rose. Then he nodded curtly. "All right, sir.

We're in good shape far as airplanes: twenty-four F6Fs, including a photo job, and eight TBMs. We're down one Turkey from our allotment but we should get a replacement before we leave."

"How's your in-commission rate?"

The leading chief straightened and looked Rogers in the eyes. "Better 'n ninety-two percent, Commander. This is a good maintenance crew."

Rogers leaned against the bulkhead and smiled. "Relax, Chief. You haven't told me anything I didn't suspect. Now, I've talked with some staff people from the *Sharpsburg*. They have one opinion of the previous CAG—what'd you make of him?"

Rimmerman paused before answering. "Well, sir, Mr. Kelso was afraid to make a decision without checking with the captain. It got pretty bad near the end. Two pilots were late recovering from a search off Kyushu and the captain was real upset. Well, these kids done a fine job: tracked a Jap convoy along the coast until another search team relieved 'em. I thought they deserved a medal but Captain Johnston was mad as hell. Wanted to ground 'em 'cause they delayed respotting the deck."

"What did Kelso do?"

Rimmerman shrugged. "Nothin', sir. He never would stand up for anybody, even when they done nothin' wrong."

Rogers merely nodded, thinking, *Albertson called it.* He pulled a folded paper from his shirt pocket and handed it to Rimmerman.

Rimmerman took the paper. "What's this, sir?"

"It's going to be my airplane, Chief. I want you to pick me the best F6F aboard—the best-maintained guns and most reliable radio. Paint those markings on it and stencil my name under the canopy rail."

Rimmerman tipped back his cap. "Aye, aye, sir. We'll get right on it. But I better tell you, Commander, the cap'n won't like this. It ain't regulation."

Rogers patted the older man's arm. "Actually, it *is* regulation, Chief. That's my point." He strode away, humming "Ac-centuate the Positive," wondering how many air group commanders had sandbagged a carrier captain within thirty minutes of meeting him.

SUNDAY, 17 JUNE
USS *CROWN POINT*

Rogers stood in the wardroom, which was crowded with some forty pilots and twenty aircrewmen from the air group's two squadrons. The formal change-of-command ceremony had just concluded on the flight deck following divine services: Johnston had insisted upon protocol, though the previous commander of Air Group 59 was metaphysically absent.

From peripheral conversations, Rogers inferred that the enlisted fliers never had been included in such a meeting before. He suspected snobbery by the deceased CAG, but those days were over. That as much as anything else was the reason for this meeting.

"Gentlemen, I am Lieutenant Commander Rogers," he began. "I was assigned here from Air Group Fifty-nine on the *Reprisal,* so this is my second command. Some of you may wonder where I come from, so I'll say that I started out as an SBD pilot in the *Saratoga* before the war." He pointed to Bill Barnes, sitting nearby. "Mr. Barnes and I flew together at Midway and Guadalcanal. In fact, he's sort of the reason I'm here, because he rode my rear seat for over a year and kept the Zeros off me."

The Avenger aircrewmen laughed appreciatively, which was the reaction Rogers wanted. "When Bill deserted to flight training, I was so depressed that I did a stupid thing: volunteered for antisub duty on a CVE." More delighted laughter. "It was a couple years before we teamed up again, but I want you all to know one thing: The white hats rate high with me. However things were done before, we're going to make maximum use of everyone in this air group." Rogers scanned the room for sign of acceptance or resistance. *Good, everybody's paying attention.*

"Second point. We'll keep our division organization until further notice. But there's a saying I subscribe to: Why let seniority lead when ability can do so much better? So from now on, if the number-four man sights a bogey, he takes the lead. I had an exec awhile back who went to the head by the numbers, and he's no longer with us. That situation will not be repeated here." Rogers told himself that a slight alteration of the Harkin saga was allowable if it helped make a point.

"Now, I've talked to Chief Rimmerman and it looks like the maintenance gang is in good shape. But you F6 pilots, remember this. We will only use water injection in two instances: a 'Gate' order from a fighter director, or to get out of trouble. Chasing down a Jap at war emergency power just isn't worthwhile. It's too hard on the engine and causes extra work for the mechs. I'll issue a written policy right away.

"Finally, I'm no trade-school boy. I came up like most of you, through the aviation cadet program. But I learned a lot from a couple of my skippers, who were topnotch Annapolis leaders. I also learned about the other kind." *Take that, Stinky Garrett.* "I think that any officer has an obligation to stand up for his men if they're unfairly treated. If it causes problems for him, well, that's the breaks. God help us if this Navy ever gets to the point where sailors and aviators take a backseat to some brass hat's career. So if you have a problem, you bring it here." Rogers punched the second button of his shirt. "I can't promise much, but I do promise that if I think you're right, I'll go to bat for you."

Rogers saw what he most wanted: smiles, nods, even some astonishment, but no obvious doubt. *Now,* he told himself, *I have to live up to that speech.*

TUESDAY, 19 JUNE

KANOYA BASE

"B-San attack on Fukuoka!" The petty officer orderly rattled doors and screamed his lungs out, spreading the news through the barracks that the B-29s were back. "All pilots report to the flight office immediately!"

Sakaida almost pulled the covers over his head. As a warrant officer he was entitled to share a room with just two others of equal rank—a major improvement on the sardine-packed hammock arrangement he had known for most of his career. Reluctantly he flipped back the blanket as Hitoshi Tachibana switched on the light. Sakaida croaked, "What time is it?"

"Almost midnight," Tachibana replied.

Pulling on his clothes, Sakaida tried to sort out the situation. "I do not think the B-Sans have come to Kyushu since April," he muttered. "We have never fought them, and Fukuoka is one hundred fifty miles away. What is different this time?"

Tachibana was almost out the door. "We will learn shortly."

In fact, no information was immediately forthcoming. The *hikotai*'s office was crowded with pilots, some still tugging on flight gear, all questioning one another. "Where is Lieutenant Homma?" Sakaida asked the duty officer.

"He has not arrived," the man responded. "He may be at headquarters seeking orders."

Sakaida sat on a bench, chin in his hands. *This makes no sense,* he reasoned. *The* Gekkos *have radar. Why are we being alerted?* He sat back and tried to remember the nearest base with Nakajima J1N1s. He knew that Air Group 210 had been posted to Kyushu after the invasion of Okinawa, but he had lost track of the twin-engine night fighters.

After ten minutes with no further information, Sakaida ran out of patience. He cornered the other warrant officer, a man in his debt from gambling, and grilled him. "What information is there on the Boeings' approach path and altitude? Are they still bombing Fukuoka?"

"I do not know, Sakaida. We are still awaiting information."

The old headache was back, the tension building behind his eyes. "In that case, maybe one or two of us should take off and try to find the Americans. We could radio information back to the base and arrange for an interception."

Spreading his hands, the duty officer explained, "We have no authority for such action. You must obtain permission to take off on a combat flight. You know that."

"I know that I am tired of waiting for somebody to tell me to go back to bed." Sakaida's mind was made up. "Inform the control tower that *Hikotai* 801 is sending up a scout to locate the enemy." He was out the door before anyone could reply.

In eight minutes Sakaida was checking his *Shiden-Kai*'s vital signs. Strapped into the cockpit, listening to the engine and scanning the instruments, his mind wandered. *We are devoted to principles of scientific fighting,* he remembered. *We should have a doctrine for coordinating regular fighters with radar-equipped aircraft.* He began thinking about a proposal to send up the chain of command. On clear, moonlit nights it should be possible to follow *Gekkos* to the enemy bomber stream. . . .

Somebody was climbing onto his port wing. He looked left, expecting to see the lead mechanic—the nervous individual who had been reluctant to cooperate. But there were two men. One was Homma. He had his pistol out and was saying something about Warrant Officer Sakaida being under arrest.

WEDNESDAY, 20 JUNE
USS *CROWN POINT*

Barnes was playing solitaire in "boys' town," the forward junior-officer bunkroom, when another ensign, James Ready Haliburton, entered the compartment. He was known as Junior, and Barnes understood the moniker: He looked just about fourteen years old, stocky, almost pudgy, with freckles and a gap-tooth smile. Barnes learned that Junior was just five years older than he looked.

As other aviators returned to the berthing space from lunch, shoptalk resumed. "It's gonna be real chummy in here with a full crew again," ventured a jaygee named Perle. "We've been short-handed the past coupla weeks."

Barnes laid down his cards and stood up. "Yeah, I heard. That's why Commander Rogers and I came over from the *Reprisal.*"

"Excuse me," Haliburton interjected. "I've been wondering why you fellows are here instead of back on the *Reprisal.*"

"Easy enough," Barnes replied. "The ship's laid up for major repairs and Mr. Rogers was offered this slot. He figured he'd rather be out here than cooling his heels in Alameda."

There were low whistles and shaking heads in the room. "Man, I'll cool my heels in Alameda any old time," offered a Southerner named Carruthers. He looked up. "What makes Rogers so eager? He's been laying plans with Wynn of the torpeckers."

Barnes scratched his head, trying to decide how much to tell his new shipmates. "Well, Phil takes the war damn serious—more than most guys. We lost some fellows at Midway and Guadalcanal, and then in the past several months Phil's lost two of his best friends. Our first skipper in VBF-59 was killed by our own gunners off Hong Kong, and a Marine from his Pensacola class went down over Indochina." Barnes looked around, gauging the reaction. "Don't get me wrong. Phil's not one of those I-fly-for-revenge guys. But he's got a hell of a lot of experience. He figures he can prevent other losses . . ." Barnes's voice trailed off as the thought crystallized in his mind. "Rogers hates just one thing more than Japs."

"What's that?" Perle asked.

The faces swam upward from Barnes's memory: Gordon Connell, Kenny Diskowski, Bernie Burnett. "Stupidity."

FRIDAY, 22 JUNE
KANOYA BASE

Sakaida had wavered between fear and anger for three days. It was bad enough, being dragged out of his fighter the night the B-29s attacked the Fukuoka urban area. But to be arrested, then charged with disobedience and "deserting his post" was bitterly galling. Now, escorted into Commander Miwa's presence by two guards, he realized that his immediate future lay in the hands of a man known as a martinet.

Sakaida was surprised to find the Mamoru Wing leader alone in his office. Miwa dismissed the guards, telling them to wait outside, then allowed the prisoner to stand at attention while he re-read the man's record and the charges against him.

At length Miwa looked up. "Warrant Officer Sakaida, you have been advised of the charges against you: disobeying standing orders and leaving your post without permission. You are guilty on both counts. Do you have any words in your defense?"

Sakaida felt his lower lip quivering. He prayed it did not show. The flunky from the provost marshal's office had given him a perfunctory lecture, then abandoned him to a questionable fate. *So this is naval justice,* he thought. He tried to concentrate. *If only Umeda were here!* "Honorable Commander, may I speak plainly?"

Miwa almost laughed. "That is your way, is it not?"

"Thank you, sir." He lowered his gaze to his commanding officer. "These charges have nothing to do with disobeying orders. The investigation established that I only meant to locate the enemy while time allowed. The real reason is . . . elsewhere." Sakaida held his breath. Even indirect criticism of a commissioned officer was dangerous in the Imperial Navy.

"Yes, I know." Miwa's voice was almost pleasant. "In fact, when I discussed your case with Captain Umeda, he provided some background information." Miwa let that information ferment in Sakaida's brain. "Between us, we arrived at a satisfactory conclusion, Sakaida. Obviously you cannot remain here—not when a superior officer has filed charges against you. But if we return you to a naval hospital, your experience will be wasted. Therefore . . ."

Somebody was inflating a very large balloon inside Sakaida's skull.

". . . your sentence is to be commuted but the conviction remains on your record. You are being transferred away from here, to Air Group 254."

Sakaida had never heard of the unit. "Beg pardon, sir, may I know where?"

"Shanghai. Dismissed."

SATURDAY, 30 JUNE

USS *CROWN POINT*

Rogers recognized the handwriting and his eyes widened in disbelief. It was like a letter postmarked from the cemetery. He tore open the envelope and withdrew a snapshot, the irregular white border framing a photo of Sunny Jim Carpenter wearing dress whites, with a good-looking blonde in a wedding dress. Rogers's mind reeled. *My God! Jim's alive—and married!*

The one-page note erased five months of grief and doubt.

"Dear Phil,

"Sorry for the delay, I've been busy. Got shot down at Saigon 12 January and was 'rescued' by the French. Walked out of Indochina and hitchhiked home from Kunming in April. Hell of a story—I'll tell you about it sometime. Met up with my high-school sweetheart and, well, the Chinese say that one picture's worth 1,000 words. (Enclosed) I'm at Miramar, running maintenance and testing new F4Us. Just checked out in the F7F-3. What a beaut: cruises at 190 knots. Will be here at least four more months. When I called your gang at Alameda, they said you're winning the war by yourself. Buck Rogers an air group commander? God help us! Drop a line, buddy.

> Yours, Jim and Candace."

Rogers re-read the letter, then put it away with the photo. He tried to order his emotions, which tugged at him from opposite directions. The confirmation of a valued friend's survival was diluted by envy of that friend's marriage. Rogers indulged in a moment of obligatory self-criticism. Carpenter obviously had been through a tremendous ordeal—he was entitled to a good shore billet and a lovely wife. But beneath it all . . . Rogers tossed the letter onto his desk. He leaned forward, rubbing his temples and trying to conjure up nothingness.

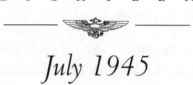

July 1945

"We're going back to Japan," Rogers announced from the head of the ready room. "Strikes against remaining fleet units have priority. After that, we'll hit the airfields." His words drew a stirring in the pilots of Air Group 56—an eager-nervous anticipation at what was now conventional wisdom: Bad places meant good targets.

As a junior officer Phil Rogers had resented not knowing what drove policies or orders. He had resolved that if he ever rose to command, he would give his men the courtesy of telling them not only of near-term operations, but the reasons for them.

"Admiral Griggs's Third Fleet call sign is Kingpin," Rogers began. "During his task group briefings, I learned some of the reasons behind this series of strikes. Basically, we're out to destroy the rest of the Japanese Navy so our convoys from the Aleutians can pass the Kuriles into Sea of Okhotsk without interference."

That information prompted an undercurrent of animated conversation. Lieutenant Foster "Windy" Wynn, skipper of Torpedo 56, raised a hand. "CAG, that's like doing a tonselectomy through the rectum, isn't it? We're already getting steady supplies from Leyte and Ulithi. The best weather up in the Aleutians is miserable."

Rogers smiled despite himself: Windy Wynn was never at a loss for words. "Remember, eventually we'll gear up for the invasion of Japan it-self. Staging through the Aleutians makes sense when you compare the circle route to the Central Pacific sea lanes." Rogers thought for a moment, pondering whether to repeat the "solid rumors" he had heard. *Well, these guys deserve to know most of what I do.* "Besides, there's a good chance that the Russians will enter the war against Japan in the next few months. If so, their navy can't even handle what little the Japs have left. So it's up to us."

Rogers turned his attention to the task force organization. "Task Force Thirty-eight remains under Vice Admiral McCain in the *Shangri-La* with Admiral Halsey running Third Fleet from the *New Jersey*." There was a resentful grumbling from the aviators, most of whom had heard of the December typhoon, which cost ships and lives. Staffers insisted that Halsey had avoided eleven other typhoons, but the losses off Japan had left a bitter taste in many mouths. Rogers decided to ignore the miniature mutiny. "We'll refuel east of Okinawa on the eighth and hit the Tokyo Plain on the tenth. It'll be the first time since February. We had real fine hunting then, so expect more of the same."

Following the briefing, Rogers conferred with Wynn and Lieutenant Lin Swanson, the fighter executive officer. "Windy, I think we're going to have more shipping than ever before. So make sure your ordnance folks have a full deckload worth of torpedoes accessible at all times, starting the seventh."

Wynn's square jaw thrust forward. "It's a pain to upload them from the magazine, but we'll be ready. I'll plan on a half dozen fish, minimum."

"Good," Rogers replied. Then he asked, "Are these torpedoes worth a damn?"

Wynn shrugged, raising his eyebrows. "Beats the hell out of me, Skipper. We run routine maintenance but we haven't dropped a one in combat yet. Maybe we could drop one or two just to see if they run hot, straight, and normal."

"I'll see what I can do." Rogers turned to Swanson. "Lin, if we get into a real heavy period of launching strikes, I won't be able to lead every mission. So I expect that Windy and I will alternate, but you'll have to take up the slack."

"Fine by me, sir. But you ought to know—I've never led a coordinated strike. Mr. Kelso always did that. Actually, I think he'd have been willing to let me, but Captain Johnston seems to insist on seniority."

Rogers was not surprised. "Seniority—it'll be the death of us all. Well, maybe I can sell it to him on the basis of professional development or something. You ever notice how he never talks about aviators? Always officers. I'll stress the leadership angle—developing the abilities of his junior officers."

Wynn's expression told Rogers that something irreverent was coming. "Skipper, while you're at it, how about changing the signal numbers for Halsey and McCain?"

"Why, whatever do you mean?" Rogers's expression was deadpan.

"Word is that the chief of staff and Jimmy Thach are actually running things, and Thach is just a four-striper!"

"He's a damn good man," Swanson interjected.

"I miss Pete Mitscher," Wynn replied. "He's a carrier aviator from the word go. Nobody else has his experience. And we always got results under Spruance, even if he is a blackshoe." Both officers looked to Rogers for comment.

"Well, I can't say as I'm a big Halsey fan," Rogers began. "But you have to give the guy credit for one thing—he's in favor of killing Japs. And that's four-oh with me."

MONDAY, 2 JULY

PILGRIM ONE-ONE

Rogers felt his Hellcat pitch slightly nose-down as he lowered his flaps at 130 knots indicated. He fell back on the old acronym and double-checked the basics. GUMP: gas (fullest internal tank), undercarriage (down and locked), mixture (rich), prop (low pitch). Touching the tailhook handle, he felt that he was ready for landing.

Rolling out on short final, Rogers was struck by the deck's appearance. Though he had seen Independence-class carriers almost daily for months, their look continued to bother him. The foreshortened profile was a structural concession to the original light-cruiser design, whose hull could not support the additional weight of a full-length flight deck. Consequently, the 670-foot deck ended fifty feet short of the bow. *Well, no matter,* he told himself. *There's seven wires to catch me.* He had landed on shorter decks— *Alazon Bay*'s measured 442 feet long—but the Independence-class deck was two feet narrower.

Checking his lineup, Rogers was satisfied. He was less concerned about the size of the deck than with his current proficiency. He had flown only twice while at Leyte, and not from shipboard. This would be his first carrier landing in ten weeks, and he wanted to look good.

He responded to a "low" signal from the LSO—arms drooping below shoulder level—and moved to correct. He began talking himself through the approach. *There, looking better.* But now the LSO's paddles were waving back and forth above his head: a wave-off, which carried the force of law.

Rogers experienced an instant of disbelief, rear-ended by concern. *What's the matter? Foul deck?* He shoved up the power, passing close aboard to port. *Nothing in the landing area. What the hell?* He sucked up his wheels, retracted the flaps—and realized he had not lowered his hook.

Shaking his head, he knew he would live with the error for months— maybe years. *New CAG, hot carrier pilot, double ace and then some. God, my first landing aboard my new ship!* The fact that the LSO had failed to give the "no hook" signal did nothing to alleviate Rogers's embarrassment.

Ten minutes later Rogers was climbing from his cockpit, the last pilot aboard, when the flight-deck bullhorn boomed. "Air group commander, report to the bridge."

Rogers accepted his plotting board from the plane captain and trudged toward the island. He walked past Barnes, who was standing with Perle and Haliburton. "Not a word," Rogers intoned. "Not one word!" Barnes smiled while the others studied their shoes.

Rogers presented himself on the small wing of the bridge, an open-air galley overlooking the flight deck. Jerome Johnston turned, his face impassive, unreadable. *Here it comes,* Rogers thought.

"Mr. Rogers, I have just noticed the nonregulation markings on your airplane. You will please explain the gaudiest paint job I have ever seen on a naval aircraft."

Astonished, Rogers sought to comprehend the captain's sense of priorities. He shot a glance downward, where the F6F was being moved forward over lowered barriers. "Captain, I am not aware that any of the markings on my plane are illegal." He did wonder, however, why Johnston had not mentioned the personal paint before.

Johnston leaned forward, hands on hips. "Don't play innocent with me, Rogers! All those meatballs, that air group marking, and"—he sputtered briefly, like a lawn mower engine—"that obscene pinup girl!"

Rogers actually relaxed. "Captain, the victory flags are completely legit. In fact, I have the AirPac authorization letter in my stateroom. It was issued about this time last year. I don't know of any regulations that prohibit the CAG markings, sir. As for the pinup, well, that was done as a surprise for me by one of the mechanics."

Johnston pointed a damning finger at Pilgrim One-One, and Rogers involuntarily followed the gesture. Thirteen rising suns and the swimsuited Varga girl behind the cowling were vividly set off against the standard gloss-blue paint. "CAG" was stenciled in three-inch white letters on the vertical stabilizer.

"I shall personally check on this matter, Mr. Rogers," Johnston was saying. "You will oblige me by producing the circular authorizing victory flags. But I will not have my aircraft adorned with such pornography."

Rogers thought: *Well, what sort of pornography will you tolerate, Captain?* Before he could voice the sentiment, Johnston ordered, "Remove the girlie picture. Now."

Rogers stepped back, saluted smartly, and barked, "Aye, aye, sir." Then he got the hell off the bridge.

Descending to the hangar deck, Rogers found Chief Richard Rimmerman, who walked up to him wiping his hands on an oily rag. "Sorry to hear about the painting, sir. The boys like to give her a little pat on the behind."

Rogers shook his head. "Word travels fast, Chief."

Rimmerman laughed. "Well, sir, this is a pretty small ship." He thought for a moment. "Commander, if you don't mind, we'll just replace the access panel on your plane. Crandall worked awful hard on that pinup—be a shame to ruin it. We can stash the panel somewhere the cap'n won't never see it."

"Okay by me, Chief. But doesn't Johnston ever check your work area?"

"Hardly ever, sir. He just passes through from time to time. Likes to inspect the engineering spaces more 'n anything else."

A thought occurred to Rogers. "Does he ever walk around the planes on the flight deck?"

Rimmerman shook his head. "Well, sir, I don't recall. Not much, I guess."

So that's why he hadn't seen the paint job before. Rogers decided he could make use of this intelligence. "Thanks, Chief." He turned to go, then pulled up short. "Say, do you have a spare tailhook laying around? Maybe one that's been surveyed?"

"Uh, yessir. A TBM broke the dashpot awhile back. We've still got it back here somewhere." He looked querulously at the CAG. "Why, sir?"

A tight little smile played around Rogers's lips. "Get it."

When Rogers trudged into Ready One, an Avenger's tailhook slung over one shoulder like a twentieth-century penance, the pilots erupted in laughter. Somebody had chalked a hasty cartoon on the blackboard, labeled COMDR. ROGERS'S FIRST LANDING but the jibe was forgotten as he lowered the hook to the deck.

"God, this is heavy," he moaned. "Today we're starting a *Crown Point* tradition. The next sad sack who forgets to lower his hook gets to lug this thing around for the rest of the day. Including one lap around the flight deck." Hoots and cheers arose from the aviators.

"Following a suitable award ceremony, of course."

Ensign Haliburton risked a question. "When are you circling the flight deck, sir?"

"Don't push it, son." Rogers glanced around. "Where's Roach?"

"Here, sir." Lieutenant (j.g.) Bud Roach rose with his LSO logbook in hand.

"Okay, I screwed up," Rogers began. "But why didn't I get a 'no hook' signal and save myself all this embarrassment?"

Roach glanced around. "No excuse, Commander. My fault."

"I don't care whose fault it was, damn it. I want to know what happened."

"Well, sir, I'm breaking in a new spotter. He didn't catch it until too late."

"Okay. I'm confident it won't happen again." Rogers allowed that sentiment to sink in. Then he asked, "What was the average interval on this recovery?"

Roach thumbed his pages, quickly consulting the data recorded by his writer. "I'd guess around thirty seconds, sir. I haven't computed it yet."

"That's to be expected after a layoff. But from now on, I want the overall average with division and individual pilots' intervals as well. I know this air group has been concerned with safety more than intervals, and that's fine. But I think we can shave a few seconds and still have room to spare. If we start getting too tight, we'll know by the increase in wave-offs. Meanwhile, I want us to close it up. Understood?"

A chorus of "Aye, aye"s rang off the bulkheads. Rogers winked at Barnes, who smiled knowingly. *Bill's got it,* Rogers told himself. *All these guys needed was somebody to show some interest in them, show them he knows what he's doing.* Little things like a hot-rock paint job and some minor theatrics went a long way toward building confidence—and building a competent war machine for what lay ahead.

TUESDAY, 3 JULY
APPROACHING SHANGHAI

The five thousand–ton transport turned out of the Yangtze River and entered the mouth of its tributary, the Huangpu, with the village of Shijiazhai on the riverbank to port. Leaning on the rail, Sakaida mused that the forty-hour voyage from Kyushu had been blessedly uneventful. American submarines apparently had forsaken the Yellow Sea for better hunting in recent months. He could recall a time when he had been flown from the floatplane conversion unit at Oppama to his combat unit in the Solomons as a priority passenger. *But that was three years ago,* he recalled. *Much has changed in that time.*

Four miles along, the creaky old *Maru* passed Jiangwan Airport. Sakaida shielded his eyes against the glare, trying to identify the two or three aircraft in the traffic pattern. As yet he did not even know where his land-based air group, *Kokutai* 254, was stationed; his orders merely said Shanghai. He would have to find his new unit largely on his own.

Hiroyoshi Sakaida had never been to China. In a way, he looked forward to the opportunity. But as he inhaled the mixture of saltwater, rotting fish, and rice-paddy fertilizer, a thought occurred to him: *Welcome to the mainland of Asia.*

WEDNESDAY, 4 JULY

USS *CROWN POINT*

Captain Jerome Cheney Johnston IV may have been a brass-hat s.o.b., but he was also profoundly patriotic. Therefore, Rogers carefully knotted his tie before reporting to the wardroom for the officers' Independence Day celebration. The ship's executive officer, a sycophantic commander named Delbert Howard, had insisted on "proper attire." The pilots called him "Dilbert," after cartoonist Robert Osborne's inept aviator.

Looking in the mirror, Rogers smiled at the recollection of Jay-Bob Yakeley, a Southerner who had exclaimed, "Hell's fire, boys. My little ol' hometown didn't start observin' the Fourth of Ju-ly till just last year." Some Americans had trouble remembering that the War Between the States had ended only eighty years ago.

On an impulse, Rogers swung by the ready room to ensure that all his officers would appear at Johnston's party. A dozen malingerers sat around, listening to Armed Forces Radio or swapping tales. The announcer had just repeated that Okinawa had been declared secure while New York City sweltered in 94.7° heat. Rogers was about to herd his people out when the announcer's next subject brought conversation to a stop: "Dateline Washington: President Truman has seized Texas Company refineries at Port Arthur, which produce ninety-one– and hundred-octane gasoline. In a smoldering labor dispute, a reported 175 strikers are threatening 4,900 jobs. Meanwhile, 15,000 workers are out at Firestone, and 16,700 Goodyear em-

ployees remain idle because twenty-two Negro janitors reportedly have refused work at the minimum wage. Firestone management says the janitors
have been suspended for three days."

Lin Swanson turned to the duty officer. "Shut that damn thing off."

Barnes sneered. "I remember after Pearl Harbor the AFL-CIO
promised no strikes for the duration. The mine workers have struck, what,
three or four times now?"

A Democrat fidgeted. "Don't you suppose working men have the right
to improve their lot? Isn't that something we're supposed to be fighting
for?"

"Hell, no!" Barnes exclaimed. "Not in the middle of a war! In the first
place, the unions said they wouldn't strike, and they lied. In the second
place, how the hell are we gonna build more ships or planes or even rifles
without steel?"

Rogers felt a small shiver climb his spine. "You know, Burnett never
carried any strain. The only thing that got him worked up was labor
unions—his dad's a manager at Ford. It didn't make any difference: Aus-
tralia, New Zealand, San Francisco, he hated 'em all. Never did stop talking about John L. Lewis leading the coal miners on strike in '43." He shook
his head in recollection. "The only good thing I ever heard him say about
Roosevelt was when F.D.R. sent federal troops in to the mines. When I think
what Bernie would say now—"

"Ungrateful, money-grubbing bunch of bastards. You don't hear about
any labor strikes in Japan, that's for sure." Barnes could have been Burnett.

Rogers turned toward the exit. "Well, happy Fourth of July, gentlemen. See you at the party."

FRIDAY, 6 JULY
SHANGHAI

Sakaida was appalled at what he found in Air Group 254.

The *kokutai* was badly under strength, with barely enough Zero 52s
for a *hikotai*. Of those fighters, only a few were airworthy at any given time,
owing to a shortage of spare parts, fuel, and generally mediocre maintenance. The division officer, Lieutenant Kenji Matano, had been forthright:
"We can use someone of your experience, Sakaida. We have very few
Class A combat pilots. But if you came here expecting to fly, forget it.
You'll be lucky to get six hours in a month."

With minimal duties, Sakaida quickly settled into the Shanghai routine. The warrant officers' quarters were decent enough, the food was tol-

erable, and laundry service was quick and cheap. Sitting outside the hostel, Sakaida struck up a conversation with a warrant officer from another *hikotai*—a long-term China veteran named Teigo Amari.

"What is the situation here?" Sakaida asked. "Are you flying combat operations?"

Amari laughed derisively. "Ha! If only we were, to break the monotony. There has been no combat activity since early April. Tachang, Woosung, and Lunghwa airfields were attacked by Chinese and American planes. They strafed the fields, shot down a few airplanes and left." He shrugged. "Almost nothing since then."

"Well, what does the enemy fly? Where are they based? I have heard nothing."

"Oh, that's not unusual," Amari replied. "None of the commissioned officers is very concerned about passing along intelligence. We just do what we are told." The spite in his voice was audible. "But as for your question, I can tell you little. The Chinese and the Americans operate together, apparently sometimes flying in the same formations. Their aircraft are quite good: North American fighters and twin-engine bombers, although there are still some old Curtiss fighters. Their bases are west of here because our army still controls most of the area from the coast into the interior."

Sakaida absorbed that information for a moment. He had heard about the North American long-range escort fighter, type P-51. He did not relish tangling with one of those while flying a worn-out Zero Model 52. *And Yankees always fight in pairs.*

"Amari, how long has the *kokutai* been here?"

"Oh, Air Group 254 fought at Formosa and Leyte before coming here. It was badly cut up in those battles—most of our current pilots have joined since then. We sometimes worked with Air Group 901 at Ya Hsien on Formosa. We flew some ground-support missions over this area but I can tell you they were not successful. We lost six aircraft in January, then retreated to Shanghai in April. Since then we've had almost no new spare parts, and our fuel allotment is below minimum."

Amari regarded Sakaida closely. "I hear that you were in a *Shiden-Kai* unit. You must be disappointed to be sent here."

He's probing, Sakaida thought. "I had a disagreement with a lieutenant."

Amari laughed again, allowing a hint of warmth into his tone. "Well, in that case, welcome to China!" He rose from his chair. "Come, Sakaida. I can show you how we enjoy life in this part of the empire." Amari's indefinite but vaguely lecherous gesture told Sakaida that perhaps exile in this land of barbarians might be tolerable after all.

TUESDAY, 10 JULY, 0500
PILGRIM ONE-ONE

Rogers felt the kick in the small of the back as the Type H, Mark II catapult threw the lead Hellcat off the deck and into the night. The sensation
was one of being fired from a powerful slingshot into a huge, black barrel
that permitted no light to enter. His sole reference in the inky void was the
truck light of the destroyer *Stuart* a mile ahead of the carrier. He was glad
of the forty-five minutes he had spent letting his night vision adapt by
wearing red-tinted goggles in the ready room.

As he cleaned up his airplane, retracting flaps and wheels, Rogers
began a gently banked turn away from the ship. He transitioned to instrument flight, forcing himself to concentrate on his artificial horizon in the
cockpit's soft, red lighting. For a chilling fifteen seconds he fought a self-
contained battle of willpower, his training and intellect clashing with his
human instincts that demanded he correct a nonexistent descent. For a moment he covered his right hand with his left on the stick to steady the controls. Then the vertigo passed and he was fully in command of himself.

Like every carrier pilot on earth, Rogers hated nothing so much as
predawn catapult shots, but this was worse than most: an 0400 launch into
poor weather 170 miles from the Honshu coast. *The only good thing about
it,* he mused, *is that we're still undetected because of the storm front.* The
fact that submarines and Okinawa-based aircraft had disposed of most
Japanese picket boats also ensured surprise up to the point that the carrier
planes might appear on land-based enemy radar.

With navigation lights running, Rogers began a slow climb overhead
the ship. He discerned the exhaust flames of other aircraft below; in minutes he was joined by Barnes; next, by his second section; and finally, the
other two divisions. Then, beneath gloomy, lowering skies, he set course
for Tokyo.

The target was Tachikawa Airfield, twenty-two nautical miles inland
and just west of the capital. The low, easterly sun cast a dismal light through
the murk as Rogers led twelve fighters in a descent, seeking the distinctive
parallel runways. Navigation was hampered by low clouds and haze, but
finally Rogers sighted Tachikawa to starboard and called his flight.

"Pilgrim chicks from One-One. I'm attacking. Two-One, take the
eastern runway as briefed. Three-One, you're top cover until I call you
down." The other team leaders, Lin Swanson and Jay-Bob Yakeley, acknowledged.

Phil Rogers normally preferred high-angle strafing: The extra time and
overhead view of the target yielded optimum results. But under a two thou-

sand–foot ceiling, he chose a 30-degree dive, slanting toward Tachikawa
from the southwest. He shoved up the power, ran his precombat check, and
was satisfied. *Gunsight on, master arm on, rockets selected. Here we go.*

There was no flak, not even any visible movement. Rogers exulted:
Got 'em! He took time to compensate for his HVARs' trajectory and sent
two five-inchers smoking into the nearest hangar. Without checking results,
he raised the nose slightly and fired his next pair into another large structure farther down the flight line. Crossing the northern boundary, he pulled
up left and established a Stateside gunnery pattern. Jake Jacobs and Junior
Haliburton, his second section, were pulling off target, leaving satisfactory
fires behind them. Rogers shot a glance to the west, saw similar results from
Swanson's team, and made a quick decision. *No fighters up here today—
we own this place.*

"Pilgrim One-One to flight. There's no AA fire yet. Go for the parked
planes." Then he remembered Yakeley, still overhead. "J. B., this is Buck.
Watch our next runs, and if there's still no flak, take your turn. Otherwise
take out the guns."

"Roger, Skipper."

Rogers bent the pattern as tightly as possible, topping out at fifteen
hundred feet before allowing the nose to drop. He adjusted his dive heading slightly to avoid an identical repeat of his first pass, in case some alert
gunner had reached his weapon. Then Rogers was concentrating on his sight
picture, framing a row of twin-engine aircraft in his Mark VIII reticle. With
the pipper one diameter beneath the nearest plane, he clamped down on the
trigger.

The high rattle came to him as six M2s churned up the concrete mat,
then disintegrated the olive-drab airplane, which absorbed nearly eighty
half-inch bullets per second. *God, I love strafing.* Rogers flattened out of
his dive, making almost 300 knots, and realized he'd had target fixation.
At fifty feet altitude, he hosed a long burst at a second line of aircraft, saw
pieces fly, then was over the fence again.

Rogers pulled up, glanced back, and saw lazy white motes spiraling
through the gloom. *Somebody's shooting at us.* He keyed the mike to inform Yakeley, when two dark, blunt shapes flashed across the field, parallel to the runways, muzzle flashes illuminating their wings. *J. B.'s on the
ball. Good deal.*

After the third pass, Rogers called for a joinup. Barnes was closed up
tight, and Jacobs had slid wide in combat spread just beneath the clouds.
Rogers craned his neck. *Where's Junior?* Barnes was rocking his wings,
pointing downward. Pilgrim One-Four expended the last of its ammunition
into another twin-engine job, which flared, burned, and exploded. Then, al-

most sheepishly, Ensign Haliburton trailed his commanding officer south-ward.

Rogers resolved to have a word with the lad, for there is a great deal of independence, and a confident immunity to risk, in a teenager flying a fighter plane.

THURSDAY, 12 JULY
USS *SHARPSBURG*

Rear Admiral Jacob Griggs believed in planning. Therefore, he had gathered all four air group commanders from his force aboard his flagship while refueling was under way. He got straight to the point.

"Gentlemen, I suppose most of you have read *Victory Through Air Power.* Well, Mr. Seversky has been right about many of his air-power lessons for America, but he's dead wrong in his eleventh point: that carriers cannot go head to head with land-based air. We're going to disprove that again, not that it needs proof."

He tapped the map of Japan. "Starting tomorrow—weather permitting—we're going to hit targets north of Tokyo. These are areas that so far have been immune to B-29 attacks, so it'll be a feather in the cap of Navy Air. Over the next two days we'll hit Honshu and Hokkaido, concentrating on naval units and merchant vessels. Apparently our submarines have all but bottled up the Japanese merchant marine, so it's largely confined to coastal waters." He looked over his small audience. "You all know what that means: Without her sea lanes, Japan will dry up as an industrial power."

Alliance's CAG, Lieutenant Commander Richard Morgan, raised a hand. "Admiral, what opposition can we expect? A lot of us were surprised that no Jap fighters came up day before yesterday."

Griggs looked at Tom Albertson, and the operations officer took the cue. "We think that was a combination of factors: surprise, poor weather, and probably a decision to save their strength for the invasion. But we're not getting complacent, Rich. We'll have the usual CAPs and escorts assigned." Albertson chuckled to himself. "Maybe your brother will let you shoot down another Jap." Appreciative laughter rippled through the compartment. It was a standing joke that the Morgan boys, Richard and Marcus, had a minor rivalry. After the five Sullivans were lost in the cruiser *Juneau* off Guadalcanal, the Navy insisted on separating close relatives. But the policy had lapsed, and now more brothers were requesting and being granted duty in the same ship—occasionally even the same squadron.

When Griggs ended the meeting, he invited Rogers and Albertson to his quarters. Rogers could guess why.

"Sit you down, son. Tell me about things in the good ship *Crown Point*."

Rogers thought for a moment. He was chilled by the thought that he may have been sent to the *Crown Point* as a staff spy. "Well, sir, I don't know what to tell you. I don't have any complaints, if that's your concern."

Jacob Griggs laughed and slapped a knee. "Hell, son. Don't you suppose I'd have known about any complaints? After all, Captain Johnston could relieve you anytime. Of course, I'd have to approve it, but I haven't heard a peep."

Rogers looked to Albertson for help. Receiving none, he plunged ahead. "Frankly, sir, I think he sees me as your fair-haired boy. If he has any resentment, he's keeping it pretty much to himself." *Like you planned, you sly old seadog.*

"Your guys did all right at Tachikawa the other day," Albertson offered. "What was it—twenty-odd planes destroyed on the ground?"

"Yes, sir. We made out okay. But mainly I'm working on changing the way the air group operates. I want to close up the landing intervals, try different tactics, that sort of thing. Of course, I tell Johnston—er, Captain Johnston—what I plan to do."

Griggs interjected. "He's a hands-on kind of leader. How's he taken to your newfangled ways of doing things?"

Rogers shrugged. "So far, so good, sir. I think he sees that we can do things better than they were before, under Kelso. I also think he realizes now that I'll stick up for my people if need be. And—" Rogers bit off the words.

"And that I'll stick up for you?" There was warmth and humor in Griggs's voice.

Rogers exhaled. "Admiral, I sure hope so!"

"Ha! I will, as long as I'm convinced you're getting results and doing right. It takes some officers awhile to realize it, but often that's what leadership is about: sticking up for your men when they're right. Some officers never learn that at all."

Griggs's flag lieutenant entered the room. "Sir, you're requested on the flag bridge. Some sort of snag in the refueling."

"All right." He made a show of rising from his chair. "An admiral's work is never done. Tom, you and Mr. Rogers may as well stay here." He stuck out his hand. "Keep up the good work, son. Sink me some ships the next few days."

Rogers grasped the old man's hand. "I sure will, sir."

As a steward poured coffee, Albertson asked, "Phil, I'd like to catch up more on the old gang. How much time do you have?"

"Oh, nearly an hour, I guess. I'm supposed to high-line back to the oiler and then to the *Crown Point* before 1400."

"Swell. Tell me, how'd things go in the *Reprisal*? Did Pat do a good job?"

Rogers nodded. "Yeah, he really did. I never warmed up to him—that's just not Pat, I guess. But we had a good air group." He looked at his former CAG. "You'd have been proud of us, Tom."

Albertson stared at the tablecloth. "Thanks. I don't mind telling you, I wondered more about Ralph than Pat. I knew that Leo and Barry were solid."

"I think Ralph grew into the job. Things got better after we got rid of Harkin."

"Yeah? What happened?"

Rogers explained and Albertson's face went blank. "Holy—"

"Yeah. Gambini lost a leg and Platco had to can Harkin. Otherwise my wingman would have committed mutiny and murder."

"Your wingman? Who's that?"

"Bill Barnes, my old gunner in Bombing Three. He replaced, ah, Diskowski."

Albertson could tell. "What happened, Phil?"

"Oh, gosh. Our first mission against the Philippines, Kenny's bomb exploded in flight. You remember, that nice kid you taught to mix drinks at North Island."

Albertson sat speechless while Rogers decided to change the subject. "Are we really going after targets the B-29s haven't hit?"

"Well, for some damn reason we're supposed to lay off four cities. My guess is the Air Force has some claim on them. One's Kokura, on Kyushu near the Inland Sea. Three are on Honshu, though one of 'em is too far north to bother with: Niigata. Then there's Kyoto, near the southwest shore of Biwa Lake. About all they have in common is they're fairly large cities and all are on or near water."

"What's the fourth one?"

"Oh, down here." He reached over and tapped the map. "Hiroshima."

SUNDAY, 15 JULY
USS CROWN POINT

Rogers eased from the cockpit onto the port wing and paused a moment. He appreciatively eyed the new pinup girl that Seaman Crandall had painted on a portside access panel—the side away from Jerome Johnston's view from the bridge. This cutie was even cuter than the first, especially without her swimsuit. Rogers chuckled to himself, appreciating the irreverent humor of the American sailor. *If J. C. ever hears about this . . .*

Trotting across the flight deck, Rogers dropped into the port catwalk, then descended to the torpedo ready room. He entered just in time to see Windy Wynn's hands raised, fingers splayed in the universal pattern that meant "boom." The intelligence officer was scribbling hasty notes.

Rogers put a hand on Wynn's shoulder. Both men still wore flight gear, and the compartment smelled like a high-school locker room. "Hey, Phil. How's it feel to sink a convoy on your first strike?"

"Chickens and eggs, Windy. We don't know if all four ships actually went down."

"Trust me," Wynn gushed. "When ol' Fos sinks a ship, it stays sunk."

"We'll sort that out later," Rogers insisted. "What about Bill Millikin?"

"I'm sure he's all right, sir." Rogers turned toward Ensign Roland Siegfried, Wynn's wingman. "He made a water landing about halfway back to the destroyer screen. I circled until everybody got out."

"Could you tell if anybody was hurt?"

Siegfried shook his head. "No, sir, but both crewmen were in the raft. That's Jackson and Matthews."

"Thanks," Rogers replied. Turning to Wynn, he added, "We shouldn't have had a loss on this one, Windy. It's these damn standardized tactics of Kelso and Johnston. I've seen it before: You establish a pattern and some AA gunner catches on real fast." He shook his head in frustration. "I should've moved faster for a change."

"If you want, I'll go with you to talk to the captain. Maybe we can gang up on him. In fact, let's wait until I get the pictures. Chief Thomas was riding with me, and I think we'll have good strike photos." He grinned at Rogers. "Even if we only sank two small ones and the bigger one, it's hard to argue with success."

Rogers stared at the blackboard with plane assignments chalked up. "Yeah. Maybe it'll make up for canceling yesterday's schedule—"

A boisterous cheer arose in the room. Rogers and Wynn looked up as a message trailed across the teleprinter screen: AVERAGE INTERVAL WAS 22.8 SECONDS. CAPTAIN IS TICKLED PINK.

Wynn punched Rogers's shoulder. "I've never known J. C. Johnston to be tickled about anything. Maybe we should see him now, while he's in a good mood."

Rogers headed for the exit. "Sometimes, Windy, you show real promise for a rewarding naval career."

MONDAY, 16 JULY
SHANGHAI

Flying over China was a revelation. Sakaida had never experienced the sense of immensity that the continent presented him, even from three thousand meters. He recalled that Honshu's widest point, from Choshu on the east coast to Kanazawa on the west, was merely 418 kilometers, or 216 nautical miles. In consulting the large map of China in the *hikotai* operations office, he had spread his fingers an equal distance and only made it to huge Lake Chaou beyond the bend of the Yangtze. Beyond that, Asia beckoned insolently as if to say, *Take me if you can, imperial soldiers.* Well, Japan had been here since 1937 and was little closer now to owning the vast interior. Chinese guerrillas were known to be operating throughout the interior, a constant threat to fliers downed in remote areas.

The clapped-out Zero Model 52 clearly needed an engine overhaul. Better yet, it needed a new engine. But Lieutenant Matano had made it plain: no new aircraft, few spares, and almost no more fuel could be expected anytime soon. Sakaida would have to be content with a half-hour familiarization flight and hope that things improved.

Ordinarily Sakaida would have received a unit checkout before being turned loose, especially since he had not flown in four weeks. But Matano had insisted that authorized flight time was too scarce to indulge in such luxuries. With a perfunctory warning to "Be careful," he had sent Sakaida aloft to feel out the airplane once more, indulge in some sedate aerobatics, and make some practice landings.

Mindful of that advice, Sakaida remained within gliding distance of the field. He trimmed for level flight, cleared himself port and starboard, and rolled into 360-degree turns in each direction. He was pleased to see that the altimeter remained within ten meters throughout each circle. Next he experimented with slow flight, power-on and power-off stalls, then a couple of loops. He missed the satisfying bump at the bottom of the first one, but caught the mild turbulence the second time, telling him that he had flown through his own slipstream—a perfectly symmetrical maneuver.

Nearing the end of his allotted time, Sakaida entered the traffic pattern in a 45-degree angle onto downwind. Gear down, flaps down, prop in low pitch, canopy locked back, seat belt tight. He rolled out on final, allowing the old Zero to settle toward the runway while he milked the stick back. Feeling for the ground, he fished for the pencil-point balance that would coordinate the stall within a meter of the ground. Sakaida felt that consistently good landings were the best measure of a pilot's skill, and he prided himself on being able to hit a spot eight times out of ten.

The Zero paid off and dropped onto the runway, bouncing twice. Sakaida berated himself while advancing throttle, offsetting torque with rudder and lifting off once more. *Too long,* he cursed. *Too long away from the cockpit.*

It was looking more and more like an endless war.

TUESDAY, 17 JULY
USS *CROWN POINT*

The mood in Ready One seemed ambivalent—an eagerness to get on with the job, yet a willingness to put it off. The ship's movement in worsening seas spurred an attitude that was almost palpable: *I do* not *want to fly today.*

Rogers seldom flew CAPs anymore, calculating that his experience was better used in leading sweeps or strikes. Consequently, he had not put himself on the schedule for the day's first launch when the task group's light carriers drew combat patrol. He had given Lin Swanson lead of the small *Crown Point* contingent in Strike Baker and was sweating out the group's return.

For lack of anything else to do, he ambled down the aisle, checking his pilots' collective mood. Junior Haliburton was engrossed in a dated issue of *Pacific Stars and Stripes.* "Hey, Ensign, what are you learning?" Rogers asked.

Haliburton looked up. "Oh, I'm reading *Terry and the Pirates,* Skipper. Milt Caniff seems to know what we're gonna do before we ever do it."

Rogers shook his head in amusement. "Okay, I'll bite. Where do we go next?"

"Well, sir, Terry has linked up with Marine scouts at a place called Pyzons Island and he's in radio contact with the Navy. Hotshot Charlie's there with April Kane."

Rogers waved a hand. "Belay that. What's the original Buck Rogers doing?"

While Haliburton tried to reply, Rogers glimpsed a headline. A guard had gone berserk at a Utah POW camp and shot twenty-eight Germans, killing eight.

Rogers heard voices at the entryway and looked up. *Perle! What the hell—*

Lieutenant (j.g.) Dave Perle entered the ready room with two of his pilots. Rogers stalked up to him. "What're you doing back? Recovery isn't for half an hour."

Perle pulled off his cloth helmet, revealing moist, black hair. His face had a clammy appearance. "Sir, we turned around. Weather's just too rough."

Conversations stopped; heads turned. Rogers was aware of a pounding in his ears. "Are you with Swanson?" He looked over Perle's shoulder. "And where's Britton?"

The team leader shook his head. "Sir, we got separated from Mr. Swanson in the soup. I decided . . ." He licked his already-moist lips. "I decided to come back. It looked like the weather was getting worse so I got a Charlie signal and came aboard." He looked down at the gray deck. "Britton went into the barrier. His plane nosed over but he's not hurt bad. I followed him to sick bay before coming here."

Rogers was not surprised of the news. *Britton's a weak sister. Kelso should have got rid of him.* Rogers was acutely aware of the silence around him, the accusations building behind expressionless faces. "You better come with me, mister—"

"Ready One from bridge." The intercom squawked as the duty officer responded. "Lieutenant Commander Rogers, report to the bridge. Immediately."

Rogers grasped Perle's parachute harness and pulled him from the room. In the passageway, he leaned close and hissed to the division leader. "Perle, in about two minutes the captain's going to ask me some pointed questions. Now, have you anything else to tell me?"

Perle sniffed loudly, and not from the cold. "Skipper, you don't know what it's like up there. Clouds, wind, can't see a damn thing." He finally looked in Rogers's eyes. "Okay, I got scared. For me and for my team. Maybe I should have tried to find Swanson. Maybe I should have dogged until recovery time. But I didn't know if we'd still get aboard in thirty minutes."

"Mr. Perle, I don't know what Captain Johnston will say to you, but I'd worry more about what Mr. Swanson's going to think. You let him down."

Perle's face flushed red. "Goddammit, Rogers! They don't pay anybody enough to do this frigging job!" His voice cracked—Rogers feared the man might break down in front of him. He touched Perle's shoulder. "Go see the flight surgeon. Stay there until I send for you."

Rogers leaned against the bulkhead for a moment, ordering his thoughts. It was not supposed to be like this—the inevitable confrontation. Rogers had envisioned himself righteously defending his men against the petty wrath of a tyrant, but David Perle had upset that balance. Turning down the passageway, he thought, *Now we'll see what kind of leader Buck Rogers really is.*

On the bridge, J. C. Johnston stood red-faced, barely controlling his wrath. Rogers was appalled to see the captain trembling slightly. But the skipper had control of his voice. He pointed to the flight deck, where a mobile crane was righting Britton's battered F6F. "Mr. Rogers, your pilots did this against all orders! Returned ahead of schedule, landed out of sequence, blocked my deck! How do you explain it?"

"Captain, I just talked to Perle. I would like to wait until Swanson lands with the rest of the strike, then give you a full report."

Johnston took two steps closer to Rogers, reeling slightly as the ship rolled. "Rogers, I've put up with you—" He choked off whatever was next, realizing that his shrill voice carried across the small bridge. "This is an unsatisfactory performance, mister." He let the statement linger in the air like mustard gas.

Rogers felt eerily calm. He noticed the bridge watch had turned his attention outward. *Here goes.* "Captain, if Perle screwed up I'll deal with him. But whether he turned yellow or exercised good judgment, he had to have permission to come aboard."

Johnston's eyes narrowed, lupine-like. "Mister, are you insinuating that—"

"Sir, I am insinuating nothing. But we all know the procedure: Recovery doesn't begin until the ship's into the wind and the Charlie signal is given. I don't have that authority, sir."

Rogers held his breath. He saw Johnston begin to deflate like a blimp with a small leak. "Hmmm. Very well. I will expect your full written report by 1800. Is that clear?"

"Yes, sir." Rogers had a thought. "Captain, will the air plan continue as written?"

Johnston turned to port, looking at the Hellcat dangling from the crane. "No. Kingpin has canceled flight operations until tomorrow."

Rogers descended the ladder, feeling better than he had all day.

WEDNESDAY, 18 JULY
USS *CROWN POINT*

One of the wardroom tables was littered with strike and reconnaissance photos, plus target maps of the Kure and Kobe areas. Rogers, Wynn, and their execs had weighted some of the pictures with cups or saucers to prevent them from curling. Wynn tapped his pencil on a shot of the Kure Navy Yard. "Lots of good targets here—most of the Japs' remaining capital ships."

"Yeah. But the big boys will probably draw those slots. They can put more ordnance on target than we can." Rogers thought back to *Reprisal*'s powerful air group. "After all, they have more TBMs than we do, and SB2Cs besides."

Bill Millikin, back aboard only one day, recalled Phil's dive-bomber comparisons. "Sir, didn't somebody around here declare the '2C a poor cousin to the SBD?"

Rogers smiled self-consciously. "Well, don't expect an old Dauntless pilot to stand up for the Beast. But Leo Hunziker's gang finally licked the '2C into shape. Once it became reliable, they did good things with it. Flew some god-awful long searches."

Wynn interjected. "So what do you think, Phil? Bombs or torpedoes?"

"Unless we hear different, plan on thousand-pounders. There are bound to be torpedo nets around the battleships and carriers." He looked up, fixing his eyes on the torpedo skipper. "Sorry, Windy. This job won't be as easy as the convoy."

Millikin pointedly coughed. "Excuse me, sir. Who says that was easy?"

When the laughter abated, Swanson interjected. "Phil, are we likely to get replacement pilots before the Kure strikes?"

Rogers shook his head. Most personnel aboard knew only the bare outlines of yesterday's drama. "We're short two F6F pilots," he explained. "Perle passed up an opportunity for another chance. We got rid of him and Britton rather than keep them around and cause resentment from the guys who are still flying."

Wynn looked puzzled. "Where are they now?"

"Johnston wanted them off the ship immediately. I agreed, so we transferred them to a destroyer. They'll probably go to the fleet pool at Saipan." Rogers sensed the collective mood. "There's lots of good aviators itching for a chance at combat," he added. "I'd rather take the time to break them in than fly with guys we can't trust."

"CAG Rogers agrees with Captain Bligh? Look out, the sky is falling!" Wynn laughed.

Rogers produced a message form from his shirt pocket. "While you're running around like Chicken Little, look at this." He handed the flimsy to Wynn and Millikin, who read, "Well done your convoy strike fifteenth. Reconnaissance confirms fourth transport beached and burned out. Clean sweep for Pilgrim. Kingpin sends."

"That message arrived late yesterday. DiLucente of the communications division just passed it to me this morning. I meant to post it in the ready room."

A gleam appeared in Wynn's pale-blue eyes. "So Johnston's got to love us even if we're the guys he loves to hate. Like Erich von Stroheim."

Swanson uttered a gutteral "Ja-wohl" and held two fingers below his nose while raising the Nazi salute.

Rogers chortled. "Johnston's coming around, but can you imagine the exec? A professional ass kisser like Dilbert Howard will turn inside out trying to adjust to that kind of change."

Wynn reached for his hip pocket. "I'd give twenty bucks to watch that show."

SATURDAY, 21 JULY
SHANGHAI

Air Group 254 was starved for news from the homeland, and as the newest arrival, Sakaida was pumped for information. Lounging outside the operations office, seated in chairs or sprawled on the grass, pilots asked about everything: What is happening at the home front? Is it true that food is growing scarce? How much of Tokyo has been destroyed? Are we coping with the Boeing bombers?

Inevitably, the discussion centered on personalities. "What of the old-time fighters," asked Flight Leading Seaman Matsumoto. "Who is still flying?" Everyone knew that he meant: Who is still alive?

Of the super aces and leaders, few remained. Sasai, Ota, Ishii, and Okumura had died in '42 and '43. And of course Hiroyoshi Nishizawa had perished ingloriously over the Philippines the previous October. Ogiya and Nagano also had been killed in '44. More recently Sugita, one of the tough old-timers, had been caught by F6Fs while taking off from Kanoya in April. He had been given a posthumous double promotion to ensign and his name was published in an all-units bulletin.

Sakaida shifted in his chair. He felt vaguely uneasy about the cult of personality among aviators—especially fighter pilots. The greater a man's reputation, the more devastating the effect on morale when he died. Nishizawa was proof. Furthermore, the whole question of battle results was fraught with danger: Japanese pilots made extravagant claims that even the professional optimists in Tokyo revised downward. Hiroyoshi Sakaida remained a confident fighter pilot, certain that few aviators were substantially better than he. But still . . .

"Iwamoto and Sakai are now our top men," he replied. "They have both been commissioned, though Sakai's wounds prevent him from flying combat. Of the others"—Sakaida thought hard—"Muto and Kanno are with Genda's *kokutai* and Sugino is a Special Attack instructor."

Tetsuzo Iwamoto and Saburo Sakai now were junior-grade lieutenants—a dramatic reversal of the previous norm, when all the top aces were NCOs. Iwamoto, whatever his extravagant claims, clearly was gifted along the lines of a Nishizawa. The youngest fighter pilot to fly in China, he had emerged in 1938 as the top ace of the campaign. Later he was hailed as the "Richthofen of Rabaul," where he piled up enormous victory claims, including forty F4Us. He called himself "Kotetsu," after a famous swordsmith. At last word he had joined Air Group 203.

Sakai, despite the loss of one eye at Guadalcanal, had returned to combat after a two-year convalescence but had barely survived an aerial massacre near Iwo Jima a year ago. Perhaps the most professional among the survivors, he was now devoting himself to passing along invaluable knowledge to rookie pilots.

Kinsuke Muto, all skill and fight, was still active with Captain Minoru Genda's Air Group 343. His tally was thought to be at about thirty, though victory scores no longer meant much, if ever they had, since the Imperial Navy had stopped crediting individual victories two years ago. Naoshi Kanno, a rara avis who built a large score as a commissioned officer, led a hikotai for Genda.

"What about Akamatsu?" somebody asked.

"The stories are incredible," Sakaida gushed. Sada-aki Akamatsu was among the high-time pilots in the Imperial Navy; he had logged six thousand hours in fighters since 1931 and was another China veteran. "They say he wallows in a geisha house with a special phone line to his hikotai near Atsugi," Sakaida continued. "When enemy planes are reported, he drives like mad to the field, climbs in his Raiden, and takes off roaring like a demon. He's drunk all the time and says he has shot down three hundred planes."

"He won't last much longer at that rate," Amari ventured.

"On the contrary," Sakaida countered. "That type lives forever." Glancing around the circle, Sakaida was startled by a realization. He had not seen a face with The Look for several weeks now.

TUESDAY, 24 JULY
PILGRIM ONE-ONE

"Pilgrim One-One from Ninety-nine Carbine. The port-hand cruiser, the one to the west. That's yours. Acknowledge."

Rogers depressed his mike button. "Roger, Andy. Pilgrim out." Commander Andrew Crewson, Sharpsburg's air group commander, was the target coordinator for Strike Able, and Rogers mused that he had plenty of targets from which to choose. The Kure anchorage contained three battle-ships, three carriers, and six cruisers, including three antiques—something for everybody in the task group. As Rogers led his twelve fighters and six bombers toward the south shore of Etauchi Bay, he heard Crewson directing Vampire One-One to the nearest cruiser. *Rich Morgan getting in his licks,* Rogers surmised. *Wonder if Marcus is flying today.*

With major portions of four air groups committed, radio discipline was crucial. Therefore, Rogers called Wynn to confirm the target and the plan. "Windy from Buck. We'll proceed as briefed. You confirm? Over."

"That's affirmative. Here we go."

Rogers watched *Crown Point*'s strike go to work. As planned, the Avengers slanted down from 6,300 feet—Rogers insisted that they keep away from even altitudes—their bomb bay doors opening. Simultaneously, Yakeley's and Ludwig's divisions accelerated ahead to suppress flak with rockets and strafing. Rogers swiveled his head, scanning for the fighters that had to be there. *Nothing yet,* he marveled. *Nothing but AA.*

The flak was dense but inaccurate. Ugly brownish-black bursts speckled the sky over the wide anchorage, mingling in midair with glints that looked like windblown tinsel. Rogers knew the strike plan called for "window," lengths of aluminum cut to match frequencies of enemy search and fire-control radars. He concluded that the simple deception worked, as no flak seriously threatened the VT-56's planes. He shot a glance at the tight little formation and saw thousand-pounders tumbling down from 3,500 feet to erupt in a long string close aboard the cruiser.

With a start, he recalled the distinctive silhouette. *Four turrets, all forward. Tone-class. Nothing else looks like that.* His mind recoiled to August 1942, the Eastern Solomons battle. This ship, or one just like her, had escorted IJNS *Ryujo,* which Ensign Rogers and Bombing 3 had put on the bottom.

Rogers thought: *Almost three years.* At Guadalcanal the U.S. Navy had barely begun to fight its way back. But now American carrier planes owned the sky over Kure Naval Base. Down there was virtually all that remained of the Imperial Japanese Navy. That island, Etajima, was home of the enemy's naval academy. Rogers speculated, *How would we feel if the Japs bombed Annapolis?*

Circling overhead, he saw mud stirred up from the shallow bottom. He realized that if any of these ships sank, they would settle only a few feet. *But that's good enough, long as they don't go anywhere.*

He returned his gaze to the TBMs, counted them, and cut the corner to resume close escort as they turned south. Passing Kurahashi Island, he saw a small cloud of blue planes over the north shore, pasting two carriers and a battleship. He felt a tiny spark of resentment. *The* Sharpsburg *and* King's Mountain. *The big boys get the biggest targets.* Then professionalism returned. *Well, they can do more than we can.*

Rogers eyed his formation and ensured the F6Fs had resumed escort position on the TBMs. Deciding a straight-line egress was warranted, he overflew the Iyo Sea, continuing south-southwest over the long neck of land jutting from Shikoku's west coast. He monitored the radio frequencies continually and heard combat ahead. Another air group was tangling with bandits over Bungo Strait. He shifted in his seat, tugged again at his shoulder harness, double-checked his switches. He knew the previous strike had encountered Jacks and Franks—*Raiden*s and Nakajima Ki-84s.

Rogers began thinking. *What do I know about Jack and Frank? Jack: looks like a P-47: fast, rugged, not very maneuverable. Frank: new army fighter, a hot ship; maybe as good as a Mustang. But the Jap navy pilots are better.*

He switched back to the strike group's B channel. "Pilgrim flight from Buck. I'm taking my team southwest to run interference. J. B., take 'em home."

Before Yakeley could acknowledge, Rogers led Team 1 into a shallow right turn. He fishtailed by booting the rudder pedals, sending his division into combat spread. Looking for his second section, he saw Barnes and Woodul well abeam. *Bill's overdue for section lead,* Phil thought. He swiveled his head, took in Junior Haliburton, and was satisfied as the Kyushu coast appeared through the haze.

Rogers traced his course on the chart. Coming abreast of Kanoya, thirty miles west, he decided it had been a good try. Apparently the fight had broken up. He eased a few degrees port, intending to trail Wynn back to the force.

Barnes's voice came on. "Bogeys four o'clock high!" He sounded excited. As Rogers searched right of his tail, the voice was back. "Phil, do you see 'em?"

Damn it to hell! Rogers glanced back, momentarily confused by the name "Phil." Because there were three Bills and another Phil in the air group, Rogers preferred "Buck" on the radio. Then he saw: *Fighters, too frigging close!* Rogers answered Barnes by initiating a defensive weave, trusting that Haliburton was the astute young man he seemed. Rogers's mental computer calculated that the bandits were no more than six hundred yards out. The three-dimensional problem in spatial geometry whirred through his circuits and spit out the answer: *We're gonna get shot at.*

Time compression kicked in. Rogers saw that the closest fighter—

probably a George—was flying a good pursuit curve on him. The bandit already had pulled lead and Rogers knew: *He hasn't fired yet, knows what he's doing.* Phil hunched his shoulders, trying to fit all of himself behind the armor plate.

Bedlam on the radio. Then Haliburton's voice alone: "Hot damn!"

Phil reversed his turn, checked the spacing and his pulse—about 220, he guessed—and saw his wingman's huge grin. Then realization set in. *Junior blew that guy off my tail with a full deflection shot!* Rogers tossed Haliburton a heartfelt salute, then clamped a trembling hand back on the stick.

Behind the four Hellcats, drifting debris and wafting smoke were all that marked the earthly passage of Lieutenant Hajime Homma, late of the Mamoru Wing.

SATURDAY, 28 JULY
PILGRIM ONE-ONE

The porkchop-shaped island of Awaji-shima pointed a long spit of land toward Kobe on the coast of Osaka Bay, where Rogers saw elements of two air groups running in to bomb the docks and shipyard. He wondered again whether to thank Tom Albertson, Jake Griggs, or someone else for the gravy portion of this meaty mission: providing roving cover for *Reprisal* and *King's Mountain* TBMs and SB2Cs closely escorted by their own fighters.

Whatever the source, Phil Rogers was not about to question the gift that the op order had given him. Nor did he feel much sentiment at seeing *Reprisal* back with the task group. Crystal Base now belonged to a new air group, and he was mildly surprised to learn that his complete allegiance went to *Crown Point* and Air Group 56.

Rogers remembered to alter course 15 degrees—never fly straight and level in a combat zone, he told his pilots. *Wouldn't do for the CAG to get bagged violating his own orders,* he mused. The flak was pattern or barrage style, some of it possibly radar-directed, but it was largely ineffective. Orbiting northwest of the strike group, ready to pounce on any Japanese interceptors, he was determined to make the initial sighting this time. Barnes had excellent vision and knew how to use it, but Rogers felt the urge to match his section leader in calling out bogeys. He felt a prickling between his shoulders as he relived the ephemeral terror off Kanoya four days before. *Thank God for Junior and Bill. But that won't happen again—not ever.*

He shot a peek at the dock area, now blossoming a series of large, oil-fed fires that lifted dense smoke thousands of feet into the air. He reckoned the bombers should be pulling off target any moment, and began planning which of two possible routes he would take to cover their withdrawal.

On A channel the attackers were concluding their business. Rogers heard, "Ninety-Nine Crystal from Eighty-Six Zebra. We're heading out." *Reprisal*'s CAG acknowledged as the *King's Mountain* Helldivers egressed southward.

Rogers took the cue and, wordlessly, led his two teams into a crossover turn. He planned to roll out southeasterly, cutting the corner of the strike group's egress in hopes of catching any bandits trailing the bombers home. He raised a gloved thumb to cover the sun, reducing glare for a moment, and squinted behind his amber lenses. He lowered his hand just as his brain registered dark specks. He looked again and there they were. He felt eerily calm.

"Pilgrim flight from One-One. Bogeys, eight o'clock and slightly high. Team One, with me. Team Four, hold tight a minute in case there's more." He did not want to commit his entire force to combat when another group might appear elsewhere.

As the range closed, Rogers discerned seven or eight Kawasaki Tonys. *Jap army fighters, look like Me-109s. Good for maybe 320 knots.* The numerical disparity did not bother him. It did not even occur to him as he led Team 1 through the enemy formation, scattering Kawasakis to either side. A few tracers sparkled past but there was too little time for accurate gunnery. He held his fire.

Rogers was sliding around in a vertically banked turn after the closest Tony. The sleek fighter half rolled and pulled through in a split-S from twelve thousand feet. Rogers went hard after it, unconscious of up, down, port or starboard, earth or sky. There was only the bare-metal glint of his target and his own relationship to it. As the Tony began pulling out, Rogers mentally licked his chops, knowing a kill was coming. *He's predictable. If he was sharp he'd have rolled away from me in the recovery.*

Phil eased back the stick, felt the onset of gravity, placing his pipper where experience told him the Tony had to be. When the victim appeared in his sight, wingtips almost touching the 100-mil ring, he depressed the trigger for two seconds.

The .50-caliber tracers converged slightly ahead of the Tony's liquid-cooled engine, then arced backward along the top of the airframe. The belting was one tracer in three: Rogers saw aluminum hacked out of the skin and white lights erupting where armor-piercing incendiaries struck. The Kawasaki lurched visibly, recovered, and decelerated abruptly. Rogers estimated a 50-knot overtake, assessed the time available, and shoved forward on the stick.

Lifted partially off his seat-pack, he abruptly pulled back, sank toward the bottom of the seat, and saw the Tony streaming smoke and glycol. At less than two hundred yards he fired again. Almost every round seemed to slam home as the fighter coughed flame, dropped a wing, and plunged from sight. Haliburton's high voice was calling. "Flamer, Skipper!"

Rogers crammed on full throttle, striving to regain lost altitude while heading south. Abruptly he remembered his top-cover division. "Pilgrim Four from Buck. Curt, come on down."

There was no reply and briefly Rogers wondered if he had keyed his mike. Then Haliburton was back. "Skipper, check ten o'clock!"

Two miles away, a pair of F6Fs were reeling in one Tony while pursued by another. Rogers did not know who they were. It didn't matter. "Pilgrim Hellcats heading east, keep going. You got one behind you!"

Rogers knew that the Kawasaki was slower than an F6F-5. He nosed down slightly, intending to open fire at extreme range to force the predator off his two pilots. Well ahead, the lead Tony came apart in a distant sparkle of sunlight on polished metal. Apparently the Hellcats had heard Rogers, as they extended to the east. As if frustrated, the trailing Tony pilot abruptly rolled left and dived toward shore.

Rogers briefly wondered: *Should I or shouldn't I?* He had already decided to give Haliburton first shot. *Hell, why not? We came here to kill people.* He depressed the mike button and shouted into his oxygen mask. "Pilgrim flight from Buck. We're taking the last one inland. Watch for us coming out."

Despite the Tony's head start, Rogers had geometry and 30 knots on the Japanese. He cut across the radius of the Kawasaki's 90-degree turn and came within half a mile. He realized: *This will be a long chase.* They were already nearing the beach—no place to be with only two fighters.

Rogers was tempted to shove his throttle through the gate, calling on war emergency power. But he had laid down the law: water injection only on FDO orders or to get out of trouble. *There's one other way.* He drew a bead on the Tony, raised his nose, and triggered a short burst. Tracers fell short—just behind the bandit. He eased back a little more and tried again. *Looks good,* he thought. *Once more.*

This time the enemy pilot reacted. Obviously concerned that he was unaccountably in range of his pursuers, he banked left, then right. Rogers fired again. Once more the Tony evaded, losing distance. In a handful of seconds the range closed to four hundred yards. "Get him, Junior."

Haliburton opened fire prematurely, quickly corrected, and then began hitting. More tiny motes of light appeared atop the Kawasaki. Convinced he had to fight, the Japanese turned to face his attackers. Rogers slid wide to the outside of the turn, ready to nail him if he reversed away from Haliburton. Junior fired again, missed close astern, then pulled more deflection. His next burst tore the side out of the Tony.

The canopy came off, the fighter rolled inverted and the pilot dropped free. Rogers watched the parachute open at four thousand feet, wondering if he should execute an enemy who could have another fighter this very day. Instead, he depressed the trigger halfway, shot some film of the chute, then called his wingman.

"Let's get out of here, son."

Haliburton appeared one hundred yards off Rogers's starboard wing, rejoining in combat spread. "Thanks, Commander. Thanks a lot."

Rogers thought he had worn out his neck, checking the sky for other fighters. But Pilgrim One-One and One-Two owned the air over Osaka Bay en route home.

1–15 August 1945

WEDNESDAY, 2 AUGUST
SHANGHAI

The shadows lengthened in the long summer evening as men filed out of the mess hall after dinner. Sakaida had taken to strolling along the flight line just to be near the airplanes, and he discovered two or three other pilots shared his interest. Surprisingly, one of them was Lieutenant Matano, who at first had struck Sakaida as a moderately tolerable officer. But the *hikotaicho* had shown an increasing interest in Sakaida's observations and, more surprising, his opinions.

"You were with the Special Attack Corps," he began. "How did you draw that assignment? Or did you volunteer?"

Sakaida carefully considered his response. "Sir, I was requested by the commanding officer of the Shinkai Unit, Lieutenant Kono. He and I had served together in a sea-fighter unit in the Solomons. He assigned me as leader of the escort section until he body-crashed." Sakaida realized that he had not thought of Yusuke Kono in weeks. *And he has only been dead since March.* An eerie question left tracks across Sakaida's mind. *Is Yusuke a sky god now?*

"I see," Matano replied. "Was the unit effective?"

"Honorable Lieutenant, I did not observe any successful attacks."

Matano shifted his sword to the opposite hand. Sakaida had noticed that the officer seldom wore the sword suspended from a belt, but preferred to carry it. Amari had hinted that Kenji Matano was a well-regarded swordsman.

"What good is there in drafting boys into the Special Attack Corps?" Matano asked. Sakaida had to assume it was a rhetorical question. It was dangerous ground.

"What point in promoting dead officers two grades and noncoms three? It makes no difference to their families," Matano continued. "The Army Air Force began conscripting suicide pilots last month, and not all are eager to become 'broken gems.' " He looked at Sakaida. "You may speak confidentially here, Warrant Officer. I wish to know your observations."

Sakaida's mind whirled. If he was being set up, there was no escape. He had never voiced his thoughts on the *kamikazes* but he had heard reports of refusals and even opposition. There was the story of the suicide pilot who strafed his command post after takeoff and disappeared out to sea. How well known were those incidents? Sakaida realized he had but one choice: to trust Kenji Matano.

"Sir, my limited experience gave me little confidence in the practice of *tai-atari*. But some men chose such body-crashing even though they were skilled fliers. Lieutenant Kono was such a man."

"The others also went gladly?"

Sakaida nodded. "*Hai!* Most of them seemed resigned by then. They were pleased when we sent them off, waving our caps and singing 'Umi Yukaba.' " "The Hymn of the Dead" had been the obvious choice at such moments.

Matano's voice took on a flat tone. "My brother volunteered for the *kamikazes*. All we know is that he went bravely, without flinching." He looked at Sakaida. "That is enough for my parents, who are steeped in the old way of thinking. But I often wonder: Did Kazuo accomplish anything with his death?"

Sakaida had no answer. He waited for his division officer to continue.

Matano said, "I have always studied history, and the comparisons between now and ancient times are obvious. The military leaders in the Meiji era knew the value of human life. They were veteran warriors who knew what it meant to fight and die in battle so they would not throw away lives needlessly. Our 'leaders' now"—he sneered derisively—"are all politicians. They know nothing of war and think nothing of wasting our lives."

The vision returned to Sakaida's mind: the flak-studded sky over the American task group, the probing tracers, Kono's Zero torn apart and spinning wildly to fruitless destruction.

"I'll tell you something, Sakaida. You were fortunate to be sent here. The war cannot last indefinitely, and we are relatively safe." Matano looked eastward, over his shoulder. "Someday, before long, I think most of us will go home."

TUESDAY, 7 AUGUST
USS CROWN POINT

"Three years ago today we hit Tulagi and Guadalcanal. Now yesterday there's this super bomb from the Air Force and a lot of guys seem to think it'll end the war tomorrow." Rogers surveyed his pilots and aircrews in the wardroom, sensing the overconfident mood. "Well, maybe so. Meanwhile, I want you to concentrate on your job; take the missions one at a time." He forced a smile. "Easy does it."

As the meeting broke up, Rogers took a chair and thought of all he had not said. He glanced at Barnes, who had flown with him from Saratoga in August of '42. Operation Watchtower had been the first step on the road to Tokyo, and it had felt good to be on the offensive for a change. But Rogers also remembered his unreasoning optimism that the war would be over sometime soon. As he had just noted, that was thirty-six months ago.

Windy Wynn slipped into a chair beside Rogers. As an ordnance enthusiast, he had been trying to grasp the principle behind what President Truman had called "the basic power of the universe." Rogers, who had been exposed to the periodic tables in college, could only attempt a vague explanation about splitting atoms. The news accounts had been surprisingly detailed otherwise: a two-billion-dollar project brought to fruition in barely three years. The Hanford plant in Washington State had been mentioned, causing Rogers to wonder what Juanita Connell was doing now.

"Do you suppose the B-29s will drop another of those things?" Wynn mused.

Rogers shrugged. Thus far nobody aboard knew for certain whether XXI Bomber Command had in fact delivered the atom bomb, but it was a logical conclusion. "I guess it depends on the Japs. If they throw in the towel, there's no need. Otherwise . . ." He almost laughed. ". . . one city, one bomb."

"Yeah," Wynn responded. "Imagine trying to intercept every single plane approaching the Japanese coast. Just can't do it."

Rogers looked around the room. Fliers were filing out, returning to shipboard routine. "Well, I'd rather get back to flying myself. I'm tired of riding out another damn typhoon for a week." The task group had taken its turn at replenishment during the lull, and *Crown Point* now was topped off with 100,000 gallons of aviation gas and seven thousand gallons of engine oil.

"You know, I'd like to get a look at Hiroshima," Wynn added. "It'll be interesting to see just how much damage this new bomb actually does."

Rogers made no reply. He was trying to remember the conversation of three or four weeks ago when Tom Albertson had mentioned Hiroshima and three other cities that were off limits to Navy attacks. Now it was obvious. *What were the others?* Rogers wondered. *Kokura, Kobe?* He shook his head. "Well, I guess we don't need to know, and by now the Japs know more than they ever wanted to."

THURSDAY, 9 AUGUST
PILGRIM ONE-ONE

Rogers sized up the small convoy of three coastal freighters escorted by a frigate. *Easy meat,* he thought. *They probably don't expect us this far north.*

He took his division down from eight thousand feet and paralleled Honshu's north coast while leaving Yakeley's team as high cover. "We'll take the escort," he called, knowing that Wynn's six TBMs would tackle the freighters without being told.

The lone frigate leading the procession obviously posed the greatest threat. Rogers waggled his wings, sending Barnes and Woodul wide to starboard while taking Haliburton in a hooking turn to port. Rogers resisted the urge to cram on combat power, to blaze in at 350 knots. *We're a long way from the ship,* he reasoned. *Better save our fuel in case we need it.* He permitted himself forty-five inches manifold pressure and 3,050 r.p.m., blower in neutral, mixture auto-rich. A quick check of his armament switches—rockets selected, master arm on—and he nosed down.

The Japanese captains were aware of their peril. On the slate-gray sea, four wakes turned off their base course, the frigate reversing its helm to circle back toward its charges. In his steep descent, Rogers admired the move. *It'll put him in a better position to cover the freighters, but they're scattering. He can't protect them all.* He shook his head in silent disapproval. *Not much discipline down there.*

Approaching five thousand feet, Rogers began tracking the frigate, which was already shooting. Light-caliber flak sparkled through the atmosphere, no threat to the Grummans yet. He had decided to ripple-fire his six HVARs beginning at three thousand feet slant range, allowing Haliburton to strafe on the way down.

Geysers spumed alongside the dark-gray ship, indicating that Barnes and McCabe already were firing. One or two flashes strobed on the escort's superstructure—rocket strikes already—but the flak hardly abated. Haliburton's guns now were churning the water, a good concentration around the bridge and fo'c'sle. Slanting in from the port quarter, Rogers coordinated stick and rudder, got the sight picture he wanted, and pressed the button atop his stick.

The first five-inch HVAR smoked off the rail, corkscrewing awkwardly. Rogers ignored the errant round and thumbed the button again. The next HVAR snaked out, guiding properly. He fired again, now approaching two thousand feet. Tracers arced ahead of him but he focused on his target. Fire again—and again.

The water rippled visibly, a concentric shock wave radiating outward from the frigate's stern. Microseconds later an orange-white flash erupted, strewing the air with smoke and debris. Instinctively Rogers shoved on full throttle, honked the stick back, and bent into a hard left turn. In stop-frame motion, his mind told him that a rocket had impacted the quarterdeck and he wondered what he had hit.

Escort vessels. Antisubmarine mission. Depth charges stored aft. It made perfect sense. Astonished, gleeful shouts on the radio confirmed Rogers's impression.

He rolled out of his steeply banked turn, passing astern of the small ship. Already down by the stern, it was rapidly losing way and the shooting had stopped. The surprising violence of his attack momentarily checked his elation, and he concentrated on priorities. *Instruments—okay. Junior's in position.* He swiveled his head and looked for the rest of his strike group. Wynn and Millikin were working over two of the freighters while the third had turned for shore, four miles away.

The tracers were back—25-millimeters, Rogers guessed. The aim was poor—off in altitude and deflection—but he was mildly astonished that any gunners remained active. Increasing his banked turn, unconsciously neutralizing the controls to minimize drag, he saw lifeboats and floater nets pushing off from the ill-fated ship. The blood rose in his brain. *Those bastards think they can have it both ways: abandon ship and keep shooting.* Without further thought, he rolled wings-level and pointed his nose at the sinking frigate.

He gauged the range nicely. At four hundred yards he triggered a short sighter burst that impacted among some rafts on the port side. A muzzle flash caught his attention. *Two for the price of one,* he thought. He depressed the trigger again and held it down, steering a .50-caliber swath through more rafts, up the hull and across the gun mount. It was not good fire discipline, but Phil Rogers no longer cared about saving ammunition.

As he pulled off, wooden wreckage mingled with floating bodies, and the twin AA mount was stained crimson. One glimpse and Rogers knew he would always keep the visual snapshot in the scrapbook of his memory.

Regrouping his team, Rogers thought: *This was good. Better enjoy it, though. This war may be over soon.*

When he landed aboard *Crown Point* that afternoon, he learned that an atom bomb had been dropped on Nagasaki and that Russia had declared war on Japan.

FRIDAY, 10 AUGUST
USS *CROWN POINT*

Rogers sensed trouble. Johnston rarely invited the air group commander to his cabin, and only then on business. Motioned to a chair, Rogers folded his hands across his abdomen and waited.

Johnston rubbed his balding head while studying an air combat action report form. Finally he laid down the ACA-1 and spoke in his clipped, formal manner. "Mister Rogers, I wish to discuss this report." He tapped the papers. "You clearly state that you strafed lifeboats and Japanese crewmen who were abandoning a sinking ship."

Rogers was taken aback. He had never figured Jerome Cheney Johnston IV as a squeamish type. "Read the rest of the report, Captain. The Japs were still shooting at us. Besides, that ship was maybe three miles from shore, and there were other ships in the area. If I had left the rafts, those sailors could still be fighting us next week."

Johnston cleared his throat. "I do not dispute that fact, Commander. I only wish to caution you about the wisdom of . . . ahem . . . committing it to paper. Understand?"

Rogers's left eye narrowed, as if peering through a gunsight. *Damn right I do, you hypocritical bastard. You've got to endorse the action report.* Phil thought for a moment. "Captain, if you disapprove of my action, it's your job to say so—in writing." Tom Albertson's warning came back to him: *Make him put it on paper.*

Johnston nearly came out of his chair. His pudgy hands pressed the top of his desk until the fingernails turned white. "I don't need any . . . *reservist* to tell me my duty!"

An icy calm settled over Rogers's brain—snowfall cooling a campfire. Choosing his words, he said, "No you don't, Captain. You only need us reservists to make your combat record for you." Johnston was stunned into silence so Rogers pressed his advantage. "We shot up two more airfields today, got through some pretty heavy flak, and added to your scoreboard. Since I've been your CAG, sir, we've lost just three planes in combat and one accidentally. We cut loose some of the deadwood and we're doing more with less." He almost smiled. "That's a damn sight better record than this ship had before. Sir."

The captain's chunky frame sagged back in the chair. Rogers again was reminded of a punctured balloon slowly deflating. *Nobody's ever stood up to this guy,* he told himself. *Now he doesn't know how to handle it.* Rogers decided to await a response.

"Harrumph." Johnston picked up the report again. "Before this misunderstanding goes any farther, I'm merely asking if you want to change any aspect of your report."

Rogers kept his gaze on his superior's florid face. "No, Captain. As I understand it, sir, you needn't approve my actions in your endorsement. You can say whatever you think is appropriate." *And I'll keep shooting Japs until Jake Griggs relieves me.*

Johnston had opened his mouth in reply when an urgent pounding on the door cut him off. After four loud raps, Commander "Dilbert" Howard poked his head inside. "Excuse me, Captain. We've copied an urgent message from CinCPac: Japan has sued for peace via the Swiss embassy in Washington. Admiral Nimitz on Guam has ordered a stand-down, effective immediately!"

Rogers and Johnston exchanged disbelieving glances. "My God, it's really happening" Johnston croaked. He looked up at his exec. "I didn't think they would give up after rejecting the Potsdam declaration."

"Apparently they have, sir." Howard stepped farther into the cabin. "The atom bombs, the Russians coming in—it's all happening so fast."

Rogers was on his feet almost without realizing it. "Captain, with your permission I would like clarification from Kingpin. I assume we're keeping our CAP on station."

Johnston nodded brusquely. "Permission granted."

Just as Rogers reached the door a thought reined him in. "Excuse me, gentlemen. I don't understand the phrase 'sue for peace.' Is that different from surrendering?"

Howard was a blank; Johnston slumped in his chair again. "Theoretically, yes, it is different. It probably means Tokyo wants terms."

Rogers nodded and stepped into the passageway, where he heard gleeful cheering. He felt that American sailors and aviators in the Pacific might jump at the chance to end the war: they had lost 7,489 dead, wounded, or missing in the past week. But after Pearl Harbor, after Bataan, after more than three and a half years and 1,068,216 casualties, he was certain of one thing: The public would accept nothing short of unconditional surrender.

Harry S Truman, obviously sensitive to the voters' mood, had voiced that opinion yesterday—Japan could surrender or be destroyed.

Philip Rogers was far less certain of something else. Pacing down the gray corridor, it struck him: *Oh, my God. What will I do after the war?*

SUNDAY, 12 AUGUST
SHANGHAI

Sakaida knew that Christians believed the world was created in six days. Apparently the Americans had arranged for it to end in a similar length of time.

"Is there any further word?" Sakaida asked the leading radioman in the operations office. The rating knew what the warrant officer meant; he gave a barely respectful negative answer and turned back to his set.

Sakaida glanced around the room where off-duty fliers stood against the walls. *It has been this way since last Sunday,* he mused. *Since word of Hiroshima.*

Radio Tokyo had been broadcasting to the world, presenting an irregular series of reports on some horrible new weapon that destroyed whole cities. The men of Air Group 254 sat in morbid entrancement around the communications office, hardly willing to leave for fear of missing the next broadcast. According to the radio, the Americans said that "practically all living things were seared to death" in Hiroshima, a city of some 343,000 souls, and, in addition, 60 percent of Hiroshima was destroyed—over four square miles. And now, most recently Nagasaki.

Lieutenant Matano had arranged for a watch schedule to monitor the radios. But Sakaida, with relatively little to do, had found himself studying his men as if through a microscope. Some handled the stress better than others. Flight Leading Seaman Inoyue, for instance, whose father and two sisters lived near the Ota River. After word of the disaster the young man had alternated between ravings for revenge and sobbing in despair. He had not been seen for two days.

Sakaida slumped into a chair and tried to appear decisive. He had never received instruction in military leadership—by the time he was promoted to warrant officer there was no time for such things. However, he knew instinctively that the depressed atmosphere in the unit would only worsen unless he, Matano, and a few others gave some sense of purpose to the *hikotai*'s existence. *But what can we do? Few aircraft, little fuel, only rumors from home as the empire shrinks.*

Booted footsteps announced Matano's approach. Everyone but the radioman stood to attention as the *hikotaicho* entered the room. He returned the salutes in a perfunctory manner and strode directly to Sakaida. "Come with me," he said, then spun about and walked out.

At the foot of the stairs, Matano turned to Sakaida. "Seaman Inoyue has been found."

Sakaida suspected the worst. "He deserted?"

"No. He was near the eastern perimeter fence. He shot himself."

MONDAY, 13 AUGUST

PILGRIM ONE-ONE

Rogers circled at 1,200 feet and watched Pilgrim One-Two splash down. Trailing an oily smoke plume, Junior Haliburton's F6F skipped once, twice, then lurched to a stop. It rode nose low, parallel to the waves, while the pudgy teenager scrambled from the cockpit.

Phil Rogers felt torn by conflicting emotions. He uttered a heartfelt prayer of thanks that Haliburton was safely out of the sinking Hellcat, but the leaden weight in his stomach sat like a cold, accusing lump. *I know better than that. Damn it to hell, I never should have gone back for a third pass.*

It had seemed a reasonable risk. Fighting 56 had caught the flak gunners napping and had burned several planes on the first pass. The airfield, southeast of Tokyo, had been flush with aircraft, mainly fighters and twin-engine types, with no airborne interceptors. The second pass had been equally profitable. There were still undamaged aircraft parked around the perimeter when Rogers led his team in from a different direction. But by then one or two 25-millimeter mounts were in action, and the gunners had tagged Haliburton as he followed Rogers across the field boundary.

Rogers made another orbit, wagging his wings as Junior waved from the water. Rogers then adjusted power for a climb and pulled his plotting board from beneath the instrument panel. He took a quick fix on coastal reference points and, satisfied with the plot, flipped his four-position frequency switch to D channel.

"Danny, this is Pilgrim One-One. Pilgrim One-One calling Danny. Over."

There was no reply from the submarine. "Oh, God, please." He checked the radio, assured himself he was transmitting, and tried again. The circuit crackled as the lifeguard submarine responded. "Pilgrim One-One, this is Danny. I read you four by four. Over."

Thanks, God. I'll take it from here. "Danny, Pilgrim. You sure sound good. I've got a pilot in the water . . ." He looked at his chart again and read the coordinates. "We can stay for half an hour. Over."

The submarine skipper apparently took his time assessing the risk. Haliburton was down four miles off Honshu—well within range of shore batteries—and there were six more hours of daylight. A surface approach would certainly draw fire, and there was little doubt that the lieutenant commander in Danny's conning tower would not lightly risk his eighty-man crew for one aviator. But Rogers was equally sure that the pigboat would at least try.

"Pilgrim, this is Danny. I can be there in twenty minutes. Let me know of any surface activity. Over."

Rogers acknowledged. Replacing the microphone, he led Barnes and Jacobs in a slow climb eastward. He wanted to remain far enough offshore to minimize Japanese ability to track the flight, while keeping within sight of Haliburton.

Level at three thousand feet, Rogers fought for emotional control. He had never experienced this—not Midway, nor Guadalcanal, nor Kenny Diskowski's death, nor even the awful thirty minutes he had spent with Juanita Connell. *Junior's down there because of me. I'm responsible for him. If the Japs get him, it's my fault.*

Rogers inhaled. Suddenly he wanted it over. The war was no fun anymore—not the thrill of low-level strafing, not even the satisfaction of combat leadership. The recent United Press report was wrong—there was no peace. Nobody was sleeping, tempers were growing short, and mistakes would surely be made. *Like the one I made, that third pass.*

Rogers shot a glance westward, toward shore. Danny had said to inform him of any surface vessels. Well, no problem with that. Phil Rogers and his team would cheerfully kill anybody or anything threatening their friend. He imagined that now he knew how wild animals felt when their young were imperiled.

He raised his left hand from the throttle, studying his fingers. There was the faintest trembling. He slid back the canopy, resting his arms on the rails. *God, I wish I could—what? Sleep?* He inhaled deeply, allowed himself the luxury of closing his eyes for a few seconds. Then Danny was back in his ears. "Pilgrim, I want to try a submerged approach. Is your pilot familiar with periscope rescue procedure? Over."

"Danny, this is Pilgrim. Affirmative. I'll give you a final position when you're ready to start in. Pilgrim out."

Rogers felt better: Danny had a plan. But the periscope rescue was still fairly new to the fleet. It had only been tried a few times, and Rogers was uncertain of how successfully. But it offered the best compromise between saving a downed flier while minimizing risk to the submarine close to enemy shores.

The next several minutes were busy ones, and Rogers was thankful for the diversion. He contacted 99 Vampire, inbound with an *Alliance* strike, and told him of Haliburton's location in case Danny was delayed. Next he called the submarine again, providing Junior's bearing and approximate distance from two landmarks, a lighthouse and the point of a small inlet. With that, his work was nearly done.

Several minutes passed, molasses-slow drops of time. Then Ensign Jacobs was on the air. "Pilgrim One-One from One-Four. There he is, Captain. Just east of us."

Rogers looked down and caught the white wake of the periscope glinting against the blue-gray water. Danny was headed almost directly for Haliburton's yellow raft, parallel to the coast. Rogers's final position report had been good.

Rogers eased back the throttle and descended toward the spot. The periscope moved with agonizing slowness, but Haliburton seemed to have spotted it. Rogers tried to recall the briefing on PRP; he could not remember the submarine's approach speed, but obviously it was not too fast. Otherwise the downed flier could not grab the periscope or hang on.

Fuel! Rogers felt an electric prickling as he remembered to check his gauges. He had told Danny that the F6Fs could remain overhead for thirty minutes. That had been more than half an hour ago. Rogers rolled wing-low, saw the white wake approaching the yellow dot, and glimpsed a movement. Junior had just made his play for the scope. If he grasped it, he would hang on while the sub skipper watched the Mortimer Snerd face through the prisms. If he missed, Danny would either circle slowly for another try or have to risk surfacing.

Rogers forced himself to reverse his turn. Climbing outbound, he felt the onset of a hellacious headache.

TUESDAY, 14 AUGUST
USS *CROWN POINT*

The unexpected rap on the door startled Rogers. He looked up from his notepad and called, "Come."

Barnes stepped into the room and closed the hatch behind him. "Skipper, is it true we're standing down for a couple days?"

Rogers sensed something—an edge to Barnes's voice. He decided to play it straight. "Yeah. The replenishment schedule has been moved up twenty-four hours."

Without awaiting an invitation, Barnes sat on the bunk. "That's swell. We can break out your booze and have a powwow."

Rogers shifted his chair away from the small writing desk. "Mr.

Barnes, you have been in the United States Navy as long as I have. You know that alcoholic spirits are forbidden except for medicinal purposes." He almost smiled.

"I've got a sore throat," Barnes rasped, touching his neck.

Without comment, Rogers twirled the dial on his wall safe and produced a fifth of Old Overholt. He poured a finger in the bottoms of two glasses, handed one to Barnes, and raised his own. "Happy days."

"Are they, Skipper?"

Rogers took a sip and set the glass down. "All right. What's eating you?"

"Hell, just look around," Barnes replied. "Every guy on this ship is a nervous wreck. Nobody's sleeping and they're turning into zombies. They hear the war's over, then it's not. They can't wait for the Air Force to drop another of those bombs so the Japs will throw in the towel. All but you."

"What does that mean?" Rogers's voice carried an edge that he regretted.

"I think you're afraid the war *will* end, Phil. That's what's bothering me." Barnes grasped his glass, tightly. He knew the next five seconds would determine the outcome of the conversation. He held his breath.

Rogers leaned back and closed his eyes. When he opened them, his voice was barely a whisper. "Bill, you think I don't know why you volunteered for this tour? You're trying to keep me alive. Aren't you?"

Barnes swallowed his scotch. He felt better. "Well, how am I doing? Sir?"

"Belay that 'sir' business." Rogers poured another finger in his glass and held out the bottle until Barnes extended his own. After he replaced the fifth in the safe, he sat back again and regarded his former gunner.

"Bill, you kept me alive at Midway and Guadalcanal, and over Japan. I'd say you're doing four-oh. So why the concern now?"

"C'mon, Skipper. You're making repeat passes at targets that are hardly worth one. You're pulling out lower than necessary so you can shoot longer. Once you chewed out Haliburton for practically the same thing. And you were right. But now he's probably aboard that sub—"

Rogers interrupted. "And now you're chewing me out."

"An ex-aircrewman's privilege, sir." Sensing an advantage, Barnes pressed it. "Look, I think I know why you're here. Burnett, Diskowski, all those guys. And your girl wouldn't marry you." Rogers's face flushed and Barnes knew the risk. But he pressed ahead. "I think there's something else. Phil, I think you *like* this work, because it's all you know anymore."

Phil Rogers sat motionless. His reddened face grew a twitch at the jowls.

"It's either that," Barnes pressed, "or you don't care about saving some of these guys like you said. And I know you well enough. You do care." He shrugged. "So it's got to be the combat. You came back because you love it. I just don't want to see one of these kids get killed because they can't keep up with you."

Barnes's words hung in the small compartment like a brooding rain cloud. It was up to Rogers whether the argumenative dew point lowered and swept away a four-year friendship in an outraged downpour. At length, Phil intoned, "You're right."

Thank you, God. "So you'll take it a little easier?"

Rogers's eyes widened in recognition of Barnes's intent. "No, Bill, I meant you're right: I do love the combat. Every minute of it." He regarded his friend. "Don't you?"

Barnes stood up. "I don't mind killing Japs, if that's what you mean. But I'd rather get one of my pilots home than notch up another meatball. I remember when that's how you felt. Sir."

Rogers came out of his chair, fists clenched. "By god, if you—" He caught himself, biting off the hateful words that lurked behind his tongue. He trembled visibly, fighting for control. *Christ, I'm about to toss my best friend off this ship.*

"Phil, you're tired, way down deep. You're taking chances that aren't worth it. Now tell me something: Will the goddamn war end one day sooner because you kill one more poor Jap bastard?"

Rogers slumped into his chair. He shook his head. "No, of course not." He sat in silence. *But it makes me feel better.* When he looked up, Barnes was leaving.

"Bill?" Barnes stopped and looked back. "Thanks." Barnes nodded and left.

Rogers slid into his bunk, one arm across his face. He forced himself to focus his mind. *Make your decisions carefully; weigh them and reweigh them. If you're going to lose people—and you know you will—make each loss worth the price. Think of it yourself: How would I like to die for no benefit? Like Gordon and Bernie and Kenny and even that ambitious sad sack, Kelso—and almost like Junior.*

God, I've been out here too long.

WEDNESDAY, 15 AUGUST
USS *CROWN POINT*, 0633

The first launch had gone as scheduled at 0415. While the big-deck carriers recovered night fighters, *Crown Point* had launched two teams on dawn

ForceCAP. Meanwhile, Torpedo 56 contributed six TBMs to a mining mission led by Rich Morgan off *Alliance.*

Rogers had analyzed the day's air plan and determined that Strike Charlie—the 1100 hours launch against industrial targets near Tokyo—offered his best prospects for tangling with Japanese aircraft. He checked his watch. "Hmm, Windy and the boys should be near the coast about now."

Jay-Bob Yakeley looked up from his chair, adding navigation data to his chartboard. "Yeah, I wonder if—"

The ready-room loudspeaker blared unexpectedly. "Attention, all hands. This is the captain speaking. Now hear this: Shipmates, the war is over!" Johnston paused long enough to allow his crew to absorb that message. "I repeat, the war is over. I am informed that the Japanese government has agreed to unconditional surrender. Hostilities will cease immediately!"

Bedlam in the ready room. Raucous, joyful shouting. Men were pounding Rogers's back, pumping his hand. Johnston was saying something else but nobody paid attention. Then, swimming through the sea of noise and motion, Barnes's face slowly came into focus.

"It's been a long war, Skipper." Barnes extended his hand.

"It sure as hell has, Bill." Phil clinched the handshake, then wrapped his free arm around Barnes's shoulders. In the past four years they had flown together from four carriers and from Guadalcanal; they had killed men, sunk ships, shot airplanes from the sky. They had never hugged—until now.

USS *CROWN POINT,* 0745

"Hey, is the war over or not?" Ensign Woodul's question, voiced in "vulture's row," on the small island, was understood by all who heard him. Taxiing forward over the lowered barriers was a strange Hellcat bearing an XX tail code, recently painted over the old geometric air group symbol. The visitor stood out from the crowd on *Crown Point*'s deck, where Air Group 56 planes sported a bold white C on their tails. Twenty-one Zebra, the *King's Mountain* F6F, had visible battle damage.

Rogers clapped Woodul on the shoulder. "Maybe this war's over and maybe it isn't. I'm gonna find out." He descended past the small bridge where Jerome Cheney Johnston IV, Captain, USN, was into the third minute of an apoplectic tirade against Foster W. Wynn, Lieutenant, USNR, for barrel-rolling his Avenger overhead the ship.

Rogers dashed across the flight deck and met the *King's Mountain* pilot at the tie-down spot. The visitor took in Rogers's insignia and tossed off a salute. "Ensign Bob Powell, sir. Thanks for taking me aboard."

Rogers fingered a 20-millimeter hole in the F6F's fuselage. There were several 7.7 holes as well, and half the rudder was tatters. "No problem, son. What the hell happened?"

Powell rolled his eyes. "We just got the recall order and jettisoned ordnance, sir. We'd turned back, just off the coast, when we were jumped by a bunch of Zekes and Oscars, I think." He shrugged. "Hell, Commander. I never seen an airborne Jap before today."

"Did you lose anybody?"

"Ah, I don't think so, sir. My exec, Mr. Knutson, got the guy who clobbered me, and I think I winged one." He thought for a moment, trying to control the rush of adrenaline. "I don't think we were the only ones that had to shoot our way clear, sir. There was a lot of excitement on one of the other channels, too."

Rogers absorbed that information. *Maybe the shooting's not over yet.* As he led Ensign Powell toward the ready room, he had already decided to put himself on the roster for the next CAP.

SHANGHAI, 1200

Sakaida lazed on the steps of the *hikotai*'s flight office, basking in the early afternoon sun. It was two P.M. local time, but the Imperial Navy kept its clocks set to Tokyo, and the noon radio broadcast was due any moment. Sakaida was content to remain outside, enjoying some solitude, when he heard shouts from inside. Curious, he jogged up the steps and turned into the radio room.

He arrived in time to hear the announcer's familiar voice intone, ". . . the Emperor will now read his imperial rescript to the people of Japan. We respectfully transmit his voice." Every man in the room rose to his feet as the national anthem began.

Sakaida gave the appearance of standing rigidly at attention, but he furtively scanned the room. Lieutenant Matano's face was a blank, as befitted an Etajima graduate. A few others were equally sanguine, but many showed emotion: eyes watering, a trembling lip. It was not difficult to guess the reason for the unprecedented broadcast—but it was impossible to believe. Finally the last strains of "Kimigayo" drifted away.

"To our good and loyal subjects," began the ruler of the Greater East Asia Co-Prosperity Sphere. None of the listeners had ever heard Hirohito's voice before. The high, reedy tone seemed unbecoming an emperor, let alone the Son of Heaven.

"After pondering deeply the general trends of the world and the actual conditions obtaining in our empire today, we have decided to effect a settlement of the present situation by resorting to an extraordinary measure."

Sakaida strained to grasp every word. The transmission quality was only fair, and he missed entire phrases. There was something about the United States, Great Britain, China, and the Soviet Union, then, ". . . accepts the provisions of the joint declaration."

It is true—Japan is surrendering! That knowledge struck with violent ambivalence. Sakaida had suspected for years—first after Midway, then after Guadalcanal, but certainly after Saipan—that the war was lost. But to hear it from His Imperial Majesty! Sakaida tried to listen, fighting for comprehension of the garbled words. It occurred to him that the rescript was a recording, and not a very good one at that.

"We declared war on America and Britain out of our sincere desire to ensure Japan's self-preservation and the stabilization of East Asia . . . the gallant fighting of military and naval forces . . . the enemy has begun to employ a new and most cruel bomb . . . we are keenly aware of the inmost feelings of all ye, our subjects . . . beware most strictly of any outbursts of emotion . . ." And finally, "Cultivate the ways of rectitude (static) nobility of spirit; and work with resolution so as ye may enhance the innate (static) of the imperial state and keep pace with the progress of the world."

Three and a half minutes after he first heard the Voice of the Crane, Hiroyoshi Sakaida's universe had imploded.

PILGRIM ONE-ONE, 1342

Leading Lieutenant Lennox's division, Rogers orbited at twelve thousand feet, twenty miles west of the task group. The hasty briefing had stressed two salient points: Japanese fliers, either ignorant of the surrender or choosing to ignore it, had engaged several air groups during Strike Able. Therefore, when Admiral Halsey confirmed the surrender to Third Fleet, he had issued a typically bullish style: "Investigate and shoot down all snoopers . . . in a friendly sort of way."

Rogers would be pleased to comply. His "CAG bird" had not been spotted for launch so he took the F6F available on deck. But he envisioned the fourteen rising suns stenciled on his personal airplane and relished this last chance to round out the scoreboard. The irony came to him: *I may kill a man in a war that's already over.* He nudged the thought aside: *Any Jap pilot out here today wants to die, anyway.*

Phil would have preferred one of the higher CAP stations, but he could not argue. Under control of Crystal Base, he went where he was told. However, it was comforting to hear the familiar voice of *Reprisal*'s fighter direction officer, Henry Lang, on the fighter-direction circuit. He had reluctantly handed off a bogey shortly after Rogers's team arrived on station, as another ship had a better radar picture. Rogers shifted in his seat. *Whoever Salvo is, I hope they didn't muff the vector.*

Following the initial bedlam early this morning—indulgent aerobatics and joyful tooting of ships' whistles—relative calm had returned. Bombers and torpedo planes had been disarmed and defueled, then struck below to hangar decks. Task Force 38 was now almost entirely a fighter organization, devoted solely to fleet defense. Rumor had it that a *King's Mountain* Corsair had crash-landed inland day before yesterday, and there was concern that IFF had been compromised. Therefore, single radar blips showing as friendly were being intercepted and identified visually. Nobody was taking unnecessary chances, today of all days.

The radio circuit crackled again. "Vampire Six-One, Crystal Base. Heads up! Single bogey, angels one-six, bearing two-eight-five. Your signal buster. Over."

Rogers heard the Vampire division leader acknowledge the vector. *Damn! Those* Alliance *guys are smack in the Jap's way.* Rogers found himself urging the lone intruder to nose over, shove the throttle to the stop, and dive under the high CAP. He double-checked his arming switches and adjusted the gunsight rheostat—just in case.

Moments later, Lang was back on the air. "Ah, Vampire Six, your bogey is now angels . . . ah, one-four. Still two-eight-five. Look ten o'clock low."

Rogers looked at his instrument-panel clock. The sweep hand ticked off six seconds. "Crystal Base from Vampire. No joy. Repeat, no joy." The disappointment was audible in the man's voice.

Looking up toward the high, thin overcast, Rogers realized he was going to get a chance. He pulled his goggles over his eyes and the sky became crisply amber. Lang was calling for the *Alliance* team to split left and right in descending turns, apparently now above and behind the bogey. Rogers was ready when the call came. "Crystal Base to Pilgrim One-One. Bogey closing on your nose, bearing now two-seven-zero, three miles. Bracket, now."

Rogers pressed the mike button and spoke into his oxygen mask. "Crystal, Pilgrim. Roger." He waggled his wings and saw Lennox's section break away to the northeast while he led Ensign Woodul to the southwest. Envisioning the problem in high-speed spatial geometry, he realized what Lang had done. *Whatever way that Jap turns, we've got him.* The bogey was now a lone mouse in a three-mile-high Hellcat box.

There he was. Rogers pressed the button. "Pilgrim One-One. Tally-ho!"

He sized up the situation. It was a single-engine type, still too far off to identify, but undoubtedly hostile. He would get a crossing shot from about a thousand feet altitude advantage.

As if seeing his peril, the Japanese pilot banked away. Then, perhaps realizing he had no time for evasion, he reversed back toward his original heading. Rogers eyeballed it as a Zeke 52—probably carrying a bomb. *This is a zoot-suiter,* he told himself. *He's alone with no escort.*

Since the Zeke held to its fast descent, it offered a predictable target. Rogers rotated the throttle, placing the diamond reticle around the silhouette. He let the gyroscope in the K-14 sight settle for two seconds, established the tracking rate, and pressed the trigger.

Tracers lanced out ahead of the Mitsubishi's nose. Hits sparkled across the dark-green airframe as armor-piercing incendiaries struck. Rogers was into boresight range now and fired again. The Browning chorus came to him, the distance closed, and he saw he was on a collision path. More hits, smoke streaming from the engine, a gout of flame that flared, abated, flared again.

Rogers waited as long as he dared. Then he was too close—the dirty red suns on the wings and fuselage were all too visible. He brought the stick back, angling nose-high, glancing down and behind himself. Oily brown smoke marked the spot where the Zeke had dropped abruptly away. Woodul was calling, "You got him, Skipper! Nice shooting!" Rogers could tell from the ensign's voice that the boy did not even get a shot. But it was almost anticlimactic. The enemy pilot had taken no evasive action, offering an experienced shooter a wide-deflection shot. Rogers regarded the episode as little more than a gunnery exercise—nothing exceptional.

A number registered in Rogers's consciousness. *That's fifteen—and I'll probably never get to do that again.* He leveled off, brought throttle, prop and mixture back to cruise, and checked the sky. Snyder and his wingman were rejoining. "Pilgrim, this is Crystal Base, confirming your splash. Clara. Resume patrol."

Rogers pushed his goggles up on his forehead. "Thank you, Crystal." He pressed the button again. "Good job, Hank."

A microphone double-clicked in his earphones. For Lieutenant Commander Philip Rogers—twenty-seven-year-old aviator, friend, lover, enemy, killer, and leader—that electronic break ended what had become known as the Second World War.

PART V

"I wouldn't take a million dollars for the experience. But you couldn't pay me that much to do it again."

Lt. Cdr. Blake Moranville, USN (Ret.)
Fighting Squadron 11, 1944–1945

16–31 August 1945

SATURDAY, 18 AUGUST
SHANGHAI

Sakaida knew it was now or never.

Definitive orders had arrived: Gather together all aircraft, drain the fuel, remove the propellers and lay them in the grass. After one or two nights, they would begin to rust.

While taxiing the last Zero Model 52 across the field, Sakaida's mind was clear. Faced with the end of flying and the uncertainty of life in a new Japan, he had reordered his priorities. He had considered suicide, and decided against it, though the samurai code of honor demanded suicide to avoid the humiliation of surrender.

Sakaida would probably return to the mountains on the island of Honshu and live the rest of his life in his rude little village, scratching an existence out of the earth. He would try to forget his life in the sky—and definitely would expunge the names and faces of the past four years. Lieutenant Azumano from cruiser *Tone,* Mizuno from Air Group 932 at Truk, a handful of others—they may yet live. Of the seventeen other pilots who had graduated from his reconnaissance floatplane course in 1940, he knew of three still alive. So many were dead, from the Solomons and Truk, from *Junyo* and *Zuikaku,* from the Shinkai Unit and the Mamoru Wing: Kono, Minami, Yoshimura, Yamamoto, Nakaya, Uchida, Doi, Kurusu, Tachibana, Inoyue—even those bastards Ono and Homma—on and on and on.

But whatever the future held, he would fly one more time.

Almost without conscious thought, Sakaida put the power to the oil-spattered Sakae engine. The weathered A6M5 bounced along the ground in a crosswind takeoff, its pilot compensating with slight upwind aileron. Then he was climbing away from the earth, raising his wheels for what would surely be the last time. He hoped that Matano would understand. If not—well, what of it?

Airborne, Sakaida turned west toward the vastness of China. He climbed slowly, adjusting prop and boost for economical cruising. A glance at the fuel gauge showed he had enough gasoline for three hours—more than sufficient for his purpose.

Passing south of Suzhou twenty minutes after takeoff, Sakaida was drawn farther west to Tai Hu, the immense lake that seemed to stretch to the horizon. Level at 2,500 meters, he gaped at the expanse of water that spanned forty nautical miles north to south. Smaller lakes—still good sized—glimmered to the northwest in the direction of Nanking. The world had become extremely agitated over events there in December 1938, and Sakaida had to admit that the Imperial Army probably had behaved poorly. He wondered: *Will the Chinese and others take retaliation against us?*

No matter. For the present I still have a fighter plane in my hands. Above the huge lake he indulged in a joyful aerobatic display, savoring the sensation of inverted flight, three- and four-G maneuvers, reveling in his mastery over a splendid machine. Even a scaly, worn-out two-year-old machine.

After passing from Chekiang into Anhwei Province, Sakaida decided to turn back. He gazed wistfully to the west, where the immensity of Asia beckoned him like an accomplished geisha, flirting coyly for his attention. Reluctantly, he eased into a 180-degree turn.

He had not yet rolled out on the reciprocal heading when a blackness spattered his windscreen. Instantly, Sakaida's attention went to his instrument panel. *Oil pressure dropping. I must find a landing spot.* Another thought crowded out the first: *Lieutenant Matano will think I have deserted.*

Sakaida scanned the countryside, seeking a place to set down. He was not overly concerned; he felt that the engine would keep running long enough for a controlled landing. Even if it seized, he had ample altitude. So far, it was not an emergency.

No major roads appeared, but the landscape was crossed by several small rivers that undoubtedly drained into the Yangtze. *If I follow one of those I will find help.* He determined to land near a stream running north-south, which he guessed was forty kilometers west of the huge lake.

Down to eight hundred meters, Sakaida had his spot in sight. An open area parallel to the river offered clear approaches, but there appeared to be large rocks. He decided to make a belly landing rather than risk flipping inverted. Beginning an intentionally high approach, he slid back his canopy, lowered flaps, and set up a rectangular traffic pattern. His early flight training came back to him: forced-landing drill in the ancient biplane, Petty Officer Nomura shouting instructions from the open cockpit.

Downwind, Sakaida judged his altitude. *Three hundred meters—a little high for a powered landing but perhaps not high enough if the engine quits.* His windscreen now was coated with a scum of oil, only partially dissipated by the slipstream. He smelled smoke in the cockpit and that made up his mind. Mixture to idle-cutoff, throttle back, fuel selector off. The prop windmilled, inducing unwanted drag. Sakaida raised his flaps, allowing the Zero to settle a bit as he prematurely began his base-leg turn.

Rolling out on final approach, he lowered his goggles and stuck his head out of the cockpit. It looked good—maybe even a bit high. He nudged back the stick, inducing a slight descent on the powerless airplane, then eased the nose down to regain airspeed. The wind whippered past his cockpit. Fifty meters' height and all of Asia extended before him. Then, sensing the ground as much as seeing it, Sakaida braced himself in the seat and allowed the aged fighter to descend into ground cushion.

His experience told him when he was there—a faint lifting as air compressed between the airframe and the earth. Gently he milked back the stick, felt the elevators respond, sensed the tug as the tailwheel dragged.

The Zero decelerated, skipping once. Then its useless propeller dug in and slewed the aircraft nose-down. The port wingtip caught a boulder, swerving the plane into a whirling skid. Sakaida was thrown forward as the fighter lurched to a halt, but he quickly braced himself with an outstretched hand.

He unbuckled and stood up in the cockpit. No people or animals could be seen, but somewhere there must be a village. Sakaida walked around to the nose and, out of curiosity, removed an inspection panel. He found what he suspected. In the hot-smelling accessory section he found a dangling oil line. A small hose clamp—a fitting worth no more than a few sen—had let him down. *Well, my last landing was not a very good one.*

As he turned to begin walking north he sensed something approaching fast behind him. A slight tremor in the ground. He looked over his shoulder, saw mounted men galloping toward him, and his spirits rose. *I did not know we had cavalry here.* He turned and waved to them and, getting no response, studied the riders as they neared. At seventy meters distance he discerned they were not cavalry—there was no uniformity to them. The realization sprung upon him with a chill: *These men are not even Japanese.*

An instinctive reaction took over. Sakaida turned and ran toward a large boulder on the edge of the field. He had left his Nambu pistol behind— he could not even kill himself to avoid capture. His heart now was racing with his feet, awkwardly covering ground in his lined flying boots. Hoof- beats behind him, audible shouts but no gunshots—yet. He glanced back, saw the lead rider bearing down. An enemy guerrilla no doubt, armed with a rifle. Sakaida heard the jingle of harness, could smell the sweaty tang of horsehair and leather. Then he was knocked off his feet as the horse col- lided with him. He was rolling across the ground, rolling and rolling as the earth traded places with the sky.

WEDNESDAY, 22 AUGUST
USS *CROWN POINT*

The ship's band played "The Daring Young Man on the Flying Trapeze" as Junior Haliburton high-lined across from destroyer *Stryker.* Some of the other ensigns held aloft a cartoon showing the baby-faced Haliburton, cling- ing to a periscope speeding through the water and crying "Whoa, dammit, whoa!" The drawing was titled "His first command."

The bosun's crew reeled in the high-line cage and held it in place while the passenger disembarked. Still wearing most of his flight gear, Junior took three brisk paces toward Rogers and saluted crisply. "Ensign Haliburton, reporting back from detached duty with USS *Tigershark,* sir!"

Rogers's return salute deteriorated into a come-on wave. He laughed despite himself and simply shook the boy's hand. "Welcome back, mister." Rogers forced himself to look into the eyes of the wingman whom he had allowed to be shot down. "Are you all right, Junior?"

The Mortimer Snerd smile was back. "Oh, yes, sir. They took real good care of me. Those submariners eat pretty well."

"Ahem." Rogers put on his commanding officer's voice. "Yes, there's the matter of our paying for your room and board."

Haliburton's eyes went wide. "Sir?"

Rogers produced a message form and began to read. " 'From: Com- manding officer USS *Tigershark* (SS-496). To: Commander Air Group 56. Subject: Compensation for care and feeding of Haliburton, J.R., Ensign, USNR. In the seven days subject officer was aboard this boat, he did eat and consume four gallons of ice cream, two each, vanilla and chocolate. Replacement of afore-mentioned strategic material in a combat zone is ur- gently required in order to maintain operating efficiency of this command. Reply by flash message requested.' "

CAG-56 lowered the traffic sheet. "Well, Mr. Haliburton?"

Junior searched for help from his friends, some of whom were doubled over in laughter. "Well, sir. Ah, that isn't all." He reached inside his flight jacket and withdrew a note from the destroyer captain.

Rogers took the handwritten message from *Stryker*'s skipper. "Sir: Ens. Haliburton is quite a boy. I fear that our galley crew overindulged his taste for ice cream. We had him aboard two days and ran out of what little we had left. Can you send over a few gallons?"

Rogers looked Haliburton up and down. "Junior, you may be the only man in the Third Fleet who's actually *gaining* weight."

"Well, gee, sir. I was the first guy the *Tigershark* ever rescued. When they transferred me to the *Stryker,* it sort of got to be a tradition." He shrugged like an embarrassed teenager, as indeed he was. "Besides, I didn't want to be rude to them, you know?"

CAG-56 smiled. "I know, Junior. I know."

THURSDAY, 23 AUGUST

ANHWEI PROVINCE, CHINA

Sakaida concluded that the Chinese were going to let him live. At least they were feeding him once or twice a day. After the first two days in captivity his hands had been untied, with an unmistakable pantomime of his fate should he try to escape. Two of the bandits—he decided they were not patriotic guerrillas—spoke a few words of Japanese. It was hard going, but Sakaida inferred that the group's leader intended to sell the captive to the highest bidder.

Sakaida took awhile to decide whether that was good news or bad. Obviously, if a Japanese unit would pay his ransom, that was preferable to going elsewhere. He would have some tall explaining to do back in Shanghai, but he was not concerned about that. The Americans might be interested, or they might not. That left only the Chinese factions, and Sakaida did not relish any of those options.

Thus far the biggest problem was transportation. The bandits had no spare horses, so Sakaida alternately rode double with one of the two Japanese "linguists." With no equine experience, Sakaida was at a loss to do anything but hang on to the man, who smelled just as bad as his mount. The group numbered eight men, a rough-and-ready bunch who seemed to live by their own law. Their leader was a compact, stone-faced man of indeterminate age who wore a large Mauser pistol and never spoke in less than a shout. Most commands were screamed, whether directed at men or beasts.

Though the bandits wove back and forth across the landscape, usually in search of food, their general track remained northwesterly. With each passing day, Sakaida's hopes sank a little lower, for the Japanese-occupied cities lay to the east. To the north was a largely unknown region, reportedly dominated by Chinese Communists.

MONDAY, 27 AUGUST

USS *KING'S MOUNTAIN*

It was crowded in flag country. Rear Admiral Griggs was concluding a briefing for Operation Airshow, the upcoming victory flyover of Tokyo Bay.

"It's going to be a mighty impressive sight," Griggs said with obvious enthusiasm. "Between us and the Army, there'll be about fifteen hundred planes in the air. Combined with the battlewagons and other ships in the harbor, the Japs will finally realize they've lost the war." He had already explained plans for the formal surrender ceremony on USS *Missouri.* Briefly Rogers wished that he could be on deck when the surrender was signed, but the desire passed. *I'd rather finish this war where I fought it—in the air.*

Griggs opened the meeting for questions and Rich Morgan of *Alliance* raised a hand. "Admiral, some of us are wondering why the surrender's being signed on a battleship. Why not a carrier? There's more space and . . . besides." He looked around. "Aircraft and submarines have done more in this war than the rest of the Navy." There were murmurs of assent in the room.

Raising a hand, Griggs waved down the dissent. "Gentlemen, I raised that very question. There's three reasons. First, Halsey doesn't want to risk the carriers inside Tokyo Bay—not yet, anyway. We'll stand off, ready to react if some Japanese fanatics try anything. Secondly . . ." He was grinning now. "You can't get enough people aboard a sub for a signing ceremony." Laughter tittered through the khaki audience.

Griggs held up a third finger. "Last, it's political. Truman's from Missouri, and since battleships are named for states, that's it. Until they start naming carriers for politicians, we'll have to be content just with winning wars instead of holding ceremonies on board."

The aviators seemed satisfied with Griggs's answer. Everyone knew that aircraft carriers had a fighting tradition—they were named for battles or famous warships. True, the new *Midway*-class ship, CVB-42, was to be christened *Franklin D. Roosevelt,* but surely that would remain an exception. Rogers felt certain that the Navy Department never would pander to

mere politicians for ship names. Tradition meant a great deal in the sea services.

As the meeting broke up, Tom Albertson eased Rogers aside. "The admiral would like you to stay awhile," Albertson whispered. Phil nodded and
sat at the table littered with coffee cups and ashtrays.

Griggs sat beside Rogers and poured another cup. He indulged in an
extra teaspoon of sugar, then folded his hands on the table. "Rogers, I have
an offer for you," the admiral began. "I need a courier to take some official documents to NavAirPac. You're senior enough for the job, but it
would mean leaving your command. What do you say?"

Rogers was taken aback. "Well, I'm flattered, sir. But I'd hate to miss
the flyover on Sunday. When would I leave?"

Jacob Griggs gave a knowing grin. "I know it's been a long war for
you, son. I can understand that you want to see it through. Suppose you leave
next Monday? I can have your travel orders and priority cut by then."

Options cycled through Rogers's mind. Naval Air Forces Pacific:
Hawaii, San Diego and then—where? Then another question forced its
way to the front of his consciousness. "I'd like that, Admiral. But . . . why
me? There must be others . . ."

Griggs shoved his coffee cup aside. "Consider it my thanks for a job
well done. You stepped into a difficult position and got results. I'll tell you
straight out, Commander. You're my junior air group commander but you
did as fine a job as my most experienced one. You should consider making the Navy a career."

So that's it, Rogers told himself. *The sly old fox. Make me feel indebted
to him, then recruit me to go USN.* "Actually, sir, I considered applying for
a regular commission back in '43. They were accepting USNRs then. But
to tell you the truth, between Captain Layman and Commander Garrett on
the *Alazon Bay,* I just wasn't interested." He shrugged. "Besides, Admiral.
They're saying there won't be any more wars—not like this one, anyway.
I'm not sure I'd enjoy the peacetime Navy."

Griggs cocked his head. "Then why'd you enlist? You were in the fleet
almost a year before Pearl Harbor."

"Well, sir, I knew we'd have to fight. Besides, naval air looked like
an adventure."

"Three combat tours, fifteen Zeros, ships sunk from under you. Isn't
that adventure?" Griggs looked up at Alberston. "By God, they don't make
young aviators like I used to know!" The mirth in his voice did not hide his
disappointment.

Rogers smiled in spite of himself. "I'm just saying, sir, that right now it looks like I've done as much as I can in the Navy. Four years ago I was a boot ensign and now I'm an air group commander. What do I really have to look forward to?"

The admiral pressed his point. "Why, new airplanes—jets, for instance. And there'll be new carriers. The *Midway*s, and no doubt some others." He waved a hand. "Oh, I'm not saying that there won't be some thin times ahead. There always are after a war. But in peace or war, son, the Navy always needs good leaders. Officers who have the integrity to put their men before themselves. There's already too many of the other kind."

Rogers could not argue the point. He thought of the ones he had known—the ambitious bastards and the careerists, always chasing more brass. *Harry Garrett, Ron Harkin, Dilbert Howard, even J. C. Johnston. Their type always lands on their feet.* "I just don't know, sir." He locked eyes with the admiral. "But I'll promise you one thing. I'll keep my reserve commission. Just in case."

"Good enough!" Griggs exclaimed. He stood and escorted Phil to the door. "But fair warning, Mr. Rogers. I'm not giving up on you!" He extended his hand. "Smooth sailing, son." Rogers grasped it, sensing the old man's heartfelt words.

Albertson walked Rogers down to the flight deck to say good-bye. "Buck, you were a fine junior officer and you became a fine combat leader. I hope we'll serve together again." Rogers thought: *They're double-teaming me.* But knowing that neither Jake Griggs nor Tom Albertson indulged in false flattery, he felt as if he'd just received a third Navy Cross. Climbing into the TBM that would return him to *Crown Point,* he realized: *It's going to be hard to stay out of this man's Navy.*

TWENTY-ONE

September 1945

SATURDAY, 1 SEPTEMBER
ANHWEI PROVINCE

Sakaida's moods alternated between relief and concern. Ignorant of his captors' intentions, he had spent the past two weeks wondering where he was being taken, but now that he had arrived, more questions arose.

Sitting near the horses, acutely aware that he no longer noticed the equine odors, Sakaida glanced around. His "escorts" had pointedly left a guard to mind him while they reported to whoever held authority at the remote village. Sakaida estimated that a few hundred people lived here: a well-organized outpost apparently run along military lines. Women and children mixed with armed men bearing a mixture of Japanese and foreign weapons, but no uniforms were evident. Still, there was order and purpose to the place. He inhaled deeply, savoring the aroma of evening cook fires and hot food.

A tall Chinese approached, prompting Sakaida to stand. The man carried himself well, and the guard's deferential demeanor confirmed Sakaida's suspicions. *This is a leader,* he told himself. The peaked cap and Nambu pistol on his belt said as much.

The Chinese bowed and intoned, *"Konichi wa."* It was the wrong time of day for that greeting, but Sakaida bowed in return.

"Kombana wa." He introduced himself in Japanese order. "Sakaida Hiroyoshi," adding his rank, *"hiko heisocho."*

"I am Wei Fieu," the educated barbarian continued. "My father, General Wei Wang, wishes to receive you tonight." He motioned with one hand. "Until then, please use our poor facilities. You may bathe as long as you wish, and suitable clothing will be provided."

Sakaida started when he heard the title, "general." But Wei Fieu had used the term *rikugun shosho,* equivalent to a rear admiral but denoting a two-star army officer. Sensing the flier's confusion, Wei Fieu added, "Rest assured, you are not a prisoner. In fact, the war is over so we hope you will choose to join us."

Sakaida looked around. The bustling activity amid crude buildings bespoke nothing his talents could contribute to General Wei's service. "Beg pardon, but what would I do here?"

Wei Fieu's jaw tightened slightly in the slanting sunlight. "Why, you will fly our airplanes, of course." Sensing Sakaida's doubt, he added, "We have three machines now: two small ones and another with two motors." He nodded to the west. "Over there, hidden away." Then he added, "All will be made clear at dinner tonight."

So the rumors are true! Sakaida recalled the bizarre reports: local warlords who bribed Chinese Nationalist or even American pilots to deliver P-40s or B-25s. It was a simple process—land at a designated site, pocket the gold, and walk back with one's parachute under one's arm. Sakaida suppressed the urge to ask the pertinent questions: How many other pilots were there? What about mechanics and spare parts and gasoline? He decided to wait until his dinner meeting.

Bowing again, Sakaida marveled at the fates that had brought him to this time and place. Whatever General Wei Wang had in mind, he was nothing if not ambitious. But he was going to have his hands more than full once the Nationalists and Communists began ripping out each other's guts for control of China.

Sakaida shook off his filthy jacket as he entered the bathhouse. A glance over his shoulder showed a crimson sunset behind the hills to the west.

SUNDAY, 2 SEPTEMBER
PILGRIM ONE-ONE

The weather was lousy—that was the good news. The bad news: some 1,200 high-performance aircraft were crowded into a relatively narrow section of the cloudy sky, with low ceilings and periodic rain showers. Visibility was poor, and Rogers found it almost impossible to maintain formation near the tail end of the 450-plane Navy contribution to Operation Airshow.

Trying to guide his lead division on a formation of *Reprisal* SB2Cs, Rogers bit his lip in frustrated concentration. The trailing Helldiver disappeared in a wisp of cloud, and when Rogers whisked through the cottony veil, the '2C filled his windscreen. He chopped the throttle all the way back, reaching for the flap lever when the Helldiver accelerated once more. In his peripheral vision he glimpsed a TBM with an N tail code sliding past to port. Apparently separated from its formation, the *Sharpsburg* Avenger had tacked onto the *Crown Point* contingent in order to avoid getting completely lost. Rogers had seen a huge parade of B-29s a half-hour before, escorted by a herd of Mustangs, but God only knew where they were now. *Probably headed back to Iwo and the Marianas, I hope.*

Breaking into the clear again, Rogers was relieved to see Tokyo Bay a few thousand feet below. He was struck by the number of ships at anchor—more tonnage than he had seen anywhere except Ulithi. He tried to spot USS *Missouri,* knowing that at this moment the Japanese delegation should be signing the instrument of surrender. The irony struck him: *I wanted to see the big show, but if I look down for a few seconds I'll probably hit another plane.* Jockeying throttle again, he imagined what his family would say if he were killed on the first day of peace in six years—2,191 days after Nazi Germany invaded Poland.

From Tokyo Bay back to the task group was a relatively short flight, and Rogers motioned for his team to close up. With Haliburton to port and Barnes with Woodul to starboard, he felt better. He pointedly turned to his right, waved to his section leader, and dramatically wiped his brow. *Whew! We made it!* Barnes flashed an "okay" sign and nodded vigorously, obviously laughing.

Over the task group, Rogers was concerned about the unaccustomed number of planes in the air. He slowed his approach, allowing things to thin out somewhat before leading his flight toward the side of the disposition where he knew *Crown Point* would be steaming into the wind.

Pilgrim One-One entered the carrier's traffic pattern, flying up the starboard side as the Charlie flag snapped from the halyard. Rogers looked back as his team slid into line astern, gaining interval for the landing, and busied himself with his checklist. By the time he had turned left on his downwind leg he was on speed, at altitude, hook down, wheels down, flaps down. It occurred to him that he may never make another carrier landing, and the thought struck him with an unexpected sadness. *Better make this one the best ever.*

Bending the Hellcat into a curving descent, Rogers picked up the LSO's paddles as Bud Roach's arms extended either side of his canvas windscreen. One bobble of the yellow-orange flags told Rogers, "You're a little low." He nudged the throttle, eased up a matter of feet, and stabilized as the paddles returned to the LSO's shoulders.

Now Rogers was seconds from touchdown, slightly left-wing-low. The impossibly narrow deck disappeared beneath his nose as he rolled wings-level. Roach's flags slashed down and Rogers neutralized the controls, chopped the throttle—and waited.

The impact came as it had more than two hundred times before, like the surprise break of a proper trigger release. Thrown forward against his straps, Rogers straightened in his seat and allowed the Hellcat to roll backward. He knew that the hook runner was disengaging him from the arresting wire. *Number three wire,* he thought. *Good landing.*

Guided up the deck by white-jerseyed sailors, Rogers eased his pet Hellcat into the forward parking spot. On signal, he jabbed the brakes, ran up the throttle, and cut the mixture. He would never enter another "1 CL" in his logbook, signifying a carrier landing aboard USS *Crown Point,* nor stamp another rising sun, indicating a confirmed victory.

Nor would he scrape by on eighteen gallons of water a day, live with the same faces, the same smells—fuel oil, aviation gas, unwashed bodies and backed-up heads—for weeks at a time.

Whether he ever made another carrier landing, Rogers knew that he would never fly this airplane again. He listened to the tinkling, whirring noises of an aircraft relaxing after flight. Handing his chartboard to the plane captain, he climbed out and stood on the wing, feeling the ship's relative wind in his face. He took in the fifteen red-and-white flags and gave a farewell pat to the nude's shapely bottom. Then he winked at the plane captain and dropped off the wing.

Now he believed it. His war truly was over.

Bibliography

Francillon, René J. *Japanese Aircraft of the Pacific War*. London: Putnam and Company, 1979.

Friedman, Norman. *U.S. Aircraft Carriers*. Annapolis: Naval Institute Press, 1989.

Grumman Aircraft Engineering Corp. *Pilot's Handbook for Navy Models F6F-3 and F6F-5 Airplanes*. Bethpage, N.Y., 1944.

Hata, Ikuhiko, and Yasuho Izawa. *Japanese Naval Aces and Fighter Units in WW II*. Annapolis: Naval Institute Press, 1989.

Mears, Lt. Frederick. *Carrier Combat*. Garden City, N.Y.: Doubleday Doran, 1944.

Mikesh, Robert C., and Rikyu Watanabe. *Zero Fighter*. New York: Crown Publishers, 1981.

Monsarrat, John. *Angel on the Yardarm*. Newport: Naval War College Press, 1985.

The New Yorker Book of War Pieces. New York: Schocken Books, 1988.

Polmar, Norman. *Aircraft Carriers*. New York: Doubleday, 1969.

Raven, Alan. *Essex-Class Aircraft Carriers*. Annapolis: Naval Institute Press, 1988.

Reynolds, Clark G. *The Fast Carriers*. New York: McGraw-Hill, 1968.

Sakaida, Henry. *Winged Samurai: Saburo Sakai and the Zero Fighter Aces*. Mesa, Ariz.: Champlin Fighter Museum Press, 1986.

Tillman, Barrett. *Corsair: The F4U in WW II and Korea*. Annapolis: Naval Institute Press, 1979.

———. *Hellcat: The F6F in WW II*. Annapolis: Naval Institute Press, 1979.

———. Coaching the Fighters." *U.S. Naval Institute Proceedings*, January 1980.

———. "The Day the Shooting Stopped." *The Hook*, August 1990.

———. "The Forgotten Flattops." *The Hook*, Fall 1980.

Toland, John. *The Rising Sun*. New York: Random House, 1970.

U.S. Navy. Air Combat Action Reports (ACA-1) and/or war diaries for Fighting Squadrons 2, 6, 9, 11, 14, 15, 17, 19, 20, 29 and 30, various dates, 1944–45.

——. *Campaigns of the Pacific War.* Washington, D.C.: Strategic Bombing Survey (Pacific), Naval Analysis Division, 1946.

——. *C.I.C. Magazine.* Various issues, 1944–46.

——. *Introduction to Naval Aviation.* Washington, D.C.: NavAir 80R-19, 1946.

——. *Tactical Orders and Doctrine, United States Fleet (USF-10), Part 6.* April 1945.

Warner, Denis, and Peggy Warner, with Sadao Seno. *The Sacred Warriors: Japan's Suicide Legions.* New York: Van Nostrand Reinhold Co., 1982.

Watts, Anthony J. *Japanese Warships of WW II.* Garden City: Doubleday, 1970.

Wilmot, H. P. *Zero A6M.* Secaucus, N.J.: Chartwell Books, 1980.

Y'Blood, Thomas. *Red Sun Setting: The Battle of the Philippine Sea.* Annapolis: Naval Institute Press, 1981.

ABOUT THE AUTHOR

BARRETT TILLMAN began flying World War II aircraft in high school and writing about them in college. He has won five writing awards for history and fiction, including the prestigious Admiral Radford Award for Naval History and Literature. Formerly managing editor of *The Hook* magazine, he is executive secretary of the American Fighter Aces Association and an honorary member of Navy squadrons VA-35 and VF-111. With Commander John B. Nichols, he wrote *On Yankee Station: The Naval Air War over Vietnam,* which has become a widely read military text. His twelve nonfiction works include operational histories of several naval aircraft, which have become standard references. His previous novels are *Warriors, The Sixth Battle,* and *Dauntless,* the first in a trilogy to which *Hellcats* is the second. An Arizona resident, Barrett Tillman now is writing the Korean War conclusion to the series.